The Language of Inclusion and Exclusion in Sports

Language and Social Life

Editors
David Britain
Crispin Thurlow

Volume 26

The Language of Inclusion and Exclusion in Sports

Edited by
Stephanie Schnurr and Kieran File

DE GRUYTER
MOUTON

ISBN 978-3-11-221419-0
e-ISBN (PDF) 978-3-11-078982-9
e-ISBN (EPUB) 978-3-11-078988-1
ISSN 2364-4303

Library of Congress Control Number: 2023941374

Bibliographic information published by the Deutsche Nationalbibliothek
The Deutsche Nationalbibliothek lists this publication in the Deutsche Nationalbibliografie;
detailed bibliographic data are available on the internet at http://dnb.dnb.de.

© 2025 Walter de Gruyter GmbH, Berlin/Boston
This volume is text- and page-identical with the hardback published in 2024.
Cover image: Tim Perdue/Moment Open/Getty Images
Typesetting: Integra Software Services Pvt. Ltd.
Printing and binding: CPI books GmbH, Leck

www.degruyter.com

To Janet and Tony

Acknowledgments

Like every research project, this book is a collaboration that would not have been possible without the help, support, encouragement and patience of a lot of people – some of whom we would like to mention and thank here specifically.

The idea for this book arose from a panel that we organized at a conference of the International Pragmatics Association, which took take place online while the world was battling with the global COVID-19 pandemic. Many of the chapters included in this book benefited from the discussions we had during the conference and afterwards with authors and other interested colleagues – academic and professional. We would like to thank everyone who came to our panel and who participated in our discussions and helped shape our thoughts and ideas long after the conference.

As our ideas formed and the chapters were written we have benefited immensely from ongoing conversations with Amanda Coulston (England Boxing), Stuart Cain (Warwickshire Country Cricket Club) and Alan Rapley (UK Coaching), who have not only agreed to co-author some of the chapters in this book, but who also generously shared their time in talking to us about the important inclusion work they do every day when interacting with athletes, fans, and other stakeholders.

A very big thank you also to Natalie Fecher at Mouton de Gruyter for approaching us after the conference and inviting us to bring together our ideas and discussions in the form of an edited volume; and for providing constant support and believing in the book throughout the process. And to the Department of Applied Linguistics at Warwick University for its financial support towards the creation of this book.

And last but not least, we are very grateful to Yesim Kakalic for fearlessly and endlessly formatting the various parts of this book and putting in extra hours so that we would meet our deadline. All remaining infelicities are, of course, entirely our own.

Contents

Acknowledgments —— VII

Stephanie Schnurr and Kieran File
Approaching issues of inclusion and exclusion in sports through language —— 1

Part I: Creating inclusion/exclusion in authentic interaction

Frances Rock
Chapter 1
'Dribble dribble dribble! Dribbling is the most elementary in football': Doing inclusion in park-based children's sport —— 17

Ozde Ozinanir and Louise Mullany
Chapter 2
#StillWeRise: The sociolinguistics of race, inequalities, and athlete activist identities in Formula 1 social media —— 43

Kieran File, Stephanie Schnurr, Amanda Coulson, and Alan Rapley
Chapter 3
Do collective pronouns construct inclusive coach-athlete relations? —— 65

Anastasia Stavridou and Kieran File
Chapter 4
Constructing inclusive team management structures: Evidence of multiparty participation in the leadership of a university basketball team —— 83

Fergus O'Dwyer
Chapter 5
Banter as a tactic of inclusion in sports organizations —— 105

Rachel Chimbwete-Phiri and Stephanie Schnurr
Chapter 6
"Sisters are hot". Denying netball players their athletic identities through sexualisation practices in online fan groups in Malawi —— 125

Part II: Inclusion/exclusion in the sports media. The representation of female and transgender athletes

Melissa Kemble
Chapter 7
Good girls and bad boys? A corpus analysis of gendered discourses in Australian media coverage of "masculine" team sports —— 147

Yasemin Erdoğan-Öztürk, Esranur Efeoğlu-Özcan, and Hale Işık-Güler
Chapter 8
From "the National Pride" to "the Daughters": Media representations of Olympic sportswomen in Turkey —— 171

Aimee Bailey and Lucy Jones
Chapter 9
"Fairness versus inclusion": Representations of transgender athletes in British newspaper reports —— 193

Part III: Reflecting on the language of inclusion and exclusion by athletes and coaches

Eva-Maria Graf and Melanie Fleischhacker
Chapter 10
Within binaries instead of beyond? The discursive (self-)exclusion of young female football players from football as a male and masculine space —— 217

Richard Pringle and Erik Denison
Chapter 11
A critical examination of homo-negative language use and the pragmatics of inclusion and exclusion of gay rugby players —— 253

Farhana Abdul Fatah
Chapter 12
"*Ha ha ha you don't cover you aurat*": Exploring modesty, prayer, and Malaysian Muslim women gymnasts' experience of inclusion and/or exclusion —— 271

Kieran File, Stephanie Schnurr, and Stuart Cain
Chapter 13
Putting inclusion into practice: A sociolinguistic lens on institutional practices for establishing an inclusive sports organisation —— 291

Kieran File and Stephanie Schnurr
Chapter 14
Bringing everything together: Considering the role of language in effecting inclusion and exclusion in sport —— 309

List of contributors —— 323

Index —— 327

Stephanie Schnurr and Kieran File
Approaching issues of inclusion and exclusion in sports through language
An introduction

1 Introduction

In this volume we explore the role language plays in the context of contemporary debates around issues of inclusion and exclusion in the sports domain. Sport is a sociocultural activity where inclusion and exclusion are omni-present. Whether we look at media reports of big international sporting events – such as the FIFA World Cup or the Olympic Games – or stay closer to home and take a stroll through the local park on a weekend to watch kids play football or basketball, issues of inclusion and exclusion are embedded in the fabric of sport. Questions around who is allowed to play on a particular team, or discussions about whether boys and girls are perceived to be equally skilled athletes, or whether athletes' dress is too revealing or just attractive enough are evident at grassroots and competitive levels of sports. These discussions take place on the side lines of sports events, as well as in the news and on social media. They involve, parents, fans, coaches, athletes, sponsors, and other stakeholders.

Language plays a crucial role in this context as it constitutes the medium through which many of these debates around inclusion and exclusion take place. Language choices inform and create specific practices of inclusion and exclusion. For example, the pronouns coaches use when talking to their athletes, the adjectives fans use to describe and comment on the performance of their favourite team, the ways in which the media report (or do not report) on the successes of men's and women's teams are all important indicators and contributors to inclusion and exclusion. It is precisely in and through these linguistic practices that inclusion and exclusion are being exercised. Staying with our examples, coaches may decide to strategically use the first person plural pronoun "we" in an attempt to signal and create a sense of inclusion with their athletes (see File et al. this volume), and through the ways female players are being talked about in the media (see Kemble this volume) or on online fan fora (see Chimbwete-Phiri and Schnurr this volume) they are either portrayed as skilful and successful athletes or as objects of desire. In the former, they are included in mainstream sports discourse,

Stephanie Schnurr, Kieran File, The University of Warwick, United Kingdom

https://doi.org/10.1515/9783110789829-001

while in the latter they are excluded, often overlooked, and denied the status and acknowledgement of professional athleticism.

And yet, despite the significance of language to debates around inclusion and exclusion in the sports domain, its role remains largely under-researched. This lack of linguistic engagement with these issues is particularly surprising given that recent discourse analytic and pragmatic research has identified inclusion and exclusion as important elements in the sports domain (e.g., Gavin and Simpson 2015; Wolfers et al. 2017; File, 2018; Wilson 2019; File and Schnurr 2019). These studies have established that on the one hand, team spirit and values of collaboration and togetherness – that lie at the heart of many sports – create and celebrate inclusion. But on the other hand, competitiveness and competition – which are also central characteristics of sports – often have the opposite effect. More specifically, the strong focus on performance and success that can be observed not only on the international stage but also at many grassroot level events, often results in the exclusion of athletes who are (perceived as being) weaker and/or different – regarding their physical abilities, sexual orientation, ethnicity, gender, religious beliefs, and many more. For example, in a study of football players in a German club, Wolfers et al. (2017) find that through their use of racial humour, team players on the one hand, express an appreciation of the cultural diversity within their team, thereby creating team cohesion and inclusion, but on the other hand, the humour also often creates exclusion by fragmenting the team and emphasising the players' different racial identities.

Issues of language and inclusion and exclusion in the sports domain are also reflected in recent media headlines. There has been a spate of news stories that have highlighted sexist, racist or bullying language used by coaches in the course of ordinary and everyday coaching interactions with players. Other news stories have portrayed high-performance sports as a context where certain kinds of exclusion are highly problematic – for example in the form of racism and sexism among athletes and fans, expectations and practices around heteronormativity and hegemonic masculinity, as well as sharply stratified social structures which give rise to bullying practices by those in power (Grierson 2016; Roan 2016, 2017; Roan and Nathanson 2017; Wolfers et al. 2017; Hope 2019). During the time that this introduction was written, for example, the sports news contained stories about racial discrimination in Formula 1, discussions about the different expectations for men and women regarding uniforms in sports like volleyball and gymnastics, and the perceived need by sports administrators to create separate categories of competition for transgender athletes. In each of these cases, specific language or semiotic resources are referred to as being culpable in or contributing to issues of in/exclusion in these sporting environments.

This edited volume contributes to these debates, as well as the growing research on the language of sports by focusing specifically on how issues of inclusion and exclusion manifest themselves in the language used by coaches, fans, athletes and the (sports) media. Zooming in on different sports in different sociocultural contexts, the chapters in this book explore a wide range of issues relating to the inclusion or exclusion of different groups, paying particular attention to the role language plays in promoting inclusion or exacerbating exclusion. However, the authors of the chapters not only explore what particular patterns of language use reveal about the practices of inclusion and exclusion in sporting contexts, but they also outline ways in which their findings can be used – and in some cases, have already been used – to inform and often improve current practice displayed by coaches, fans, athletes and the media.

2 Inclusion and exclusion in sports

Social inclusion is often understood as an expression of social equality (e.g., Chen and Liu 2020), while social exclusion typically refers to social inequality (e.g., Elling and Claringbould 2005). Both concepts are multi-dimensional (Masanovic 2019) and closely linked to "the different possibilities and opportunities available to different groups in society based on socioeconomic status (income/education), age, gender, ethnicity, religion, sexuality, and/or physical and mental abilities" (Elling and Claringbould 2005: 499).

Viewed more specifically in the context of sports, Chen and Liu (2020: 598) conceptualise inclusion "as an ongoing relational process whereby people and organizations actively and collaboratively co-create spaces and structures that enable community members to make decisions about how and when to participate in physical activity and sport." Collins and Haudenhuyse (2015: 6) distinguish between two dimensions of social inclusion in sport: "inclusion in sports" and "inclusion through sport". While the first dimension refers to activities and policies aimed at increasing the participation of groups who "are less likely to participate", the second dimension includes programmes or activities targeted at "deprived, poor or disadvantaged people" in the hope of including them more systematically in sports. Most of the chapters in this book fall into the first category, but some also touch on the second (e.g., Rock; Bailey and Jones).

However, as Kelly (2010: 127) remarks, the notions of social inclusion and exclusion are "contested concepts" and have been (ab)used for political and ideological purposes (see also Morgan and Parker 2017). She thus calls for further investigation of the specific processes and activities through which inclusion and exclusion are enacted, as well as the ideologies and assumptions that inform these practices. This book contributes to this ongoing endeavour by exploring and discussing some of the specific language choices that inform and create practices of inclusion and exclusion in a variety of different sports in different socio-cultural contexts.

Although there is a growing body of literature on social inclusion and exclusion in sporting contexts (e.g., Elling and Claringbould 2005; Collins and Haudenhuyse 2015; Masanovic 2019), most of this previous research focuses on sports management and explores the effectiveness of specific policies and programmes targeted at under-privileged groups (e.g., Morgan and Parker 2017; Ekholm and Dahlstedt 2017; Pandya and Marino 2018). For example, in their study of the Dutch sports landscape, Elling and Claringbould (2005) identified six factors that impact inclusion and exclusion in the context of sports. They found that an early sport socialisation via school, parents and friends resulted in higher levels of inclusion. Moreover, formal and informal exclusion and discrimination (e.g., messages around certain sports being "for boys" of "for girls") as well as athletes' physical abilities and sporting talent had an impact on the levels of inclusion. Other factors impacting the level of inclusion involved the availability and accessibility of sporting facilities, the existence of spare time and money, as well as what other social groups athletes belong to (e.g., referring to gender and religion).

Many of these previous studies on social inclusion have maintained that, on the one hand, sport is "an effective tool to increase social inclusion", but on the other hand, they also identified several limitations of sports-based intervention programmes (Chen and Liu 2020: 3). For example, McConkey et al. (2012), in a study of the effectiveness of a specific sport programme targeted at the inclusion of children and adults with intellectual disabilities in Germany, Hungary, Poland, Serbia and Ukraine, found that although the programme did promote social inclusion within the specific sporting context, it was less successful in increasing inclusion in the athletes' wider community. Similar observations were made by Ekholm and Dahlstedt (2017: 232) who investigated "a sports-based social intervention performed in a 'socially vulnerable area' in Sweden". They found that inclusion was successfully achieved by the intervention "as long as the 'excluded' adapt to the 'inside' [i.e., a set of Swedish norms]". But the authors also pointed out that the overall social policy – which includes the sports-based intervention programme – maintains and reinforces rather than challenges and reforms the social order that creates the specific inequalities and tensions the policy was designed to address and overcome in the first place. Moreover, in one of the few studies in non-Western contexts, Chen and Liu (2020: 597) examined "the effects of community sports provision on social inclusion and public health" in rural China. They also found that the community programme was only partially successful in that it promoted inclusion in the rural areas where it was implemented, but it did not enhance public health.

Based on these findings, recent research cautions not to over-estimate the effectiveness of intervention programmes and their "transformational potential", and to provide "theoretically informed explanations as to how participation in sport may contribute to social transformation" instead of making generalisations (e.g., Morgan and Parker 2017: 1028). A similar argument is made by Kelly (2010: 126) who points out that many sports-based intervention programmes focus exclusively on exclusionary processes while overlooking others, thereby often "highlighting individual deficits and de-emphasizing structural inequalities."

3 Doing being inclusive or exclusive in sporting contexts

This book aims to contribute to debates about the different forms and effects of inclusion and exclusion in the sports domain and how to best address them by providing a different perspective that focuses on and emphasises the role of language. Rather than examining the effectiveness of intervention programmes and policies, the subsequent chapters focus on different aspects of language use and explore the discursive and pragmatic processes through which individuals and groups are being included or excluded. They thus provide a better understanding of the specific processes through which issues of inclusion and exclusion are understood, constructed or perpetuated by different sports stakeholders in different sporting and socio-cultural contexts.

Drawing on authentic, naturally occurring interactions – in written, spoken and multimodal form – the chapters identify and unpack issues of inclusion and exclusion in sport by presenting empirical evidence of inclusion and exclusion *in action* from a range of different contexts. The authors of the chapters largely understand inclusion as referring to the processes of accepting others who may initially be members of an – often marginalised – outgroup and welcoming them into their own in-group. These processes of inclusion may, for example, apply to girls who play football (Graf and Fleischhacker), transgender athletes who strive for recognition and inclusion (Bailey and Jones), as well as young women exercising a particular religion in gymnastics (Abdul Fatah). Some of the chapters take an explicitly critical angle and have an openly political agenda calling for change. For example, Ozinanir and Mullany base their research on the United Nations' (2016: 20) definition of social inclusion as "the process of improving the terms of participation in society for people who are disadvantaged on the basis of age, sex, disability, race, ethnicity, origin, religion, or economic or other status, through enhanced opportunities, access to resources, voice and respect for rights". Similar understandings of inclusion are also operationalised, among others, in the chapters by Rock, Erdoğan-Öztürk et al., Abdul Fatah, as well as Pringle and Denison. As these chapters show, doing inclusion means giving a voice to members of marginalised groups and acknowledging them as legitimate athletes. This can be achieved, as is illustrated throughout the chapters in this book, for example, by changing the ways in which the media report (or do not report) about female and transgender athletes (e.g., Kemble; Bailey and Jones; Erdoğan-Öztürk et al.) or the language they use to represent these athletes in media stories.

But inclusion and exclusion do not only take place in media coverage. On the contrary, as several chapters convincingly demonstrate, inclusion and exclusion occur in everyday practices, which are "both embodied and linguistic" (e.g., Rock). These processes may take place online (e.g., Ozinanir and Mullany) as well as offline (e.g., Stavridou and File); they may involve fans (e.g., Chimbwete-Phiri and Schnurr), players (e.g., O'Dwyer), as well as parents and coaches (e.g., Abdul Fatah; File and Schnurr), and other stakeholders (e.g., Graf and Fleischhacker; Bailey and Jones). But regardless of who is involved in doing inclusion and exclusion, as the subsequent chapters illustrate, the processes involved are always collaboratively performed. While some chapters focus on inclusion and exclusion practices in formal settings, guidelines and rulings (e.g., Bailey and Jones), others explore more informal practices in fan interactions and on the playing field (e.g., Chimbwete-Phiri and Schnurr; Stavridou and File) or analyse the interplay between formal and informal practices in player reflections and media reports (e.g., Graf and Fleischhacker; Erdoğan-Öztürk et al.).

The chapters in this book bring together research conducted in different sporting and socio-cultural contexts and involve a wide range of sports. As editors, we have also aimed to be inclusive when compiling this volume. The chapters report on different sports in different socio-cultural contexts – such as rugby in Australia and the UK, football in Austria, basketball and boxing in the UK, volleyball and boxing in Turkey, netball in Malawi, gymnastics in Malaysia, Formula 1, swimming, and many more. However, they all showcase some of the benefits of approaching issues of inclusion and exclusion from a discourse analytic and pragmatic angle. In doing this, the chapters take different methodological and analytical approaches, including, for example, discourse analysis, interactional sociolinguistics, multimodal discourse analysis (MMDA), Critical Discourse Analysis (CDA), corpus-based discourse analysis, Feminist Critical Discourse Analysis (FPDA), thematic analysis, and Critical Discursive Psychology.

In their analyses, the authors work with different language data – i.e., German, English, Malay, Turkish, Arabic and Chichewa – and explore different facets of the language of inclusion/exclusion in sports. They thereby provide an account of how different forms of inclusion and exclusion are being constructed, negotiated, and sometimes even rejected by athletes, coaches, fans, and the media.

In unpacking the language of inclusion/exclusion, the chapters in this edited volume address the following questions:
- Where and how is inclusion relevant in the everyday practices of sports teams, and in what circumstances does exclusion appear?
- What linguistic and pragmatic practices threaten or help to accomplish inclusion in sports contexts?
- How are issues or practices of inclusion and exclusion negotiated among athletes, coaches, fans, and the media?
- What are the benefits of approaching inclusion and exclusion through a focus on language?
- What deeper, underlying ideas or ideologies about inclusion/exclusion in sport can be located in the everyday, ritual patterns of language use by coaches, athletes, fans and the sports media?
- How can we translate the theoretical findings of our linguistic research for sports practitioners?

The chapters in this volume contribute in a number of ways to advancing our understanding of inclusion and exclusion in sport. They also advance our knowledge of language and the ways in which it functions in a sporting context. By drawing attention to the role of language in constructing inclusion or exclusion in a range of sporting contexts, this edited volume makes important contributions to the burgeoning field of sports discourse (e.g., Wolfers 2017; Wilson 2019). Each chapter identifies and describes a specific aspect of the language and pragmatics of inclusion on the micro-level of an interaction while at the same time linking these observations to (often problematic) issues of inclusion and exclusion in team sports on the macro-level. The chapters also illustrate how different linguistic approaches and methodologies can help make the processes of inclusion and exclusion more visible. Capturing a wide socio-cultural diversity and looking at different sports will make important contributions to current scholarship which remains largely limited to studies on football and rugby in Western contexts.

However, as well as being a topic of interest to linguists and other academics, issues of inclusion and exclusion are managed by sports practitioners every day. Sports organisations, in particular, are increasingly being required to demonstrate the steps they are taking to be more inclusive. With this in mind, we have asked the authors of the chapters to consider the implications of their work for sports practitioners.

The practical implications explored in each of the chapters are targeted at specific stakeholders who were studied within the chapter. In this regard, the chapters of this volume offer practical implications for journalists and media organisations, governing bodies, social media companies, athletes, coaches and people more generally when performing their own fan identities, to help drive reflection on how sport – through its various practitioners – can better enact inclusion. Chapter 13 and the Epilogue to the book, we also engage directly with practical implications of linguistic analysis and what studies of the kind collected together in this volume offer as a driver for change. We do this with the help of insights from an experienced leader in professional sports, one who has been a CEO of multiple sporting organisations and who is in their own right a champion for inclusion. Using their experiences and reflections, we highlight how sports organisations can put inclusion into practice, implementing, where relevant, insights and discussion from the other chapters in this volume to ground strategy in material linguistic action. By ensuring academic findings are presented in the chapters of this volume in ways that are of relevance to practitioners and that highlight practical applications, this book also makes improving current practice a core mission.

4 Overview of the book

The book is divided into three sections each focusing on a particular aspect of inclusion and exclusion and exploring it through analysis or discussion of language. The chapters in the first part explore how inclusion and exclusion are created in naturally occurring interactions among athletes, coaches and others, while Part II focuses on the role of the sports media with particular attention to the ways in which female and transgender athletes are represented. The chapters in Part III demonstrate reflections on the language of inclusion/exclusion as expressed by athletes in different sports and different socio-cultural contexts.

In the first chapter in Part I, Rock demonstrates how an inclusive atmosphere and team spirit is created in a grassroot football context in the very local context of a park in Cardiff (Wales), where young boys from all over the world meet weekly to play football. Analysing audio-recordings, photographs and videos from these grassroots training sessions conducted in both English and Arabic, combined with field notes and interviews with the coach, Rock illustrates how inclusion is locally managed and performed both within individual training sessions and as an accomplishment across sessions. Throughout the analysis of these local forms of inclusion and exclusion, the chapter asks important questions that are picked up in subsequent chapters. It provides a critical discussion of the notion of inclusion and demonstrates that the linguistic concept of translanguaging is particularly useful for capturing and understanding the specific processes of inclusion at play in this context.

Moving from the local grassroots level to the global level, Ozinanir and Mullany examine the role of language and other semiotic resources on social media for constructing activist identities designed to fight inequality. They ground their study in the globally influential motorsport of Formula 1 (F1) and analyse Instagram posts by Lewis Hamilton for insights about how he uses linguistic, semiotic and multimodal discourse strategies to construct a Black athlete activist identity that rejects social exclusion in F1 and racial injustice in the wider society, as well as negotiating a language of inclusion as a vision for the future.

In chapter 3 File, Schnurr, Coulson and Rapley explore the language of inclusion in the context of coach-athlete communication during boxing bouts at different national and regional events in the UK. Applying a linguistic lens, they analyse the coaches' use of the collective pronoun "we" during authentic face-to-face interactions with boxers recorded during competitive boxing bouts. Their findings challenge the assumption that the use of the collective "we" always signals and constructs inclusive relations between the coaches and boxers, and point to various other meanings and functions of this linguistic device.

Chapter 4 stays in the UK and provides a case study of a university basketball team in which Stavridou and File explore inclusion with regards to team governance and the establishment and enactment of an inclusive, participatory team management structure in which various players of the basketball team are involved. Analysing interactional and ethnographic data collected from a university basketball team, they observe that leadership in this team is a collaborative activity, and that interactional rights are claimed by and distributed among different players, regardless of their notional role or their status in the team. Insights gained from their analyses are then used to formulate specific criteria for inclusive team management structures.

Also mainly focusing on players, chapter 5 by O'Dwyer explores the various forms and functions of collaborative humour with regards to creating and maintaining inclusion in the team and the wider context of a Dublin Gaelic Athletic Association club in Ireland. Drawing on naturally occurring interactions that occurred in training sessions, matches and social activities between team members, this chapter argues that regularly participating in humour and banter is one way for players to release tensions while also confirming their status in the team and the wider club. Collaborative humour is thus one strategy of bringing the team together and creating inclusion. Making space and time available for such humour to occur is thus important for stakeholders in any sporting organisation.

The final chapter in Part I by Chimbwete-Phiri and Schnurr analyses issues of inclusion and exclusion in the online context of fan fora – with a particular focus on netball in Malawi. Exploring posts in Facebook fan groups of the national netball team, Chimbwete-Phiri and Schnurr identify and critically discuss the discrimination and sexualisation that the netball players experience. When talking about the sport and commenting on the athletes' performance the fans in their posts often – more or less explicitly – mobilise gender stereotypes and evaluate the players based on their body, looks, dress and attractiveness. Through these practices they at the same time portray netball as an exclusively feminine domain in which women are often sexualised and assigned the stereotypical roles of mother, wife, and object of desire, rather than celebrated for being successful athletes on the playing field.

Zooming in on the topic of gender, the chapters in Part II provide important case studies on the language of inclusion/exclusion used in the sports media with a particular focus on the representation of female and transgender athletes. Not only have women's sports historically received relatively little media coverage, but existing media reports often undermine women's status as successful professional athletes. The chapters in this part of the book take this background as a starting point and explore a range of relevant issues of inclusion and exclusion in different socio-cultural and sporting contexts.

The first chapter by Kemble explores how gender bias and sexism in professional sports are reported on and negotiated within the Australian print media. Analysing the occurrence of the discursive strategies of gender marking, infantilisation, sexualisation and trivialisation of the athletic performance of female athletes, Kemble observes positive developments. For example, unlike Chimbwete-Phiri and Schnurr in their chapter, she finds no evidence of sexualisation, with the women instead being represented as skilful and successful athletes. But in spite of this positive trend, the chapter provides strong evidence of asymmetrical gender marking whereby gender labels are added to women's but not men's teams (such as "women's football" versus "football", and "female athletes" versus "athletes").

Similar trends are observed in chapter 8 by Erdoğan-Öztürk et al. which presents the findings of an analysis of the discursive strategies of inclusion and exclusion displayed by Turkish media outlets when reporting on sports women who represented Turkey in the 2020 Tokyo Olympics. Drawing on news texts, opinion pieces and columns published in different Turkish newspapers with different readerships and different political alignments, the authors observe that the media outlets create multiple, complex and sometimes conflicting representations of these athletes based on their ideological and political stances. Across the different outlets, the sportswomen are often portrayed as national icons, heroines and model citizens with a marked absence of sexualized representations. This inclusion of the female athletes in these media texts is achieved through a nationalist ideology celebrating national values and ideals. Through the use of ideological perspectivation strategies and other discursive processes, the women are instrumentalised as ideological symbols to affirm political ideologies and to validate the standpoints of the ruling party. As such, the inclusion and exclusion of sports women during the 2020 Olympic Games is fundamentally shaped by political ideologies and reflects the controversial political atmosphere in the country.

The final chapter in Part II, chapter 9 by Bailey and Jones, zooms in on the news reporting in the British press of one particular athlete, namely the transgender swimmer Lia Thomas, in the run-up and aftermath of her championship win and FINA's landmark ruling about the inclusion of transgender athletes. Analysing a corpus of 225 articles totalling over 160,000 words compiled from ten British newspapers with different readerships and different political agendas, the authors observe a clear trend for journalists and commentators to shape the debate on transgender athlete participation in sport as resting on issues at the intersection between inclusion and fairness. Positioning these processes in opposition to each other, creates and reflects an ideological binary between cis and transgender women that does not allow for any crossover between them. Moreover, cis-normative ideologies are prevalent portraying cis women athletes as potential victims of trans athletes who are systematically constructed as stronger and faster, and as displaying predatory behaviour in the changing rooms. As a consequence of this portrayal, a potential inclusion of trans athletes in sport is constructed as unfair to cis women, thus reflecting and reinforcing implicit transphobia.

The third and final part of the book presents three case studies in which the authors analyse athlete reflections on their own or other sports stakeholder's language use in relation to issues of inclusion and exclusion. In chapter 10 Graf and Fleischhacker report on in-depth focus group interviews conducted with the players of a U16 girls football team in Austria. Focusing on ideological rather than structural forms of inclusion, the authors explore the different and opposing discourses and subject positions (co-)produced by the players when reflecting on the gendering of football. Their findings demonstrate that the players still very much perceive and experience football as a male and masculine space which disadvantages and excludes women in many regards. Thus, in spite of some changes and improvements, this research study clearly shows that football remains an extremely gendered sport and that any structural and ideological changes have led to an accommodation of women rather than a transformation of underlying structures and ideologies.

In chapter 11, Pringle and Denison examine how homo-negative language use in rugby teams in the UK and Australia can contribute to an exclusion of male players who identify as gay or bisexual. Drawing on eight focus group interviews and survey questionnaires conducted with gay and straight rugby players from different amateur clubs, the authors observe that competing discourses surround the multiple understandings of homosexuality, and that homonegative practices and overt language appear to be publicly known by players as problematic and unacceptable. Although the players who participated in their study did not want to appear homophobic and commented that they would call out such behaviour, at the same time many of them acknowledged that they used such language in their rugby clubs.

In chapter 12, Abdul Fatah explores the ways in which former professional female Muslim gymnasts in Malaysia occupy and negotiate their troubled and untroubled subject positions as Muslim women and professional gymnasts. Drawing on in-depth interviews with former gymnasts who competed in national and international championships, this study identifies and analyses a range of linguistic features which give raise to specific religious Discourses that constitute prominent sites for identity struggles around being "good, practicing Muslims" and "good gymnasts". In the recounted experiences of these women, religious, gender and athlete identities intersect in complex ways, placing the gymnasts in troubled and marginalised subject positions thereby excluding them from fellow – non-Muslim – gymnasts and/or denying them the religious identity of good Muslims. Based on these findings, Abdul Fatah argues for the need to promote the inclusion of Muslim athletes in national and international sports without undermining their religious and cultural values.

Chapter 13, the last chapter in this part of the book, outlines a concrete example of how inclusion was put into practice in a Cricket Club in the UK. Co-written by the editors of this volume and an experienced leader of sports organisations (Stuart Cain), it presents an organisational account of inclusion by considering how a sports organisation might go about putting inclusion into practice. The chapter describes six key strategic actions or practices to foster and promote greater inclusion particularly in terms of creating a welcoming stadium environment for all fans.

The volume is brought to a conclusion by the final chapter written by the editors of the book, in which we take a look across the previous chapters and reflect on their contributions to wider discussions about inclusion/exclusion in sport. This chapter returns to the questions posed above and answers them in light of the findings presented throughout this book. We also take stock of the applications for practice discussed in the previous chapters and reflect more broadly on how sports practitioners can mobilise the power of language to instigate and drive efforts to promote inclusion and reduce exclusion in the sports domain. The chapter ends with a brief outline of future research and a call for more empirical studies on the language of sports.

References

Chen, Qiu & Tianbiao Liu. 2020. The effectiveness of community sports provision on social inclusion and public health in rural China. *International journal of environmental research and public health* 17(2). 597–610.

Chovanec, Jan. 2009. "Call Doc Singh!": Textual structure and coherence in live text sports commentaries. In Olga Dontcheva-Navrátilová & Renata Povolná (eds), *Cohesion and Coherence in Spoken and Written Discourse*, 124–137. Cambridge Scholars Press.

Chovanec, Jan. 2016. 'It's quite simple, really': Shifting forms of expertise in TV documentaries. *Discourse, Context & Media* 13. 11–19.

Collins, Mike & Rein Haudenhuyse. 2015. Social exclusion and austerity policies in England: The role of sports in a new area of social polarisation and inequality? *Social inclusion* 3. 5–18.

Ekholm, David & Magnus Dahlstedt. 2017. Football for inclusion: Examining the pedagogic rationalities and the technologies of solidarity of a sports-based intervention in Sweden. *Social Inclusion* 5(2). 232–240.

Elling, Agnes & Inge Claringbould. 2005. Mechanisms of inclusion and exclusion in the Dutch sports landscape: Who can and wants to belong? *Sociology of Sport Journal* 22(4). 498–515.

File, Kieran A. & Stephanie Schnurr. 2019. "That match was a bit like losing your virginity". Failed humour, face and identity construction in TV interviews with professional athletes and coaches. *Journal of Pragmatics* 152. 132–144.

File, Kieran A. 2018. "You're Manchester United manager, you can't say things like that": Impression management and identity performance by professional football managers in the media. *Journal of Pragmatics* 127. 56–70. https://doi.org/10.1016/j.pragma.2018.01.001

Gavins, Joanna & Paul Simpson. 2015. Regina v John Terry: The discursive construction of an alleged racist event. *Discourse & Society* 26(6). 712–732. https://doi.org/10.1177/0957926515592783

Grierson, Jamie. 2016. June 30. BBC Wimbledon commentator accused of 'creepy sexism'. *The Guardian*. https://www.theguardian.com/society/2016/jun/30/bbc-wimbledon-andrew-castle-marcus-willis-girlfriend-sexism

Hope, Craig. 2019. March 6. Peter Beardsley no longer employed by Newcastle after investigation. *Mail Online*. https://www.dailymail.co.uk/sport/sportsnews/article-6777565/Peter-Beardsley-no-longer-employed-Newcastle-investigation-alleged-racism-bullying.html

Kelly, Laura. 2011. 'Social inclusion' through sports-based interventions? *Critical social policy* 31(1). 126–150.

Le Boutillier, Clair & Anna Croucher. 2010. Social inclusion and mental health. *British Journal of Occupational Therapy* 73(3). 136–139.

Masanovic, Bojan. 2019. The effects of sports-recreational activities on the inclusion of young montenegrins in society. *Journal of Anthropology of Sport and Physical Education* 3(3). 21–24.

McConkey, Roy, Sandra Dowling, David Hassan & Sabine Menke. 2013. Promoting social inclusion through unified sports for youth with intellectual disabilities: a five-nation study. *Journal of intellectual disability research* 57(10). 923–935.

Morgan, Haydn & Andrew Parker. 2017. Generating recognition, acceptance and social inclusion in marginalised youth populations: the potential of sports-based interventions. *Journal of Youth Studies* 20(8). 1028–1043.

Pandya, Tej & Katherine Marino. 2018. Embedding sports and exercise medicine into the medical curriculum; a call for inclusion. *BMC Medical Education* 18(1). 1–3.

Ponic, Pamela & Wendy Frisby. 2010. Unpacking assumptions about inclusion in community-based health promotion: Perspectives of women living in poverty. *Qualitative Health Research* 20(11). 1519–1531.

Roan, Dan. 2016. October 28. Shane Sutton: Jess Varnish's sexism allegations upheld by British Cycling. *BBC Sport*. http://www.bbc.co.uk/sport/cycling/37804761

Roan, Dan. 2017. March 23. British Swimming: Bullying claims by Paralympians are investigated. *BBC Sport*. http://www.bbc.co.uk/sport/disability-sport/39368319

Roan, Dan & Patrick Nathanson. 2017. June 13. Great Britain Olympic bobsleigh coach accused of racism by athlete. *BBC Sport*. http://www.bbc.co.uk/sport/winter-sports/40252620

Wilson, Nick. 2019. When we means you: The social meaning of English pseudo- inclusive personal pronouns. In Paul Bouissac (ed.), *The social dynamics of pronominal systems- a comparative approach*, 35–56. John Benjamins Publishing Company.

Wolfers, Solvejg, Kieran File & Stephanie Schnurr. 2017. 'Just because he's black': Identity construction and racial humour in a German U-19 football team." *Journal of Pragmatics* 112. 83–96.

Part I: Creating inclusion/exclusion in authentic interaction

Frances Rock

Chapter 1
'Dribble dribble dribble! Dribbling is the most elementary in football': Doing inclusion in park-based children's sport

1 Introduction

Piller and Takahashi observe that the applied sociolinguist should not try to ascertain what inclusion is or should be. Instead, we must strive to "account both for the complexity of social inclusion as well as its complex intersections with language" (2011: 374). This chapter accordingly considers a grassroots children's football club and uses analyses of data from that setting to critically evaluate notions of inclusion. It focusses on a park in drizzly, cold, autumnal Cardiff, Wales, where young boys play football together. They are organised and galvanised, chastised and chivvied by a wiry, charismatic figure who seeks to share with his young charges his enthusiasm for the game and for its potential to enrich lives. A detailed, multilingual, visual team ethnography of this informal sports club permits examination of a setting so small and fragile that it could easily be overlooked. Despite being understated, this setting unites children from various locations worldwide and features practices which index and, I argue, accomplish multiple potential forms of integration.

The chapter recognises that the coach, himself, had experienced various forms of exclusion. Indeed, the coach responded by creating opportunities to *do inclusion*, on his own terms developing "an alternative sense of belonging" (Bradbury, 2011;

Acknowledgements: This work was supported by the Arts and Humanities Research Council (AH/L007096/1), Large Grant, 'Translation and Translanguaging. Investigating Linguistic and Cultural Transformations in Superdiverse Wards in Four UK Cities' (2014–2018, £1,973,527, Principal Investigator: Angela Creese, Cardiff Research Team: Amal Hallak and Piotr Wegorowski. Wider research team: Mike Baynham, Adrian Blackledge, Jessica Bradley, John Callaghan, Lisa Goodson, Ian Grosvenor, Jolana Hanusova, Rachel Hu, Daria Jankowicz-Pytel, Agnieszka Lyons, Bharat Malkani, Sarah Martin, Emilee Moore De Luca, Li Wei, Jenny Phillimore, Mike Robinson, Frances Rock, James Simpson, Jaspreet Kaur Takhi, Caroline Tagg, Janice Thompson, Kiran Trehan, Zhu Hua). Assistance with transcription was gratefully received from Zeen Suad Nafie Al-Rasheed, Zayneb Elaiwi Sallumi Al-Bundawi, Reem Al Madani, Katy Brickley and Harriet Lloyd. The editors and reviewers of this chapter are thanked for their generous work.

Frances Rock, Centre for Language and Communication Research, Cardiff University, Wales

Burdsey, 2007, cited in Spaaij 2015: 313). I characterise doing inclusion as an everyday practice which is both embodied and linguistic. Through scrutiny of audiorecordings, photographs and videos from training sessions featuring English, Arabic and other languages, data analysis reveals how inclusion is locally managed, performed and accomplished within and across training sessions. Through fieldnotes, understandings and contextualisations of this practice are examined and different researcher perspectives brought to bear. Through interviews with the coach, his representations of activities and intentions around inclusion become accessible and are here laid out against the naturally occurring data and fieldnotes. This makes for a multidimensional analysis.

Through this analysis this chapter asks, in this particular setting: What is inclusion? What are participants potentially included in? How is inclusion accomplished through discursive means and, broadly defined, communicative practices? This provides for a critical re-appraisal of the notion of inclusion which picks apart both ideological and teleological dimensions. This, in turn, gives insights into the potent position of community sports coaches as potential sources of innovation and change in social life. For coaches, this chapter will consider their role and influence and for parents and children it will illustrate the value of everyday sports and its leaders.

Although much of the coach's activity could be seen as simply coaching, I argue that specific configurations and realisations of features presented in this chapter construct a form of coaching which entails *doing* inclusion. This inclusion is an interactional project, co-produced with players. Translanguaging provides a lens through which to view this project by considering: multilingual practices; gesture and movement; repetition at various levels; use of and dissemination of sporting lexis, phrases and actions; analogy with elite football; and flexibility around routine structural elements such as session times, sports kits and fees.

2 Key concepts and connections

2.1 Inclusion

Humans may universally need inclusion, (e.g., Bredtro, Brokenleg and Van Bockern 1990; Andrews 1998:420). Inclusion of newcomers in dominant language cultures can foster such advantages as language learning and feelings of welcome and respect (e.g., Yates 2011: 457–458). Sport, specifically, is considered a site for social inclusion as it can permit construction of institutions, identities and social networks, for example (Cortis 2016: 92). However, problems with the substance or use of highly political and politicised terms like "inclusion" and "integration" have been observed and their distinctions variously debated and overlooked. This is complicated by these being "ordinary words" as well as technical terms. They have been appropriated in, for example, education particularly around additional learning needs and, of course, sports policy particularly around migration. Whole studies have been dedicated to untangling them from one another in relation to their use in practice (e.g., Sheehy and Duff 2009) and policy (Dowling 2020). Very crudely, integration, the older term in its polity/policy use, encourages rendering a minority or marginalised group more like their majority counterparts. Inclusion, which predominated from the 1990s in Western European countries, instead seeks to bend the majority group in some way(s) to better accommodate others.

"Integration" and "inclusion" are frequently deployed as neoliberal labels for what can be seen as a perspectivised, rather needy idealism. "Belonging" has undeniably warmer connotations, perhaps mostly because it avoids nominalisation. All these terms, however, have centralist overtones implying that there is something to which some social actors are/have already integrated, been included in or belong to whilst other individuals do not fit or, at least, not yet. There is an enforced aspirational dimension and deficit assumption here which has been widely critiqued (e.g., Beneke 2020). Yet "inclusion into what?" can be poorly specified rendering the notion insidious (Piller and Takahashi 2011: 373; Otsuji and Pennycook 2011: 414). Communicative practices are instrumental in creating categories of inclusion in particular instances and manufacturing the politics and social machinery to instrumentalise that work through such features as deixis and pronouns (Mulderrig 2012: 707–721). In relation to sport, organisations' LGBTQ+ "inclusion policies", for example, can create a statis involving "gesturing towards change but failing to implement it", "equality proofing" by doing "just enough" (Spurdens and Bloyce 2022: 507; 517; see also Bailey and Jones this volume). There is also a risk in seeing inclusion and related concepts as simply states or goals. The study of language in social contexts, however, permits or even requires recognition of inclusion as a process accomplished interactionally. As Madsen notes, "processes of integration involve micro-acts that bring about and integrate relations of different cultural frames" (2012: 84). In this chapter then, I consider inclusion as an interactional project which can be recognised outside preconceived social structures, indeed, becoming constitutive of those structures. I show how perceived exclusion leads a coach to create a social space where not only is he included, but he is integral enough that he, himself, can discursively construct inclusion using the social and communicative machinery available. Accordingly, we could see the phenomenon presented here as different from inclusion and accordingly coin or appropriate a new or alternative term. However, as I will show, the coach keeps the institutionalised and the global in view despite, in a sense, side-stepping both integration and inclusion.

2.2 Inclusion and superdiversity in Cardiff

Between 1993 and 2014 the foreign-born population in the UK more than doubled from 3.8 million to around 8.3 million" (Migrant Observatory 2016). It is not by chance then that twenty-first century sociolinguistics has witnessed the development of a wealth of research on urban language contact (e.g., Block 2010; Gregory and Williams 2000; García 2020). Some of this has developed around Vertovec's (2007) term, "superdiversity", which proposes not only that more migrants are coming to the UK from more places and with more varied backgrounds, but also that they come with a wider variety of statuses, through a wider variety of channels which leads to increasingly diverse patterns of age, gender and work/educational experience.

Multilingual, superdiverse cities are only one aspect of the linguistic and communicative life of Wales, yet as multilingual, superdiverse cities go, Wales's capital, Cardiff, with a population of almost 355,000 (Welsh Government 2016) offers a distinctive example in the UK context. Cardiff has witnessed successive waves of migration which include those of which Vertovec (2007) speaks alongside the combination of Welsh and English. Those who use the notion of superdiversity are often criticised for missing the fact that urban language contact is nothing new. Cardiff provides a case study in which various old or established diversities (migrants from England and Somalia, for example) meet superdiversity (worldwide new arrivals such as asylum seekers and international students) (Singh and Rock 2017).

Amidst superdiversity, social activities such as sport assume particular significances even as they become central to some people's lives and irrelevant to others. Amongst adults across Wales, 34% participate in sports three or more times per week rising to 43% in Cardiff (Stats Wales 2022). Such activities bring individual and social benefits. For example, UEFA estimates that football clubs and players generate £553m for Wales, helping the economy and NHS and creating social good (BBC 2021). Yet, this positive news is inconsistent. For example, of the 90,000 football players in Wales registered with Football Association Wales, only 3% are from "Black and Minority Ethnic backgrounds" (Football Association Wales 2012). It is not a revelation to assert that sports' benefits are unevenly distributed. This chapter considers one individual's response.

3 Methods

3.1 Introducing the data

The data used in this chapter were collected as autumn turned to winter in a city park in pre-pandemic Cardiff by the author with researcher Amal Hallak. They were collected within a large, multilingual, multisite, team linguistic ethnography spanning four UK cities (Cardiff, Leeds, Birmingham and London). During the project, each city's researchers moved through four multilingual research sites concerned with social activities including sport. In Cardiff, we focussed on sites where at least Arabic, English and Welsh were in play. Our sports research site featured a coach who had come to Wales from Sudan, via Holland where he had held a full-time job. As the key participant in our sports site, he joined the research team in collaborating on practical tasks such as negotiating consent, managing data collection and eventually discussing analytic themes. Throughout the data collection period, he also became the focus of our study as he shared his working life as well as his social, home and online activities via wide-ranging forms of data in which he interacted. These included:

- 38 hours of football training audio-recordings
- 11 hours of football training video-recordings
- 791 photos taken in and around training
- 69,881 words of fieldnotes
- 3 interviews with the coach
- 20 hours of audio-recordings from the coach's home and friendship networks
- 23 screenshots of social media data

Here, I will call him Captain S (CS). This derives from a nickname that he asked us to use in writing about him. People typically referred to him just as "The Captain". We shadowed CS for 16 weeks, attending sports training sessions with him in his two main areas of expertise: table-tennis and football. In this chapter, I focus on an academy that he established for football training.

CS introduced himself to researcher Amal by casting his sporting activities in relation to inclusion:

Fieldnote Excerpt 1: CS introduces himself

The coach and I started having a conversation about the research . . . He said that [translanguaging] was something he experienced with kids every day. Because of language boundaries a lot of kids feel excluded at school and feel the lack of white privilege. He said that was why he enjoyed providing a space and opportunity for kids to exercise. [CarSpoFn_0912_AH_01]

This conversation, and Amal's representation of it captured the coach's motivation for *doing inclusion*. The philosophy he expounds here turned out to underpin his work. His coaching was concerned with much more than simply football skills.

3.2 Introducing the analysis

The language of sport has already been richly characterised. For example, Heath and Langman's (1994: 85) four organisational coaching characteristics assert that:
- Language is used in a context of participation, demonstration and, hence, activity
- Accordingly, action scripts talk
- Those engaged aim to function as a group to accomplish a single objective
- The activity is constituted by rules based on the activity which, in turn, regulate the activity.

This characterises CS's coaching. Therefore, we could simply conclude that there is nothing more to say about his work. However, I argue that in combination, the specific realisations of the features I discuss below contribute to a particular, *inclusive* version of coaching

Data analysis has been iterative involving input from the wider project's local and national research teams including, of course, CS. This chapter presents a fragment of this thinking as it relates to this book's themes. The analysis has been driven by the multilingual, multimodal orientation of CS and, accordingly, of data collection. To understand how his social life is situated in contexts, societies and cultures, we use interactional sociolinguistics (Gumperz 1999; Stubbe et al. 2004) which motivates the ethnographic fieldwork (Boxer 2002; Bucholtz and Hall 2005) and analytic attention to using data to make sense of other data. *Translanguaging*, a crucial perspective for the research, is also reflected in CS's orientation. This idea of translanguaging develops from recognising *languaging* as an intentional, creative use of signs such as words, gestures, and one's wider surroundings, in sequences to convey thoughts and, in turn, to perceive them within various constraints and affordances (Debes 1981: 188). *Trans* acknowledges that all of this is "always in the making" (Khafaji 2007: 464). *Translanguaging* (Lewis, Jones and Baker 2012) points up that we have repertoires and competences that span languages, rather than separating them. It encourages us to consider how people make meanings using all of their resources, not just stuck within a particular language or, indeed, within the restrictive notion of individual, isolated languages (Canagarajah 2011: 1, see also e.g., Creese and Blackledge 2010). In this chapter I show how translanguaging can be a lens through which to recognise and interrogate inclusion. This makes it possible to look beyond dominant views of "social inclusion" which either see monoligualism as "central" and languages other than English as "impediments" or which view bilingualism as "premised on a notion of relatively fixed and stable borders between discrete languages" (Otsuji and Pennycook 2011: 414). Instead, this perspective makes it possible to "open up an understanding of social inclusion to include not only the recognition of bilingual capacity but also the fluidity and flux of the metrolingual" (Otsuji and Pennycook 2011: 415).

4 Analysis

4.1 Confronting exclusion by doing inclusion

I begin by examining how CS represents his own experiences of exclusion from the sporting mainstream because this illustrates his motivations for doing inclusion. As we will see, he presents himself as confronting and correcting exclusion by creating a new, translanguaging space for inclusion, his academy. Certainly, sports can contribute to feelings of social inclusion (Walseth and Fasting 2004). However, its social and cultural norms and potential to expose participants to cultural resistance, even racism, can lead "newcomers or minorities to feel alienated or marginalised" (Spaaij 2015: 304). Indeed, for CS, despite having worked full-time in Holland, similar roles were not forthcoming in Wales. CS responded by enterprisingly and proactively creating opportunities amongst ebbs and flows of paid and voluntary involvement in multiple organisations and sites mostly of hourly-paid shifts and emergency cover. Such marginalisation may lead newcomers or minorities even to "segregate themselves into separate clubs" (Spaaij 2015: 304) and CS indeed responded to his situation by launching his own football academy. When asked to introduce himself during an interview, CS's talk recognises this complexity: He casts his situation positively and emphasises not his exclusion but his multiple forms of inclusion, specifically indicating doing inclusion through the academy:

Interview Excerpt 1: CS introduces himself

1	I am er football coach and table-tennis coach
2	and tennis coach and er generally sport- sport
3	coach really and now I'm qualified to have er
4	sport leader level two football er level one level
5	two I'm doing now my B licence it's means level
6	three in football [F: mm] and er I just er I work
7	for er er Football Association Wales FAW and
8	work for Cardiff Council and I work for Cardiff
9	City and I have my own football academy and

```
10      er is my target is er er er to get one of my
11      players to play for Cardiff City or Swansea . . .
12      but I'm doing well because I I work almost
13      three years now and I have many talent players
14      now they're promising to get- to get they can
15      make it to the short ((list)) and yeah what I'm
16      trying to do I'm- do my best and yeah the rest
17      for the boys to be honest I can- I can't hold
18      them to put in Cardiff City but they have to
19      work hard and we have to work together
20      simple as that [F: mm] and I do my best and
21      with the rest I have to wait
```

[CS interview 01]

In representing his work, CS does not dwell on the absence of full-time employment. Rather he casts himself as included. In the process, or to this end, he foregrounds particular aspects of his inclusion by:

(a) labelling multiple spheres of expertise, football, table-tennis and tennis (lines 1–3),
(b) identifying and explaining his qualifications (lines 3–6),
(c) naming organisations with which he affiliates (lines 6–9),
(d) presenting his creation of a footballing "academy", not merely a "club" or "training sessions" (line 9) and casting that organisation as ambitious (lines 10–15),
(e) positively evaluating and highlighting the duration of his achievements and efforts (lines 12–13).

As well as orienting to his own inclusion, he looks to others. Specifically, he presents his academy's "target" (line 10) being inclusion for players (lines 15–16). He indexes players' aspirational inclusion as being mainstream, through reference to local professional teams (lines 11, 18) and casts that inclusion as potentially resulting from something itself inclusive: a collective effort between him and the boys (lines 16–21). This is "inclusion from below" (Werbner 2012), a grassroots "inclusive multiculturalism" which features volunteers and participatory networks (Halilovich, Boz and Kianpour 2022: 3).

Spaaij suggests that "being good at sports may be perceived by new arrivals as a way to 'make it' in a new country, especially in host societies where sport is a key site of culture production and social prestige" (2015: 303) like Wales. This resonates with CS's activities. He developed his academy by independently creating and circulating leaflets, selecting venues for his publicity strategically and building social networks in schools and sports venues. Through these literacy practices (Gregory and Williams 2000), despite his experience of exclusion in not finding full-time work, he created an inclusive play opportunity. An open orientation to membership was a constant in the operation of his academy. Indeed, fieldnotes reveal that new members could simply walk-up during training and join. So, whilst, by forming his own academy, CS has "segregated", in Spaaij's (2015) terms above, he embodies a *trans* stance both in language and in his negotiations of multiple forms of membership and inclusion for himself and players. His multicompetence extends his participation in professional clubs beyond his academy. The academy itself is not then "segregated" in being closed, exclusive or, ultimately, separate.

Having established a group of players CS sought a place for his academy to operate. He reported feeling excluded from hiring a playing space:

Interview Excerpt 2: Why play in the park?

1	F	and the places you play tend to or where we've seen are like in parks
2	CS	yes
3	F	would you prefer to be on kind of official pitch or is that quite is that =
4	CS	= er no yeah there was no er there is no any possibility to get just a proper pitch to be honest

[CS interview 01]

For financial and practical reasons, CS found himself unable to hire conventional facilities. As Cortis observes, "cultural . . . patterns of sport participation reflect underlying inequalities in access to community opportunities and infrastructure" (2016: 92). However, this restriction itself resulted from seeking to be inclusive of players. CS did not routinely charge for participation in, or membership of, his academy and indeed, as we will see later, had a benevolent approach to even one-off payments. This enabled boys to attend, irrespective of their financial circumstances but rendered conventional venues impossible. His response was to demarcate an inclusive space within a public park for his group. He thereby reconstituted the public space, making part of it inclusive in a particular way. Both fieldworkers were struck by the experience of attending sports training that was permanently locum. Both were also struck by the confidence, even audacity of claiming space, both photographing the unrestricted space where the club would pop-up to try to convey, in initial fieldnotes, its peripatetic state:

Fieldnote Excerpts 2a and b: Where is the academy?

I arrived at 3pm and walked out onto the park. I wondered where CS would be and looked around for him.

[CarSpoFn_0906_FR_01]

The weather is really beautiful today and perfect for a football game. I notice that there are cones spread around the pitch. For some time, I don't know what they are there for and where they came from. They look like they are used to mark the boundaries of where CS and the kids are going to be training. I wonder whether they belong to the park or whether he brought them with him. Seeing these cones makes me feel like I'm entering a new territory, one with which I am not familiar. They stir my curiosity, but for some reason I don't ask CS about them. Strangely enough, for a moment I feel like I don't know what I am doing here.

[CarSpoFn_0912_AH_01]

Both researchers expected a formal playing pitch. Taking cues from the presence of rugby posts, goal posts and line markings in the grass, we had not questioned whether CS's academy would have a recognisable, repeatable home. Amal found its absence positively disorientating. CS selected a space for participation according to availability each week. He enforced his claim on it through such semiotic devices as the cones and, on other occasions, simply jumpers marking corners and goalmouths. Despite his activities, the location remained public and sometimes non-players entered the informal pitch:

Fieldnote Excerpt 3: Transgressing the pitch

A woman walks through the pitch, quite oblivious to the sporting fixture underway. . . . Soon afterwards two men cycle across the pitch's corner.

[CarSpoFn_0906_FR_01]

Metaphorically, the pitch was inclusive of anyone, playing or not, at least fleetingly and practically this sometimes influenced the game as the players stopped to chat to people passing. However, the playing space was more than simply a venue for a kick-around. CS's communicative practices made it the home of his academy.

4.2 Doing inclusion in a translanguaging space

We have seen that CS creatively and inclusively invented, peopled and, somewhat paradoxically, located his academy. The following sections show how he made the academy, session-by-session, through translanguaging including multilingualism, diverse language practices and paralinguistic features such as gesture

This translanguaging in sessions was perhaps surprising, given CS's expressed language ideologies. CS had some strong folklinguistic beliefs (Albury 2014; Preston 2017) about inclusion in multilingual environments (Albury and Diaz 2021). Specifically, he articulated the dominant language ideology that migrating people must include themselves in communities they join or visit by learning their dominant language (see Meadows 2014). He characterised using newly-arrived languages as "not polite" and valorised migrant players who learn their new majority language exemplifying an elite player learning to speak "fluent" Dutch saying "I love that". He called not learning local majority languages "the disaster". However, whilst he celebrated learning English, his academy was accepting, even encouraging, of multiple languages. CS himself regularly used English, Arabic and Dutch often in tight combination and with scant separation. He also presented a need to learn languages himself to coach effectively. CS had become able to use some Somali to support players from Somalia who, he believed, tended not to know English, initially. Children also used Pashto and Bengali during training sessions. None of these languages were problematised or policed and they wove in and out of players' and spectators' activities. Despite my use of essentialist labels for languages above, the languages themselves were not treated as distinct at the academy. Indeed, the linguistic environment in training sessions was rich with translanguaging. Here, a typical fieldnote indicates the interweaving of languages and language practices:

Fieldnote Excerpt 4: Inclusive translanguaging

A 7-year-old is now standing next to CS, passing the occasional comment. He's like a commentator. Occasionally he takes a turn at the game . . . Now the boys are squabbling over the score. "I got two", "You got two, I got two". Play continues. The 7-year-old stands close to CS. He looks up at CS and asks him "are you a Muslim?" The smallest player comes over to his Mum and little brother (a 2-year-old). He cradles the toddler's head . . . and strokes the boy's soft hair very gently. He's very good with him and the toddler smiles contentedly. He speaks to his Mum in Somali and mentions CS's name. . . . The kids chatter away in either Somali or English – they seem oblivious of which and comfortable in both. . . . Some older boys speaking Spanish are leaving the field right next to us. One of them shouts back to the others, seemingly wanting the ball.

[CarSpoFn_0926_FR_07]

Even the few moments described above feature spoken English, Somali and Spanish in the context of bilingual Welsh-English signage which characterised the park. However, it is not only the range of languages but also the range of tolerable language practices which is notable. CS is happy for a player to cease play and engage in commentary, doubtless a rich learning activity for the player (Hoyle 1991). CS is also relaxed about enquiries about his religious affiliations, answering briefly but informatively (not included above). His academy features chat on the side-lines and players can drop in and out of off-pitch activities. Meanwhile, other park participants circulate. This was not ill-disciplined chaos. Rather, the complex of languages, forms of practice, use of space, participation formats and participants constituted the space as one of inclusion by allowing the boys to take the semiotic lead. CS grasped the event loosely enough that players could participate on their own terms. Examining his language ideologies and those implicit in sessions reveals the social inclusion facilitated through his take on "multilingualism within societal monolingualism" (Han 2011: 383).

4.3 Doing inclusion through repeating activities

In this section, I show how translingual, multimodal coaching resources facilitate players' involvement. In other words, the examples here evidence how CS accomplishes his version of inclusion through the multiple, micro ways he tailors his communicative practices to his interlocutors, drawing them into his inclusive, sporting space. Here, then, languages and other meaning-making systems entwine with particular outcomes for participants (Garcia 2009; Creese and Blackledge 2015). To illustrate, I focus on repetition, here a multilingually, multimodally and discursively constructed translanguaging practice. Repetition is "a resource by which speakers create a discourse, a relationship and a world" (Tannen 1987: 574). It can foster emotional involvement (e.g., Grimes 1972). CS tailors it to his specific participants. This is exemplified by a dribbling training activity which repeated across and within sessions. Whilst repetition underpins any training, here, its familiarity gained currency in building CS's relationships with the boys and making sessions inclusive by creating familiarity, irrespective of participants' understanding of English. This overcame potential communicative breakdown without foregrounding it. The fieldnote below on the dribbling task, includes a drawing:

Fieldnote Excerpt 5: The dribbling activity

CS . . . begins moving some small plastic cones . . . He seems to be making a course. . . . He now explains that [players] must run in and out of three cones before taking a shot at the goal. . . . He concludes his introduction to the task by saying "the most important thing to do is keep the ball close" [i.e., dribble]. He repeats this."

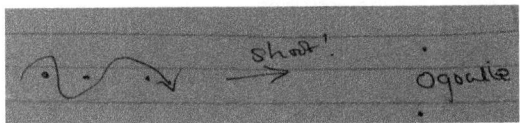

[CarSpoFn_0906_FR_01]

CS presents the intended focus of this activity as dribbling, with shooting relatively incidental. Elsewhere too, he casts dribbling as crucial to football below (line 14), in our first recording of him explaining the task to players:

Transcript Excerpt 1: The most elementary in football

1	CS	keep the ball in front of you not far
2		from you yes close your third no far
3		from here that's it outside inside
4		outside inside (.) outside your feet
5		inside your feet (.) outside inside (.)
6		no far from you no far from you not
7		far from you boys (.) that's it
8		excellent (.) well done (.) that's it (.)
9		well done yes yes yes Player-A (.)
10		well done (.) well done (.) well done
11		(.) dribble dribble dribble dribbling
12		is the most elementary in football

[CarSpoTr1_0919]

We see that delivering and explaining the task involves talking through it whilst one player does it (lines 1–7) with multimodal coordination between his words and the boy's actions (Callaghan, Moore and Simpson 2018: 40). Narration (lines 1–7), evaluation (lines 8–10), elaboration (lines 11–12) and summary (line 11) (cf. Delin 2006: 46) recall the commentary genre, invoking inclusion in larger structures by referencing the wider context of professional play, a move which we will see featured elsewhere, too. Through these, CS creates a sense of inclusion for the narrated player by lavishing detailed attention on his actions thus legitimating them. The evaluation features praise (lines 8–10). Such approval has been linked to fostering inclusion (e.g., Wehling 2017). In lines 11–12, CS provides something akin to a coda in Labov and Waletsky's (1972) terms when he indicates that the initial explanation is over, summarising it and connecting the explanation with participation in the wider footballing world (cf. Johnstone 2016: 546). Thus, the minutiae of his talk, whilst it could have occurred in any training session, here contributes to *doing inclusion* by including in multiple ways.

CS repeated this task and the talk and gesture which accompanied it, within and across sessions, creating familiarity for the boys, some of whom were new to Wales and/or the academy, and drawing them into a Community of Practice (Wenger 1998). Indeed, such was their comfort with the activity that they became able to subvert it. Its occurrence became a source of contest which, far from indicating problems, created communicative opportunities for negotiation. This ultimately allowed the boys to be heard and the coach to accommodate to them: through this repetition and its development, they collaboratively co-produced integration. This subversion of the task is described, as it occurred, over successive weeks in fieldnotes from both observers. Here is one example:

Fieldnote Excerpt 6: Cheeky

[CS] tells the boys to dribble and then try to score. . . . The boys are really cheeky. They keep moving closer to the goal and CS tries to push them back and asks them to focus.

[CarSpoFn_1025_AH_14]

Subversions were typified by CS admonishing the boys to move further back in their playing space. Such turns featured lexical and semantic repetition with excerpts like the one below, which tries to foreground dribbling, occurring repeatedly:

Transcript Excerpt 2: I'm looking for a dribbler

1	CS	Player-C
2	Player-C	my turn
3	CS	dribble listen listen [inaud. 1 syllable]
4		dribble from here

Chapter 1 'Dribble dribble dribble!': Doing inclusion in park-based children's sport

5	Player-C	where
6	CS	From where you are (.) from here until
7		here and from there you tackle from there
8	Player-C	my goal
9	CS	yes
10	Player-C	((here))
11	CS	dribble Player-D you didn't dribble no is
12		no goal you have to dribble
13	Player-D	not goal?
14	CS	no you have to dribble listen listen up
15		you have to listen carefully to me
16	Player-D	you have to dribble?
17	CS	I'm looking for a dribbler you dribble
18		from here to here here easy peasy
19	Player-D	oh
20	CS	that's it

[CarSpoTr_20151017]

In the excerpt above, CS nominates a player to commence the activity and the child brightly takes up that invitation for this most local form of inclusion, announcing "my turn" (line 2). Soon, however, it becomes clear that neither Player-C (lines 1–10) nor Player-D (lines 11–20) recognise the importance of dribbling. In communicating this, CS's talk is highly repetitive. Even in this short excerpt he says "dribble" nine times and "listen" or "listen up" five times which was typical. This lexical repetition facilitated inclusion through familiarity and drew the boys into learning English-language footballing terms. As well as featuring repetition, CS's negotiations also considered his interlocutors by being multilingual as the following notes on CS's talk shows:

Fieldnote Excerpt 7: Go back

CS: 'Player-E go back a bit go back {لورا ارجع شوي لورا ارجع ه اللاعب}'. The kids have slowly come closer to the goal despite CS's attempt to make them stick to where he's asked them to line up, 'boys you are not allowed, stay where you are, stay here.'

Players who were not included by understanding either the repetition in English or the Arabic are included through movement around the pitch and gesture. Sequential photos in Figure 1 exemplify:

In image 1, CS places his hands before the boys, miming pushing them back. In image 2, he begins to reverse away from them, illustrating the space where shooting should take place before, in image 3, turning to indicate the goal posts with his gaze before stopping, bending and pointing to both cones to emphasise

Image 1

Image 2

Image 3

Image 4

Image 5

Figure 1: "You dribble from where you are until here". All images in figure 1 are from [CarSpo_1017].

that shooting should only occur at the close of each player's turn (image 4). He then stands behind the shooting target and, through a resting stance, invites play (image 5). Our impression was that ultimately, CS was relaxed about the extent to which the boys complied. Over multiple observations, including the boys in the play seemed to be much more important to him than compliance despite his repetitive, multilingual, multimodal labouring of the explanation.

This section has illustrated translanguaging in the sense of multiple languages and ways of saying along with physical demonstration. This enables all boys to be included, despite their current understanding of English, without diverting attention from football to communication. In Li's terms, the academy is a "translanguaging space" "where language users break down the ideologically laden dichotomies between the macro and the micro, the societal and the individual, and the social and the psychological through interaction" (Li 2018: 23). It is an ideal space for inclusion to arise from such breaking down. Despite so much multimodal work, CS only *attempts* to achieve compliance. Apparently, his academy is not about inclusion at any cost. Rather he works concertedly through different forms and practices to assert his authority whilst ensuring that the boys enjoy play.

4.4 Doing inclusion through utterance-level repetition

Whilst coaching, CS used several short comments, exclamations and paralinguistic moves repeatedly. These are almost jarringly frequent throughout the spoken data, as fieldnotes from different sessions, below, exemplify:

Fieldnotes set 1: Lexical and phrasal repetition

CS continues to speak "yes, kick the ball", "unlucky",
"good shot", "happy days", "finish". [CarSpoFn_0906_FR_01]

CS is giving instructions as usual: "you can't miss this one. Finish! Unlucky!" [CarSpoFn_0919_AH_04]

CS is shouting encouragement again "A good goal", "What a quality Player-C" "What a quality". High fives are exchanged amongst the boys and with CS. [CarSpoFn_0919_FR_05]

The repetitive, formulaic vocabulary, phrases and physical rituals (high fives, in this case), potentially include the boys even if they do not immediately know all the English words. The tokens mapped onto repetitive on-pitch activities such as kicking and scoring and qualities such as trying hard ("unlucky") and playing well ("what a quality"). Through the repeating talk and actions CS saturates the boys in communicative practices that typify football. Tannen (1987, 2007) proposes four functions for repetition, which are illustrated in fieldnote set 1 and potentially construct inclusion through what Tannen calls "interpersonal involvement". I summarise this in the table below:

Table 1: Analysis of inclusion through repetition based on Tannen (1987: 581–585, see also Tannen 2007: 58–62).

Tannen's four functions of repetition	Summary of Tannen's point	Reflections on the data
Production	Through repetition, speakers "produce language in a more efficient, less energy draining way" (1987: 581).	CS provides continual feedback during play and evaluative responses afterwards. As the sport is repetitive and the effort of constant multilingual, multimodal feedback considerable, repetitive feedback offers a practical way for CS to support himself in supporting players.
Comprehension	Likewise, semantically thinner information and redundancy allow hearers "dead space" to absorb information. (1987: 582)	Some players are unfamiliar with English. All players frequently play whilst simultaneously listening. Repetition provides rest-bite from understanding and opportunities to understand and even learn repeated items.
Connection	Repetition brings cohesion having a "referential and tying function" and conveys meaning through "comment", "evaluation" and "so what" (1987: 583).	The coach creates emphasis and perspectivises his talk by foregrounding key activities (e.g., scoring) and orientations (e.g., we can be unlucky but it's good to have tried). Through this function he also connects different parts of training sessions.
Interaction	Repetition "functions on an interactional level – accomplishing social goals". It ties parts of discourse, and "ties participants to the discourse and to each other" (1987: 583–584).	CS's repetition creates a sense of listenership, shows appreciation, persuades, links ideas and ratifies players' on-pitch contributions. This consistent backdrop gives all participants common ground and, as we will see, recourse to meaning-making apparatus.

Repetition "sends a metamessage of involvement" (Tannen 1987: 584) which constructs inclusion in CS's talk. Furthermore, the boys take up his formulations, through re-use or recontextualisation, suggesting that these repetitive phrases were significant to them and created inclusion which they could replicate:

Fieldnotes set 2: Recontextualisiation

Whenever there's a goal, CS smiles, broadly. He exclaims "what a goal" and applause follows. Player-A walks past us as a goal succeeds and takes up CS's phrase "what a goal". [CarSpoFn_0926_FR_07]
One of the boys says: "Oh what a save". He points at the goal whilst he says this. [CarSpoFn_0919_FR_05]
"Oh what a block" says one of the boys in goal. He seems to be innovating on one of CS's favourite phrases "what a goal". [CarSpoFn_1003_FR_10]

By rendering CS's words, phrases and actions "extractable" (Bauman and Briggs 1990: 73) the boys draw on discourse's reflexive capacity (Silverstein and Urban 1996), indexing affiliation and aspiration, and implying "look at me! I'm on! Watch how skilfully I express myself" (Bauman 2004: 9). They invoke professional and global football, regular training and their relationship with and membership of the academy by (re)indexing (cf. Sarangi 1998: 306) as they transfer and transform CS's tokens which, itself, transfers and transforms tokens from beyond this academy.

4.5 Doing inclusion through connections to international, professional football

CS and his players referenced international, professional football in ways which flagged inclusion within those wider footballing communities. In football, long-established expectations about inclusion "filter down from, or are reinforced by the professional game", potentially shaping expectations about who "can" participate in play (e.g., Spaaij, Farquharson and Marjoribanks 2015: 403), decision-making, coaching and administration (e.g., Loy and Elvogue 1970; Hallinan and Judd 2009). We saw, when discussing the boys' enthusiasm for shooting rather than dribbling, that they too orient to messages from the professional game and CS seemed aware that invoking this "glamourous" world was a powerful communicative resource.

One way that CS drew on this resource was assigning professional players' names to the boys, during training. One, for example, was consistently referred to by CS as "Ronaldo", invoking the elite footballer, Cristiano Ronaldo dos Santos Aveiro who was, at the time, at the peak of his international career. This resource had further meaning-making potential in implying ongoing approval of the boy's play. Additionally, it enabled CS to exploit the boys' understandings of professional players. For example, in the excerpt below, he plays on the boy's Ronaldo identity to position inclusion in international football as being about more than play. We join excerpt 3 as CS explains his award of this week's "man of the match":

Transcript Excerpt 3: Not enough

1	CS	listen up I give this ((each)) week for the best
2		man the best man
3	Player-A	[inaud. 2 syllables]
4	CS	of behaviour attitude and performance
5	Player-A	okay
6	CS	performance is not enough you are Ronaldo
7		but you have to behave
8	Kids	[laugh]
9	CS	if you are not behaving you can't get it

[CarSpoTr_20151210]

Here, CS characterises sporting discipline as comprising "behaviour attitude and performance" and presents this as more important than just "being Ronaldo". Such talk allows us an insight into how inclusion for CS extends to instilling sporting values. This recalls Heath and Langman's observation that coaches' "language relates to . . . working with individuals so that they become team players" (1994: 84).

4.6 Doing inclusion through accommodation

In this chapter, we have encountered linguistic and multimodal actions which I have suggested could foster a sense of inclusion for the boys who, as I have illustrated, hear instructions in languages which are familiar to them, experience talk coordinated with gestures as well as purely visual communication, encounter repetitive tokens and are drawn into an appealing world of international football. However, not all of CS's efforts swung towards including the boys by drawing them towards him and towards sporting norms. He also moved away from some norms of sports training in ways that included the boys by accommodating them. Institutionalised, policy-driven sport for integration agendas "paradoxically can lead to a sense of alterity and exclusion" (Dowling 2020: 1152). CS was unfettered by such top-down interventions. The final examples in this chapter show how CS fitted to the boys, rather than requiring them to fit to him. The examples relate to time-keeping, wearing sports kit and paying fees.

Turning first to time-keeping, sports training sessions usually depend on punctuality because of their collectivity. Usually, coaches and a quorum of players, whose time might be valuable and/or expensive must all participate simultaneously. However, in these training sessions, late arrivals joined in without comment or censure. Sometimes the whole group would arrive almost an hour late. Far from chastising them, the coach simply delayed until they arrived before delivering the whole session, irrespective of start time. He even phoned around on one occasion before running the session almost an hour adrift of its intended start time. CS eventually changed the session times, accommodating the boys attending Saturday Madrasah sessions at a local Mosque. The new start time was inclusive but also arose iteratively with CS fitting around the boys rather than *vice versa*. Similarly, kit was never mentioned as far as we were aware. Indeed, a fieldnote observes that it does not seem to be a consideration for CS or the players, saying "The boys are variously dressed. One has football socks and a full football kit . . . Others are in trousers and shirts, jumpers, and T-shirts looking only prepared for sports by their shoes. Like the timing, the clothing is relaxed." [CarSpoFn_0912_FR_02] Non-sports-kit featured frequently, as two photos from different dates, indicate:

CarSpoPho_1003_FR_0013   CarSpoPho_1108_FR_0011

Finally, a regular and often inescapable feature of many sports clubs is fees. These can be an unforgiving deterrent to participation. Yet in CS's academy, as I noted earlier, fees were barely mentioned and when they were proffered, handled unpredictably:

Fieldnote Excerpt 8: Fees

I wonder whether the boys pay to be here. I then remember that I asked CS about this and he said that they just give him £10 every now and then. I see one of these exchanges go on at the end of the session and he insists on giving the money back.

[CarSpoFn_0912_FR_02]

CS had no draw towards an inclusion which was framed in terms of what Dowling calls "becoming like 'Us'" (2020:1162). Thus, he does not insist on punctuality, kit or fees nor the resulting fixities these bring. The norms of his football academy seemed barely to be norms at all. Rather the academy was inclusive in its flexibility and the communication which scaffolded that.

5 Conclusion

Sports contexts are ideal for observing micro acts which bring about integration and inclusion (Madsen 2012: 84). The football training examined here exemplifies micro acts which, rather than executing policy-driven agendas, instead sidestep integration and inclusion in their conventional senses. Finding no means to access initiatives connected to either, CS creates something different. It seems productive to still call this *inclusion,* but his players are included in something of his making, so this is not inclusion in the more usual sense. Whilst he aspires to feed players into mainstream competitive football, this is balanced with his wish to simply provide a place for play and learning for all. He thus creates an academy which is shackled to the majority and to global football yet quite distinct. This is driven by his own values, rather than formalised policy. Thus, examining CS's academy illuminates a very localised yet highly globalised understanding of inclusion. As Han observes:

> For centuries immigrants and their children have lived multilingual lives, and sometimes have carved out alternative spaces that help them to survive and thrive socioeconomically . . . These alternative spaces may have a lot to offer to mainstream institutions regarding policies, practices and conditions that are conducive to furthering social inclusion and multilingual development, which may help us to discover and envision creative responses to linguistic diversity (2011: 383–384).

CS's academy potentially answers questions that mainstream inclusion initiatives did not know they had. At the beginning of this paper, I asked three questions which I include here with some answers which arise:

What is inclusion? In this paper, inclusion has been viewed as a process, bottom-up, rather than an institutional agenda. It has been shown to be discursively constructed through evolving and often collaboratively produced multimodal practices. The chapter has shown how one individual, who, himself had experienced some exclusion in the sporting sphere took control of his own and others' inclusion where he could and created inclusion, on his own terms.

What are participants potentially included in? In CS's academy, participants gain a sense of being in CS's team through shared linguistic practices which bring familiarity when used by CS and joint ownership when used by the boys. They are also inculcated into wider footballing and sporting contexts which operate internationally and can be transferred at a variety of scales. This is likely to bring individual benefits to players in practical ways such as providing the skills and confidence to participate on their own terms in wider sports activities and in more personal ways, perhaps creating a way around the white privilege which CS discussed when he first met us.

How is inclusion accomplished through discursive means and, broadly defined, communicative practices? Mechanisms for accomplishing, or at least providing for, inclusion discussed in this chapter were translanguaging including multilingual practices, gesture and movement, repetition at various levels, use of and dissemination of sporting lexis, phrases and actions, analogy with elite football and flexibility around routine structural elements such as session times, sports kits and fees.

Despite concerted, long-term effort to provide a fit for the players, the coach remained a lone figure without a support structure for his academy at sessions or beyond. Previous research advises that "those who are denied belonging within 'mainstream' football club contexts can develop an alternative sense of belonging" (Bradbury, 2011; Burdsey, 2007, cited in Spaaij 2015: 313). This is exactly what CS has done although the question raised at the opening of this chapter in relation to macro-institutional inclusion remains relevant here: inclusion into what? Furthermore, the question of "inclusion for whom" is tricky even in this very specific instance. The end of the story for both the boys and the coach is unclear. Even the coach was thinking of moving to a new country towards the end of our data collection period. I therefore conclude by revisiting the coach's wider experiences through an excerpt from a vignette produced as the fieldwork period ended:

> [It was difficult to get things set up and moving in the sports site]. I . . . began to wonder whether these problems (as we perceived them at the time) told us something about the world of a sports coach – on the edges of other institutions, peripatetic in every sense of the word and keen not to make any "sudden moves" in case work from a particular source dries up. [FR's vignette]

In summarising and characterising our participation in this site, the coach's precarity, stemming from a lack of inclusion, was central. We can see CS as being on a fulcrum balancing his own lack of inclusion with his efforts to create or, at least, simulate inclusion for his players.

Appendix

Transcription and fieldnote conventions

{words}	Indicates the surrounded words were originally said in Arabic. In transcripts the Arabic is reproduced in one set of curly brackets and an English version appears italicised alongside also in curly brackets.
(.)	A pause of any duration (often action was occurring as, we suggest, a second pair part. This action is not displayed in the transcripts above so pauses are indicative).
Player-A	All player names have been anonymised with consistent alphabetic labels.
[inaud. 2 syllables]	This marks the position of the number of syllables specified of inaudible talk.
. . .	Indicates the text has been edited for brevity and focus.
((word))	A 'best guess' at somewhat inaudible talk! Alpha-numerical codes (e.g. [CarSpoTr1_0919]) Indicate the origin of each excerpt or photograph in our dataset.
!	Excitable or exclamatory speech.
Alpha-numerical codes (e.g. [CarSpoTr1_0919])	Indicate the original of each excerpt or photograph in our dataset.

References

Albury, Natan. 2014. Introducing the folk linguistics of language policy. *International Journal of Language Studies* 8(3). 85–106.

Albury, Natan & Max Diaz. 2021. From perceptual dialectology to perceptual multilingualism: a Hong Kong case study, *Language Awareness* 30(2). 152–175.

Andrews, Sharon E. 1998. Using inclusion literature to promote positive attitudes toward disabilities. *Journal of Adolescent and Adult Literacy* 41(6). 420–426.

Bauman, Richard. 2004. *A World of Others' Words: Cross-cultural Perspectives on Intertextuality*. Malden, MA: Blackwell.

Bauman, Richard & Charles L. Briggs. 1990. Poetics and performance as critical perspectives on language and social life. *Annual Review of Anthropology* 19. 59–88.

Griffiths, Iwan. 2021. November 4. Football: Wales' grassroots game worth £550m, report says. *BBC*. https://www.bbc.co.uk/news/uk-wales-59152584

Bergh, Gunnar & Sölve Ohlander. 2020. From National to Global Obsession: Football and Football English in the Superdiverse 21st Century. *Nordic Journal of English Studies* 19(5): 359–383.

Block, D. 2010. Problems of portraying migrants in applied linguistics. *Language Teaching* 43. 480–493.

Boxer, David. 2002. *Applying Sociolinguistics: Domains and Face-to-Face Interaction*. Amsterdam and Philadelphia: John Benjamins.

Brendtro, Larry K., Martin Brokenleg & Steve Van Bockern. 1990. *Reclaiming youth at risk: Our hope for the future*. National Educational Service.

Bucholtz, Mary & Kira Hall. 2005. Identity and interaction: a sociocultural linguistic approach. *Discourse Studies* 7: 585–614.

Callaghan, John, Emilee Moore & James Simpson. 2018. Coordinated action, communication, and creativity in basketball in superdiversity, *Language and Intercultural Communication* 18(1). 28–53.

Canagarajah, Suresh. 2011. Translanguaging in the classroom: Emerging issues for research and pedagogy. *Applied Linguistics Review* 2(2011). 1–28.

Creese, Angela & Adrian Blackledge. 2010. Translanguaging in the bilingual classroom: A pedagogy for learning and teaching? *Modern Language Journal* 94(1). 103–115.

Debes, John L. III. 1981. It's Time for a New Paradigm: Languaging. *Language sciences* 3(1). 186–192.

Delin, Judy. 2000. *The language of everyday life: An introduction*. London: Sage.

Dowling, Fiona. 2020. A critical discourse analysis of a local enactment of sport for integration policy: Helping young refugees or self-help for voluntary sports clubs? *Sociology of sport* 55(8). 1152–1166.

Football Association Wales. 2012. "Additional evidence from the Football Association of Wales" http://www.senedd.assemblywales.org/documents/s8499/Additional%20Written%20Information%2600-%20CELG4%20Football%20Association%20of%20Wales.pdf (accessed 17 January 2023)

García, Ofelia. 2021. 'What is translanguaging? Interview with Ofelia García'. In François Grojean. *Life as a bilingual. Knowing and using two or more languages*, 171–175. Cambridge: CUP.

Gregory, Eve & Ann Williams. 2000. *City literacies, learning to read across generations and cultures*. London: Routledge.

Grimes, Joseph E. 1972. Outlines and overlays. *Language* 48. 513–24.

Gumperz, John J. 1999. On interactional sociolinguistic method. In Srikant Sarangi & Celia Roberts (eds), *Talk, Work and Institutional Order: Discourse in Medical, Mediation and Management Settings*, 454–471. Berlin: Mouton de Gruyter.

Halilovich, Hariz, Tuba Boz & Masoud Kianpour. 2022. Fields of play: Refuge(e)s in youth multiculturalism on the fringes of Melbourne, *Journal of Immigrant and Refugee Studies* 1–13.

Han, Huamei. 2011. Social inclusion through multilingual ideologies, policies and practices: a case study of a minority church, *International Journal of Bilingual Education and Bilingualism* 14(4). 383–398.

Heath, Shirley Brice & Juliet Langman. 1994. Shared thinking and the register of coaching. In Douglas Biber & Edward Finegan (eds.), *Sociolinguistic perspectives on register*, 82–105. Oxford: OUP.

Hoyle, Susan M. 1991. Children's competence in the specialised register of sportscasting. *Journal of Child Language* 18(2). 435–450.

Johnstone, Barbara. 2016. 'Oral versions of personal experience': Labovian narrative analysis and its uptake. *Journal of Sociolinguistics*. 20(4). 542–560.

Khafaji, Adil H. A. Al. 2007. Translanguage. *Journal des traducteurs / Meta: Translators' Journal* 52(3). 463–476.

Labov, William & Joshua Waletzky. 1997 [1967]. Narrative analysis: Oral versions of personal experience. *Journal of Narrative & Life History* 7(1–4). 3–38. Orig. pub. In June Helm (ed.). 1967. *Essays on the Verbal and Visual Arts*, 12–44. Seattle/Washington: University of Washington Press.

Wei, Li. 2018. Translanguaging as a practical theory of language. *Applied linguistics* 39(1). 9–30.

Madsen, Lian Malai. 2012. Discourses on Integration and Interaction in a Martial Arts Club. In Barbara Segaert, Marc Theeboom, Christiane Timmerman & Bart Vanreusel (eds.), *Sports Governance, Development and Corporate Responsibility*, 74–88. London: Routledge.

Meadows, Bryan. 2014. Nationalism in folk theories of language. *International Journal of Applied Linguistics* 24. 337–356.
Migrant Observatory. 2016. *"Migration and Brexit"*. http://www.migrationobservatory.ox.ac.uk/projects/migration-and-brexit/ (accessed 17 January 2023)
Mulderrig, Jane. 2012. The hegemony of inclusion: A corpus-based critical discourse analysis of deixis in education policy. *Discourse and Society* 23(6). 701–728.
Piller, Ingrid & Kimie Takahashi. 2011. Linguistic diversity and social inclusion, *International Journal of Bilingual Education and Bilingualism* 14(4). 371–381.
Preston, Dennis R. 2017. Folk linguistics and language awareness. *The Routledge handbook of language awareness*, 375–386. New York: Routledge.
Sarangi, Srikant. 1998. Rethinking recontextualization in professional discourse studies: An epilogue. *Text* 18(2). 301–18.
Sheehy, Kieron & Hester Duffy. 2009. Attitudes to Makaton in the ages on integration and inclusion. *International Journal of Special Education* 24(2). 91–102.
Silverstein, Michael &Greg Urban. 1996. The natural history of discourse. In Michael Silverstein & Greg Urban (eds.), *Natural histories of discourse*, 1–17. Chicago: University of Chicago Press.
Singh, Jaspal Naveel & Frances Rock. 2018. Changing Landscapes: Cathays in Cardiff. Working Papers in Translanguaging and Translation WP. 3. https://tlang754703143.files.wordpress.com/2018/08/changing-landscapes-cardiff.pdf (accessed 17 January 2023)
Siuty, Molly & Margaret R. Beneke. (2020) Authoring dis/ability identities mapping the role of ableism in teacher candidate identity construction. *Critical Education* 1. 26–48.
Spaaij, Ramón. 2015. Refugee youth, belonging and community sport, *Leisure Studies* 34(3). 303–318.
Spurdens, Bradley & Daniel Bloyce. 2022. Beyond the rainbow: a discourse analysis of English sports organisations LGBT+ equality diversity and inclusion policies. *International Journal of Sport Policy and Politics* 14(3). 507–527.
Stats Wales. 2022. "Percentage of people participating in sporting activities three or more times a week by local authority" https://statswales.gov.wales/v/MZRT (accessed 17 January 2023)
Stubbe, Maria, Chris Lane, Jo Hilder, Elaine Vine, Bernadette Vine, Meredith Marra, Janet Holmes, & Ann Weatherall. 2003. Multiple discourse analyses of a workplace interaction. *Discourse Studies* 5. 351–388.
Tannen, Deborah. 1987. Repetition in conversation. *Language* 63(3). 574–605.
Tannen, Deborah. 2007. *Talking voices: Repetition, dialogue and imagery in conversational discourse*. Cambridge: Cambridge University Press.
Vertovec, Steven. 2007. Super-diversity and its implications. *Ethnic and Racial Studies* 30(6). 1024–1054.
Walseth, Kristin & Kari Fasting. 2004. Sport as a Means of Integrating Minority Women. *Sport in Society* 7(1). 109–129.
Welling, Elisabeth. 2017. Discourse management gestures. *Gesture* 16(2). 245–276.
Wenger, Etienne. 1998. *Communities of practice: learning, meaning, and identity*. Cambridge: Cambridge University Press.
Werbner, Pnina. 2012. Multiculturalism from above and below: Analysing a political discourse. *Journal of Intercultural Studies* 33(2). 197–209.
Yates, Lynda. 2011. Interaction, language learning and social inclusion in early settlement, *International Journal of Bilingual Education and Bilingualism* 14(4). 457–471.

Ozde Ozinanir and Louise Mullany

Chapter 2
#StillWeRise: The sociolinguistics of race, inequalities, and athlete activist identities in Formula 1 social media

1 Introduction

This chapter examines the sociolinguistics of race, inequalities, and identities in the understudied yet globally influential motorsport of Formula 1 (F1). Undertaking a qualitative, case study approach, we apply a multimodal discourse analytical (MMDA) framework to language and semiotic resources used in social media posts by the first and thus far only Black F1 driver, Sir Lewis Hamilton, who holds the record for the most wins in the sport. We focus in particular on Hamilton's feed on the international image and video-sharing platform Instagram, where he currently has 30.3 million followers, the most of any F1 driver. Our interest is on how Hamilton uses a series of semiotic and multimodal discourse strategies to construct a Black athlete activist identity which rejects social exclusion in F1 and racial injustice in wider society. We also demonstrate how Hamilton advocates for and negotiates Black inclusion and racial justice in F1 and wider society as a vision for the future using linguistic, multimodal, and social semiotic strategies.

Data has been selected from the 2020 season because this unique time period offered a useful context in which to investigate the sociolinguistics of identity in motorsport and online media. Firstly, it took place during the global Covid-19 pandemic, at a time when much of the world was still in a sustained period of lockdown, with fans unable to attend sporting events, including F1. Therefore, we argue that, without being able to physically attend any races as spectators, fans were ever-more reliant on the media and social media particularly to keep them connected to the sport. Secondly, and most importantly, six weeks before the 2020 F1 season started, a video of a white police officer murdering George Floyd, a Black man who was in police custody in Minneapolis in the United States, sparked protests against racism and marked the significant growth of the Black Lives Matter (BLM) movement. As TePoel and Nauright (2021: 695) have noted, race relations in sport "have a renewed urgency and intensity due to BLM and the COVID-19

Ozde Ozinanir, University of Warwick, United Kingdom
Louise Mullany, University of Nottingham, United Kingdom

https://doi.org/10.1515/9783110789829-003

pandemic, shining a light on continued inequities and injustices in sport and society".

We focus on a series of posts from Hamilton's Instagram profile. We examine how, as a high-profile sporting celebrity, Hamilton uses his Instagram feed to partake in socio-political activism. We focus in particular on highlighting the complex array of multimodal discourse strategies that he uses to construct a Black athlete identity for himself, and to position himself against racism in wider society and the exclusion of Black identities in F1. We analyse Hamilton's posts by locating social semiotic elements and the language strategies selected in the social media feeds through an MMDA approach (Kress and van Leeuwen 2021), further contextualised through sports media studies (Wenner 1998), thus expanding the heavily under-researched area of F1 sports language research (see File and Schnurr 2018). Through our analyses of the textual choices of Hamilton's Instagram posts, combined with the social semiotics of how significant sporting artefacts are displayed and discussed, we aim to demonstrate how Hamilton uses several discourse strategies to construct a leading Black athlete activist identity to engage audience members, and to advocate for racial inclusion in F1 and activism in racial justice movements.

We will now outline the background to the study in section 2, focusing on establishing the sport-media-identity nexus and its relationship to F1, alongside an interdisciplinary consideration of social inclusion and exclusion, and Black identities and activism in sport. The methodology of the study is given in section 3, and the data analysis of the Instagram posts are presented in section 4. It is our intention that the findings can be of applied linguistic value to those working within F1 and sports, and we discuss this further in section 5, along with emphasising the role that sports personalities can play in human rights activism through the identities they perform on social media platforms and in sporting contexts. We conclude with a consideration of future directions for studies of F1 and the sociolinguistics of identity in relation to athlete activism via social media.

2 Background

In this section, we outline our key terms and areas of study, covering the relationship between sport and the media, Black athlete activism, identity construction on social media, and social inclusion and exclusion. We also outline previous research on F1 and characterise the under-researched area of linguistics in F1 to date. It is well-established in sports studies that media and sport have a complex dialogic relationship. Wenner (1998: xiii) argues that this is a result of "the cultural fusing of sport with communication", caused in part by the rapid mediatisation of sport, and "the interaction of institutions, texts and audiences" (1998: 9). The relationship between media and sport is increasingly important (Rowe 2009), especially with the emergence of digital and online forms, which have deepened the wider influence and reach of sport. Digital social media features such as hashtags have also received scholarly attention recently due to their prominence as audience engagement strategies, therefore highlighting social media as a critical medium for sports (Horky and Meyer 2021; Wang 2021). Identity, defined here as "the social positioning of self and other" (Bucholtz and Hall 2010: 18), has long been viewed as a key feature in sports media, therefore forming a prominent sport-media-identity nexus. Despite the dominance of political neutrality discourse in sports, sport has also historically acted as a fertile site for socio-political messaging, and particularly those supporting marginalised and under-represented identities. This has been observable in the case of Black activism in sport; since Edwards' (1969) influential work, Black identity, socio-political activism and sport have had a complex relationship in sporting contexts and their scholarship.

In our analysis of the inclusion of the Black athlete activist identity in F1, we follow the United Nations' (2016: 20) definition of social inclusion as "the process of improving the terms of participation in society for people who are disadvantaged on the basis of age, sex, disability, race, ethnicity, origin, religion, or economic or other status, through enhanced opportunities, access to resources, voice and respect for rights". Issues of social inclusion are particularly relevant to F1, as the sport is notorious for its exclusivity and high expenditure. Hamilton identifies as the "only Black, working-class person in his field" (Mission 44 2021), defining F1 as a "billionaire boys' club" (BBC 2021). While the sport does not openly discriminate in recruiting drivers, F1 has historically been infamous for the exclusion of marginalised groups, including women, and people of colour. This diminishes the supposed global influence of the sport, which currently includes races in every inhabited continent excluding Africa.

However, most of the pre-existing social scientific research into F1 has focused predominantly on the impact of the sport on host countries and local communities from sociocultural or economic perspectives (Cheng and Jarvis 2010; Gezici and Er 2016), or on criticisms around F1's environmental impact (Miller 2016). F1 also provides complexities for the sport-media-identity nexus: teams and drivers use sports gear as important semiotic devices to promote sponsors and develop their personal sporting brands, including logos on race helmets and overalls, and team-issued merchandise worn by drivers during media interviews. The body is thus used as a key medium in the sport, creating a complex sport-media-identity nexus, providing excellent opportunities for multimodal linguistic analysis.

Much of the research conducted on athlete activist identities, and the relationship between sports and race more broadly has focused on more traditional forms of broadcast and written media (Farrington et al. 2012; Lamb 2016) or has come from fields outside of sociolinguistics (see Carrington and McDonald 2001; Nauright and Wiggins 2016). However, by highlighting the importance of online social media analysis, some scholars are beginning to examine online media to explore identity through notions of the sporting celebrity and athlete activism. LeBron James (basketball) and Colin Kaepernick (American football), whose anti-racism activism is similar to Hamilton's approach, have notably received media and academic attention as athlete activists for their platforming of Black identity and social movements including BLM (Coombs and Cassilo 2017; Marston 2020). However, Hirschfelder (2020) argues that media representations of Black sporting celebrities who are established as athlete activists can be damaging as they often isolate Black athlete activists within their sporting contexts, thus maintaining and reproducing discourses of social exclusion.

Only a handful of studies in media and language research has examined F1 or Hamilton's role as a leading athlete. Farrington et al. (2012) discuss racism towards Hamilton during one race, or Grand Prix (GP), as well as accusations of Hamilton using the "race card" during a post-race broadcast interview in 2011, where he joked that he may have received a penalty during the race because of his Black identity, explicitly highlighting the impact of Black exclusion in F1. File and Schnurr (2018) approach the latter incident from the linguistic perspective of failed humour in sports discourse. They focus on the mixed responses Hamilton received from other participants, including the interviewer and online audience, noting again the reception of the incident by critics as Hamilton "playing the race card". Hamilton's comment about his race in 2011 took place almost a decade before the focus of the current study, where for the first time he consistently makes explicit his sociopolitical stance against racism and inequalities (Younge 2021). More recently, Tyrkkö and Limatius (2019) have focused on team radio communication within F1 from a corpus linguistics perspective, thus further demonstrating the emergence of F1 as a fertile site for linguistic analysis. However, despite an emerging interest by sociolinguists and discourse analysts into the languages, discourses, and identities of sport (Caldwell et al. 2016; Butterworth 2021), racial justice activism in motorsport and sports generally continues to remain understudied in these disciplines, a knowledge gap which this study intends to address.

3 Methodology

In a media interview with sociologist Gary Younge, Hamilton reflected on the start of the 2020 season being a critical moment for his own position as a Black athlete. He comments that the BLM movement triggered the following:

> This wrath of emotions came up and I couldn't contain myself . . . I was in tears. And this stuff came up that I'd suppressed over all these years. And it was so powerful and sad and also releasing. And I thought, 'I can't stay quiet. I need to speak out because there are people experiencing what I'm experiencing, or 10 times worse. Or 100 times worse. And they need me right now. And so when I did speak out, that was me letting the Black community know: 'I hear you and I stand with you.' (Younge 2021: 1)

Because of the importance of this particular moment in time to Hamilton and his developing role as a Black athlete activist, we decided to focus our analysis at this pivotal point in Hamilton's F1 career. We have focused on the opening two races of the 2020 season which took place in Austria, analysing Instagram posts from the Austrian and Styrian Grands Prix. Our data consists of the first Instagram posts where Hamilton uses the linguistic, multimodal, and social semiotic conventions of the platform and a series of F1 artefacts, including helmets, visual footage and clothing to comment directly on racial in/exclusion and racial justice in F1 and contemporary society.

We have also selected these Instagram posts as they were posted at the start of the 2020 season where Hamilton, for the first time, deliberately backgrounds his usual stance as a successful F1 driver, to instead foreground his identity as a Black athlete activist. An F1 race weekend typically covers Thursday through Sunday, during which F1 drivers, all of whom have active social media accounts, often post on each day. It is also common for drivers to post reflections about their race performance on Monday, to explain any incidents that may have occurred and to publicly thank team members. Despite often following this trend, Hamilton notably abstains from posting reflections exclusively or explicitly about sporting performance for the first two races of the 2020 season post-race, curating his social media feeds instead around activism, particularly focusing on BLM. The first post in the data set, Extract 1, marks the beginning of the season through Hamilton's 2020 season helmet reveal post, whereas Extracts 2 and 3 were released shortly after the two races. The first race of this season also saw the launch of an all-black car for Hamilton's team Mercedes including the command "End Racism" written on the car, and the launch of F1's #WeRaceAsOne initiative, which involved the inclusion of rainbows on cars to honour COVID-19 frontline workers, a manifesto detailing sustainability goals, and "visual displays of support in the fight against racism" (Formula 1 2020). This initiative also included some drivers taking the knee before races and was controversial due to the divided opinion of drivers. While #WeRaceAsOne has received some scholarly attention (Khan 2021), this study addresses Hamilton's reflections on these demonstrations through fine-grained analysis.

The sociocultural influence of BLM across several continents demonstrates the important role played by Hamilton as not only the sport's most popular personality, but as the emerging athlete activist striving for Black inclusion in a predominantly white sport. As we will demonstrate further below, through his social semiotic choices within the sporting context, including crash helmets and pre-race clothing, as well as embedding BLM into his social media persona, Hamilton uses the start of the 2020 season to align himself and his team directly with racial activism. By locating our study within this context, we aim to illustrate how sports professionals utilise textual and visual strategies online and in sporting contexts to advocate for social inclusion through engagements with audiences and constructions of their own social, professional, and activist identities. Therefore, our analyses will demonstrate how social media and professional sporting platforms can be used to further social inclusion causes. This adds to the growing area of professional communication research which examines how linguistic analysis can be used as a tool of political intervention (see Mullany 2020), as well as having practical implications for sporting professionals and sports media practitioners who are interested in how social media sites can be used as successful platforms to further activism and advocacy around issues of inclusion for mass international audiences.

3.1 Analytical framework

In order to illustrate the strategies that Hamilton used in his posts to position himself as an emerging Black athlete activist, we deemed a qualitative, multimodal discourse analytical approach (MMDA) necessary to ensure that the intricacies of these strategies could be given full attention. We combine this framework with the analysis of social semiotic elements present within the images, including clothing, gear, hair, logos, and other forms of non-verbal communication and kinesics, including body language and gestures, e.g., taking a knee and raised fists. These are accompanied by discourse analyses of written captions under images, hashtags, emojis, and slogans to investigate how Hamilton uses his Instagram feed to construct identities for himself and his team, and precisely how he disseminates his activist messaging through the discourse strategies that have been chosen.

We integrate a series of key principles from sociolinguistics and discourse analysis in our analytical framework. Central to our analyses of Hamilton's Instagram posts are Bucholtz and Hall's (2010) principle of indexicality (Ochs 1992), and Fairclough's ([1989] 2014) conceptualisations of intertextuality and synthetic personalisation. We follow Bucholtz and Hall's (2010: 21) assertion that identity emerges through "indexical processes" which includes identity indexes in the form of explicit use of identity labels, implicatures, and presuppositions, and "the use of linguistic structures and systems that are ideologically associated with specific personas and groups". In the context of our analyses, we demonstrate how Hamilton makes use of certain identity indexes through social semiotic elements such as hair and clothing. We are defining intertextuality in this chapter as the articulation of other texts (written or otherwise) within different texts (Fairclough 2014). As such, our analyses of Hamilton's Instagram posts explore intertextual links that Hamilton embeds within his posts to notable Black athletes and activism, and Black identity indexes to represent himself as a notable Black athlete activist. Finally, synthetic personalisation is defined as "the simulation of private, face-to-face, person-to-person discourse in public mass-audience discourse" (Fairclough 2014: 65), and we analyse how Hamilton uses textual and visual synthetic personalisation strategies to establish an argumentative rhetorical style and engage his audiences to highlight his racial justice messaging.

The discourse analyses of captions are supported by van Leeuwen's (2008) network for the critical discourse analysis of the representation of social actors and legitimation in discourse. For the MMDA approach, we follow Kress and van Leeuwen's (2021) model. MMDA provides an ideal framework for qualitative social semiotic resources including videos, photographs, and text, with these resources including displays of the body such as clothing and various sports accessories which are central to F1 Instagram posts. The Instagram posts primarily include representations of human participants in the images, predominantly Hamilton himself; we therefore focus more specifically on features including gaze, angle, and size of frame. Table 1 summarises the key analytical terms which we have used to code the visual features in our data, adapted from Kress and van Leeuwen (2021).

Table 1: Summary of key effects and features under a multimodal discourse analytical framework, adapted from Kress and van Leeuwen (2021).

Demand	Gaze at the viewer
Offer	Absence of gaze at the viewer
Personal distance	Close shot
Social distance	Medium shot
Impersonal distance	Long shot
Involvement	Frontal angle
Detachment	Oblique angle
Viewer power	High angle

Table 1 (continued)

Equality	Eye-level angle
Participant power	Low angle
Action orientation	Frontal view neutralizing central perspective
Observer orientation	Top-down view neutralizing central perspective

We will now analyse the Instagram data from the two GP in Austria, starting with the longest post, used to launch Hamilton's 2020 season.

4 Analysis

Our analyses of Hamilton's Instagram posts aim to demonstrate how a series of multimodal discourse strategies work together strategically to establish an argumentative rhetorical style designed to engage audience members, to raise their awareness of racial inequality and simultaneously to advocate activism in racial justice movements. The first Instagram post which fulfils our data collection criteria went live on 2 July 2020. It consists of video footage where Hamilton reveals his new helmet. This is the first post which explicitly launches Hamilton's activist stance for the 2020 season, and so it is analysed in full.

Extract 1: Austrian GP, Media Day post, with embedded video, 02/07/2020
https://www.instagram.com/tv/CCJu_I7hXqF/?utm_source=ig_web_copy_link

Caption: Still WE Rise ✊ #BlackLivesMatter
Video transcript:

1	*[close up shots of helmet details]*
2	*[Hamilton shown in front of his poster at the Mercedes motorhome, wearing a black and green*
3	*"END RACISM" t-shirt under a checkered overshirt, in a face mask and sunglasses, looking to*
4	*the side]*
5	*[Hamilton shown in the motorhome, wearing jewellery, black mask, and Mercedes team gear]*
6	*[Hamilton looks down and then directly at camera]*
7	Hamilton: I've just arrived at the track here in Austria. For a long time we've been planning
8	for uhm the livery change with the car... uh for the suit change... and I'd also designed... and
9	my helmet is black... and purple this year.
10	*[holds helmet up to the level of his shoulders and towards the camera]*
11	So I've only just seen this for the first time... *[pauses, looks at helmet]*
12	And uh, normally my helmet is white, my suit is white, and obviously the car is silver. On the top
13	here *[points at BLM raised fist logo and BLM writing with index]*
14	*[camera back on Hamilton who alternates between looking down at the helmet and directly at the*
15	*camera]*
16	*[camera alternates between helmet details and Hamilton]*
17	This is the whole reason that the helmet has changed its colour, like my suit has and also the car.
18	It's supporting equality above all and just really continuing to solidify that important message.
19	As we currently now have the mic and people are starting to listen so it's an opportunity to continue
20	to push that message and really hold people accountable... brands, and the teams at Formula 1,
21	and everybody here needs to be held accountable and be open to educating themselves, to being
22	open to uhm understanding why the Black Lives movement is happening and why around the
23	world we need to be pushing for equality. Uhm because it's not good enough. Even if someone
24	says to you "we've been doing something" uhm or "we've been trying" *[shakes head side to side]*
25	they need to try harder because it is still a big issue that the world is fighting, you know, 60 years
26	later after Martin Luther King uhm was fighting for it and gave his life so uhm...
27	That's what it's about I think, I've kept the purple from what I've planned to start with the season.
28	It's my favourite colour and uhm... yeah I hope you get to see it when I'm in the car

Starting with the post's caption, the first piece of language the viewer sees, it is notable that Hamilton makes an intertextual reference to Maya Angelou's poem *Still I Rise*, an iconic piece of Black literature, with a strategic pronoun shift, changing the singular personal pronoun "I" in Angelou's poem to collective pronoun "we". This pronoun change draws attention to a shift from individual to collective Black identity. Hamilton's use of intertextuality to index Black identity is further seen in the addition of the raised fist emoji in the caption, in the darker brown colour of the five different options, arguably signifying Hamilton's mixed-race Black identity. This emoji is another reference to a key moment in Black athlete activism: the first notable use of the Black Power salute in sports, when African-American athletes Tommie Smith and John Carlos raised a black-gloved fist on the podium at the 1968 Summer Olympics. The emoji also works as an intertextual device to align Hamilton with BLM, as the gesture has become a prominent symbol of the movement. In this short caption, Hamilton positions himself with two key moments in Black histories and assigns himself the authority to change Angelou's original phrase, arguably demonstrating an awareness of the power of his voice and platform. In his reference to the Black Power salute, he explicitly aligns himself with fellow Black activist athletes and BLM. Finally, Hamilton's use of the #BlackLivesMatter hashtag shows him explicitly positioning himself with the movement, whilst simultaneously targeting future audiences for potential engagement through the hashtag choice.

This is paralleled by the video transcript of Hamilton demonstrating the motivation behind stylistic choices for the 2020 season, including switching from the famous Mercedes silver to black in honour of BLM. In claiming that the change was planned "for a long time" (line 7), he also uses collective pronoun "we" to refer to the Mercedes team. His switch to the singular pronoun "I" (line 8) suggests that while Hamilton was active in the Mercedes team's stylistic decisions, he was responsible for his helmet design. This highlights Hamilton's awareness of the power of his platform both on social media and on track. His emphasis on the colour changes (lines 9 and 12) alongside his declarative "so I've only just seen this for the first time" (line 11), as well as use of the adverb "normally" marks the uniqueness of the circumstances and creates anticipation for the explanation that follows, further emphasising the message. Hamilton is explicit in demonstrating his motivation behind the changes, directly citing the BLM movement (line 17).

Hamilton then shifts his collective personal pronoun use to refer arguably to Black communities, using a voice-related metaphor "as we currently now have the mic" (line 19). This adds to the argument that Hamilton explicitly uses his platform to drive forward inclusive and anti-racist ideology, further and explicitly foregrounding his role as a voice for the Black community. His increased use of temporal deixis ("currently", "now") marks the intensity of the time-period as an opportunity to take action, highlighting the urgency and importance of the message. Lines 19–20 assign power to the Black (activist) communities with which Hamilton aligns himself through the use of the active voice in conjunction with the continued voice metaphors, thus platforming collective Black (activist) identities.

His contextualisation of anti-racist causes within F1 through naming, and collectivisation and spatial deixis ("everybody here", line 21) in his specific references to F1 settings focalises his social inclusion efforts around the sport. The switch to the active voice in discussing the awareness of racial justice issues " . . . be open to educating themselves" (lines 21), assigns white individuals the responsibility to develop race consciousness, a prominent discourse of BLM and other social movements. Hamilton echoes this assignment of responsibility to previously uninvolved individuals through vague and non-technical language ". . . why the Black Lives movement is happening and why around the world we need to be pushing for equality" (lines 22–23). This demonstrates Hamilton's efforts in indexing his athlete activist identity by reproducing prominent activist discourse. In order to create further audience engagement, Hamilton utilises the second person pronoun "you", synthetically personalising his audience, and directly positioning them alongside himself in the fight against racial exclusion and injustice (line 24). Hamilton then delivers a call for action against racial exclusion and injustice to launch his season. In his use of collective third person pronoun "they" (line 25), he separates himself and his audience from those he criticises. His use of evaluative language through adjectival "big", modifying the noun "issue", as well as the choice of "fight" as a metaphor for anti-racist efforts, further emphasises the importance of his cause. This is also the case in line 26, where Hamilton constructs Martin Luther King Jr. as the active participant in continuing the fight metaphor. In his direct address (line 28), Hamilton finally attempts to create engagement with and attention for the sport "I hope you get to see it when I'm in the car", referencing the on-board camera shown during F1 broadcasts, from which the helmet would be visible, aligning F1 directly with his platforming of social inclusion causes.

Multimodal and semiotic elements in the video and on the helmet itself support the messages in the transcript through a strategic use of intertextuality. The back of Hamilton's helmet shows the words "Still We Rise", written in the same font as Hamilton's "Still I Rise" tattoo. It is an adaptation of Hamilton's previous helmets, which showed "Still I Rise" in the same font, directly referencing his past uses of the phrase. This use of font, and the shift of pronouns again demonstrates intertextuality as a key strategy in Hamilton's call for his audiences to join in collective action against racism and for inclusion of Black identities into a sport otherwise notorious for its social exclusion. Taken together, these semiotic and textual features highlight the importance of F1 helmets as tools for Black athlete activist identity construction, with the overarching goal of promoting racial justice and inclusion.

Hamilton's use of multimodal synthetic personalisation strategies throughout the video, including the *demand images* achieved through direct eye contact with the camera (and thus his audience), further supports his use of synthetic personalisation strategies in the transcripts, therefore further solidifying his call for racial inclusion and justice. Hamilton's eye contact also shifts between the camera and towards the helmet, further supported by hand gestures (line 13) towards details on the helmet, inviting the viewer's gaze to follow Hamilton's to the BLM logo and slogan, therefore overall strengthening his call for his audience to join him and support his call for action against racial exclusion in F1 and wider society as a whole.

Extract 2: Austrian GP, post-race post on Race Day, 05/07/2020
https://www.instagram.com/p/CCReSLFBu1C/?utm_source=ig_web_copy_link

```
1   Today was an important moment for me and all the people out there who are working
2   for and hoping for change. For a more equal and just society. I may get criticism in the
3   media and elsewhere, but this fight is about equality, not politics or promotion. To me it
4   was an emotional and poignant chapter in the progress of making F1 a more diverse and
5   inclusive sport. I want a better future for our generation and the ones after us. There is
6   so much that needs to be done. No one is perfect but if we all chip in and do our part,
7   we can see change. I truly believe that. Thank you to my team for their incredible
8   support and hard work this weekend and thank you to all who supported. Let's keep
9   pushing, guys. See you next week. Love. #EndRacism #BlackLivesMatter
```

This post consists of two images from the first #WeRaceAsOne demonstration taking place. There are a number of features in the images used which are analysed here using Kress and van Leeuwen's (2021) MMDA framework. In the first image, Hamilton is shown taking a knee whilst wearing the Mercedes race overalls up to the waist, a black t-shirt with "BLACK LIVES MATTER" written in the centre in white block capitals, and a black Mercedes hat. This first image achieves a sense of equality between Hamilton and the viewer through an equal eye-level shot. The image also signifies a common cause between Hamilton and his audience through *involvement* achieved by a frontal angle, indexing collective identity and efforts in the pursuit of racial justice and inclusion. This is supported by Hamilton's choice of clothing, as the BLM t-shirt and the team-issued Mercedes hat continue to demonstrate the importance of semiotics in promoting the sport's brands and Hamilton's social inclusion causes. The *offer image* in the first photograph, presenting Hamilton to the viewer as an "item of information, object of contemplation", while traditionally considered to take power away from the participant, arguably solidifies Hamilton's position as a symbolic voice for the Black activist community (Kress and van Leeuwen 2021: 118).

The second image shows the demonstration and Hamilton taking a knee from a wider angle, with fellow drivers, five of whom are taking the knee, five of whom are not. While the image shows a higher angle, which under our MMDA model would assign the viewer power, historically, taking the knee for Black activism has been viewed as a reclamation of power in the form of opposing oppression. This demonstrates the continued importance of intertextuality and contextual knowledge in Hamilton's activism. This is also true of the wider angle and long shot, which allows the viewer to see Hamilton taking a knee amongst several athletes who are not. This echoes other athlete activists, notably Colin Kaepernick, who can be said to have popularised the gesture in sport, as well as other athletes, including footballers, who followed. Arguably, it also references the earlier instances of the gesture by Martin Luther King Jr, who took the knee during protests in Selma in 1965, and whom Hamilton has already cited in the helmet reveal post. Notably, by fitting the photograph into the square specification on Instagram, the other drivers who are kneeling in the image are cropped out (including Hamilton's teammate Valtteri Bottas) but the majority who did not kneel are included. This creates the effect that Hamilton is differentiating himself from fellow drivers, constructing a lone athlete activist identity in contradiction with his captions. This is substantiated by Hamilton's choice of clothing; he is shown to be the only driver wearing a BLM t-shirt in comparison to other drivers' End Racism t-shirts, thus directly aligning himself with the specific social movement as opposed to a more generic command.

Despite being released shortly after the race, Hamilton does not use this post's caption to reflect on race performance or his first win of the season, as would be expected, but instead reflects on the demonstrations which took place beforehand. Notably in this extract, Hamilton assigns himself the authority to represent activists in the same utterance ("all the people out there who are working for and hoping for change", lines 1–2), indexing a collective activist identity. Hamilton's use of strategic ambiguity in line 3 ("this fight"), continuing the fight metaphor prevalent in Extract 1, enables him to reject politics and promotion claims towards his activism. This continued use of intertextuality in representing other activist voices, combined with Hamilton's repeated acknowledgment of his own individual athlete activist voice, "for me" (line 1), "to me" (line 3) combines individual and collective voices in social inclusion efforts, adding weight to Hamilton's activist messaging. This is further reflected in his use of collective personal pronouns (line 6), as well as in his expressions of gratitude towards his team and supporters (lines 7 and 8). Therefore, Hamilton's athlete activism is constructed as multilayered, and as representing individual and collective voices in racial justice efforts within both the specific sporting contexts of F1 as well as broader social inclusion movements.

Hamilton continues to develop his multilayered athlete activist identity through associations of emotive language with issues of diversity and inclusion, for instance, through the noun phrase "emotional and poignant chapter" (line 4). This association legitimises and assigns authority to Hamilton's message and his position as a leading Black athlete activist, representing himself as an athlete motivated by morality above politics or promotion as he claims his critics suggest. Such expressions of emotion alongside personalisation strategies (through direct address in lines 8–9) not only enables Hamilton to construct an emotive ethical athlete identity for himself, but also strengthens the personalised relationship with both his audience and his team, thus ultimately strengthening the outreach of his racial justice messaging. His use of the

"#EndRacism" and "#BlackLivesMatter" hashtags further assist in this pursuit, marking continuity and consistency in his activist messaging using social media features as well as other semiotic elements (e.g., clothing choices), and aligning Hamilton once again with the BLM and other racial justice movements, as well as with fellow drivers through the "#EndRacism" hashtag, to solidify the foregrounding of the collective activist voice.

Our final extract, similar to Extract 2, takes the form of a written reflection of the race weekend, accompanied by an image, which was posted shortly after the Styrian GP on 12 July 2020, where Hamilton secured his first win of the season.

Extract 3: Styrian GP, post-race post on Race Day, 12/07/2020
https://www.instagram.com/p/CCjOzm4sfF6/?utm_source=ig_web_copy_link

The single image shows Hamilton on the Styrian GP podium in Mercedes driver overalls decorated with team sponsors, Hamilton's car number, surname, and the British flag. Hamilton is pictured looking down, wearing braids and a black mask, with a raised right fist.

The following text accompanies the photographic image:

1 We stand together and fight ✊ the team today took the knee which was just amazing to see that
2 together we can learn, be open minded and conscious of what's going on in the world. Today we
3 won but we have a long way to go. Thank you so much to everyone in my team, here at the track
4 and back at the factory. I hope you are proud of what we are standing for and achieving together.
5 A huge thanks to all of you #TeamLH, I appreciate all of your support and your positive messages,
6 you've really kept me going 🙏 #StillWeRise

In this extract, the multimodal strategies found in the first photograph strengthen Hamilton's platforming of the Black athlete activist voice. Power is assigned to Hamilton through a lower eye angle, emphasising the Black Power salute. The photograph also shows an *offer image*, with Hamilton's gaze pointing downwards and out of shot, further guiding the viewer's gaze to the raised fist, thus increasing its power. Hamilton looking down also allows the viewer to observe his tightly braided hair, often considered to be a significant index of Black identity (Dabiri 2019). The image further adds weight to Hamilton's messaging through targeted audience engagement using *involvement* achieved through a frontal angle, signifying alliance and commonality between Hamilton and the viewer.

Hamilton begins the caption with a continued emphasis on inclusive collective identity and efforts (through first-person plural pronoun "we" in line 1) and "fight" as a metaphor for racial justice activism. His use of the first-person plural pronoun is ambiguous, and could be in reference to the Mercedes team, Black or activist communities, or his fans, which allows multiple groups to consider themselves as the target audience. He also continues his use of the raised fist emoji, and therefore direct reference to the Black Power salute also found in the image.

The following sentence suggests that the pronoun use refers to the Mercedes team taking the knee against racism. The ambiguous use of the first-person plural pronoun continues in lines 2 and 3, and arguably simultaneously represent participants within F1 and wider society, thus demonstrating Hamilton's contextual and broader social sensibilities, and his advocacy for social inclusion on multiple levels. Line 2 specifically sees Hamilton using his social media platform to disseminate a call for action in the development of racial consciousness ("together we can learn, be open minded and conscious of what's going on in the world").

The use of vague language in reference to the racial justice causes ("what's going on in the world") alludes to the design of an assumed audience with previous knowledge of the subject, emphasising the importance of a collective identity in furthering social inclusion causes. The blurred lines between sport and activism in lines 2–3 ("today we won but we have a long way to go") aligns sporting success directly with social inclusion causes. The strategic ambiguity in the use of the collective personal pronouns in this line acts as a possible synthetic personalisation strategy, bringing together different camps Hamilton aligns himself with, including his fanbase, his team, and other activists, under causes of social inclusion and racial justice. The prominence of a collective identity persists alongside the repeated emotive expressions of gratitude (lines 3–5), continuing to construct personalised relationships between not only Hamilton and the Mercedes team, but also Hamilton and his audience. This is supported by his use of the hashtag "#TeamLH", as a collective term of address for his fanbase, used to create further engagement. Using synthetic personalisation strategies including direct address, Hamilton credits "TeamLH" as active catalysts in his success, therefore solidifying the personal relationship he constructs between himself and his audience through social media features, working to strengthen his activist causes in the process.

It becomes clear that Hamilton approaches efforts for inclusion through a variety of ways, most directly through the explicit and public articulation of his racial justice activism, but also through inclusion of audiences within sporting processes, and through a public acknowledgment of team hierarchy. Hamilton's use of the hashtag "#StillWeRise" intertextually links back to multiple levels of semiotic and multimodal elements, including Angelou's original poem, his tattoo and helmet, as well as his past social media posts including repetition of this phrase in Extract 1, therefore demonstrating Hamilton's intertextual sensibilities, and continued contributions to racial justice activism discourse.

5 Discussion

Our detailed analysis of Hamilton's Instagram posts has shown how the combination of several multimodal discourse choices enables Hamilton to construct a Black athlete activist identity and to address issues of inclusion and exclusion. Khan (2021: 175) claims that, "when Black athletes protest today, their speech is neither purely spontaneous nor purely derivative". Hamilton's constructions of his Black athlete activist identity accordingly represent his sensitivities towards the use of his voice for the social inclusion of Black identities in both his sporting context and in wider society. Hamilton uses a whole set of diverse multimodal discourse and sociolinguistic features, primarily intertextuality, synthetic personalisation, and indexicality, to address a designed audience, to construct athlete activist identities for himself and members of his team, and to position himself directly as a Black athlete against racial injustice and exclusion. The analysis clearly demonstrates Hamilton's desire to position himself as directly speaking out against racism in wider society and the exclusion of Black people in F1, evidenced through the direct indexicality of Black identity and the multiple metalinguistic strategies about race and racism, which he consistently makes the core focus of his Instagram feed throughout the 2020 F1 season and beyond.

Hamilton suggests at multiple points that his efforts are applicable to both his specific sporting contexts and to wider societies, therefore echoing scholars who emphasise the blurred lines within the sport-media-identity nexus. Hamilton further blurs the lines between sport and culture through his strategic use of intertextuality. He utilises both traditional and contemporary media (helmets, clothing, social media) and art forms (references to Angelou), highlighting the argument that sport does not exist within a vacuum, and is affected by and affects cultural processes and products. Hamilton using a wide range of discourse features for identity construction and racial justice activism within the unique contexts of F1 therefore offers a distinctive set of opportunities and challenges for scholars and practitioners, and adds to a growing body of research analysing the activism of other Black athlete activists (Coombs and Cassilo 2017; Marston 2020).

Athlete activism in F1 appears to be particularly significant for Hamilton in the two races we examined, in the sense that it makes up part of wider international efforts for social change. Hamilton associates symbolic gestures directly with social change, therefore not only increasing the sociocultural importance of athlete activism and the sport-media-identity nexus, but also putting further value on F1 and its semiotic and media conventions. For Hamilton, his existence in such an exclusive sport appears to function as an inclusion strategy, shown by the changes he enacts within his team at the start of the 2020 season, and using his own body as a key medium. Hamilton contributes to discourses of inclusion and exclusion within F1 and wider sociocultural contexts by discursively establishing identity positions for himself as a Black athlete activist, and for his team members, fellow drivers, teams, and fans as either in opposition to or as sharing his activist values in the scope of the two Grands Prix. He embeds Black identity into F1 through his own identity construction through both explicit and implicit adaptation of Black histories and indexes. He also includes BLM as a social movement in F1 contexts explicitly through the use of its slogans and logos and implicitly through voice and fight metaphors, therefore arguing against exclusion and so-called political neutrality in sport. Finally, through collective identity construction and synthetic personalisation of his audience, he includes otherwise invisible participants within the processes of F1.

Hamilton's continuous awareness, direct address, and synthetic personalisation of the viewer enable him to strengthen his activist messaging to engage his audience, supported by the consistency of the message through different modes. He uses his popularity and curates a social media presence, which continues during the season and beyond, to establish a firm position for him as an athlete activist foregrounding Black identity. Hamilton's dissemination of his activist messaging through semiotic and multimodal discursive features continues beyond the two races analysed here; whilst heavily concentrated around racial justice, he also includes environmental activism, gender equality, and LGBTQIA+ rights, demonstrating an ongoing commitment to the use of social media platforms as social inclusion tools.

Hamilton's consistent use of direct indexicality and metacommunication about the language of racial exclusion and activism shows his awareness of his social media platform in furthering causes of Black inclusion. These observations also support the argument that sport and media have a critical dialogic relationship; more specifically, they support arguments from researchers in other disciplines, including Finn (2021), in establishing the increasingly important role of mediatised motorsport in wider society. The omission of sporting performance reflections by the sport's most popular athlete also reflects the role of F1 beyond the sporting level, therefore highlighting the importance of athlete activists in burgeoning social media platforms with such significant audience reach, which is now being increasingly acknowledged by scholars and critics.

5.1 Sporting bodies, athlete activism and identity control

As highlighted above, the Instagram data analysed here has been taken from the 2020 season. In late December 2022, during the F1 off-season, and just prior to this book's publication, the ruling body of F1, the FIA (Fédération Internationale de l'Automobile) announced a ban on "the general making and display of political, religious and personal statements or comments" by professionals in F1 without prior written permission from the FIA from the 2023 season (Noble 2022). The FIA's justification for this action was cited as wanting to abide by "the principle of neutrality". The sudden inclusion of such a clause and the ambiguity of its conditions not only demonstrate the complex entanglement of the sport-media-identity nexus and socio-political messaging in F1 motorsport, but also problematise the affordances offered by the sport and its platforms for drivers to advocate for socio-political causes or foreground religious or personal aspects of their identities.

This controversial decision has already generated significant criticism and resistance from drivers working under the FIA, as well as journalists and fans of the sport, while Hamilton has not yet offered a comment on the matter, as of January 2023. Such a drastic decision from the FIA has real-life implications for the practitioners of Formula 1 motorsport, and this development emphasises the timely importance of this type of athlete activist research. Hamilton's prominence in F1 and his use of F1 for activism and identity construction clearly demonstrate his arguments against any claims that sport should strive to be "politically neutral". Hamilton instead questions and rejects the very existence of political neutrality, constructing sport more broadly, and F1 in particular, as inherently culturally and socio-politically significant in propagating the inclusion and exclusion of specific groups, e.g., the exclusion of Black people in F1 and the exclusion of Africa in the so-called World Championship. What happens next in this now potentially hostile F1 environment for Hamilton and others will be crucial to observe and assess, particularly around how much control the FIA will attempt to have around athlete activists' personal social media accounts and their behaviour within F1 contexts.

6 Conclusion

This chapter has demonstrated how the textual and visual choices of Instagram posts can be strategically used by athlete activists online to index under-represented identities and to get political activist messages across to mass global audiences. Lewis Hamilton establishes an argumentative rhetorical style, representing himself as a Black athlete activist leader at the helm, raising awareness for racial inclusion in F1. He effectively positions himself as a leading advocate of global racial justice within an otherwise exclusive, elitist, and predominantly white sport. This study demonstrates how Black identity inclusion in F1 motorsport can be achieved by analysing the linguistic strategies that athlete activists choose on social media platforms. Through an analysis of multimodal choices, textual analysis of captions, and analysis of semiotic elements, we have shown how athlete activists can help advance awareness of and act as advocates for social inclusion in a sport which is notorious for its social exclusion.

We have also shown how F1 provides rich datasets for multimodal discourse analysts and sociolinguists interested in marginalised identity and activism in sports, contextualised by the limitations and affordances offered by the sport. As the extensive mediatisation of sport continues, and sports such as F1 attempt to balance the promotion of certain social and environmental causes against their arguments of political neutrality, the analyses of Hamilton's use of different social media features, images, and semiotic elements in his role as an athlete activist help establish a framework for other athlete activists, sports journalists, or media organisations, including those using online media for audience engagement, socio-political messaging, and identity construction.

This chapter ultimately contributes to an emerging body of sports discourse which demonstrates the importance of social media data in analysing the negotiation of identities and the socio-political messaging of athlete activists from underrepresented communities. Athlete activism through and for previously underrepresented voices, facilitated via social media platforms, is a growing and crucial discourse type and thus provides compelling grounds for further analysis of issues of inclusion and exclusion in sport. Our findings are of practical relevance to those working within digital media, motorsport, and to sports professionals interested in activism and advocacy. Our analysis of Hamilton's use of Instagram demonstrates the value of how direct indexicality, intertextuality, and synthetic personalisation can connect with mass audiences past and present. Hamilton's posts aim to make his followers aware of historical and systemic racial injustices as a way of framing current social exclusion in F1 and across other sports.

In light of the FIA's 2023 ban of personal, religious, and political demonstrations in F1, our analysis of Hamilton as a leading Black athlete activist, advocating for social inclusion and racial justice arguably presents sports professionals with a set of useful and effective tools for subverting dominant discourses. This will be particularly useful if they are operating within restrictive sporting contexts, with a sporting body attempting to exert control over the individual voices and socio-political beliefs of participating athletes. Our analysis demonstrates how leading athlete activist identities can be successfully foregrounded and how wider, global audiences can be reached in their rejection of social exclusion and advocacy for social inclusion within their sporting contexts and beyond.

In overall conclusion, we believe that our study of social media in professional motorsport empirically demonstrates a set of key multimodal strategies which sports professionals can use to move away from established ritualistic social media practices about their sporting ability and successes to instead become advocates for social change and resist discourses of political neutrality in their sporting contexts. In Hamilton's case, this is achieved through inclusion awareness-raising through his posts positioning himself as a Black athlete activist. Hamilton clearly and consistently argues for improving social inclusion within F1, in sports more generally, and also across societies in these social media posts. Indeed, these posts have operated as an important launch pad for Hamilton's shift from a highly successful F1 driver to a notable athlete activist who advocates for the eradication of social exclusion on the grounds of race and ethnicity in sport and the world.

Appendix

Transcription conventions
Italics in transcripts denote video directions and details

Data sources

Extract 1: https://www.instagram.com/tv/CCJu_I7hXqF/?utm_source=ig_web_copy_link

Extract 2: https://www.instagram.com/p/CCReSLFBu1C/?utm_source=ig_web_copy_link

Extract 3: https://www.instagram.com/p/CCjOzm4sfF6/?utm_source=ig_web_copy_link

References

BBC. 2021. "Lewis Hamilton says Formula 1 is a 'billionaire boys' club'". https://www.bbc.co.uk/sport/formula1/57189132 (accessed 20 May 2021)

Bucholtz, Mary &Kira Hall. 2010. Locating Identity in Language. In Carmen Llamas & Dominic Watt (eds.), *Language and Identities*, 18–28. Edinburgh: Edinburgh University Press.

Butterworth, Michael L. 2021. *Communication and Sport*. Berlin: DeGruyter.

Caldwell, David, John Walsh, Elaine W. Vine & Jon Jureidini. 2016. *The Discourse of Sport: Analyses from Social Linguists*. London: Routledge.

Cheng, Elaine & Nigel Jarvis. 2010. Residents' Perception of the Social-Cultural Impacts of the 2008 Formula 1 Singtel Singapore Grand Prix. *Event Management* 14(2). 91–106.

Coombs, Danielle Sarver & David Cassilo. 2017. Athletes and/or Activists: LeBron James and Black Lives Matter. *Journal of Sport and Social Issues* 41(5). 425–444.
Dabiri, Emma. 2019. *Don't touch my hair*. London: Penguin Books.
Edwards, Harry. 1969. *The Revolt of the Black Athlete*. New York: Free Press.
Fairclough, Norman. 2014 [1989]. *Language and Power*, 3rd edn. London: Routledge.
Farrington, Neil, Daniel Kilvington, John Price & Amir Saeed. 2012. *Race, Racism and Sports Journalism*. Oxon: Routledge.
File, Kieran A. & Stephanie Schnurr. 2018. That match was "a bit like losing your virginity". Failed humour, face and identity construction in TV interviews with professional athletes and coaches. *Journal of Pragmatics* 152. 132–144.
Finn, Mark. 2021. From accelerated advertising to Fanboost: mediatized motorsport. *Sport in Society* 24(6). 937–953.
Formula 1. 2020. "Formula 1 launches #WeRaceAsOne initiative to fight challenges of COVID-19 and global inequality". https://www.formula1.com/en/latest/article.formula-1-launches-we-race-as-one-initiative.3s2AhNDApNDzrCoQDc1RY8.html (last modified 22 June 2020)
Gezici, Ferhan & Serran Er. 2016. What has been left after hosting the Formula 1 Grand Prix in Istanbul?. *Sport Marketing Quarterly* 25. 166–181.
Hirschfelder, Nicole. 2020. "Change Starts with Us": The Issue of Media Representation of Athletes' Activism for Black Lives. In Frank Jacob (ed.), *Sports and Politics: Commodification, Capitalist Exploitation, and Political Agency*, 101–118. Berlin/Boston: DeGruyter Oldenbourg.
Horky, Thomas & Robin Meyer. 2021. #Rio2016 and #WorldCup2018: social media meets journalism. In Michael L. Butterworth (ed.), *Communication and Sport*, 693–708. Berlin/Boston: Mouton.
Khan, Abraham I. 2021. The ethos of the activist athlete. In Michael L. Butterworth (ed.), *Communication and Sport*, 161–178. Berlin/Boston: Mouton.
Kress, Gunther & Theo van Leeuwen. 2021 [1996]. *Reading Images: The Grammar of Visual Design*, 3rd edn. London: Routledge.
Lamb, Chris. 2016. *From Jack Johnson to LeBron James: Sports, Media, and the Color Line*. Nebraska: University of Nebraska Press.
Marston, Steve. 2020. The Revival of Athlete Activism(s): Divergent Black Politics in the 2016 Presidential Election Engagements of LeBron James and Colin Kaepernick. In Frank Jacob (ed.), *Sports and Politics: Commodification, Capitalist Exploitation, and Political Agency*, 119–140. Berlin/Boston: DeGruyter Oldenbourg.
Miller, Toby. 2016. Greenwashed sports and environmental activism: Formula 1 and FIFA. *Environmental Communication* 10(6). 719–733. mission44. "About." 2021. https://www.mission44.org/about (accessed 24 May 2022)
Mullany, Louise. 2020. *Professional Communication: Consultancy, Advocacy, Activism*. London: Palgrave.
Nauright, John & David K. Wiggins. 2016. *Routledge Handbook of Sport, Race and Ethnicity*. London: Routledge.
Noble, Jonathan. 2022. December 20. FIA bans drivers from political statements without approval. *Autosport*. https://www.autosport.com/f1/news/fia-bans-drivers-from-political-statements-without-approval/10413112/
Ochs, Elinor. 1992. Indexing gender. In Alessandro Duranti & Charles Goodwin (eds.), *Rethinking Context: Language as an Interactive Phenomenon*, 335–358. Cambridge: Cambridge University Press.
Rowe, David. 2009. Media and Sport: The Cultural Dynamics of Global Games. *Sociology Compass* 3(4). 543–558.

TePoel, Dain. and John Nauright. 2021. Black lives matter in the sports world. *Sport in Society* 24(5). 693–696.

Tyrkkö, Jukka & Hanna Limatius. 2019. "When did I do dangerous driving then?": Structures and functions of Formula One race radio messages. In Marcus Callies & Magnus Levin (eds.), *Corpus Approaches to the Language of Sports: Text, Media, Modalities*, 111–138. London: Bloomsbury.

United Nations. 2016. *Leaving no one behind: the imperative of inclusive development: Report on the World Social Situation 2016*. New York: United Nations.

Wang, Yuan. 2021. Building relationships with fans: how sports organisations used twitter as a communication tool. *Sport in Society* 24(7). 1055–1069.

Wenner, Lawrence A. 1998. *MediaSport*. London: Routledge.

Younge, Gary. 2021. July 10. Lewis Hamilton: 'Everything I'd suppressed came up – I had to speak out'. *The Guardian*. https://www.theguardian.com/sport/2021/jul/10/lewis-hamilton-everything-id-suppressed-came-up-i-had-to-speak-out

Kieran File, Stephanie Schnurr, Amanda Coulson, and Alan Rapley
Chapter 3
Do collective pronouns construct inclusive coach-athlete relations?
Exploring the use of "we" in communication during boxing bouts

1 Introduction

In this study we explore the language of inclusion in the context of coach-athlete communication during sporting events. The issue of how inclusive coach-athlete relationships has so far largely escaped academic scrutiny (Hammond et al. 2019). Yet, in light of current trends towards more athlete empowerment (e.g., Schofield 2017; Morrow 2021; House 2022; Kennedy 2022), issues of inclusion and exclusion between coaches and athletes warrant greater attention and more theorising so that we can better understand what these concepts mean in a sports coaching context. With more research attention to this issue, we can begin to understand what inclusive relationships between coaches and athletes may or may not look like, how they might be accomplished and, indeed, whether they are able to be accomplished within the mainstream ideologies of inclusion and solidarity that underlie and inform much coaching.

In this study, we apply a linguistic lens to unpack the issue of whether (and to what extent) inclusion can be achieved between coaches and athletes in the sport of boxing. We do this by studying instances of the collective pronoun "we" as it was used by boxing coaches in their face-to-face communication with boxers during competitive boxing bouts. Our analytical goal is to assess the extent to which the use of this pronoun by coaches can be seen to help them signal or construct inclusive relations between themselves and the boxers they are communicating with. The collective pronoun "we" is a linguistic resource commonly associated with reflecting or constituting inclusive relations between people (e.g., Vertommen 2013, DuBois 2012, Gardelle and Sorlin 2015) making it a useful resource to study for clues about the accomplishment of inclusive relations between coaches and athletes.

As we will illustrate, "we" was frequently used by the coaches when communicating with the boxers during boxing bouts. However, when we looked more

---

Kieran File, Stephanie Schnurr, University of Warwick, United Kingdom
Amanda Coulson, England Boxing, United Kingdom
Alan Rapley, OLY; UK Coaching, United Kingdom

https://doi.org/10.1515/9783110789829-004

closely at these instances, using the tools of discourse analysis and pragmatics, we found evidence to suggest that the way these pronouns were being used did not always index an inclusive relationship between the coaches and the boxers. In what follows, we present and support this claim with the help of examples from a data set of authentic face-to-face coach-boxer communication. We use the findings to discuss issues of inclusion and exclusion in coach-athlete relationships more widely.

2 The issue of inclusion in sports coaching

This chapter reports on the findings of a study on language use in high performance sport carried out together with England Boxing's Performance Pathway Programme (File et al. 2021). During a communication workshop in which coaches assessed their actual linguistic practices in real coaching settings through transcription analysis activities, a number of comments were raised about a perceived division being constructed between the coach and the boxer in and through their ritual language choices, particularly concerning the selection of pronouns (discussed further below). These observations were identified as problematic in the eyes of the coaches based on philosophical and cultural changes that the organisation wanted to enact with the aim of establishing a more unified team approach to boxing.

While validating this philosophy more generally is beyond the scope of the current chapter, on the surface at least, there do appear to be a number of contextual and cultural realities that might make establishing an inclusive team ethos between coaches and athletes rather challenging in the context of boxing. For example, in a high-performance sporting context, coaches and athletes have been found to enter into hierarchically distinct roles (File 2022). As a consequence, coaches maintain a significant amount of power over athletes in and through the management of their interactions with one another, a process which, in turn, can construct social distance between them. Moreover, despite having the same goal (i.e., to win a match/fight) and despite being on the same side, coaches and athletes play distinct roles during a boxing fight, with the boxer ultimately taking responsibility for the actual physical performance and the coach playing more of a supporting but not executing role.

In this chapter we explore some of the discursive strategies that coaches use to create an inclusive team ethos with the boxers. Our overarching research question is thus *how (if at all) are the coaches establishing an inclusive team ethos between themselves and the boxers during actual sporting competitions?* In addressing this question, we hope to contribute more broadly to understanding the challenges of creating and enacting inclusion between coaches and athletes. Our particular focus is the use of the first-person plural pronoun "we", which was one of the discursive strategies that the coaches identified in the communication workshop as enabling them to enact the more inclusive philosophy and more unified team approach to boxing described above. However, while there seemed to be consensus among workshop participants that the use of "we" (rather than "you" and "I") would be a relatively quick and easy way to put this philosophy into practice, previous research on "we" emphasises the complexity of this pronoun (Pavlidou 2014).

2.1 "We" – more than an inclusive pronoun

Previous research has shown that "we" is one of the most flexibly used pronouns in the English language (Pavlidou 2014: 3) and "the most complex category of all person categories" (Helmbrecht 2002: 33). On the one hand, "we" may be used as a plural pronoun referring to collectives. For example, it may refer to a collective that includes the speaker and addressee (inclusive "we"), as well as a collective that includes the speaker but not the addressee (exclusive "we"). On the other hand, "we" may also be used in its singular meaning and refer to the addressee only (similar to the second person singular "you") or to the speaker themselves (similar to the first person singular "I"). "We" in these meanings is also often called "pseudo-inclusive we" (e.g., Wilson 2019).

In its meaning as singular "you", "we" is a frequently occurring feature of doctor-patient interactions (e.g., De Cock and Kluge 2016; Chimbwete-Phiri and Schnurr 2020), and nursery or classroom discourse (e.g., Pavlidou 2014). It has also been observed in care home settings as a feature of elderspeak (Williams, Kemper and Hummert 2003; Marsden and Holmes 2014), as well as in talk with children (Ervin-Tripp 1976). Moreover, "we" in its meaning as "I" frequently occurs in political discourse (e.g., Vertommen 2013) and academic writing (e.g., Krapivkina 2015). While some researchers have pointed to the condescending connotations of using "we" when meaning "you" (e.g., Wales 1996; Williams et al. 2003), others have argued that "we" in this meaning actually contributes to establishing solidarity between speaker and addressee (e.g., Marsden and Holmes 2014).

This last function of "we" was also observed by Stavridou (2022) in a study of a basketball team. She found that the team captain and other players frequently used this pronoun to "create[..] and maintain[..] team cohesion and mutual engagement" (Stavridou 2022: 149). Similarly, Fransen et al. (2012: 641) in a study of volleyball players also observed that "positive supportive communication" –

which included the use of the pronoun "we" – was the strongest factor influencing the team's positive beliefs in collective efficacy. These findings are further supported by research in sports psychology more widely which argues that "we" often contributes to reinforcing solidarity and creating team spirit (e.g., Grandzol, Perlis and Draina 2010; Cotterill and Fransen 2016).

In a discourse analytical study of coaches' use of "we" in a New Zealand rugby team, Wilson (2019) observed that by including themselves and their addressees in their choice of pronoun, the coaches were able to mitigate the force of negatively affective speech acts (such as directives and criticisms), while still being relatively direct in getting their message across. Analysing the pronoun use of three coaches in different interactional contexts – including team meetings and half-time huddles – and various speech events – i.e., compliments, criticisms, and control acts – Wilson (2019) found that through their use of different pronouns, the coaches successfully balanced a more authoritarian stance with creating solidarity. Using "we" in these contexts enabled the coaches to get their message across and display their authority and expertise, while at the same time maintaining a positive relationship with the players. This was particularly the case in the team huddles, in which players and coaches were in close physical distance to each other. This close physical proximity, Wilson (2019) argues, might be one of the reasons why the coaches favoured the use of "we" over other pronouns in this context.

These observations are of great relevance to our study as they demonstrate not only that "we" is a very complex and ambiguous pronoun, but also that through their choice of pronouns coaches are able to minimise the distance between themselves and the players, thereby creating a more inclusive environment in which a collective team identity is foregrounded. However, while Wilson's (2019) study focused on rugby – a team sport where creating a collective team identity may be particularly pertinent – in our study we analyse the coaches' pronoun usage in the context of boxing, where more emphasis is put on individual athletes and their performance. The particular focus of our study is to explore whether through their use of "we" the coaches indeed manage to create the inclusive team ethos that they discussed during the communication workshops. In the next section we introduce our methodology and provide a brief overview of the data that we collected.

3 Methodology

In this chapter we use the toolkit of discourse analysis, specifically linguistic pragmatics, to unpack the meaning and functions of "we" in the specific context of boxing bouts. Pragmatics is a subfield of linguistics that is concerned with locating meanings that are being made by linguistic forms in their contexts of use (for an introduction see e.g., Scott 2023). Pragmatics, as an approach to discourse analysis, is particularly well suited for our study as we are interested in identifying the various potential meanings or functions of the pronoun "we" in a given context (e.g., Thomas 2014).

The data set that we draw on in our analyses below consists of authentic interactions between England Boxing's talent pathway coaches and their boxers that occurred during two national age-group boxing tournaments. In these tournaments, a number of talent pathway boxers from different age categories compete against those from Scotland, Wales and Ireland in three-round boxing bouts. This age-group element is important to highlight as the dyads we analyse in this study involve adult coaches and young adult boxers, which may be important to consider when interpreting the findings discussed here.

For each bout in a tournament, a boxer would be accompanied by two talent pathway coaches, with one coach leading and another performing a support role. Two participation frameworks were therefore evident during the course of a boxing bout: the coach-boxer framework, which saw the coaches and boxers communicate with each other in the boxer's corner (1) before and after the fight, (2) in the breaks between rounds, and (3) during a fight as the coaches shouted out to the boxer to give instructions and feedback while they were engaged in the bout itself. The other participation framework evident in our data was talk between coaches, which could occur with the boxer as a legitimate overhearer or out of earshot of the boxer while the boxing bout was ongoing. With respect to the goals of this paper, our focus here is on the coach-boxer participation framework.

Data was collected by attaching audio recorders to the coaches during these tournaments. This enabled us to capture everything they said without being too intrusive and allowing the coaches and their boxers to go about their typical coaching activities as they normally would. The microphones on the audio recorders were sensitive enough to also pick up any replies from the boxers. However, due to the physically demanding nature of the boxers' activities during the fights, the interactions that we recorded were largely dominated by the coaches and afforded only relatively minimal opportunities for the boxers to contribute as they were usually exhausted and used the one-minute breaks between the bouts to catch their breath.

Overall, we recorded 25 boxing bouts (each consisting of three rounds) across two competition weekends. Within these 25 bouts, there were 11 different coaches and 25 different boxers involved. Of the 11 coaches recorded, 10 were male and one was female. Of the 25 boxers recorded, 23 were male and two were female. Additional personal information about ethnicity and regional background of the coaches or boxers were not collected. From an interactional perspective, each bout followed a similar format with talk happening between the boxers and the coaches before the bout, during the break between rounds and after the bout. Our recordings also captured talk between the coaches and the boxers during the actual bout, as the coaches shouted out instructions and supportive remarks to the boxer.

This data set resulted in roughly four hours of interactional data. Following this data collection phase, we then transcribed these interactions using transcription conventions influenced by Interactional Sociolinguistics (listed at the end of the chapter) to facilitate a more in-depth analysis of the coaches' use of pronouns.

4 Analysis

As alluded to above, we set ourselves two interrelated analytical missions when analysing coach-boxer interaction during the boxing bouts: (1) to analyse and unpack the way "we" is being used by coaches, assessing, in particular, the extent to which these uses of "we" construe a collective and inclusive sense of "we" between coaches and boxers, and (2) to use these insights to comment more broadly on the challenge of accomplishing inclusive relations between coaches and athletes. In order to achieve these aims, we performed two closely related analytical steps. In the first step, we identified and summarised the use of different pronouns by the coaches. Table 1 provides an overview of our findings.

As can be seen from Table 1, the main pronoun used in our data set is the second person singular pronoun "you", predominantly marking the boxer as the subject of feedback and instructions being issued by the coach. However, interestingly, regarding the first-person pronoun use, where we might find the coach as the primary speaker referring to themselves, "we" was used considerably more often than the individual pronoun "I". We explored this use of "we" and the various other functions this pronoun may perform in the context of the boxing bouts in more detail in the second step of our analysis.

In this second step, we paid particular attention to the context in which the pronouns occurred and what functions they performed. More specifically, we analysed what the message was doing, who the audience for the message was, and what implications the message had and for whom (e.g., does the message concern something the boxer needs to do or something that both the coach and the boxer are responsible for). In this analytical step, we also drew on additional contextual insights (e.g., who the boxer was, their gender, how the fight was going etc.) in

Table 1: Overview of pronoun use in our data set by coaches when communicating with boxers during boxing bouts.

First person personal pronouns	Pronoun	Amount	Third person personal pronouns	Pronoun	Amount
	I	12		He	34
	Me	25		Him	52
	My	1		His	4
	Mine	0		Himself	0
	Myself	0		She	11
	We	24		Her	4
	Us	3		Hers	0
	Our	0		Herself	0
	Ourselves	0		It	66
Second person personal pronouns	You	148		Its	0
	Your	67		Itself	0
	Yours	0		They	0
	Yourself	3		Them	9
	Yourselves	0		Their	0
				Theirs	0

order to further investigate and interpret the pragmatic meanings of "we" in our data, particularly who the "we" included or referred to.

Two key patterns in the coaches' use of "we" were identified, namely (1) instances where "we" included the boxers but (at least partly) excluded the coaches, and (2) instances where "we" included the coaches but excluded the boxers. No uses of the pronoun "we" by coaches in our data set clearly referenced both the boxers and the coaches as a collective. We illustrate and discuss the two patterns we did observe below.

4.1 Including the boxer but (at least partly) excluding the coaches

The most prominent pattern regarding the use of "we" by the coaches in our data and the most significant for the purposes of this chapter, was its use as a variant of the second person singular pronoun "you" to refer to the boxer alone (excluding the coaches). As extracts 1 and 2 below illustrate, often "we" was used instead of "you" to give specific instructions and tell the boxers what moves exactly they needed to do during the fight. In the transcripts, all speakers are coaches, and all names are pseudonyms.

Extract 1

1	Brian:	nice and sharp (.) nice and long
2		(5.0)
3		good bo::y
4		(12.0)
5		good boy (0.5) **HOW BOUT *WE* FOLLOW IT UP ONCE *WE* TURN**
6		(6.0)
7		good boy

Extract 2

1	Gillian:	nice (0.5) c'mon
2		(10.0)
3	Brian:	good more (.) **more than one when *we* get there Kate**
4	Will:	get your head moving

In both of these instances, the coach uses "we" to refer exclusively to the boxer. There is little doubt that it is the boxer alone – rather than the boxer and the coaches conjointly – who is expected to enact the instruction, e.g., "to follow it up once we turn" (line 5, extract 1). The use of "we" here, thus seems to be purely rhetoric and potentially functions to mitigate the force of the direct feedback shouted at the boxer during the fight (see also Wilson 2019). A more complex picture with regards to the functions and meanings of "we" is illustrated in extracts 3 and 4, which occurred in the breaks between rounds.

Extract 3

1	Gillian:	so every time *you* adjust your feet after *you*'ve punched (.) be ready because if he comes (1.0) counter that (1.0)
2		does that make sense
3	Stuart:	yeah ((breathing heavily))
4	Gillian:	because every time *you*'ve adjusted don't just punch and adjust and wait (0.5) punch and be ready (0.5)
5		and if comes (0.5) hit him (2.0)
6		**which way *we* gonna move eh (0.5) after *we've* punched**
7	Stuart:	right
8	Gillian:	***we're* gonna move right (.)**
9		***we're* gonna keep away from his backhand aren't *we***
10		good boy
11		think about that cos he's landed a couple of them **and *we* don't need all of them do *we***

12	Stuart:	yeah
13		((announcer calls fighters back into the middle))
14	Gillian:	clever boxing using your feet and stepping off to the right Ok (1.0)
15		good boy

Extract 4

1	Brian:	go::d (ki::d) (0.5) move your legs up ((Brian taps Fred's foot with his own))
2		give yourself some (room) (1.0)
3		head up ((Brian gently taps Fred's chin))
4		(4.0) spit this one out ((Gillian holds bucket for Fred))
5		((Brian holds water bottle for Fred to drink))
6		(3.0) few cracking rounds there Fred (0.5)
7		**we're listening (.) and we're working (.) and we're staying nice and sharp and engaged** (unclear)
8		but he's gonna come a bit harder (.)
9		he needs this last round (0.5)
10		**we're just gonna stay nice and switched on** (.)
11		remember what's coming back (.) score (.) **adjust your feet and then we go again every single time**
12		**single shots are good but we have to adjust** ((claps hands))
13		and go again (unclear) make sure you do not admire or anything (.)
14		that head stays chin down (.) (nice and tight)
15		work (0.5) yeah?
16		up ya get ((Fred and Brian stand up))
17		((Fighters called to centre))
18		one more one more good round this one Freddy (1.0)
19		stay nice and sharp ((Brian leaves ring))

In extracts 3 and 4 we see examples of the coach issuing the boxer performance directives, checking *their* knowledge and giving *them* positive or critical feedback. For example, in extract 3, lines 6 to 9, the coach quizzes the boxer on which way they are going to move during the fight, in order to avoid the opponent's strong hand in the next round, and in extract 4 the coach remarks positively on what the boxer is doing in the ring and what they need to do or keep doing in the upcoming round. In both extracts, "we" and "you" seem to be used interchangeably – with the coaches sometimes addressing the boxer with "you" (e.g., lines 1 and 4 in extract 3; lines 1 and 13 in extract 4) and then shifting to "we" (e.g., lines 6, 8 and 9 in extract 3; lines 7 and 10 in extract 4). This shift seems noteworthy as, strictly speaking, the referent of the pronouns does not change. In spite of the use of the inclusive pronoun "we" there is little doubt that the actions associated with the referent (e.g., moving, punching, staying alert, listening etc.) will be performed exclusively by the boxer.

However, the functions and meanings of "we" are more complex in these extracts and harder to explain. As we can see, "we" is often used in the context where the coaches have just referred to the opposition boxer (e.g., lines 8 and 9 in extract 4). By using "we" – rather than "you" here it could be argued that the coaches construct a "we versus him/her" dichotomy. By using singular pronouns to reference the opposition boxer but the pronoun "we" when addressing their boxer, the coaches may be establishing the opposition as an unaided individual and their boxer as part of a larger and potentially more powerful collective. On the one hand, this use of "we" thus – at least metaphorically – includes both boxer and coaches and constructs them as jointly responsible for the outcome of the fight. However, at the same time, a closer look at the actions assigned to the "we" undermines this effect to some extent as – just like in extracts 1 and 2 – it is clearly the boxer alone who is expected to perform the tasks (such as listening, working, adjusting their feet etc.).

Extract 5 provides further evidence that the coaches often used the pronouns "you" and "we" interchangeably to refer to the boxer. However, in contrast to excerpts 3 and 4, in extract 5 below, the different pronouns were used without previous reference to the opposition boxer.

Extract 5

1	Brian:	((Brian addressing Will)) Will can you bring that bucket over
2		spit this first one out for me ((Brian Holds water bottle for Kate))
3		(2.0)
4		goo::d deep breath (1.0) and this one ((Brian Holds water bottle for Kate)) (1.0) goo::d (0.5)
5		Ok (.) all the right things are there Kate (.)
6		**we just need to be a little bit tighter when we get in there on the inside (.)**
7		**we're taking a couple on the way in (0.5)**
8		**nice and tight with your guard**
9		**keep nice and compact**
10		**your head's gotta move**
11		**when you're there you're scoring one punch but one isn't enough**
12		**you've gotta put a couple together**
13		**you've gotta have a little adjust ((Brian mimics bobbing and weaving))**
14		**don't just stay in front of her**

15		nice and tight (.) head move (.) score
16		**and then *you've* gotta go again as you're circling round**
17		((Fighters called to centre))
18		come in with the backhand over the top
19		***we* gotta be aggressive with** (unclear) ((Fighters
20		called again))

Throughout this excerpt "we" and "you" are used interchangeably to refer to the boxer. Both pronouns occur when the coach provides feedback (e.g., lines 8 and 11), evaluates the boxer's performance (e.g., line 8), outlines future actions (e.g., lines 12, 13 and 19), and gives concrete instructions (e.g., lines 6 and 10). What is particularly noteworthy in this extract is the ways in which the second person "you" seems to be used when the coach provides positive feedback (e.g., lines 8 and 11) and "we" when the feedback is more critical (e.g., line 6). There may also be a tendency for "we" to be used in instructions to the boxer that are more forceful or challenging for the boxer to enact, such as instances where the coach asks the boxer to be "more aggressive". However, like in the extracts above, it is clear that in all cases it is the boxer alone who is expected to perform these actions and put the coach's instructions into action.

4.2 Including the coaches but excluding the boxer

Another pattern we noticed in the data, one that was perhaps less ambiguous to unpack, was messages where "we" was used to refer to the coaching team only (i.e., both coaches in the corner). "We" often occurred in these instances when the coaches were performing typical coaching tasks, like reminding the boxer of important points previously discussed or perhaps explained or outlined by the coaches that are relevant to the current and unfolding fight or giving feedback to the boxer during the fight. Extracts 6 to 8 are illustrations of this use of "we" across our data set.

Extract 6

[shouted out during a round]
1	Steve:	now go again Moe (.) go again (2.0)
2		remember **what we said about** going again when you spin off (1.0)
3		GOOD BO::Y

Extract 7

[said during a between round talk]
1	Bob:	take deep breaths
2		you're getting there you backing (.) you're backing off a little bit (.)
3		you're kind waiting for your breath (.)
4		**what did we say earlier**
5	Francis:	move off and work
6	Bob:	yeah (.) yeah 100% man (.)

Extract 8

[shouted out during a round]
1	Gillian:	clever boxing cle::ver boxing (1.0)
2		**that's what we're looking for Stuart** (.)
3		clever boxing son

The use of this feature was most evident while the fight was in progress and was used in messages that coaches shouted out to boxers during the unfolding boxing bout (as is the case in the three extracts presented above). In extracts 6 and 7 above, the coach who is speaking reminds the boxers of an instruction, comment, piece of feedback or advice that was raised during a previous interaction and that the coaches would like to see acted upon in the current fight. In extract 8, line 2, the coach is shouting out positive feedback to the boxer, perhaps to reinforce certain boxing actions being displayed by the boxer.

In all of these instances, the coach who is speaking deploys the collective "we" to encode him/herself and the other coach but not their boxer. In the context of these messages, "we" is thus referring to a more knowledgeable authority who is in a position to give instructions and evaluate the boxer's performance. More specifically, the referents of "we" in these extracts are active – they are giving instructions ("we said" [extract 6]) and have clear expectations ("what we're looking for" [extract 8]), while the addressee – the boxer – is positioned as a responsive receiver who may repeat but not decide on strategies (extract 7). As has been suggested elsewhere (File 2022), we may be seeing the distinctive roles and power differences that underlie the social activity of coaching in action. However, as far as a resource for promoting inclusion between coaches and boxers, the use of "we" in these instances arguably does not function to establish a collective between coaches and the boxer and instead signals that the boxers are not included in key activities like decision-making and performance evaluation. We pick up this point further below when we discuss these findings.

5 Discussion

It was the aim of this chapter to explore the coaches' use of the pronoun "we", and to investigate how (if at all) their use of this pronoun contributes to establishing an inclusive team ethos between the boxers and themselves. Our analyses of several instances of "we" in authentic coach-boxer interactions once more illustrated the complex and multi-faceted nature of this pronoun (see also Helmbrecht 2002). Like in previous research in other sporting contexts (e.g., Wilson 2019; Stavridou 2022), the coaches in our data also used "we" when referring to a range of different collectives and individuals, including (1) the boxers only (similar to the second person singular "you"), (2) themselves only (similar to the first person singular "I"), as well as (3) both the boxers and themselves (inclusive "we"), or (4) when referring to the coaching team but excluding the boxers (exclusive "we").

As we have shown throughout our analyses, the specific meaning and referent of each instance of "we" was very much context dependent – sometimes "we" referred to the boxer only (extracts 1 and 2) and at other times it referred to the coaches but not the boxer (extracts 6 to 8). Moreover, the coaches often switched seemingly effortlessly between different pronouns (typically "you" and "we") when referring to the boxers (extracts 3 to 5). This diversity in terms of the referents and meanings of "we" clearly points to the complex nature of this pronoun, which in turn, renders it very difficult – if not impossible – to make generalising claims about the functions of "we" with regards to constructing inclusive coach-athlete relationships. Thus, in contrast to what the coaches at the communication workshop suggested, "we" is not an easy and straightforward solution to address issues of inclusion and a lack of solidarity and sense of team spirit. Quite the opposite – "we" is much more than an inclusive pronoun, and its complex and multifaceted nature demands more attention.

Our analyses have shown that on the one hand, by using "we" rather than "I" or "you" the coaches emphasised a more intimate and inclusive relationship between themselves and the boxers and created an interactional environment where – at least rhetorically – responsibilities, instructions and decisions are portrayed as collective – rather than individual – tasks. As a consequence, directions and criticisms could be uttered more explicitly and directly while still maintaining harmony, downplaying the power differential between coaches and boxers, and mitigating the illocutionary force of the criticism or directive (see also Wilson 2019). In light of the coaches' comments in the communication workshop, these functions of "we" could be interpreted as reflecting the coaches' attempts to minimise status and power differences between themselves and the boxers (see also File 2022) and to establish the desired inclusive team ethos.

However, on the other hand, our observations have also demonstrated that not everything that looks like inclusion does actually do inclusion. In other words, because of its complexity as a pronoun, not every instance of "we" is actually inclusive. Rather, as our examples above have shown, in many cases, "we" was used to exclude (rather than include) the boxers. This was particularly the case in those instances where "we" was used in the meaning of "you" (extracts 1 to 3). Taking a more critical angle, it could even be argued that in these instances, using "we" disguises or obscures the power differential that exists between the coaches and their boxers.

Similarly, the coaches' decision to use "we" in an attempt to create a more inclusive team ethos could be regarded as merely window-dressing since adopting this linguistic practice alone does not really contribute to creating an inclusive coach-athlete relationship or increase athlete empowerment. Quite the opposite – as our analyses have shown, in spite of using the pronoun "we", coaches and boxers maintain different roles vis-à-vis their actual physical performance during the fight, and despite the coaches' efforts the boxers hardly contributed to and participated in any strategic discussions or decision-making processes.

Our findings are thus in line with Wilson's (2019) observations that the coaches' use of "we" constituted the norm in the specific context of the rugby huddle – and we would argue, also in the context of boxing bouts. After all, in spite of all the caveats mentioned above, "we" – like no other pronoun – is particularly suited to communicate potentially difficult and threatening messages (like a criticism or a directive), while at the same time – at least metaphorically – creating an inclusive environment in which solidarity and team ethos are valued and strived towards. However, as we have demonstrated throughout, due to its complex nature, "we" can convey several meanings and is thus not an easy solution when attempting to create greater levels of inclusion between coaches and athletes.

5.1 Using a linguistic strategy for accomplishing greater inclusion: A warning for practitioners

One of the insights from our analyses that we believe is particularly relevant for coaches and other practitioners, who aim to create greater inclusion with their athletes and teams, is the fact that using "we" – or any other linguistic strategy – without paying close attention to its potential meanings and the wider context, is not advisable as there is no one-to-one relationship between linguistic form and function. Rather, as we have shown above, context is crucial in the meaning making process.

A tenet of discourse analytical work is that language forms do not create meaning in isolation and on their own. Rather, their meaning potential (Halliday 2013) is flexible and only able to be retrieved fully when linguistic forms are interpreted within their contexts of use. As a consequence, "we" cannot and should not be thought of as a decontextualised resource that communicates or creates a sense of inclusion when added to the subject position of messages and interspersed in coaching interactions with athletes. Like any linguistic feature, pronouns gain their meaning, especially regarding their referents, when interpreted in their specific context of use. As our analyses above have demonstrated, sometimes "we" may contribute (metaphorically, at least) to fostering inclusion and a team ethos, while at other times it may have the opposite effect and may actually function to single out individuals.

It is therefore imperative that any linguistic strategising by sports coaches, teams and organisations, with the aim of fostering greater inclusion and creating team ethos, needs to consider language choices within the specific context in which they are made. It is important, for example, to take into consideration the nature and constraints of current coach-athlete relationships, and the power differential that exists between them, as well as the different responsibilities and expectations associated with the different roles. There is no question that particular language choices can reshape contexts, for better or worse, and that social or interpersonal goals and improvements can be accomplished in and through changes to linguistic practices (see, for example, Sarangi and Candlin 2003; Williams, Kemper and Hummert 2003; Holmes, Schnurr and Marra 2007; Mullany 2020). However, language changes devised in isolation and based on generalised interpretations and meaning may end up having adverse or unintentional effects that may harm any progress people or groups may be attempting to make.

Looking forward, an unknown but important piece of this puzzle is, however, how the athletes feel about these actions. For example, do the boxers (or other athletes more widely) interpret the use of the pronoun "we" as a replacement for "you" as different, relationally or interpersonally, to the use of more unmarked second person pronoun "you"? While we do not have any reflective data from the boxers, this might prove a useful basis for future research. Some researchers who have seen this "we" as "you" phenomenon in other professional contexts, have identified it as an exclusive form of "we" and have viewed it pejoratively as patronising or condescending (e.g., Williams, Kemper and Hummert 2003). Others view the practice as nurturing or as an attempt to establish solidarity with the addressee (e.g., Marsden and Holmes 2014; Chimbwete-Phiri and Schnurr 2020). Collecting and analysing more reflective data that can reveal the interpersonal meanings addressees associated with the use of this pronoun could help to advance knowledge of the use and effects of this feature in coach communication. Additionally, questions remain about whether or how gender interacts (or not) with the use and interpretation of pronouns in coach-athlete communication of this kind. Future research might find nuances in the use of pronouns in different gender dyads that might help to shine further insight on the function of collective pronouns in coach-athlete communication.

6 Conclusion

Our analyses of coach-boxer interactions have demonstrated that although coaches did use "we" in their interactions with boxers, the status and function of this pronoun as a resource for fostering inclusion are questionable. Thinking of "we" as a device to foster isolation and using it in an uncritical and unconsidered way is not likely to create a more inclusive environment on its own. Rather, as we have argued throughout, considering linguistic actions in their contexts of use is of utmost importance. Should greater inclusion between coaches and athletes be desired, examining the context, including the deeper ritual communicative practices and social structures that guide behaviour and interpretation processes, and considering how these can be linguistically reconstructed in and through communicative action – whether in pronoun use or other discursive strategies – is going to prove more fruitful.

We hope that the research processes and findings presented and discussed in this chapter also point to the value of a pragmatic toolkit for unpacking and facilitating deeper discussions around issues of inclusion and exclusion in sport. In a profession that thrives on generalisable truths, the opportunity to engage in in-depth analyses of language in specific contexts, modelled in this and many other chapters in this volume, offers a chance to better understand the complexities of issues of inclusion and exclusion, while at the same time providing concrete measures to address these issues or problematise currently used measures and processes.

Transcription conventions

(.)	A short pause (less than a second)
(5.0)	A longer pause or break in speech (length marked in seconds)
good bo::y	:: mark an elongated sound
Work yeah?	? marks rising intonation
HOW BOUT WE FOLLOW IT UP ONCE WE TURN	All capitals represented increase in volume where message was shouted

((breathing heavily))	double parentheses offer meta commentary of the unfolding event, particularly speaker actions
(nice and tight)	single parentheses Marks speech that was hard to transcribe and represents our best account of what was said

References

Chimbwete-Phiri, Rachel &Stephanie Schnurr. 2020. "We are breastfeeding, right?" Exploring the discourse of male healthcare providers in antenatal consultations in Malawi. In Joanne MacDowell (ed.), *De-gendering Gendered Occupations: Analysing Communicative Practices in the Workplace*. Abingdon: Routledge.

Cotterill, Stewart T. & Katrien Fransen. 2016. Athlete leadership in sports teams: Current understanding and future directions. *International Review of Sport and Exercise Psychology* 9(11). 116–133.

De Cock, Barbara. 2011. Why we can be you: The use of 1st person plural forms with hearer reference in English and Spanish. *Journal of Pragmatics* 43(11). 2762–2775.

De Cock, Barbara & Bettina Kluge. 2016. On the referential ambiguity of personal pronouns and its pragmatic consequences. *Pragmatics* 26(3). 351–360.

Du Bois, Inke. 2012. Grammatical, pragmatic and sociolinguistic aspects of the first person plural pronoun. *Subjectivity in Language and in Discourse* 319–338.

Ervin-Tripp, Susan. 1976. Is Sybil there? The structure of some American English directives. *Language in Society* 5(1). 25–66. https://doi.org/10.1017/S0047404500006849

File, Kieran. A. 2022. *How Language Shapes Relationships in Professional Sports Teams: Power and Solidarity Dynamics in a New Zealand Rugby Team*. Bloomsbury Academic.

File, Kieran, Stephanie Schnurr, Daniel Clayton, Solveig Wolfers & Anastasia Stavridou. 2021. *Focus on coach talk: How do boxing coaches communicate in breaks between rounds on fight night?* Warwick University. https://www.englandboxing.org/wp-content/uploads/2020/11/Coach-Communication-in-Boxing-Kieran-File-Warwick-University.pdf

Fransen, Katrien, Norbert Vanbeselaere, Vasileios Exadaktylos, Gert Vande Broek, Bert de Cuyper, Daniel Berckmans, Tanja Ceux, Maarten De Backer & Filip Boen. 2012. "Yes, we can!": Perceptions of collective efficacy sources in volleyball. *Journal of Sports Sciences* 30(7). 641–649

Gardelle, Laure & Sandrine Sorlin (eds.). 2015. *The pragmatics of personal pronouns*. Vol. 171. John Benjamins Publishing Company.

Grandzol, Christian, Susan Perlis & Lois Draina. 2010. Leadership development of team captains in collegiate varsity athletics. *Journal of College Student Development* 51(4). 403–418.

Halliday, Michael Alexander Kirkwood. 2013. Meaning as choice. In Lise Fontaine, Tom Bartlett & Gerard O'Grady (eds.), *Systemic Functional Linguistics: Exploring Choice* 15–36. Cambridge: Cambridge University Press. https://doi.org/10.1017/CBO9781139583077.003

Hammond, Andrew, Ruth Jeanes, Dawn Penney & Deana Leahy. 2019. "I Feel We are Inclusive Enough": Examining Swimming Coaches' Understandings of Inclusion and Disability. *Sociology of Sport Journal* 36(4). 311–321. https://doi.org/10.1123/ssj.2018-0164

Holmes, Janet, Stephanie Schnurr & Meredith Marra. 2007. Leadership and communication: Discursive evidence of a workplace culture change. *Discourse & Communication* 1(4). 433–451. https://doi.org/10.1177/1750481307082207

House, Alfie. 2022. October 19. Anything is possible as Saints continue mission to empower through success. *Daily Echo*. https://www.dailyecho.co.uk/sport/23060514.southampton-head-coach-team-mission-empower-community/

Kennedy, Ciarán. 2022. September 11. 'He'll empower the players' – The GAA legend taking on a key role with Leinster Rugby. *The42*. https://www.the42.ie/declan-darcy-leinster-5862246-Sep2022/

Krapivkina, Olga A. 2015. Pragmatic effects of first-person pronouns in academic discourse. *European Journal of Social and Human Sciences* 1. 35–39.

Marsden, Sharon & Janet Holmes. 2014. Talking to the elderly in New Zealand residential care settings. *Journal of Pragmatics* 64. 17–34. https://doi.org/10.1016/j.pragma.2014.01.006

Morrow, Michael. 2021. May 1. 'You don't put a limit on a person' – O'Gara's La Rochelle project bearing fruit. *BBC Sport*. https://www.bbc.co.uk/sport/rugby-union/56885756

Mullany, Louise (ed.). 2020. *Professional Communication: Consultancy, Advocacy, Activism*. Cham: Springer International Publishing.https://doi.org/10.1007/978-3-030-41668-3

Pavlidou, Theodossia-Soula. 2014. Constructing collectivity with "we": An introduction. In Theodossia-Soula Pavlidou (ed.), *Pragmatics and Beyond New Series*, 1–20. Amsterdam: John Benjamins Publishing Company. https://doi.org/10.1075/pbns.239.03pav

Sarangi, Srikant, & Christopher N. Candlin. 2003. Introduction Trading between reflexivity and relevance: New challenges for applied linguistics. *Applied Linguistics* 24(3). 271–285. https://doi.org/10.1093/applin/24.3.271

Scott, Kate. 2023. *Pragmatics in English: An introduction*. Cambridge: Cambridge University Press.

Schofield, Daniel. 2017. June 5. Eddie Jones: I want to make myself redundant by letting England players take control. *The Telegraph*. http://www.telegraph.co.uk/rugby-union/2017/06/05/eddie-jones-want-make-redundant-letting-england-players-take/

Stavridou, Anastasia. 2022. *Challenging traditional understandings of leadership and followership through discourse: A sociolinguistic case study of a basketball team*. Unpublished PhD thesis. The University of Warwick.

Thomas, Jenny A. 2014. *Meaning in interaction: An introduction to pragmatics*. London: Routledge.

Vertommen, Bram. 2013. The strategic value of pronominal choice: Exclusive and inclusive "we" in political panel debates. *Pragmatics* 23(2). 361–383.

Wales, Katie. 1996. *Personal pronouns in present day English*. Cambridge: Cambridge University Press.

Williams, Kristine, Susan Kemper & Mary Lee Hummert. 2003. Improving Nursing Home Communication: An Intervention to Reduce Elderspeak. *The Gerontologist* 43(2). 242–247. https://doi.org/10.1093/geront/43.2.242.

Wilson, Nick. 2019. When *we* means *you*: The social meaning of English pseudo-inclusive personal pronouns. *The Social Dynamics of Pronominal Systems*. 35–56.

Anastasia Stavridou and Kieran File

Chapter 4
Constructing inclusive team management structures: Evidence of multiparty participation in the leadership of a university basketball team

1 Introduction

In this study, we explore the notion of inclusion as it pertains to team management and the establishment of an inclusive, multiparty, participatory team management structure. The focus for this chapter emerged from interactional data collected and analysed during an ethnolinguistic study of a university basketball team (Stavridou 2022). In the interactions of this team, we noticed a number of peculiarities about the way important team talks played out. One of these was the open, multiparty interactional floor that the players constructed in and across timeouts during games. In these timeout talks, it was common to see a range of individuals actively contribute to important team management or leadership tasks in these game-day talks. Previous research has suggested that, in sporting contexts, rights to the interactional floor, and with it rights to manage or lead the team, can pattern in quite restricted and structured ways, often being dominated by a small number of individuals with notionally powerful roles in a team structure (File 2022). However, in the data analysed here, the interactional patterns showed multiple individuals claiming rights to address and, by extension, lead (or manage) the team.

In this chapter, we use this case study to explore the notion of an inclusive team management structure in practice. We use the case study to locate examples of linguistic behaviour (mainly in the form of particular interactional practices) that we argue reflect an inclusive team management structure in action and consider why an inclusive, multiparty participation structure is oriented to by members of this particular team. In the next section, we ground the complex notion of inclusion in relation to leadership and team management structures. We do this by suggesting that a wider distribution of interactional rights to lead the team, by individuals with different roles and status (particularly in relation to experience levels in the team), can be viewed as a criterion of an inclusive team structure on

---

Anastasia Stavridou, University of Manchester, United Kingdom
Kieran File, University of Warwick, United Kingdom

https://doi.org/10.1515/9783110789829-005

the simple basis that more people are *included* in management of their team. We also discuss the theoretical toolkit of discourse analysis used in this study to help examine the construction of an inclusive team structure. The findings section will present three extracts that help to illustrate how interactional rights in important team talks were claimed by and distributed to different individuals, regardless of their notional role or their social status in the team. We wrap this chapter up by considering why a more multiparty, participatory approach to leadership was evident in our specific team context, as explanatory insights at this level can help with the theoretical development of ideas about inclusive team structures. We also consider a key linguistic implication for practitioners wishing to support or establish more of an inclusive team structure in their own contexts.

2 Literature review: Framing our study of inclusion at a team structure level

To set a conceptual frame for the discussion we have in this chapter, we need to ground and connect several important concepts, particularly the notions of an inclusive team management structure, leadership, role and status. We attempt to pull these concepts together in this section.

The central concepts for this study are the notions of an inclusive team management structure and leadership. More generally, the notion of a team management structure is deployed here as a macro-level concept that helps to define or characterise the way members of the team go about the running of their group activities interpersonally. The concern here is very much social structure and in locating patterns in the way rights to manage the team are distributed interpersonally. For the purposes of this chapter, we define an *inclusive team management structure* as a macro-level shared understanding, within a group or community of practice (Lave and Wenger 1991; Eckert and McConnell-Ginet 1992; Wilson 2011), that the right to direct or manage the team is afforded to, claimed by, and more widely distributed across a wider array of individuals within the team. In other words, more people are *included* in the management of their team. The concept of *leadership*, particularly an understanding of leadership as a performance or process (Schnurr 2009), is strongly implicated in the above definition and is a central tool through which claims about team structure are developed in this chapter. In essence, the way leadership rights are claimed or distributed in material team management tasks – such as addressing the team, driving problem and solution identification, decision making, performing evaluative commentary on team and individual player performance, and leading the team's bonding rituals – can be considered instrumental in the construction of a team's management structure as more or less inclusive or exclusive.

In this chapter, we will locate practices of and claims to leadership in interaction and use the patterns we unearth to help us develop an understanding of the more macro-level team management structure that is being indexed and constructed through these practices. Stereotypically, sports teams are understood more as *exclusive* structures, where rights to lead the team are afforded to a small number of individuals with institutionally assigned leadership roles in the team, like the coach and captain (Cotterill 2012; File 2022). Such a structure might be considered top-down or authoritarian in nature, with certain individuals claiming the right to perform team management tasks. As noted above, an *inclusive* team structure could (in relation) be conceptualised in contrast to this whereby a greater number of members in the team, with different roles and degrees of social status (discussed below), claim and enact rights and responsibilities to manage the team, constructing leadership identities in the process. In other words, instead of one leader at the top of a pile (i.e., the coach or captain), the team distributes or accepts the distribution of leadership rights and responsibilities as a more inclusive process, whereby a variety of individuals emerge in the team's interactions to lead the team's management tasks and have their leadership identities ratified in the process. In this chapter, then, we conceptualise team structure as locatable on a continuum whereby there is more or less inclusion of team members in the material management of a basketball team.

However, to be able to examine the nature of team management structures in this way, we also need to know more about the make-up of the team. In this chapter, we have used the notions of role and status to help us with that task. In this study, we take *role* to mean more concrete, institutional labels assigned to individuals that demarcate certain rights and/or responsibilities to that individual (Stevanovic and Svennevig 2015). The most obvious roles in team sports are the roles of coach or captain, but there are others we can locate in a sporting team structure including previous captain, player, starting player or bench player. Status, on the other hand, while it can be connected to role, is seen in this study as a broader category that includes a range of competencies and experiences within the sociocultural context of sport that elevate an individual, giving them greater standing in comparison to others in the group (Stevanovic and Peräkylä 2014). High degrees of status might be claimed or assigned to individuals if they have, for example, played many games, have a well-regarded amount of talent or have been in previous leadership roles. Status can also work in reverse, with those not deemed to have valid competencies or experiences likely to have, at least on the surface, less status within a team.

Both role and status are crucial concepts for helping to locate and understand inclusive and exclusive team management structures. With an understanding of the different roles and levels of status individuals lay claim to in the team, we can more closely interpret the significance of any action taken by these individuals in the management tasks of the team. For example, in analysing the team's management encounters, evidence of significant and consequential action taken by a greater number of individuals, regardless of their role and status, could be seen as the basis for claims that a team is constructing an inclusive team management structure.

2.1 Using discourse analysis to locate and explain leadership and social structure in action

To be able to locate in/exclusive team structure in action in our basketball team (as per the above conceptual framing) we deployed the theoretical and analytical toolkit of discourse analysis. Discourse analysis is a useful theoretical toolkit for locating structure underlying everyday human interactions in context (Jaworski and Coupland 2006). Through a close analysis of the way language is being used by people in their purposeful activities, discourse analysts can bring into focus the deeper, underlying and unspoken patterns of social structure that constitute and are constituting the surface level interactional dynamics on show. In this chapter, we use discourse analysis to frame an analysis of social structure in our basketball team by attempting to understand the extent to which interactional practices in our team reveal and/or construct a more or less in/exclusive team management structure in action.

Discourse analysis has already been used to study interaction in sporting contexts and has been used more broadly to study issues of leadership and team management in action (Fairhurst 2007; Tourish 2007; Larsson 2017). Sociolinguistic and discourse analytical work in the domain of sport has begun to explore leadership behaviour and, perhaps more tangentially, issues of inclusion and exclusion in sports teams. Wilson (2011), for example, in a study of an amateur New Zealand rugby team, found evidence in the interactional data of the group constructing more of a shared leadership dynamic or what might be construed of as a leadership teams. While this work did not discuss inclusion at a team management level per se, the evidence presented in this study at least suggests leadership may in fact be a more distributed phenomena in sports teams than might be stereotypically understood.

In a more recent study, Schnurr et al. (2021) looked at a case in which members of a UK netball team emerged as leaders when their coach was absent from a training session. In recordings taken from a training session that the coach did not attend, the players were left to lead themselves, offering a unique opportunity to explore how leadership emerged in the team's interactions. In this context, various players are included in the leadership performance and claim, assign, reject and eventually accept leadership by different team members at different points throughout an interaction (Schnurr et al. 2021). While this study was more concerned with unpacking the notion of emergent leadership, it does suggest that teams can depart from more rigid leader-follower dynamics and that individuals can emerge to claim rights and responsibilities to lead, perhaps when the context allows for it.

However, these previous studies aside, the question of sports teams as in/exclusive structures (from a team management perspective) remains largely unexplored. This includes the key issue of whether an inclusive approach to managing the team is actually valued within the wider institutional context of sport. While there is anecdotal evidence to suggest that inclusion of players is valued within sports teams, largely due to the perception that it supports the development of more leaders in a team (see, for example, Schofield 2017; Morrow 2021; Reason 2021), there are likely to be counter arguments built around the idea that multiparty leadership structures may lead to disorganisation or undermine chains of command and values of discipline and respect deemed important in the sporting domain.

In this chapter, we explore different but equally important questions regarding inclusive team structures, ones that are more aligned with the discourse analytical lens we are deploying in this chapter. Our goal in this chapter is to explore and discuss *what* an inclusive team management structure might look like in practice. We do this by highlighting patterns of language use and social interaction in our basketball team that illustrate a multiparty approach to managing the team's everyday tasks. We also consider the features of our specific case (i.e., the makeup of our basketball team) in greater depth to unpack aspects of this context that might have influenced the enactment of this more widespread inclusion of multiple team members in the management of the team's activities.

3 Methodology

3.1 The team context and data set

This chapter is based on data collected from a university basketball team – The Tigers (a pseudonym) – during 2018–19 academic year (Stavridou 2022). Included in this data set are approximately 69 hours of observations and 38 hours of video-recordings from a total of 19 training sessions and match days (see Stavridou 2022). For the recorded interactions (our primary data set in this chapter), one of the researchers put recording equipment on our team's bench located at the sides of the court and captured the team's pre-game, in-game and post-game interactions. Unfortunately, a great deal of atmospheric noise – the constant dribbling of the balls, the echo of the bouncing balls and crowd noise – impacted the audibility of the data in a number of places. However, from these recorded interactions it was possible to see how individuals in the team contributed to the interactional performance of training session and match day tasks.

The subset of data we draw on in this study consists of the timeouts on match days. A timeout in the sport of basketball is a short, sixty-second (in our context) stoppage that can be called by a team when they want to take a break in play, usually to evaluate performances and discuss or diagnose issues the team are experiencing. This purpose of timeout talks makes them an interesting text through which to explore inclusion and leadership as stereotypically we might expect a leader with a notional role (i.e., a captain, coach or high-status individual) to seek and exercise greater amounts of control over the process of calling timeouts, evaluating performances, diagnosing issues and directing changes in performance (behaviour). However, as we will demonstrate in this chapter, the performance of leadership in our team in these timeouts was distributed across a greater number of individuals and this constructed what we would argue is a more inclusive approach to managing the team.

3.2 The team

Given the discussions above, it is also important to outline here the make-up of the team, particularly in relation to the notions of role and status. Table 1 below illustrates the characteristics of the team. All names, including the team's name, are pseudonyms.

Table 1: Overview of team players.

Player	Position	Games played	Current role	Previous role(s)	Years playing for the team
Owen	Point guard	7	Team captain		2
Mark	Shooting guard	7	Player	Team captain	4
Derek	Shooting guard	7	Player		1
Jay	Small forward	7	Player		2
Andrew	Power forward	6	Player		3
Jim	Small forward	2	Player		3

Table 1 (continued)

Player	Position	Games played	Current role	Previous role(s)	Years playing for the team
George	Power forward	7	Player	Team captain; Club president	6
Richard	Point guard	4	Player	Student coach	3
Alex	Centre	3	Player		1
Jackson	Centre	7	Player	Team captain	3
Nathan	Power forward	4	Player		1

As Table 1 indicates, the team consisted of eleven players. Each player's current and former roles have been noted as has the number of years they have played for the team (what we might label experience level). As can be seen in the table, several of the players (Mark, George and, Jackson) had previously been the team captain before the 2018–2019 season but were now, notionally at least, under Owen's captaincy in the team. Richard is also an important figure to highlight here as he has previously been a student coach giving him some experience in a leadership position. Additionally, the majority of the players are final year undergraduate students which, given that they have played for the team throughout their degree, arguably gives them some legitimate claim to status along experience lines, what might be viewed as a form of epistemic status (Stevanovic and Svennevig 2015).

Perhaps the most significant feature to highlight from the outset is that the team had no designated coach making it a particularly useful case study in which to explore leadership and establishment of an inclusive team structure (see also Schnurr et al. 2021). As we will argue in the discussion, this contextual feature, along with the number of team members with previous leadership experience, could be a significant contributor to the emergence of the inclusive team management practices we saw exhibited in our data.

Taken together, this contextual information, along with other finer-level contextual details about these individuals that we raise throughout the analysis, provides an important frame through which to interpret the meaning of interactional patterns in The Tigers timeout talks and support claims we make about the construction of an inclusive team structure in this basketball team. We will pay particular attention to the behaviour of four individuals from this team context: Jackson, Derek, Mark and Owen. As we will show, it was the interactional behaviour of these four individuals, who spoke the most, that provided the basis for claims we make about the more multiparty, participatory approach to the management of the team being constructed in this context.

3.3 Our analytical toolkit: Interactional sociolinguistics

When analysing the interactional patterns in our team's timeouts, we deploy the discourse analysis toolkit of Interactional Sociolinguistics (Schiffrin 1996; Gumperz 2001) – one approach to discourse analysis. Interactional Sociolinguistics allows researchers who study social interaction to track the moment-by-moment organisation of talk (in our case between members of The Tigers basketball team in their timeout talks) and link patterns at the micro interactional level to more macro-level constructs such as leadership style and (social) structure. In this chapter, we use this toolkit to locate and bring into focus interesting features of the micro-level linguistic action in our basketball team and, in turn, use these to discuss the more macro-level ideas being enacted about the leadership and management rights of individuals in the team.

When analysing the data at a micro-level, we focus our attention on four simple analytical questions which help to reveal dynamics in the turn-taking and interactional management of team tasks:

Who (i.e., which individuals, in which roles, with what status) talks in the timeouts?
Who does not talk in the timeouts?
What do they do with their talk?
How do they take turns in an unfolding interaction and position their contributions vis-à-vis other speakers?

While most of the above questions will be relatively easy for lay audiences to approach, questions 3 and 4 perhaps need some further explanation. These analytical questions are central to much of the work discourse analysts do as they focus on identifying the sometimes-opaque actions or functions being performed in and through talk. The timeout data showed speakers performing an array of actions through talk including *assessing performance* and *giving directives* to others. These actions arguably reflect some of the key purposes of timeout talk. As question 1 suggests, we also looked closely at who was performing these actions and we explored how these speech actions were being designed by speakers when making finer level linguistic choices. We paid particular attention to linguistic choices that characterised a speech action as more or less direct or indirect (Bach and Harnish 1979; Searle 1979) or as mitigated or unmitigated (Rendle-Short 2010), as directness and unmitigated force have been associated with leadership action in sporting contexts (Stavridou 2022).

Question 4 turns attention away from the more fine-grained analysis of speaker actions and explores the way speakers performed vis-à-vis one another as team talks unfolded. The focus here is very much on turn-taking, a prominent target for interactional linguists, with patterns at this level allowing us to see how the speakers work together (or do not) to manage their own and other's contributions to the floor as they attempt to achieve the communicative tasks at hand. For example, in this vein, we analysed who held the greatest amounts of speaking time, who took long turns at talk, whether people claimed the floor or were allocated it, and whether people interrupted one another or not. Insights from turn-taking analyses have helped to shine a light on power dynamics in action, making patterns of turn-taking a valuable target for exploring issues of leadership and team structure (Holmes, Schnurr, and, Marra 2007; File 2022).

In what follows, we present an account of the micro-level analysis we conducted on the team's timeout team talks, illustrating features that were both prominent in the data and that constructed what is arguably an overarching orientation to a multiparty, participatory, inclusive team structure in this particular team context. The wider significance of the patterns presented in the analysis will be picked up and discussed in the final section of this chapter, where we consider what these patterns help us to conclude, more broadly, about the nature of inclusive team structures in sports team contexts.

4 Findings: Evidencing the multiparty distribution of interactional rights to lead

In setting up the results of our analysis, what was immediately evident in our team's timeout talks was that multiple speakers claimed extensive turns at talk and performed actions through their talk that can be interpreted as attempts to lead the team. At the same time, we saw those in notional leadership roles (i.e., the captain) taking a backward step and allowing others in the team to contribute to or lead the interactional work in timeout team talks. It is this orientation to a multiparty floor, not dominated by those with powerful roles and high degrees of status in the team, that led us to claim the team's management structure was more inclusive. In the remainder of this section, we unpack three typical timeout team talks in our data set by drawing attention to the sociolinguistic phenomena (particularly the turn taking patterns) that support our understanding of this team's management structure as inclusive in nature.

Extract 1:

Context: The extract below is recorded during the 3rd quarter of an away game when The Tigers are ahead in the score, but the gap has decreased from, what they discuss below as defensive issues.

```
1                    ((the players gather around the bench))
2      Jackson:      you have to talk on defence as well
3                    like we're just quiet
4                    like they just run into us run down the court and
5                    pass where they want you know ((players nodding))
6                    just get in their way get in the way
7                    you can't just let them drive to the basket
8                    fucking foul them ( ) all right
9      Mark          let's just (.) wake up and play seriously (10.0) guys
10                   if we don't stop doing fouls yeah? and play forward
11                   you don't stop doing the first two-three minutes >of
12                   the back< and turn back (3.0) let's just cross each
13                   other let's just penetrate let's penetrate and give
14                   to [Alex
15     Owen:            [let's go let's go eh
16     Jackson:      let's pick up the intensity
17     Owen:         TEAM ON THREE ONE TWO THREE
18     All:          TEAM
```

In extract 1, we see Jackson and Mark (neither of whom are the team's captain) claim significant speaking time and take longer turns in this timeout to lead the debrief on the team's performance to date. Jackson and Mark were frequent contributors to the timeout talks in our data. In this instance, we see both players raising issues about the team's defence strategy, specifically regarding how to defend against the opposition. Topics of this nature were common during timeout communication.

On speaking time alone, the analysis of timeout talks suggests that Mark and Jackson claim rights to leadership (Wilson 2011). Stereotypically, it is a team's leaders who dominate the interactional spaces, particularly those in which significant team management tasks are being performed (File 2022). We frequently saw Mark and Jackson dominate these sixty-second timeouts claiming significant floor time and, in the process, rights to address the assembled group in what is an important and time-constrained interaction.

However, it is when we look more closely at what both Jackson and Mark are doing with their contributions to the interaction that we find what is arguably more significant evidence to support the claim that these two players are claiming and/or are afforded the right to perform leadership responsibilities in this team context. Two speech actions that are particularly evident in the talk of Jackson and Mark in extract 1, and that help to characterise their behaviour as leading in this specific interactional context, are assessments and directives (Holmes and Stubbe 2003; Schnurr 2009, 2013). Jackson, in particular, provides a series of strongly worded, negative assessments of the team's performance in the match and weaves in directives that arguably aim to oblige players being addressed to accept and attempt a change in the playing behaviour. In line 2, Jackson begins his contribution to the team talk by stating that the team *need to talk (more) on defence* before pejoratively evaluating the team as quiet.

Jackson's leadership rights in this and other instances of a similar kind are predicated on claims that he is capable of both providing a valid assessment (in this case about the appropriate level of talk required) and has the status to be able to oblige the team to change. The nods of agreement by those around him as he issues these assessments and directives support and co-construct these claims. In lines 7 to 8, Jackson goes on to make further negative assessments of the team's commitment to defending when he suggests the opposition are having an easy time of it in the match (not positive in the context of a competitive game of sport) because of the team's low intensity approach to defence. He follows these assessments with a further directive to the team to 'get in their way' (see line 6) and foul the opposition as he closes his turn at talk.

While the above analysis makes a case for why Jackson's and Mark's talk can be considered leadership in action, at this point it is pertinent to remind readers that neither Jackson nor Mark are the team's captain. Both have previously been team captain, but neither are currently in the role. In fact, throughout this extract and many other extracts in our data, the captain, Owen, is not directly afforded room to address the team by others, he does not initiate team talks, and he does not interject or force his way into the talk – all of which are behavioural norms of captains noted in other research (Lyle 2002; Cotterill and Fransen 2016; File, 2022). Instead, like others in the huddle, he provides support for the assessments and directives being issued by Jackson through nods and minimal feedback tokens (of agreement). Owen does lead the team chant, though, that brings the timeout to a close and signals a return to the floor. In this regard, Owen claims responsibility for closing the 'meeting' (lines 15, 17), an action that has in other contexts been described as a leadership responsibility (Chan 2008; Asmuß and Svennevig 2009).

What the above extract hints at is the freer adoption and performance of leadership responsibilities by players without notional leadership roles in the team. In extract 2 below, we see another individual from the team perform significant leadership actions in a timeout. This time it is Derek who claims significant floor time and performs similar actions that arguably index claims to leadership, again by issuing negative assessments and directives to the assembled group.

Extract 2:

Context: This extract was recorded during a timeout in the 1st quarter of The Varsity Match, i.e., the annual fixture played between The Tigers and another local university basketball team. The extract below is one of the first timeouts of the game where the team is discussing its strategy.

```
1    Jackson:   (come on) (.) (who wants) the ball on offence?
2    Derek:     31 cannot get another clean look
3               he hit his first
4               we left him wide open
5               he hit his second
6               how is he still wide open (.) yeah?
7    Jay:       there's the screen
8               we need to switch on that screen
9               but he's on the wing if (.) so he's shot everyone
10              from the [wing yeah
11   Owen:               [yeah
12   Derek:     if the big sorry ah if the forward (.) forward needs to
13              get out first guard needs to come across
14              they're not screening both of you yeah
15   Jay:       I know but yeah but
16   Derek:     someone's got to be (.) the last two shots he's had
17              two three-meter ( )
18              that's far too much space
19   Jackson:   I'm I'm I'm sitting in the paint all right
20              just go over the screen if you're going over
21              because he's going to drive in if [you go over okay
22   Jay:                                         [yeah yeah
23   Derek:     we're good (.) we just need to stop
24              ( ) we need to set up (unclear)
25   Mark:      yeah and keep attacking the basket
26   Derek:     ( )
27   Jackson:   yeah I don't think our offence is a problem
28              we're just rushing our shots a little bit
29              like the first look we get we're (taking)
30   Owen:      let's go let's go
31   Derek:     let's go
```

| 32 | Owen: | TIGERS ON THREE ONE TWO |
| 33 | All: | TIGERS |

This timeout starts with Jackson ushering everyone into the huddle. While Jackson does try to initiate a topic of discussion, it is Derek (also not the team captain) who succeeds in claiming the floor and directing the debrief (at least initially) in this huddle. In line 2, we see Derek enter the huddle a little later than the others (who are assembling and taking on water) and claim the floor without being invited to speak and offer what turns out to be a critical assessment of the team's defence on the opposition's shooting guard.

The pattern of self-selection is interesting to reflect on further here with respect to leadership claims by Derek. One interpretation is that the rapid and uninvited, self-claimed turns at talk we saw in this and other extracts might be explained by the time-pressured nature of these timeout interactions. As noted above, timeouts are time-restricted speech events that last roughly sixty seconds. The pressure to get the team business done in such a short amount of time might be what encourages people to jump into the discussion and claim the floor uninvited. However, these self-selection patterns also simultaneously imply that this player (or speaker) feels they have the right to enter the interaction, claim the floor and directly address the group when they believe they have something relevant to say.

When we look more closely at what Derek does with his turns at talk, across the first half of the extract, we see him performing in a similar way to Jackson in extract 1 by issuing strong, critical assessments of the team's performance (lines 2 to 10) and directives to the group for fixing these issues (lines 12 to 16). The way Derek speaks (i.e., the way he designs his messages) may also suggest that he is taking some leadership liberties. In line 6, he poses (and in the process claims the right to issue) a somewhat face-threatening proposition or question to those assembled, when he asks the group how the opposition's shooting guard has been able to get clean shots away. Whether it is a question or exclamation is somewhat irrelevant as the underlying intention of this action by Derek is to criticise the team's defensive efforts and may be an invitation for someone to claim responsibility for the mistakes being highlighted by Derek. His assessment is arguably more strongly designed than the ones issued by Jackson in extract 1 as it implies that the team should have but has not been able to identify and address an obvious issue (i.e., that a good shooter on the opposition team should be more appropriately guarded against). In essence, Derek, in issuing this account of the team's play could be seen to be questioning their abilities as players, a very face-threatening action in this context, and an action we might expect to see more typically from those who have the status to be able to call out player performances, such as a coach (Lyle 2002).

Jay also joins this sequence of talk, in lines 7 and 8, and offers what appears to be a solution to the issue Derek has raised – that the players responsible for guarding need to switch positions when the opposition use a screen to help create a shooting opportunity for the shooting guard. However, Derek baldly rejects this solution in lines 9 and 10 and offers a counter solution to the group in lines 12 to 16 that involves the forward and the guard moving around the screen the opposition are creating. Jackson also plays a role in this team talk. However, he can be seen to be playing a supporting role to Derek in this particular interaction, by offering a further solution to the issue that has been raised by Derek (lines 17 to 19).

There are other points to raise here about the leadership actions of Derek in particular. Later in the extract, Derek seeks to calm the team down in line 21 by stating that they are 'good' and motions everyone to calm down with hand gestures in the process. Moderating the team's emotional pulse could also arguably be seen as an act of leadership in that the speaker claims expertise to be able to read people and demand responses of some kind from them. However, it is through his claims to expertise (either in identifying issues or proposing solutions to them) and his claims to speak frankly to others and hold addressees accountable by demanding actions the members *need* to perform to resolve these issues that Derek claims rights to lead the group.

Again, overhanging this analysis is the fact that, like Jackson, Derek is not the team captain. On the surface, Derek's status could be viewed as even lower than Jackson's. He has also not held any previous notional leadership roles in the team prior to the season this data was collected and is in his first season playing for the team. Based on this background information, we might expect Derek to adopt more of a follower role throughout team interactions. Yet, as we have illustrated in extract 2 above, we see Derek claiming rights to hold others in the team accountable (mainly those guarding the opposition's shooting guard), giving directions to members of the team to resolve the issue they are experiencing on defence and attempting to calm any feelings of pressure being felt by members of the team.

Owen, the captain of the team, again chooses not to enact any of his own notional rights to the floor. However, he does again lead the closing ritual, which may suggest he is performing important timekeeping responsibilities on behalf of the team. However, in comparison to others in this and the previous interaction, Owen has remained peripheral in his influence.

In the final extract, we see yet another player emerging to claim leadership rights in timeout talk. This time it is Mark (seen briefly in extract 1 above), a team captain from previous years, who, together with Jackson, performs a number of interactional rights and responsibilities that arguably show him claiming rights to lead the team.

Chapter 4 Constructing inclusive team management structures — 97

Extract 3:
Context: This timeout is recorded during the 3rd quarter of an away game when The Tigers are ahead by 8 points. As the excerpt below shows, members of the team feel they still need to improve their offensive tactics despite being ahead in the score.

```
1    -          ((horn))
2    Owen:      ((unintelligible due to loud background cheering))
3    Mark:      ↑what happened to the lay-up?
4    Owen:      we were nervous
5    Jackson:   ↑the lay-up didn't work
6    Mark:      o- okay I can retry we've got options (2.0)
7               and people you gotta shout like Mark I'm
8               here (.) cos if you don't shout I can't
9               really know where [you are
10   Richard:                    [we've got big mismatch, that's a full
11              press zone
12   Mark:      when you have the ball you need to shout me
13              Mark give me the ball °like acknowledge give
14              the ball°
15   Jackson:   more important use all the fouls we've got
16              especially ( ) okay? when the foul comes up
17              you cannot >fairly< get ( ) all right? stand
18              up stand up ((players stand up from the
19              bench)) we need to stop them from
20              penetrating
21   Owen:      ↑TEAM ON THREE ONE TWO THREE
22   All:       TEAM
23   Jackson:   let's go Tigers let's go ((after the timeout))
```

In this extract, which for space restriction reasons we do not discuss in too much detail, we see Mark emerge, again with Jackson, to perform what could also be considered leadership actions, namely an attempt to fix coordination issues he is experiencing with other players on the court. In line 3, Mark initiates a topic and a task for discussion by the group – considering the reasons for a lay-up chance the team missed on a previous play. In responding to Mark's lead, Owen and Jackson both issue explanations that negatively assess the team's performance in that sequence of play (in lines 4 and 5). Mark then reclaims the floor in line 6 and lays out the prospect of repeating the play and issues instructions that arguably aim to increase the chances of success with this strategic play. In lines 7 to 9 and again in lines 12 to 14, Mark indicates the importance of shouting out to one another to communicate where players are on the court and whether they are ready or open to receive the ball. Directing the strategic plays of the team can be considered a leadership action and Mark's actions in this extract perform an influential role in choosing the team's strategic plays and encouraging important competencies (in this case clear and audible communication with one another).

Looking at some of the design work in Mark's messages, the leadership status of this instance of talk, and, with it, Mark's status as a contributor to the management of team, is perhaps a little less certain. For example, Mark encodes his directive to the rest of the group to try this strategic play again in ways that shape it more as a suggestion ("I can retry" in line 6) and less as a directive for others to follow. However, there are cues in other utterances to suggest that Mark also constructs himself as a legitimate claimant to a leadership role in the team. For example, in the above extract, Mark issues directives to the team that show he is taking some responsibility for increasing the team's cohesive play (directing people to communicate more effectively when they want the ball). He also uses semimodals such as *gotta* and *need to* which directly encode an obligation to those he is addressing – a linguistic action we would associate with leadership (Holmes and Stubbe 2003; Vine 2020: 56–57). He also uses the pronoun *you* in both of these instances above which appears (from our reading of the data and video) to be issued more generically at multiple individuals (i.e., generic plural *you*) and not one specific individual (i.e., singular *you*). In this regard, Mark claims the right to address (and perhaps chide) the team for their performance inaccuracies while also distancing himself from those he appears to be chiding.

So, while his talk may be styled in less direct ways, taken together, Mark can arguably be seen as another contributor to the team's leadership performance – the fourth (including Owen) we have illustrated here. Additionally, while he was a previous captain of this team, he is again another contributor that does not currently possess a notional leadership role in the team.

In the discussion section of this chapter, we review these findings and consider what they tell us more broadly about the notion of inclusive team management structures in sports teams.

5 Discussion: Theorising inclusive team structures

In the data presented above, we have provided evidence of a multiparty participation approach to the leadership of our basketball team, which, we argue, constitutes an inclusive team management structure on the basis that more people are *included* as legitimate social actors in management of their team. From our analysis, we saw a number of different individuals (four we have specifically discussed here) contribute in varying ways to the leadership of the team and across different timeout interactions during match day events. We saw these speakers perform what are arguably key responsibilities of leaders in these interactions, including providing critical assessments, identifying solutions to these issues, often delivered in and through directives, calming the team down and leading the team's solidarity rituals. In our team, we provided sociolinguistic evidence of these leadership actions being performed by more individuals in the team than we might stereotypically expect and argue this reflects and constructs a more inclusive philosophy on leadership.

Additionally, as well as seeing multiple individuals involved in the leadership of the team, we saw a diverse array of individuals, from role and status perspectives, perform leadership tasks in the team's timeouts. This is arguably further and perhaps even more persuasive evidence of an inclusive team management structure in action. Many of the more dominant speakers in this team did not have current notional or institutional roles within the team structure (such as captain). Some had previously been in such roles (a point we pick up further below) but others were playing in their first year with the club. The captain spoke rarely and seemed comfortable allowing the other players to perform leadership responsibilities in these timeout talks. Based on this sociolinguistic fact, we would also argue that this team invites, accepts or even expects involvement in the leadership of the team from members regardless of their role or status – arguably a further dimension of what we have labelled an inclusive team structure. In our data, none of these speakers had their attempts to contribute rejected and there was evidence in the data to suggest that speaker contributions, regardless of the role or status of the speaker, were accepted in the form of minimal feedback tokens and non-verbal acknowledgement in the recordings and transcripts, although more significant analysis could be done regarding this with better quality video and audio recordings.

We would, therefore, claim that inclusive team management structures are perhaps not simply defined by the construction of a multiparty, participatory approach to leadership, but also with respect to who contributes to that leadership performance. In our case, it was not one person giving out opportunities to others to participate that characterised the management structure of this team as inclusive. Rather, it was the free-flowing claiming and acceptance of rights by multiple individuals, regardless of their (un)official status in the team, to participate actively in the leadership of the team.

5.1 Digging deeper: Explaining this orientation to an inclusive team structure

One of the main questions we asked ourselves as we processed the findings of our case study more closely was why do we see an inclusive team structure being enacted in this specific team context? Put another way, why do we see multiple players of different role and status backgrounds contributing to the ongoing management of the team and its performances? Because previous research has highlighted how leadership and management rights in sports teams is typically restricted to those with notionally powerful roles (Cotterill 2012; File 2022), some consideration of the specific context from which this data comes might be useful for building more of an understanding about inclusive team management structures.

There are a number of potential explanations and readers may have developed their own from their understanding of the context we studied here. For example, it may be that student team contexts support or encourage a more inclusive approach to team management, given they are part of a wider academic setting. Programmes of extracurricular activity within universities, such as sports teams, have been noted as specific sites where values like respecting diversity and being inclusive are particularly appreciated, fostered and developed (Foley et al. 2022). A shared understanding and orientation to overarching educational values such as these might, therefore, be one potential and/or partial explanation for the emergence of the more inclusive team management structure we saw in our data.

Another potential factor of significance here is the absence of an official coach. File (2022) in his study of a professional New Zealand rugby team found the coaches to be a dominant force in the team's interactions when they were present and that there was greater interaction between the players when the coach was away from the players (i.e., in instances when they talked on the field in huddles during stoppages). In other words, perhaps what we see here is multiple players stepping up to perform leadership in the void provided by the absence of an officially sanctioned and powerful coach. As noted above in the literature review, other studies have also explored this phenomenon of emergent leadership in similar situations where a coach has not been present (Schnurr et al. 2021).

Alternatively, the previous leadership experiences of the individuals in this team may help to explain why this more inclusive team management structure emerged in this team context. Mark and Jackson were both captains of the team in previous years and this may have given them the experience in a leadership role, namely this specific team context. This previous experience may have given Mark and Jackson a degree of comfort with issuing directives and performing other leadership actions while also contributing to an acceptance of their contributions in these interactions by the other members of the team. However, this would not necessarily explain Derek's frequent and forceful contributions to the running of the team, as he is in his first year with the team and has not previously held a position of leadership in this team.

What we may also be seeing here is evidence of new cultural or ideological norms emerging in team sporting structures. Ideology and shifting ideological belief systems are frequently cited as an explanation for linguistic patterns and change in linguistic patterns (Van Dijk 2009, 2011). Ideology is often used as a blanket term that can be applied loosely to all manner of beliefs. For our purposes here, ideologies can of course be formed around beliefs about status, power, leadership and who, in a specific setting, is responsible for leading a team, for example. Importantly, ideologies are subject to change and with a number of well-publicised examples of successful teams outlining aims to create greater involvement by the wider membership of the team (see, for example, Schofield 2017; Morrow 2021; Reason 2021). What we may see here is evidence, from one setting, of a wider, cultural move in sport towards a more inclusive understanding of how leadership, power and responsibility need to work in sports teams. While this is one potential explanation, it is put forward very tentatively, as previous research cannot support such a widespread claim at this stage.

5.2 Advice for practitioners: Defining and facilitating inclusive team structures

In closing this chapter, we consider how the findings and discussion in this chapter might be approached by practitioners in sport, particularly those who have some say over advising on or instilling a team culture or management approach in sports teams. In particular, we draw attention, as other authors in this volume have done, to issues of *how* to accomplish inclusion. In this case, we have considered how inclusive team management structures might be constructed and/or supported should teams or team advisors wish to pursue such a philosophy.

We would argue that for practitioners interested in fostering a more inclusive approach to team management, the findings presented in this chapter suggest that close reflection of ritual communication dynamics in team interactions is a useful point of departure. What initially drew us to the discussion we have had in this chapter were peculiarities in the distribution of interactional rights in typical and ordinary team management tasks. These peculiarities centred on our observations of a more widespread performance of leadership, accomplished in this instance through different members of the team leading the team's everyday interactional rituals.

Therefore, critically reflecting on the way interactional rights are being claimed and distributed, particularly in relation to how these rights pattern onto roles in the team, can provide teams and team advisors with useful data of how inclusive their structure is and where specific intervention work may need to be applied. Explicitly articulating and giving players evidence that their contributions are welcome is going to be important for fostering wider involvement to managing the team. In some situations, players may take to such an offering but in others they may need to develop comfort with leading. In our team, the fact that several of those team members who helped to construct a multiparty leadership structure in this team had previous leadership experience may explain why this practice emerged as normative in our context. For those seeking to choreograph or develop an inclusive management structure in their context, supporting players in the team develop comfort with leading team management tasks and clearly articulating that their contributions to leadership are accepted (or even expected) are going to be important actions.

Appendix

Table of transcription conventions

?	a question marks a rising intonation
,	a comma marks a slightly rising intonation but is also used when the intonation contour is hearable as incomplete
↑word	sharp rise in pitch
underlined	stress
CAPS	louder talk
°word°	talk which is quieter or whispered
>word<	talk which is noticeably faster than the surrounding talk
[word	start of simultaneous talk
(.)	very short pause
(0.3), (1.2), etc.	timed pause in seconds
(words)	problematic talk, with possible hearing
( )	talk which cannot be understood for transcription
((words))	transcriber's comment, description

Source: Liddicoat, Anthony J. 2022 [2007]. *An Introduction to Conversation Analysis*, 3rd ed. New York: Bloomsbury Academic.

References

Asmuß, Birte & Jan Svennevig. 2009. Meeting talk: An introduction. *Journal of Business Communication* 46(1). 3–22. https://doi:10.1177/0021943608326761

Bach, Kent & Robert M. Harnish. 1979. *Linguistic communication and speech acts*. Cambridge, MA: MIT Press.

Chan, Angela. 2008. "Meeting openings and closings in a Hong Kong company." In Hao Sun & Daniel Kadar (eds.), *It's the Dragon's Turn*, 181–229. Bern: Peter Lang.

Cotterill, Steward T. 2012. *Team psychology in sports: Theory and practice*. Hove, East Sussex: Routledge.

Cotterill, Steward T. & Katrien Fransen. 2016. Athlete leadership in sport teams: Current understanding and future directions. *International Review of Sport and Exercise Psychology* 9(1). 116–133.

Eckert, Penelope &Sally McConnell-Ginet. 1992. Communities of practice: Where language, gender and power all live. In Kira Hall, Mary Bucholtz & Birch Moonwomon (eds.), *Locating Power. Proceedings of the Second Berkeley Women and Language Conference*, 89–99. Berkeley Women and Language Group, University of California.

Fairhurst, Gail. 2007. *Discursive leadership: In conversation with leadership psychology*. Thousand Oaks, CA: SAGE.

File, Kieran A. 2022. *How Language Shapes Relationships in Professional Sports Teams: Power and Solidarity Dynamics in a New Zealand Rugby Team*. London: Bloomsbury Academic.

Foley, Carmen, Simon Darcy, Anja Hergesell, Barbara Almond, Matthew McDonald & Elizabeth Brett. 2022. University-based sport and social clubs and their contribution to the development of graduate attributes. *Active Learning in Higher Education*, 146978742211276. https://doi.org/10.1177/14697874221127692

Gumperz, John J. 2001. Interactional sociolinguistics: A personal perspective. In Deborah Schiffrin, Deborah Tannen & Heidi E. Hamilton (eds.), *The Handbook of Discourse Analysis*, 215–228. Oxford: Blackwell Publishers Inc.

Holmes, Janet & Maria Stubbe. 2003. *Power and Politeness in the Workplace: A Sociolinguistic Analysis of Talk at Work*. London: Longman.

Holmes, Janet, Stephanie Schnurr & Meredith Marra. 2007. Leadership and communication: Discursive evidence of a workplace culture change. *Discourse and Communication* 1(4). 433–451.

Larsson, Magnus. 2017. Leadership in Interaction. In John Storey, Jean Hartley, Jean-Loui Denis, Paul t' Hart & Dave Ulrich (eds.), *The Routledge Companion to Leadership*, 173–193. New York: Routledge.

Lave, Jean & Etienne Wenger. 1991. *Situated learning: Legitimate peripheral participation*. Cambridge: Cambridge University Press.

Jaworski, Adam & Nikolas Coupland (eds.). 2006 [1999]. *The discourse reader*, 2nd edn. London: Routledge.

Liddicoat, Anthony J. 2022 [2007]. *An introduction to Conversation Analysis*, 3rd edn. New York: Bloomsbury.

Lyle, John. 2002. *Sports coaching concepts. A framework for coaches' behaviour*. London/New York: Routledge.

Morrow, Michael. 2021. "Ronan O'Gara: La Rochelle head coach on the power of positivity and a 'no limits' approach". *BBC Sport*. https://www.bbc.co.uk/sport/rugby-union/56885756 (last modified 1 May 2021).

Reason, Mark. 2021. "Mark Reason: What Ian Foster could learn from Gareth Southgate". *Stuff*. https://www.stuff.co.nz/sport/opinion/300356027/mark-reason-what-ian-foster-could-learn-from-gareth-southgate (last modified 13 July 2021).

Rendle- Short, Johanna. 2010. 'Mate' as a term of address in ordinary interaction. *Journal of Pragmatics* 42(5). 1201–1218.

Schiffrin, Deborah. 1996. Interactional sociolinguistics. In Nancy F. Hornberger & Michael H. Long (eds.), *Sociolinguistics and language teaching*, 307–328. Cambridge: Cambridge University Press.

Schnurr, Stephanie. 2009. *Leadership discourse at work*. Basingstoke/New York: Palgrave Macmillan.

Schnurr, Stephanie. 2013. *Exploring professional communication: Language in action*. Abingdon: Routledge.

Schnurr, Stephanie, Kieran A. File, Daniel Clayton, Solvejg Wolfers & Anastasia Stavridou. 2020. Exploring the processes of emergent leadership in a netball team: Providing empirical evidence through discourse analysis. *Discourse & Communication* 15(1). 98–116.

Schofield, Daniel. 2017. "Eddie Jones: I want to make myself redundant by letting England players take control". *The Telegraph*. http://www.telegraph.co.uk/rugby-union/2017/06/05/eddie-jones-want-make-redundant-letting-england-players-take/ (last modified 5 June 2017).

Searle, John R. 1979. Expression and meaning: Studies in the theory of speech acts. Cambridge: Cambridge University Press.

Stavridou, Anastasia. 2022. *Challenging traditional understandings of leadership and followership through discourse: A sociolinguistic case study of a basketball team*. Coventry: University of Warwick PhD thesis.

Stevanovic, Melisa & Jan Svennevig. 2015. Introduction: Epistemics and deontics in conversational directives. *Journal of Pragmatics* 78. 1–6.

Stevanovic, Melisa & Anssi Peräkylä. 2014. Three orders in the organization of human action: On the interface between knowledge, power, and emotion in interaction and social relations. *Language in Society* 43(2). 185–207.

Tourish, Dennis. 2007. Themed book reviews: Communication, discourse and leadership. *Human Relations* 60(11). 1727–1740.

Van Dijk, Teun A. 2009. Critical discourse studies: A sociocognitive approach. *Methods in Critical Discourse Analysis* 2(1). 62–86.

Van Dijk, Teun A. 2011. Discourse and ideology. In Teun A. van Dijk (ed.), *Discourse studies: A multidisciplinary introduction*, 379–407. London: SAGE Publications.

Vine, Bernadette. 2020. *Introducing language in the workplace*. Cambridge: Cambridge University Press.

Wilson, Nick. 2011. *Leadership as communicative practice: The discursive construction of leadership and team identity in a New Zealand rugby team*. Wellington: Victoria University of Wellington.

Fergus O'Dwyer
Chapter 5
Banter as a tactic of inclusion in sports organizations

1 Introduction: Inclusion and the roles of humour in sporting organizations

Humour can perform many functions including the construction and maintenance of good relations with colleagues (e.g., Holmes 2006: 26). This chapter examines the ways collegial humour can create and maintain inclusion (which I take to mean being included in team or club activities) amongst sport club members. The sociopragmatic analysis of humourous interactions in this chapter finds that strategies such as engaging in banter, responding quickly to jovial insults, and telling humourous stories are ways to create a sense of inclusion in a sports team context. Data is presented from an ethnographic study of Club Fingal (pseudonym), an amateur Gaelic Football and Hurling club in Dublin, Ireland. An important point to note is that players specifically mentioned that having the *"craic"* (Irish word for fun, enjoyment, general banter and good times, see Dolan 2006: 64), in training and around games makes participation worthwhile (O'Dwyer 2020: 188). Engaging with banter is an effective way to create common ground amongst teammates as it creates shared stories and threads which can be recalled, recycled and extended when teammates gather together.

The main argument of this chapter is that collaborative humour can be used to construct and enact inclusion by fostering a sense of belonging and social cohesion within teams and clubs. The principal implications of this study are that coaches and other stakeholders in sporting organizations can choose from a range of pragmatic strategies when introducing humour in order to create a lighthearted atmosphere with the view of developing positive relationships and enhancing inclusion in team dynamics. It is important to create communicative spaces where banter is possible: threads of humour can be created and developed, forming a bond or connection between players which can be extended in future interactions. I develop these ideas by relating to literature in the next section, before detailing the methodology used, and presenting an overview of

Fergus O'Dwyer, Marino Institute of Education, Ireland

the club in question. Section 4 presents analysis of three interactions which exemplify tactics of inclusion, with the discussion section including implications.

2 Humour, identity and inclusion

In this study I illustrate how humour plays a central role in the club, acting as the social glue of the club, to enhance and maintain a sense of inclusion. Key theoretical concepts I draw on in this chapter to discuss humour are identity and inclusion. I offer a brief review of relevant literature regarding these concepts here to ground my chapter beginning with an overview of sociopragmatic issues of humour.

When analysing humour, the pragmatic question is not "what does this utterance mean?" but "why has this utterance been produced?" (Haberland and Mey 2002: 1672). A sociopragmatic perspective focuses on the factors that make certain language use more or less acceptable, in contrast to other, perhaps abstractly equivalent, but pragmatically radically different uses (Mey 2002: 8–10). This area is informed by politeness theory, in particular strategies to mitigate a face-threatening act (FTA) proposed by Brown and Levinson (1978): negative politeness, positive politeness, and bald-on-record strategies. Strategies to address negative face wants — by not imposing on speakers' freedom — include indirectness, questioning, and apologizing (O'Keeffe, Clancy, and Adolphs 2011: 69). Positive politeness strategies — avoiding threatening the addressee's positive face (desire to be liked and accepted) — can include paying attention to the addressee's interests and needs, finding common ground and using *we* forms (e.g., Wolfers, File, and Schnurr 2017; see also File et al, this volume). A bald-on-record strategy, talking directly, is used when mutual demands override face concerns, and the interlocutors act based on factors such as equality, common ground and a need to get something done. Politeness and face issues are central to the analysis of humour and teasing as it occurs in interactions amongst friends and sport club members.

The study of humour can help to understand issues such as how speakers can linguistically signal inclusion. Different groups of people develop different ways of doing humour (Schnurr and Chan 2009: 151): not only the amount of humour differs, but also the ways in which humour is used. Similarities and differences in humour are thought to derive from the setting and society in which the sociopragmatic strategy and humour is performed (Richards 2006: 95–96). When outlining the distinctive ways of doing humour in a context, specific reference can be made to issues such as topic (e.g., are certain types of topics commonly used in certain situations?), delivery (intonation etc.), direction (e.g., whether humour is self-deprecating or directed toward an out-group), orientation (e.g., derogatory), and organization (e.g., to indicate the close of a conversation) (Richards 2006: 95–96). It is also worth noting that the nature of implicit messages found in humour can range from bonding face threatening acts (FTAs) (see Boxer and Cortés-Conde 1997: 276, 279) to biting, bald-on-record FTAs. The latter are rare but note that the intermediary teasing category of nipping — friendly teases which contain both a bond and bite and an underlying message such as criticism — are common in interactions analysed below. Note that humour is viewed in this chapter as multifunctional, with several possible interpretations and overlapping functions possible during interactions (cf. Boxer and Cortés-Conde 1997; O'Dwyer 2020: 187–189). Humour can be considered as an important politeness strategy to mitigate the face-threatening nature of the criticism that leaders of sport teams often employ (O'Dwyer 2020). The specific positions and possible functions implemented through humour have been described coherently by Hay (2000), such as solidarity-building and boundary-maintaining humour. Teasing is prevalent in sporting organizations (e.g., Edwards and Jones 2018; Thompson, Potrac, and Jones 2015): participants generally perceive teases in close relationships more positively and better intentioned than those in non-close relationships; and relationship closeness increases positive perceptions of teasing (Haugh and Pillet-Shore 2018). So, teasing can also be used as a tool to indicate closeness.

Identities are constantly shifting as humourous interaction unfolds. By foregrounding certain stances and attitudes, humour can indirectly align or disassociate an individual to/from a specific social group and relate important tactics of intersubjectivity and other identity principles (cf. Bucholtz and Hall 2005). The tactic of adequation emphasizes similarities in order to align oneself with a social group to which one may not otherwise be able to claim membership, while distinction creates distance between an individual and a specific social group (Bucholtz and Hall 2005: 598). The indexicality principle sees identity relations emerge in several related processes, including overt mention of identity categories, implicatures and presuppositions regarding identity positions, and displaying evaluative and epistemic orientations to ongoing talk (Bucholtz and Hall 2005: 593). The partialness principle views constructions of identity in part deliberate and intentional, in part habitual and hence often less than fully conscious, in part an outcome of interactional negotiation and contestation, in part an outcome of others' perceptions and representations, and in part an effect of larger ideological processes and material structures that may become relevant to interaction (Bucholtz and Hall 2005: 605). This leads to identity performance and performativity: doing things with words, and the way we talk directly indexing a prediscursive self, constituting the very act that it performs (Hall 2000: 196). These identity performances, frequent in interaction, may be evaluated by an audience and often involve stylization (Bucholtz and Hall 2005: 580). Relational identity development (Boxer 2002; Chovanec and Tsakona 2018) is an important concept in relation to how humour is performed in excerpts analysed below.

In this chapter, I examine how humour relates to inclusion: the link between organizational inclusion and identity (e.g., Ortlieb, Glauninger, and Weiss 2021: 280) is a nascent area. An important consideration regarding teams is psychological safety: a shared belief that the team provides a safe environment for taking interpersonal risks such as asking a question, reporting an error, seeking feedback (Edmondson 1996), or in the case of this chapter co-constructing humour. This links to communication style and perceptions of teasing as leader incivility is thought to lead to lower team cohesion, lower psychological safety, and lower objective team performance (Smittick, Miner, and Cunningham 2019). Possibly problematic speakers' positioning of themselves and others in German sport team communications (Wolfers, File and, Schnurr 2017: 92) were counterbalanced by linguistic strategies such as use of inclusive "we", familiarizers, and laughter alongside co-construction of humour. The important findings presented below relate to inclusion and collaborative humour.

The central premise of this chapter is that co-constructing humour is a salient tactic of inclusion which enacts belonging and creates social cohesion within teams. The games and preparation etc. are not only about winning and losing: they are an important social outlet for members. An important part of this social world is the humour that makes being a member of the club enjoyable. Another point to note is that speakers referring to threads and stories are a way to find a common thread to talk about and maintain a sense of solidarity within the club. This ultimately facilitates inclusion as it is possible for all present to collaborate in the humourous interactions. This chapter goes on to analyse and interpret some salient examples before outlining important implications for practitioners, but first outlines the specific communicative setting and analytical framework adopted. The main goals of this study are to explore how humour is a sociopragmatic resource that can be actively deployed in sporting team contexts to promote inclusion. To address this, I will explore three interactions that exemplify the use of sociopragmatic strategies in Club Fingal: the methodology used in the study is now discussed.

3 Methodology: Ethnography

This data analysed below emerged from a sociolinguistic PhD project (O'Dwyer 2020) conducted in Dublin Ireland over the course of six years between 2012 and 2016. I used the ethnographic data collection method of participant observation to become involved in activities where speakers potentially perform sociopragmatic strategies. The aim of this approach was to develop an in-depth understanding of people's behaviour and observing attitudes. I began observation and taking field notes in the club through participating in training session in Club Fingal (see the following sub-section for further details about the club). My first entry into the field notes was that instead of greeting each other with a "hello", a more typical greeting is to make a joke. This observation was the starting point from which the discovery of an important sociopragmatic strategy — humour, the focus of this chapter — in Club Fingal emerged. In the latter stages of the project further observations, interviews and free recordings focused on developing a clear understanding of the functions of humour.

During my fieldwork, I interacted with club members in different capacities: as a friend, a player, a parent of a player, a spectator, and a general club member socializing during club activities (e.g., watching a game or enjoying a casual drink in the club bar). I "blended in" (i.e., did what other members generally did before, during and after training) with club practices: the principal form of observation was participating in training sessions with two club teams over the course of four years. These training sessions typically lasted for 90 minutes of drills and practice matches, with 15 to 30 players. Other observations include games that generally involved the teams I trained with. I often accompanied the team members when they socialized together after the games or training sessions in the club bar or in nearby pubs. At all times during, before and after these matches and training sessions I engaged socially with members of the teams, in a relatively natural way. Our relationship was that of a team- or club-mate. In this way, these informal interactions allowed me to develop rapport with potential study participants. This was often a case of redeveloping rapport, as I knew the members from previous interactions. I occasionally socialized with other club members before and after major Gaelic Athletic Association (GAA) events in Croke Park stadium, and in surrounding pubs. I continue to do many of these activities, along with coaching a team, since moving back to Dublin in 2018. I have been spending a lot of time involved in coaching activities, which also involves social elements like attending club fundraising events and enjoying casual drinks in the club bar. Transcriptions from memory of interactions I observed are analysed in this chapter alongside interpretations based on the extensive notes I made while conducting participant observation in the club. I now provide an overview of the club where the ethnography was undertaken.

3.1 Research context: Club Fingal

Club Fingal is part of the GAA, a nationwide organization which primarily focuses on the playing of the Irish field games Gaelic Football and Hurling. Both are relatively tough games, with much physicality. Gaelic football could be seen as a mix between soccer (the objective to score points by passing the ball through the other team's goals) and rugby (the field and posts are similar, and you may catch and kick the ball over the bar). There are no offside rules which leads to open, free-scoring play. Hurling shares a number of features with Gaelic football, with players using a hurley — a wooden stick shaped like a hockey stick but with a wider end — to hit a small ball roughly the size of a tennis ball. The club is a major social institution in the local area (see O'Dwyer 2020, chapter 2 for more details), foregrounding community involvement through the playing of games and activities in its social centre. The adult members who participated in this study are members of one of the 65 club teams, all of which are amateur: the teams I engaged with are made up of regular (i.e., non-elite) players. The very elite, talented players are selected to represent their county (in this case Dublin) in inter-county games. Many of the members though support and attend these games, which are a central part of social life in Ireland. The friendship groupings formed through involvement with the club are a large part of the attraction of the GAA and the club in question, creating a sense of community and identity for many.

3.2 Data and sociopragmatic analytical framework

The data analysed in the project spanned between 2012 and 2016, where I spent periods of three to ten weeks on a total of eight times. I participated in the region of 200 90-minute training sessions, along with attending in region of 100 matches and other club events (social activities in the club bar etc.). Alongside extensive fieldnotes, I annoted approximately 50 transcripts of interactions (see O'Dwyer 2020, 2022 for further analysis of other transcripts). The long-term participant observation — doing things that everyone else does, while trying to stay aware of what is going on (Malinowski 1961 [1922]; Milroy and Gordon 2003: 75) — made it possible to develop a deep understanding of in-game and in-training interactions that might otherwise be inaccessible to outsiders (Wolfram and Schilling-Estes 1995). Language identity issues (adequation, distinction, indexicality etc. as discussed above) were explored in Club Fingal through participant observation in a variety of contexts as mentioned above, 20 interviews and approximately 10 hours of free recordings of interactions during games and social occasions. I present below representative examples of humour as a strategy of inclusion in section 4 below. As mentioned, the initial stages of the ethnography involved creating extensive field notes on interactions, with background and interpretative information focusing on sociopragmatic strategies adopted, and types of humour employed. I made these notes on my phone as soon as possible after interactions and transferring to more detailed notes and transcriptions (from memory, by adding to phone notes) on a computer on returning home. As discussed in O'Dwyer (2022), the principal reason for adopting this strategy was that I felt that the players would not have engaged in such humour if the interaction was being audio-recorded. The transcriptions of the interactions may not be as reliable as transcriptions made from recorded data, I am confident that the interactional and pragmatic content of the speech is a realistic and authentic presentation of the exchanges observed. All the interactions analysed below were selected as they were representative of interactional strategies and humour typically employed in Club Fingal.

The transcriptions are presented using a simple transcription convention (each line represents a clause or sentence of speech), with all utterances transcribed orthographically (i.e., spelling is normalized). Each spoken segment begins with a capital letter on a new line. I do not use any punctuation like question marks, full stops, or apostrophes in words like "can't". The principal purpose of this is to draw focus to the salient sociopragmatic elements found in the interaction (Rampton 2006). Transcription devices include: = (for latched conversation), { } (for transcriber comments, e.g. {Laughter from players}), and ↗ (for rising pitch). Pseudonyms (Head, Jaysus, Free, Mentor 1, Mentor 2, Lucky and Box) are used for speakers that feature in excerpt 1 to 3 below.

The sociopragmatic analytical framework first characterizes the actions in sequence and how speakers perform communicative actions (such as the direction, orientation and organization of jokes: Richards 2006: 95–6), aiming to highlight the nature of joking (e.g., "biting", "nipping", "bonding": Boxer and Cortés-Conde 1997: 276, 279), and face concerns in terms of politeness strategies (Brown and Levinson 1978). Analysis then interprets how actions were accomplished to implicate interactional identities (Van Dijk 1997: 71; Richards 2006: 95–96), and other roles, relationships etc., before highlighting the inclusion-building functions of humour in this context.

4 Findings: Collaborative humour can create inclusion and a cohesive team culture

This section illustrates, through the analysis of three extracts, a variety of ways humour is used to enact inclusion. An appropriate collection of sociopragmatic strategies such as the use of mock insults can develop collegial relations and promote a sense of inclusion in team/club enterprises.

4.1 The bonding power of shared historical humour events

Club Fingal members collaborate in storytelling and developing running jokes to create solidarity and inclusion within teams. From observation, humorous happenings and events become a shared experience and an important resource for establishing and maintaining bonds of togetherness in the group. One illustrative example happened on the final evening of one of my data collection trips: Head (all names are pseudonyms) and I were walking along the four-metre wide outdoor corridor between the complex and fenced field, having just exited a dressing room after casually chatting with Free while changing after a training session. There was a layer of snow on the ground: Free burst out of the dressing room completely naked: "Come on yez bastards, I'll take the two of youse on in a snowball fight!". The distance of ten metres allowed a good flurry of snowballs amid yelps and screams. Jaysus did not bother coming out as it was too cold. After a minute or so Head enquires "Are you right in the head?", to which Free begins to howl at the moon. We start off for the car, and Free quickly enters the dressing room. Head and I got in the car and had a laugh about what we have just witnessed. Fast–forward to my next visit over four months later, and I find myself in the dressing room with Free and Jaysus (both assigned pseudonyms, note that I typically assigned pseudonyms based on words used by speakers in the first line of excerpts that they featured in: in line 1 of excerpt 1 Jaysus begins with the word "Jaysus"). A lull in the casual conversation is broken by Jaysus, who involves me (FOD) into the conversation (lines 1–2).

Excerpt 1 some of the players gather in dressing room after training

1 Jaysus: Jaysus the last time I was talking to you ye must have been when
2   Free was howling at the moon in the snow
3 FOD: Yeah I was thinking about that we should have lulled Free further
4   away from the dressing room so you had time to fully lock him out of

5		the dressing room
6	Jaysus:	Yeah I was thinking that myself
7	Free:	If you were that smart you wouldnt be just talking about it
8		Im too quick for ye lot
9	Jaysus:	Ye mean youre too mad for us ye mean
10	Free:	Mad quick its all the same
11	Jaysus:	How is it the same
12	Free:	If you were any way clever you could work it out yourself

This excerpt arguably functions to create common ground through storytelling and banter, and club members acknowledging that I have been absent. Free and Jaysus refer to previous humourous events to include me in team conversations through implicit invitations to collaborate in humour. It can be said that one purpose of the humour is relational identity development (Boxer 2002; Chovanec and Tsakona 2018), in the form of developing collegial relations. This humourous event (naked snowball fights; howling at the moon) is a thread that I can use to connect with Jaysus, Free and other club members who know about the story the next time we meet. The abrasive, confident assertions of Free found in line 12 is one example of stylized identity performance, which over time have been become indexed in the club. Club members may be less than fully conscious of the identity and style of humour that is commonly used in dressing rooms, and habitually fall into such joking relationships (cf. the partialness principle of identity, Bucholtz and Hall 2005: 605).

It is humorous instances like these that members of the club, when socializing, refer back to again and again. From observation, I can say that this incident alone has been referred to over ten times in the one year since the incident, even by people who were not there at the time. It becomes a running joke, and when people are reminiscing about the year they have just enjoyed with the team, it is times like these they refer to. When there is a lull in conversation it is often that they refer to these times to fill the gaps. These running jokes, conversations and shared experiences are the means by which members of the teams can express and reify their solidarity. This in turn constructs and enacts inclusion. This is the case, for example, for club members who may have been absent from activities for whatever reason: upon returning they can be included in the team banter by reverting to shared humour and collaborating on new humourous threads. When club members get together socially, from observation, they often spontaneously tell stories about the actions and comments of team members before, during or after games and training sessions. It is a type of a sociopragmatic resource that establishes a bond between the interactants that can, in turn, contribute to shaping an amiable atmosphere with teams and the club. These moments when characters express themselves are the bonds that hold the group together. It is important to highlight to sporting practitioners that it can be very beneficial to create spaces for this type of bonding work in coaching practice. These stories are the threads which tie conversations together. As a result, these humourous threads are an avenue to being included in the club. Extract 2, discussed below, illustrates how a club team coach invokes such belonging and a sense of inclusion.

4.2 An appropriate collection of sociopragmatic coaching communicative strategies

In this excerpt, a club coach (often called "mentor" in GAA circles) selects mock insults from his toolbox of sociopragmatic strategies to implicitly welcome and include a newcomer to the team in question. Mentor 1 is a very verbose and outgoing individual and likes to have the craic with the players. Mentor 2 is also likes to be upfront. During this challenge match (i.e., not an official match played as part of a sanctioned competition, but an unofficial game organized between two teams) played one evening, there was a lot of banter throughout the game among the substitutes. The interaction taking place after a poor miss by one Club Fingal attacker. There was one young player (J1er) who had just returned from California on a J1 (student visa) and did not really know a lot of the players involved in the team, so could be considered a newcomer. He had been the butt of jokes several times throughout the evening, after challenging Mentor 1 (in this and immediately previous interactions). One important underlying purpose of this teasing is to involve the unfamiliar player in the banter and team enterprises.

Excerpt 2 mentors of the first hurling team are engaging in "banter" during a game

```
1    Mentor 1:   I could have hit that over the bar with one hand {=on the hurley}
2    J1er:       You played in goal didnt you
3    Mentor 2:   I still could hit a ball over the bar
4    J1er:       Bring yourself on corner forward and see how well you get on
5    Mentor 1:   Now I dont want to hear any of your guff get back to California or
6                wherever the hell you came from
7                How long have you been coaching senior hurling teams
8    Mentor 2:   Yeah J1er none of your guff youre only a corner back
9    Mentor 1:   Leave it up to me
10               What do you reckon Mentor 2
11   Mentor 2:   Dont be listening to any of these young guns more false courage
```

12		than real balls
13	Mentor 1:	Unlike ourselves Mentor 2 the old dogs for the long road

The teasing banter clearly reproduces the vertical hierarchical structure of the group (Fine 1990), and it is interesting to see that toward the end of this exchange, the J1er was happy to let the mentors ridicule him. He challenged the main mentor in line 2 and line 4 in particular: from line 5 onward Mentor 1 and Mentor 2 take over the interaction to bombard J1er with jocular insults (inferior experience in lines 7 and 11; lack of attacking prowess: line 8; false courage: line 11–12). J1er acknowledged he was not in a winning situation, by not offering any defence in word or gesture to the insults directed at him (lines 5–13). The rest of the players were happy to bow to the hierarchy, and not offer any defence or back up their teammate against the managers. However, what can be emphasized is that the J1er has never been a central part of the team, and the slagging (=jocular abuse) Mentors 1 and 2 engage in is a strategy of inclusion: by slagging J1er he is welcomed into the group, and a theme that other players can build upon in future interactions. As a result, a sense of closeness is created through the light-hearted banter: it is up to coaches to foster an appropriate collection of strategies when engaging with players. Face concerns and direct face threatening acts are ignored in excerpt 2 for the purpose of having a laugh. There is also the underlying coaching move of developing relational identity — a joking relationship in this case — between the coach and J1er. In a wider view, this stylised performance of an indexed identity (brash and assertive) prevalent in the club by Mentors 1 and 2 also maintains a positive atmosphere between the coaches and playing group.

This friendly mocking creates a sense of social cohesion which others will want to, and are welcome to, join. The more these type of friendly interactions take place, the more vibrant the atmosphere in the club, which helps all involved. Furthermore, it is humourous interactions like these that become part of an enjoyable team and club culture. It is important for coaches to make room for this social aspect — that is not sanctioned in many contexts in Ireland and beyond — in team sports. It is also worth noting that even though one strategy may work for one player, it may not work for the next individual. It is up to the coach to "read the air" before deciding upon an appropriate interactional strategy. In this case, teasing is used to signal closeness and friendliness, which offers interactional possibilities J1er and others can exploit to claim a central place in the team. You need to facilitate a place where humour can be exchanged, which players can then fall back on. This humour exchange develops interactions and relationships between players, which leads to solidarity, collegial relations, inclusion and ultimately the motivation to continue playing. The final excerpt is an example of a coach creating opportunities for collaborative humour.

4.3 Reducing formality and mitigating face threats

The final interaction is co-constructed by Lucky and Box to foster team solidarity, and ultimately maintain a sense of inclusion. These two characters enjoy the craic together in excerpt 3, but also manage to communicate implicit messages. Lucky first provides guidance to the players, and gently encourages them to follow his guidance (i.e., to reflect on performance: lines 1–5 below). His identity is that of a serious leader, who expects players to be cognisant of their performance while training. Interactions which produce constructive criticism during training are encouraged and valued. This is the last of the contributions from the management team for this session: it is customary to finish the training session with some sort of comment, for example an assessment of the training performance, advice about what to improve, or simply signposting of future activities. As is common when this serious comment is finished, somebody will inject humour into proceedings, in order to break the ice, and also to segue toward the time after training — i.e. it is a type of conversational boundary marker (see Aijmer 2002: 42) — where people can release some "steam" by casually chatting, engaging in banter, or talk about something that is on their mind with their team mates.

Excerpt 3 lucky is wrapping up a football training session

```
1    Lucky:     Lads I have been saying it and will keep saying it
2               Be thinking when you train
3               After every training you have to think of one thing you done
4               well
5               and one thing you need to improve that youre not doing so well
6               Box what did you do well ↗=
7    Box:       =I turned up=
8    Lucky:     =Ye turned up good man
9               And what did you do not so well
10                Ye turned up
11              {Laughter from players}
12   Player A:  This is like an ongoing lovers tiff
```

Box and Lucky have been active members of the club since childhood (and hence enjoy the status of core club member) and played together on teams for over 10 years. They are very familiar with each other, and this can be seen from the jovial slagging alongside the competitive dynamic found in this extract. From observation of the training sessions this season, it was customary for these two to engage in slagging, often in an effort to create a good atmosphere by enjoying a bit of fun. Lucky expects a serious attitude, commitment and earnest effort during training, and is quick to admonish players both individually and as a group. However Lucky shows he is wary of not being overbearing and brings a fun element into the equation by introducing humour into proceedings (line 6, and then continuing on in lines 8–10).

Excerpt 3 is a good example of the use of humour as a conversational boundary marker to transition from serious training issues to less serious topics. In this case Lucky is the one who signals the transition of speech activity by starting banter with Box. In line 6 "what did you do well?", the other teammates can tell by the pitch (slightly raised) and intonation (raised at end of "do well") that slagging talk has started. Box is quick to reply, within milliseconds, with his humourous and self-depreciating reply "I turned up!" (line 7). Not to be outdone, Lucky is quick to first acknowledge the humour, and turn it back with the next question "And what did you do not so well?" (line 9). Lucky does not give his friend and teammate time to reply but replies for him with the ironic mock "Ye turned up!" (line 10). On face value, this parallelistic mocking comment infers that it was a mistake for Box to turn up, as he does not contribute anything to the enterprise. This type of nimble wit is something that is expected of players in the team and club.

This type of banter is generally considered by club members to be "harmless" and without malice and part of the enjoyment for players involved in the team. These two individuals regularly engage in such interactions, the interjection by another player "This is like an ongoing lovers tiff!" (line 12) acknowledges this, by stating that as the two engage in slagging matches habitually, they are very similar to two lovers nipping at each other. This deliberate and intentional performance of coaching identity is positively evaluated by the player group audience. Players recognise the joking performances as it can be argued it has become indexical within the club of an outgoing lad who can take a slagging. The main purposes here are to have a laugh, release tension and distract from the seriousness of training. Furthermore, similar to the two previous excerpts face concerns are ignored for the purpose of generating a positive atmosphere. This interaction is again a clear case of relational identity development between the two established members and the rest of the playing group. This further extends our understanding of the club culture and identity which has developed over time: being able to respond to jocular abuse in a suitable and humourous way is one way to be further involved in the team and club. This is an important and undervalued element of sporting club life: to collaborate in humour is a passport to further interactions in the future. The beginning of the banter (lines 7–11) by Box and Lucky is an invitation to the rest of the team to collaborate and co-create humourous threads that team-mates can pick up and extend in future meetings. This promotion of psychological safety — that the team provides a safe environment to co-construct humour (Edmondson 1996) — by the leaders of the team is one way to create an atmosphere of inclusion in clubs. There are also other important considerations.

As mentioned before, Lucky is very authoritative while taking the training session, encouraging lads to be thinking while playing. To counter this sense of serious engagement, there is also an encouragement to have a sense of fun while doing training. The two main characters, Box and Lucky, are quick to perform the "real man" persona in training in order to command respect and communicate important messages like providing constructive criticism, but often use humour to mitigate the face-threatening nature of these messages. These two leaders (Lucky and Box) signal in admonishments when training performance expectations are, or are not, being met. But they also signal when such concerns can be forgotten, and players can let their guard down, to have a bit of craic. One interpretation of the sociopragmatic strategy employed by Box and Lucky from line 6 onwards is that the formality (and social distance) is reduced through humorous remarks immediately after constructive but critical comments. One function of the humour in lines 6 to 11 is repair: to ensure any reading by players of the criticism in lines 1 to 5 is not overly negative, and that they leave training in an upbeat mood. When providing criticism of players, it is possible that leaders create an atmosphere of incivility, with negative implications for team cohesion and psychological safety (Smittick, Miner, and Cunningham 2019): the use of humour in the latter part of this interaction is to mitigate potentially damaging effects of lines 1 to 5. The final six lines of excerpt 3 are also an example of a discursive space where a collaborative style of humour (Holmes 2014) is possible. All present can contribute to the joking, thereby highlighting their solidarity and expressing ease with each other to create a laugh out of nothing. Players being present in this space can only contribute to psychological safety on an individual player level, and the implicit goal of creating a greater sense of inclusion on a team level.

5 Discussion: Banter can create inclusion

The banter that runs throughout Club Fingal activities creates an amiable atmosphere in the club and teams. Being included in the practices provides a comfortable feeling. Members value the playfulness and inventiveness involved in sharing and collaborating on humour. An important point to note is that players specifically mentioned that having the craic in training and around games make participation worthwhile. As a result, this creates motivation to continue playing. While slagging is often performed in a mischievous way to create a bit of fun and express solidarity, these practices may simultaneously function to foster a sense of inclusion in the group. The polyvalent and versatile humour most definitely contains an underlying aggression and competitiveness which is offset by the central role of creating a cohesive team culture in which inclusion is vital. It is possible for all present to contribute to humourous events — even if it is only through joint laughter — while training and playing games.

Collaborative humour fulfils the function of relational identity development (Boxer 2002; Chovanec and Tsakona 2018) and an important tactic of inclusion which creates belonging and social cohesion within teams. Some of the interactions (e.g., excerpts 1 and 2) are player-generated events which exemplify how this humour is an integral part of the club culture and identity. The snowball fights and howling at the moon events found in excerpt 1 have become threads which club members can pick up to reify their solidarity and a way to include team members in bonding conversation. The performance of participating in humour creates a great atmosphere in the club which all can enjoy. Hence, such public performances incorporate inclusion in the club and set a template for others to co-construct similar humour in future club interactions. Such habitual performances of humour can be interpreted as an outcome of interactional negotiation, and often less than fully conscious (see the partialness principle in subsection 1.1: Bucholtz and Hall 2005: 605). Nevertheless, the tenor of these slagging events become indexed via evaluative orientations of the audience/club members present (Bucholtz and Hall 2005: 593) and mentions of identity categories such as "characters" like Box and Lucky who engage in such jocular abuse. These shared experiences of club activities seemingly make an institutional habitus: values, dispositions and expectations that are acquired through activities (Bourdieu 1999). The potentially problematic nature of the direct, face threatening acts in Irish society (Kallen 2005) are counterbalanced in this co-constructed humour by implicit agreement that the face concerns can be ignored in the pursuit of having a laugh.

Teasing is salient in Club Fingal and used as tactic in inclusion in mentor-player communication as a signal of, and invitation for closeness. Excerpt 2 exemplifies how teasing is used to welcome a newcomer into team banter and offer the opportunity for J1er to adopt a more central role in the team. As I will discuss in the next sub-section, coaches may follow the lead of Club Fingal mentors to create opportunities for their players to create room for banter in their practices. Sport stakeholders can encourage inclusion and psychological safety by facilitating team sport members building bonds via co-constructing humour together. These interactions create threads to develop in future team interactions which develop relations in an atmosphere of inclusion. To tease is to walk a tightrope as levels of offense differ widely across people and situations, so coaches need to command a high level of emotional intelligence.

5.1 Preliminary recommendations to create inclusion in team enterprises

One consideration for sports practitioners is that they should actively create room and a discursive space for banter and humour in or after their sessions. It is up to the coach and other stakeholders in a sporting organization to choose from a range of pragmatic strategies when introducing humour. In order to create a light-hearted atmosphere with the view of increasing solidarity in a team. Furthermore, while increasing solidarity and inclusion through humourous exchanges around mandated training sessions and matches is to be encouraged, it is also important to create other spaces (e.g., social events) where banter is possible. Here threads of humour and other interactions can be created and developed, which can then form a bond or connection between players which can be extended in follow-on interactions in regular training, for example. A journey begins with one step: in order for players to be actively involved in a team there needs to be a space for casual interaction and creation of solidarity via engagement in communicative instances that are valued in a society. In the Irish context, collaborative humour is most definitely a key context and trigger for inclusion in a communicative context (Vaughan and Clancy 2011: 51). The J1er (in excerpt 2) had been away for a whole summer and returned to a team where he did not know many people: the mentors could have left him alone to make connections. This can be a daunting process for many. Instead, the mentors included him in interactions (even though it was done through mocking but jovial abuse). This creates the threads that other players can then pick up on when interacting with J1er, the new player on the team. It should be noted, however, that J1er is quite a confident individual who is not easily knocked back by such upfront mocking. The mentors implicitly acknowledged this and interacted in such a way. In the case of another more subdued character, the mentors need to select another interactional strategy to begin the inclusion process. That is an important take out for coaches and other stakeholders: develop emotional intelligence to understand what is appropriate for specific individuals and interactional situation, before selecting from a loosely defined but nuanced interactional toolkit that develops inclusion (and avoids exclusion) in sporting teams and organizations.

6 Conclusion

This chapter has exemplified how banter can significantly increase the enjoyment of being involved in the games, and how such strategies of inclusion are relevant in the everyday practices of sports teams. Cooperative humour is a part of the complex milieu that keeps teams coherently working together in an amiable and constructive manner. It is imperative for stakeholders in sporting organizations to make space and time available for such interaction. Coaches should aim to actively implement a collection of strategies to develop collegial relations to foster inclusion in team and club activities. After the serious business of training and games is over, it is beneficial to facilitate a discursive space to release pressure for sporting club members. Humour and play acting can fulfil an important role, providing running jokes and shared experiences which can construct and develop both inclusion and solidarity.

Which linguistic and pragmatic practices help to accomplish inclusion in this particular sporting context? In Club Fingal a sense of closeness is created through light-hearted banter: it is up to coaches to foster an appropriate collection of strategies, while being cognisant that results will vary across individuals and coaching contexts. It is important obviously for the coach to create a good atmosphere in the club and teams: rather than simply creating a space for play-acting it must be remembered that joking can communicate implicit meanings (Boxer 2002). By coaches and other stakeholders being involved in joking spaces it possible to integrate face-threatening acts or possibly awkward conversations that may be difficult to conduct directly. Beyond this covert purpose, simply having a laugh is always fun as has been demonstrated above, with mocking humour achieving inclusion and being a type of induction as a core Club Fingal member. Such understated rituals can only help the larger enterprise of creating a group of individuals working together as a cohesive unit in games.

References

Aijmer, Karin. 2002. *English Discourse Particles: Evidence from a corpus*. Amsterdam: John Benjamins. https://doi.org/10.1075/scl.10.

Bourdieu, Pierre. 1991. On Symbolic Power. In John Thompson (ed.), *Language and Symbolic Power*, 163–70. Cambridge, MA: Harvard University Press.

Boxer, Diana. 2002. *Applying Sociolinguistics: Domains and Face-to-face Interaction*. Amsterdam: John Benjamins.

Boxer, Diana & Florencia Cortés-Conde. 1997. From bonding to biting: Conversational joking and identity display. *Journal of Pragmatics* 27(3). 275–294. https://doi.org/10.1016/S0378-2166(96)00031-8.

Brown, Penelope & Stephen Levinson. 1978. *Politeness: Some universals in language usage*. Cambridge: Cambridge University Press.

Bucholtz, Mary & Kira Hall. 2005. Identity and Interaction: A Sociocultural Linguistic Approach. Discourse Studies 7(4–5). 585–614. https://doi.org/10.1177/1461445605054407.

Dolan, Terence Patrick. 2006. *A Dictionary of Hiberno-English: The Irish Use of English*. Dublin: Gill & Macmillan.

Edmondson, Amy C. 1996. Learning from Mistakes is Easier Said Than Done: Group and Organizational Influences on the Detection and Correction of Human Error. *The Journal of Applied Behavioral Science*. 32(1) https://doi.org/10.1177/0021886396321001.

Edwards, Christian Nicholas & Robyn L. Jones. 2018. Humour in sports coaching: 'It's a funny old game'. *Sociological Research Online* 23(4). 744–762. https://doi.org/10.1177/1360780418780047

Fine, Gary A. 1990. *With the Boys: Little League Baseball and Preadolescent Culture*. Chicago: University of Chicago Press.

Haberland, Hartmut & Jacob Mey. 2002. Linguistics and pragmatics, 25 years after. Journal of Pragmatics 34(12). 1671–1682. https://doi.org/10.1016/S0378-2166(02)00149-2

Hall, Kira. 2000. Exceptional Speakers: Contested and Problematized Gender Identities. In Janet Holmes & Miriam Meyerhoff (eds.), *The Handbook of Language and Gender*, 353–380. Cambridge, MA: Blackwell.

Haugh, Michael & Danielle Pillet-Shore. 2018. Getting to know you: Teasing as an invitation to intimacy in initial interactions. *Discourse Studies* 20(2). 246–269. https://doi.org/10.1177/1461445617734936.

Hay, Jennifer. 2000. Functions of humor in the conversations of men and women. *Journal of Pragmatics* 32. 709–742. https://doi.org/10.1016/S0378-2166(99)00069-7.

Holmes, Janet. 2006. Sharing a laugh: Pragmatic aspects of humor and gender in the workplace. *Journal of Pragmatics* 38. 26–50. https://doi.org/10.1016/j.pragma.2005.06.007

Holmes, Janet. 2014. Doing Discourse Analysis in Sociolinguistics. In Janet Holmes & Kirk Hazen (eds.), *Research Methods in Sociolinguistics: A Practical Guide*, 177–193. Oxford: Wiley-Blackwell.

Kallen, Jeffrey L. 2005. 'Silence and Mitigation in Irish English Discourse'. In Anne Barron & Klaus P. Schneider (eds.), *The Pragmatics of Irish English*, 47–72. Berlin, Boston: De Gruyter Mouton.

Kallen, Jeffrey L. 2013. *Irish English Volume 2: The Republic of Ireland*. Berlin: De Gruyter

Malinowski, Bronislaw. 1961 [1922]. *Argonauts of the Western pacific*. New York: Dutton.

Mey, Jacob. 2002. *Pragmatics*. Second Edition. Oxford: Blackwell.

Milroy, Lesley & Matthew Gordon. 2002. *Sociolinguistics: Method and Interpretation*. Oxford: Wiley-Blackwell.

Motor Neurone Disease Association. 2014. The MND Ice Bucket Challenge. Motor Neurone Disease Association (accessed 20 January 2023)

O'Dwyer, Fergus. 2020. *Linguistic Variation and Social Practices of Normative Masculinity: Authority and Multifunctional Humour in a Dublin Sports Club*. New York: Routledge. https://doi.org/10.4324/9781003014140.

O'Dwyer, Fergus. 2022. The functions of collegial humour in male-only sporting interactions. *Te Reo the Journal of the Linguistic Society of New Zealand*, [edited by Guest Editor Nick Wilson] 64(2). 15–36.

O'Keeffe, Anne, Brian Clancy & Svenja Adolphs. 2011. *Introducing Pragmatics in Use*. Milton Park: Routledge.

Ortlieb, Renate, Elena Glauninger & Silvana Weiss. 2021. Organizational inclusion and identity regulation: How inclusive organizations form 'Good', 'Glorious' and 'Grateful' refugees. *Organization* 28(2). 266–288. https://doi.org/10.1177/1350508420973319.

Rampton, Ben 2006. *Language in Late Modernity: Interaction in an Urban School*. Cambridge: Cambridge University Press.

Richards, Keith. 2006. *Language and Professional Identity*. Basingstoke: Palgrave Macmillan.

Schnurr, Stephanie & Angela Chan. 2009. Politeness and leadership discourse in New Zealand and Hong Kong: A cross-cultural case study of workplace talk. *Journal of Politeness Research. Language, Behaviour, Culture* 5(2). 131–157. https://doi.org/10.1515/JPLR.2009.009.

Smittick, Amber L., Kathi N. Miner & George B. Cunningham. 2019. The "I" in team: Coach incivility, coach gender, and team performance in women's basketball teams. *Sport Management Review* 22(3). 419–433. https://doi.org/10.1016/j.smr.2018.06.002.

Thompson, Andrew, Paul Potrac & Robyn L. Jones. 2015. 'I found out the hard way': Micro-political workings in professional football. *Sport, Education and Society* 20(8). 976–994. https://doi.org/10.1080/13573322.2013.862786.

Tsakona, Villy & Jan Chovanec. 2018. Investigating the dynamics of humor: Towards a theory of interactional humor. In Villy Tsakona & Jan Chovanec (eds.), *The Dynamics of Interactional Humor. Creating and negotiating humor in everyday encounters*, 1–26. Amsterdam: John Benjamins.

Van Dijk, Teun A. 1997. *Discourse as Social Interaction*. Los Angeles: Sage.

Vaughan, Elaine and Clancy, Brian. 2011. *The pragmatics of Irish English. English Today: The International Journal of the English Language*, 27(2), 49–54. https://doi.org/10.1017/S0266078411000204.

Wilson, Nick. 2022. Analysing team sports discourse: From interaction to identity. Te Reo — The Journal of the Linguistic Society of New Zealand, [edited by Guest Editor Nick Wilson] 64(2). 1–14.

Wolfers, Solvejg, Kieran File & Stephanie Schnurr. 2017. "Just because he's black": Identity construction and racial humour in a German U-19 football team. *Journal of Pragmatics* 112. 83–96. https://doi.org/10.1016/j.pragma.2017.02.003.

Wolfram, Walt & Natalie Schilling-Estes. 1995. Moribund Dialects and the Endangerment Canon: The Case of the Ocracoke Brogue. *Language* 71(4). 696–721. https://doi.org/10.2307/415741.

Rachel Chimbwete-Phiri and Stephanie Schnurr
Chapter 6
"Sisters are hot". Denying netball players their athletic identities through sexualisation practices in online fan groups in Malawi

1 Introduction

In 2020 the Netball Association of Malawi decided to change the official name of the sport to make it more inclusive. Up to this point, in Chichewa – Malawi's official language – netball had been referred to as *ntchemberembaye*, which translates into 'one who has given birth'. This name, which explicitly gendered the sport by specifying its players as women of a particular age was replaced by the more neutral and arguably more inclusive term *Mpira wa Manja* (which translates as 'Hand Ball'). According to Khungekile Matiya, President of the Netball Association of Malawi, the previous name of the team implied that "the sport is [only] for women with children" which she described as "discriminatory" (according to conversations with Mlanjira 2020). It was argued that the new name would help avoid these gendering connotations and reflect the diversity of the game (Mlanjira 2020).

However, while this name change was generally welcomed and supported by fans, athletes and officials, it only partly addressed some of the issues of inclusion and exclusion associated with netball in Malawi. For example, it did not address the discrimination and sexualization that netball – including athletes as well as officials – experience. This chapter aims to address these issues by identifying and describing some of the processes through which such discrimination and sexualization take place – often unnoticed. Our specific focus is the online domain concentrating on three official netball fans' Facebook pages for the Malawi national women's team. Through an in-depth analysis of language use on these fora, we illustrate some of the ways in which some fans – in the otherwise largely supportive posts – mobilise gender stereotypes thereby sexualising and discriminating against netball players and (female) officials when commenting on their body, looks, dress and attractiveness rather than their actual performance. Through foregrounding

---
Rachel Chimbwete-Phiri, University of Malawi, Malawi
Stephanie Schnurr, The University of Warwick

https://doi.org/10.1515/9783110789829-007

these physical aspects in these posts, the fans portray the sport as an exclusively feminine domain in which women are often sexualised and assigned the stereotypical roles of mother, wife and object of (largely male) desire, rather than celebrated for being successful athletes on the playing field.

In what follows, we first discuss relevant previous literature on sports, social inclusion and the role of gender and culture before briefly outlining the history of netball in Malawi. We then describe our methodological and analytical approaches and analyse several Facebook posts with the aim of illustrating and critically discussing some of the discursive processes through which netball, its players as well as officials are being sexualised and portrayed negatively. Through these processes, we argue, the fans discriminate (even if unknowingly) against the players and contribute to upholding and sometimes even reinstating the gender boundaries and discriminatory practices of exclusion that the name change in 2020 aimed to break down. Moreover, through these sexualisation practices the female athletes are denied their athletic – and professional – identities and are primarily portrayed as sexual objects of (largely male) desire rather than valued for their professional accomplishments.

2 Sports, social inclusion, and gender

As the editors of this volume outline in more detail in their Introduction chapter, there seems to be general consensus that sports contribute to social inclusion – for example, in the form of concrete sport-based intervention programmes and policies which directly address issues of inclusion and exclusion in specific contexts (e.g., Nogueira et al. 2018; United Purpose 2020). However, the concept of social inclusion is highly contested and different understandings exist "within policy, professional and academic discourses" (Kelly 2011: 127). It has even been argued that sports-based inclusion programmes and policies are necessarily restricted, and while they provide opportunities for some, they are often not able to reach their target group and implement lasting change (e.g., Kelly 2011). This seems – at least partly – to also apply to the name change of netball in Malawi as we illustrate below.

The relationship between sport and gender is a complex one. As Singh et al. (2010: 86) argue, sport "is a social and cultural process in which social constructions of masculinity and femininity play a key role", and in which aspects of hegemonic masculinity – such as physical strength and power – are often promoted (e.g., Shifflett et al. 2016; Nogueira et al. 2018). Sport itself is a masculine domain, in which attributes and qualities typically associated with hegemonic masculinity – such as competitiveness, strength, and athleticism – are celebrated. Moreover, in the sport domain, "beliefs about sex binary and male hegemony are dominant" (Braumueller et al. 2020: 1). Not only is sport itself traditionally associated with masculinity but gender segregation remains an important principle in the performance of many sports, and homophobia is often an issue (see also Pringle and Denison this volume).

The crucial role of gender in sports is reflected on many levels, including for example, the gendering of sport (e.g., Peng et al. 2022) where specific sports are often described as "feminine" (such as netball and ballet) or "masculine" (such as rugby and boxing) which often results in perceived (or actual) boundaries regulating access to these sports. As a consequence of this gender segregation, athletes crossing these boundaries are often discriminated against – this applies in particular to women participating in sports traditionally perceived as the domain of men, as well as transgender, intersex and LGBTQ+ athletes who often struggle with the binary system of categorising athletes as male or female (e.g., Braumueller et al. 2020; Pigozzi et al. 2022; see also Bailey and Jones this volume).

Another area where this relevance of gender in the sports domain is particularly evident is in media coverage of sports events. Ample research exists that describes and laments the continuing "underrepresentation, trivialization, and sexualization of women athletes" (Trolan 2013: 215; see also Kemble this volume). Much media coverage either overlooks or objectifies women – for example by focusing on the athletes' appearance and bodies rather than their actual performance and skills (e.g., Fink 2015; Shifflett et al. 2016; Toffoletti and Palmer 2019; Courtney et al. 2020). These issues regarding the representation and portrayal of women athletes in the media seem to be of a global nature and affect athletes in different socio-cultural contexts (see also English et al. 2019; Kemble this volume).

In this chapter we focus on the often negative and derogatory portrayal of female netball players in Malawi in the specific social medium of fan posts on Facebook. More specifically, we explore how the netball players of the country's international team, the *Malawi Queens* are being portrayed in their fans' posts on three official fan groups on Facebook. Analysing the processes of inclusion and exclusion in this domain not only provides important insights into the dynamics of the fan culture, but also makes important contributions to ongoing debates around making netball in Malawi a more gender-inclusive sport.

2.1 Introducing the context: Netball in Malawi

Netball has a long tradition in Malawi and is generally regarded as one of the country's high performing sports – especially on an international stage. The country's national team and its players enjoy high popularity, and together with the sport's governing body, the Netball Association of Malawi, they play an important role in the proliferation of grassroot netball activities. For example, in 2020 the *Malawi Queens* were sixth in the International Netball Federation netball rankings and secured second position among the African teams. Moreover, one of the team's players, Mwawi Kumwenda, was ranked as the fourth best netball player worldwide. However, despite its popularity, netball in Malawi tends to be perceived and constructed as a gendered sport which – just like its players – is often sexualized by its fans. Through this sexualization – as we illustrate below – the players are primarily portrayed as objects of desire (through a largely male gaze) while their professional identities as successful athletes and role models are often backgrounded, thereby excluding the players from the domain of professional sport.

It is widely believed that netball is a women's sport (e.g., Taylor 2001) – perhaps due to the fact that it was "invented in the late Victorian era as a de-powered women's form of basketball" (Tagg 2016: 2; see also Pulumutsa 2015). Having been developed "exclusively for women [...] it suffers from the limited fortunes of most women's sports" (Chappell 2005: 247), and in spite of recent attempts to make netball a more gender-inclusive sport, it is generally viewed as "a women's game" in Malawi (Rogers 2018: 134). Netball was introduced to Malawi by British colonialists, particularly by British Missionaries in schools in the early 1900s. Its popularity increased over the years, and in post-independent Malawi it became popular among players outside of schools (Lwanda and Phoya 2019). Today netball in Malawi is established at grassroots, national and international competitions. However, despite the netball team's success on the playing field, netball in Malawi – like so many sports associated with women around the globe (Adjepong 2021; Manning et al. 2021) – usually suffers from underfunding by the national sports fund (especially when compared to the funds assigned to the male football team, e.g., Chirwa 2016). This is particularly surprising given that *The Malawi Queens* are more successful on the international stage than the country's male football team.

Part of this positioning and perception of netball and women's sport more generally has been linked to cultural influences and role expectations for women and men in Malawi. For example, it has been observed that, in Malawi like in many other African nations, women participate less in sports than men (e.g., Fasting, Huffmen, and Sand 2014). This relatively low participation is often attributed to cultural influences (e.g., Fasting, Huffmen, and Sand 2014; Pulumutsa 2015). For example, due to largely patriarchal family structures, women often need to obtain their husband's permission to participate in certain activities (such as sports) outside the home. Moreover, traditional (and highly restrictive) roles and responsibilities which firmly position women in the domestic domain often constitute an additional obstacle for women aiming to pursue activities outside the domestic sphere. Another factor that has been identified as contributing to women's low participation in sports is the dress, which is often considered as inappropriate. This is particularly true for the shorts and miniskirts worn in netball. In fact, the wearing of shorts or trousers and miniskirts was not acceptable in Malawi until the country became a democracy in 1994; and many religious groups still consider such dress as immoral and immodest (e.g., Fasting, Huffmen, and Sand 2014; Vyas–Doorgapersad 2020).

This chapter aims to address some of these issues by identifying and describing some of the discursive processes through which the *Malawi Queens* netball players are talked about and portrayed in fan online fora on Facebook. We argue that by foregrounding the players' physical appearance, the fans contribute to their sexualisation and discrimination, which ultimately leads to a very restrictive and derogatory portrayal of the players, which in turn denies their professional identity and prevents them from being included in and recognised and celebrated for their success in a professional sport. In the next section, we briefly describe our methodological and analytical approaches before analysing selected posts from various official netball fans Facebook sites.

3 Methodology and data

We have collected posts from three official and publicly available Facebook groups of Malawi netball fans that were posted between December 2020 (after the team's name change was announced) and May 2022 (when we started writing this chapter). Some of the fans' posts are in English, while others are in Chichewa (the national language of Malawi) or a combination of both. In order to protect participants' identity, however, we only present the English translations here using the punctuation and emoticons (where applicable) as in the original posts (see also Fangen 2020). We have also replaced any Facebook names with codes.

Overall, during the period of data collection, more than 5,000 comments were posted in the fan fora. Over 60 percent of these comments are very supportive of the team, complimenting individual players on their performance, and celebrating the team's victories. However, while most fans express their appreciation of the performance of the players and coaches, and praise them for putting Malawi on the map of international netball, there are several posts in our dataset in which often negative gender stereotypes are oriented to and largely reinforced. For example, some threads – generating a total of about 600 comments – indicate how some fans are concerned with players' body and appearance, and over 1000 posts discuss the netball officials as being too emotional and overly jealous, and describe them negatively as "full of gossiping", entitled, and "shopping mongers", as well as being weak leaders and hence in need of male support. Mobilising these and other gender stereotypes not only portrays the players and coaches in a negative and unprofessional way, but it also reinforces derogatory and discriminatory gender ideologies which ultimately position netball as a non-inclusive sport.

We have selected for closer scrutiny three of these posts and the comments they received (from around 16 members of the fora where they were posted). These posts – more or less explicitly – mobilise gender stereotypes and comment on the players' body, looks, dress and attractiveness. We analyse excerpts from these comments below using Critical Discourse Analysis (CDA) as this approach enables us to combine a detailed micro-level analysis of the discursive and visual features used in the posts to portray (and often sexualise) the netball players, while at the same time, enabling us to link these observations on the micro-level to the bigger picture of issues around inclusion and exclusion in netball and the role and standing of female athletes and women in Malawi society more widely.

CDA typically focuses on the interrelationship between language, power and ideology by identifying and making visible the power dynamics and social inequalities existing in the social context in which an interaction takes place (Wodak 1997; Fairclough 2010). In other words, language is seen as a means of social construction because through texts, speakers create, sustain and legitimize inequalities and social structures. At the same time, "power relations are exercised and negotiated" (Fairclough and Wodak 1997: 258; Van Leeuwen 2008; Machin and Mayr 2012). Like other CDA scholars, we argue that texts are constitutive of the social relations of power and ideologies (e.g., Wodak and Fairclough 2010; Angouri and Wodak 2014), and we aim to identify and critically discuss some of the discursive strategies through which the post writers in the *Malawi Queens* fan Facebook groups implicitly, explicitly and potentially unconsciously contribute to a sexualisation of the netball players, thereby at the same time contributing to a naturalisation of the very limiting traditional – and often marginalising and discriminatory – roles available to women in Malawi society more widely and ultimately denying the players their identities as professional athletes.

Within CDA, the assumption is that on the surface, texts may seem plain, yet when the strategies used in their production are analysed, ideologies and collective representations of events and people within certain social relations come to the surface (Machin and Mayr 2012). In line with this assumption, we follow Van Leeuwen's (2008; 2009) CDA-informed conceptualisation of text as "social practice". In other words, in and through their posts the authors (and respondents) orient and respond to gender stereotypes and ideologies (by reinforcing or challenging them).

Moreover, authors, readers and respondents are considered to be social actors – or "doers of action", "participants to whom actions are done", as well as "participants who benefit from an action" (van Leeuwen 2009: 148). As a consequence, people never just innocently read and respond to a text, but they always "do" something or are involved – as recipients, beneficiaries etc. – in the process of producing a text and its perceptions, as well as in reproducing society's knowledge and beliefs in and through the text (Fairclough and Wodak 1997). More specifically – as we illustrate below in more detail – by talking about netball and commenting on the athletes' performance in this way, the fans at the same time portray and literally talk into being the sport as an exclusively feminine domain in which women are sexualised and assigned stereotypically gendered roles (e.g., as mother and object of desire). Such a portrayal is, of course, closely linked to issues of power and underlying gender ideologies, which Mansfield (2014) suggests, requires a recognition and examination of the networks that produce and reproduce them, by not ignoring the complex social structures that characterise netball players' experiences of gender-power relations in Malawi.

By critically discussing these issues and identifying and making visible the specific discursive strategies through which they are enacted, reinforced and often naturalised on the micro-level of the Facebook interactions, we hope to identify specific areas of concern and ultimately contribute to social change – towards establishing a more inclusive and supportive environment where the successes of the netball players are celebrated without necessarily reinforcing problematic gender stereotypes, thereby making the sports more inclusive – for fans, officials and athletes.

4 Analysis: The language of exclusion in fan posts

In what follows we identify and describe some of the discursive processes through which this is achieved. We particularly focus on posts that comment – often in problematic ways – on the players' clothes and physical appearance, and posts in which the players are – more or less explicitly – sexualised.

4.1 Commenting on players' clothes and physical appearance

Making explicit reference to the players' clothes and physical appearance is an aspect of gendered discourse which is particularly problematic in those instances where these comments are linked – more or less explicitly – to fans' expectations that the players are supposed to be attractive, feminine, and even sexy. We have chosen two examples that are representative of the data set to illustrate this.

Example 1[1]

The excerpt below is taken from a comment that was posted in response to a poster announcing a netball match between two teams in a small town in Malawi. The poster contained a snapshot of netball players. While most subsequent posts were enquiries about the game and compliments of the match organisers' contributions to the development of netball in rural Malawi, Fan 5 posted the following:

Fan 5: In Malawi aaaaaah why are girls wearing cycling shorts inside like that? In other countries your fellow players just wear a little something inside so that spectators should also feel the sight 😅😅😅😅😅
(no further comments)

Amongst the largely supportive and appreciative comments the original poster received, the comment displayed in example 1 stands out due to its focus on the players' dress and the associated sexualisation of the players and the sport. The opening statement of the comment expresses the poster's disapproval and disappointment over the fact that the players depicted on the poster wore "cycling shorts" underneath their short skirts to cover their thighs. However, by introducing this post with the location marker ("In Malawi") followed by an expression of disappointment ("aaaaaah") and positioning the players' way of dressing in opposition to players' uniforms "in other countries", Fan 5's comment is not only about the netball team pictured on the announcement in the original post but applies more widely to netball players in Malawi and elsewhere. There are about 28 similar posts in our data set where fans – who usually have a male Facebook ID – make derogatory comments about the players' clothes and physical appearance. For example, in another post, a fan with a male Facebook ID laments that "players are wearing full trousers", and another fan wrote that "These girls are keeping (having) big bums 😅". Referring to their "big bums" here can be seen as a reference to the widespread sub-Saharan African beauty ideal of the plump and round "Bantu figure" (Leseth 2014).

Posts like these are a reminder that the netball field – like many places where sports take place – is a distinct space for displaying the female body (Devonport et al. 2019; Marfell 2021; Peng 2022). However, the comments above are

---

[1] In all examples, we have used boldface typeset for those parts of the text that were originally in English, and all Chichewa posts have been translated into English for ease of reading and to preserve the poster's anonymity.

particularly noteworthy in the socio-cultural context of Malawi where women are generally expected to cover up their bodies in public, and not expose any skin above the knee, for example, by using so-called 'wrappers' (*chitenje*), which are iconic garments for women in Malawi (Mfune-Mwanjakwa 2022). Moreover, strict rules about dressing and displaying modesty apply to women, and have recently led to the ban by the Malawi censorship board of a (female) South African singer due to her perceived lack of modesty in her dress, as well as display of nudity and inappropriate dance moves on stage. Against this background, Fan 5's comment about the lamentable covering up of the players' body in example 1 is even more marked.

It is interesting to note that this post has not received any further comments in the Facebook group although it was posted over a year ago at the time of writing this paper, and so this conversational thread comes to an end, and the portrayal of the netball players as objects of desire (who should display rather than cover up their legs) remains unchallenged. The observation that this post is not responded to could perhaps also be interpreted as indirectly signalling that it is not of much interest or sanctioned by other members of the group.

This is different in the next example that we discuss here, where another fan (again with a male Facebook ID) makes a similar comment which – in contrast to example 1 – is responded to by other fans who criticise it and thereby challenge such a portrayal of women and the underlying gender ideologies that inform it.

Example 2

The following are extracts of comments to a post that announced a men's netball match in a small town.

Fan 1: Men's netball aagh very lazy, we like the ladys' one, so that we see the legs too 😂😂😂 so, you men with your very stiff calves
Fan 2: What you have just said spoils the game, you go there with a nasty mindset, your mates go to watch the game not what you are referring to
Fan 3: 😂😂😂😂
Fan 4: Kkkkkk
Fan 2: And we like to watch it heavy [a lot], and we also play the game, I love men's netball so much

The post by Fan 1 is a response to a male netball match in a lower-level netball league. He claims that male games are "very lazy". The original Chichewa expression is *"aah zaulesi"* which is translated as laziness, but which may also connote something that is weak. This negative description of men's netball is set in opposition to the fan's appreciation of "the ladys' one" (i.e., netball played by women). However, this appreciation of the women's game is explained with the players' display of their legs. Using the inclusive first-person plural pronoun "we" Fan 1 seems to include several (potentially also male) fans in his appreciative assessment, which is followed by three smiling emoticons with closed eyes and showing their teeth (due to laughing so hard) and a comparison with the male netball players who are being criticised for their "very stiff calves".

Although it could be argued that the laughing emoticons frame Fan 1's comment about the players' display of their legs as humorous, the responses it generates from other fans (also with male Facebook IDs) are very critical and not only express their disagreement with Fan 1 but also challenge the underlying gender ideologies. In particular, Fan 2's critical distancing comment that Fan 1's comment "spoils the game" and that he has a "nasty mindset" expresses strong disagreement. Using the second person singular pronoun "you" Fan 2 directly addresses Fan 1 and singles him out by putting him in opposition to "your mates" who "go to watch the game" rather than being primarily interested in the display of the players' bodies. Through creating this opposition between Fan 1 – whose behaviour is described as inappropriate and not shared by others – and "your mates" and by implication other fans of netball – Fan 2 clarifies that Fan 1's views are not widely shared. These sentiments are further supported by Fan 3 who posts three different emoticons – including two with a "not impressed" and two with a contemplative expression – and Fan 4 who responds with dry laughter ("kkkkkk"). The exchange comes to an end with Fan 2's expression of his appreciation of men's netball which he loves "so much". His choice of pronouns here is interesting, especially his use of the inclusive first-person plural "we" – which seems to include other fans in the forum but excludes Fan 1.

What is noteworthy about this thread, then, is the observation that Fan 1's focus on the players' bodies and physiques is challenged and rejected by the other fans (most notably Fan 2). As a consequence, the sexualisation of the players and a potentially derogatory portrayal of them (as discussed in more detail below) is counteracted and replaced by an expression of the love of the sport itself. This, at the same time, contributes to giving the sport credibility and reminding posters and the fan community more generally that sport rather than the players' bodies should take centre stage. In other words, the creation of sexual subjectivities which view the netball players' bodies as a source of pleasure (e.g., Marfell 2021) is challenged. Similar observations are discussed in the next section.

4.2 Sexualisation of the players

In addition to sexualising players and the sport more widely by commenting on the players' physical appearance and attractiveness as displayed in some of the posts discussed in the previous section, some posts further explicitly portray the players as sexually attractive. An example of this is the quote in the title of this chapter which is taken from the post of a fan with a female Facebook ID who repeatedly stated that she likes the name of a local netball team called *Hot Sisters* and that she indeed believes that "sisters are hot". Although her last comment in the thread is followed by a hard laughing emoticon – thus framing it as humorous – comments like this – whether they are humorous or serious – contribute to the sexualisation of the netball players. Example 3 illustrates this sexualisation further.

Example 3

The following quotes are part of the comments that were posted in response to a discussion around issues with the selection of players for the *Malawi Queens* squad for an important upcoming international competition. At this point in the discussion fans are talking about the nomenclature of netball.

Fan 23: That's the problem of sticking to ntchembere[2] instead of giving the chance to young ones
Fan 24: Actually South Africa is also using the same ntchembere. And what do you expect from the team which had only 6 days to train??? Let us be honest here our ntchembere are not receiving enough support.
Fan 25: So, you go and bring out (reveal) the virgins to us 😂
Fan 26: Bring the ones with erect breasts
Fan 27: kkkkkk you say, the ones with erect breasts?
Fan 26: Yes, is not saying ntchembere, no 😂😂😂😂
Fan 27: I am not part of this conversation, I have not joined you on this one kkkkkk
Fan 28: Kkkkkkk
Fan 27: I have a family relation among those ntchembere

This discussion occurred around three weeks before the name of netball was officially changed, as outlined above. At the beginning of this excerpt, Fan 23 utilises the negative connotations of old age and slowness often associated with the mother role when he refers to the *Malawi Queens* players as "ntchembere" ('one who has given birth') and putting them in opposition to "young ones" whom he would like to see introduced into the team. He thereby links his criticism of the current players on the Malawi national team to their relatively old age – they are mothers, according to him, who lack the benefits (which he does not specify further here) of young age.

In responding to this post, Fan 24 appears to attempt to defend the current *Malawi Queens* by reminding others that one of their rival teams – South Africa – also has older players in their team. The post then shifts the blame for the team's

---

2 Literally translated as mothers or those who have given birth.

recent poor performance to a lack of training opportunities and "support" – without specifying where and from whom the support is lacking. What is noteworthy about this reply, however, is that Fan 24 also uses the Chichewa terminology "*ntchembere*" but gives it a more positive meaning (which is further reinforced by the use of the inclusive pronoun "our") and reinstating its status as referring to netball players.

These attempts at reinstating the status quo and defending the current players on the team, however, are undermined by the next post from Fan 25 who poses a challenging – and it appears rhetorical – question. The utterance initial "So" and the fact that it is directly addressed at the previous poster (as reflected in the choice of pronoun "you") make this comment potentially threatening. However, the utterance final laughing emoticon mitigates this to some extent as it frames the comment as potentially humorous. What is noteworthy in this post is that Fan 25 uses the term "virgins" to refer to the netball players. This term is not only in stark opposition to the previously used "*ntchembere*", but it also makes the sexualisation of the players very explicit. This interpretation is further supported by the subsequent posts which pick up on this theme. For example, when Fan 26 clarifies that "virgins" refers to those "with erect breasts", which is responded to with dry laughter by Fan 27 before he echoes Fan 26's description. Fan 26 then laughingly (as indicated by the use of four laughing emoticons) agrees by once more rejecting the idea that the players should be "*ntchembere*". After this the conversation comes to an end when Fan 27 laughingly (c.f. "kkkkkk") reminds others that he is "not part of this conversation" thereby humorously and light heartedly distancing himself from the previous sexualisation of the netball players. This is met with further laughter (by Fan 28) and what could be read as an indirect criticism by Fan 27 that he has "a family relation among those *ntchembere*".

The terminology used in this thread to describe the netball players is explicitly sexual in nature and perhaps even vulgar. The humour, of course, downtones these effects to some extent while at the same time making these comments acceptable – even if borderline according to the norms of the group (as indicated by the last two comments by Fan 27). Previous research has established that humour is a double-edged sword which enables its users to make potentially inappropriate comments while being guarded against possible criticisms because of the possibility of claiming that this was all non-serious and that the poster was "just kidding" (e.g., Schnurr 2010). But nevertheless, the ways in which the netball players are described throughout this thread are clearly sexualising and emphasising the players' femininity ("virgins") and bodily features ("erect breasts") rather than their skills and abilities as professional athletes. They thereby deny the players their professional identities as netball players and instead – by referring to the women as either "virgins" or "*ntchembere*" – the posters make two other roles available to them: the role of an innocent and inexperienced potential sexual partner, and the role of an experienced but unattractive mother and potential wife. These binary limiting roles are problematic because they assign women to very restrictive and in both cases subordinate and powerless positions in relation to men and the male gaze rather than celebrating them for their athletic successes on the netball field. Other examples where the netball players are portrayed in similarly powerless and vulnerable roles include numerous posts which refer to the players through the identity category "girls" rather than women or athletes. Such address terms, however, are highly problematic as they contribute to an infantilisation of these professionals, deny them their professional status, and also construct asymmetric power relations in which the players are positioned as helpless, powerless, and inferior.

5 Discussion

It was the aim of this chapter to identify and describe some of the discursive processes through which the discrimination and sexualisation of the *Malawi Queens* netball players takes place in the otherwise largely supportive posts found on different fan groups on Facebook. Our analyses have shown that by commenting on the players' performance as well as their dress and appearance, the posters mobilise gender stereotypes and reinforce generally degrading and objectifying gender ideologies which portray the women not as successful athletes but rather as mothers or as objects of desire for the male gaze. Through these posts the fans discriminate (even if perhaps unknowingly) against the players and deny them their professional identities as athletes. Ultimately, these processes contribute to upholding and reinstating the damaging gender boundaries and excluding practices that the change of the vernacular name of netball aimed to break down.

For example, evaluating and sexualising players' bodies through the evaluative noun phrases "big bums", "erect breasts" (example 3), and commenting on their legs (example 2) portrays the women not primarily as professional athletes but rather as objects of desire. As a consequence, through these descriptions and the focus on the players' body and appearance, netball is presented as a display and sexualisation of the female body which attracts male fans. The image of an ideal netball player is thus constructed as one who is sexually attractive and desirable by the male spectators and fans (see also Devonport et al. 2019) rather than as a committed and successful professional. Similar observations were made in a study of two prominent Chinese female athletes by Peng et al. (2022). In their study of men's posts on a Chinese sports fandom platform, they also observed that these successful athletes were often sexualised by their male fans, and that their sports accomplishments were trivialised. Like the posts about the Malawi netball players that we analysed above, the Chinese athletes were also depicted as cute, attractive, and objects of (sexual) desire rather than celebrated as professional athletes who have made impressive accomplishments on the playing field.

The fact that the athletes themselves are not oblivious to such portrayals and perceptions of their (largely male) fans has also been demonstrated. For example, Devonport et al. (2019), in their study of netball players in the UK, found that the athletes who participated in their research demonstrated their awareness of constantly being exposed to the pressures of the male gaze. They expressed their concerns about their feminine body and described their efforts to portray themselves simultaneously as feminine and athletic. Similarly, in a study of netball in New Zealand, Marfell (2021) observed that in some cases the netball players themselves were engaged in (re)producing the hegemonic femininities that the (often male) fans projected onto them; for example, by accentuating certain aspects of their dress, appearance and body movement on the court. Marfell (2019: 588) argued that through the ways the players dress and move, they "are implicated in the social (re)production of [their] feminine and heterosexual subjectivities and the overall feminization of netball space".

However, in the context of Malawi, reducing the netball players – or any athletes in fact – to their physical appearance and ignoring their success on the playing field, is of course also problematic with regards to the standing of women in traditional Malawi society. More specifically, this objectification and sexualisation of the players can be interpreted as a reflection (and reinforcement) of the wider social structures and the often-subordinate positioning of women, which are further evidenced in news reports about sexual assault scandals in job recruitment and academia (e.g., Khamula 2020; Kasanda 2021; Mwale 2022). In this context, the negative and sexualising portrayal and objectification of the players as discussed above – and the underlying gender ideologies that inform them – are highly problematic as they reduce the players to traditional roles, overlooking their success on the playing field and ignoring their professional status.

Moreover, through the problematic portrayal of the netball players, their successes on the international stage are talked down, which may eventually mean that they lose their performative power to impact and change the recognition of netball and perhaps even the image of sports in Malawi more generally. By sexualising and portraying the players as objects of (male) desire, gender stereotypes are reified which position women as powerless and downplay or overlook their successes outside the domestic domain. These stereotypes make only the very limited traditional roles of mother and object of desire available to women and girls. To us, this seems like a missed opportunity, especially since these highly successful and widely regarded netball players would be prime examples of role models who have the potential to encourage and inspire not only young girls and women but an entire nation.

Focusing on how people talk about the players and analysing how they use language to portray them in specific ways is an important step to address these issues and can make important contributions to shaping societal attitudes towards the elimination of existing gender stereotypes. Our analysis and critical discussion of the specific discursive strategies through which a problematic portrayal of the netball players – even if unintended by the fans – takes place, has enabled us to gain important insights into the representation of social actors, social practices, belief systems and ideologies behind netball as a sport (e.g., Van Leeuwen 2008). We have shown that, while some of the problematic posts remain unchallenged by the fan community (example 1), others are challenged and the underlying gender ideologies that inform them are questioned and rejected (examples 2 and 3). Taking these responses into consideration is, of course, crucial as it helps us understand how the posters jointly produce and reproduce social structures and power relations (Fairclough and Wodak 1997), and how they thereby contribute to the legitimisation and delegitimisation of certain social actions and practices (e.g., Van Leeuwen 2007; 2008).

Although our focus has been on the discursive strategies used in the posts, it is equally interesting – and highly relevant for issues of inclusion and exclusion – to consider what remains unsaid and what is absent from the texts, and the ideological implications this may have (e.g., Van Leeuwen 2007). More specifically, official representatives of the governing netball bodies and administrators of the fan groups remained remarkably silent in the discussions that we have analysed. Through this silence, it could be argued, the fans' gendered, sexualised and sometimes discriminatory comments not only remain unchallenged, but are actually legitimised, and potentially contribute to the image and reputation of this sport in Malawi. As observed by Fasting, Huffmen and Sand (2014) some sports governing bodies in Southern Africa, including Malawi, have a code of conduct for its members but those do not specifically cover the important topics of harassment and gender related abuse in the sports community. These observations, of course, have important implications for practitioners, which we outline in the next section.

5.1 Implications for practice

We hope that the insights provided by our small-scale study help raise the awareness of netball fans and officials alike about the sexualisation and discrimination of the netball players that currently occurs in some of the posts on official fan fora but that has not yet been systematically picked up by netball officials, forum administrators or fans. Identifying these issues and raising people's awareness are important first steps towards addressing them and changing the ways in which netball players (as well as netball itself) are talked about and hence portrayed in these posts.

Our observations are also evidential in advocating for a diversification of images and posts of the netball players in marketing netball as a sport. We hope that netball officials, fan club representatives, media practitioners and marketers of netball sports might embrace the need to widen their pictorial and textual focus to create a more inclusive and professional representation of the players that celebrates their success and emphasises their professional (rather than sexualised) identities. There is a clear need to demonstrate that anyone, regardless of their appearance, dress and bodily image can and does participate in the sport, and that netball players – and other female athletes – are primarily professionals representing their clubs and their country. Regular and prolonged exposure to such imagery might help disrupt current portrayals of netball players as trivialised and unprofessional sexualised objects of desire and help challenge associations of netball players with idealised forms of femininity (see also Devonport et al. 2019).

We thus hope that the research presented here will be used to support calls to establish rules for posting in these fora, and for developing and implementing consequences for those who break them (such as being blocked from further participation). Making sure these rules are adhered to could, of course, in the first instance be considered the responsibility of officials from the Netball Association of Malawi, but we would argue that all members of the fora should be made aware of the consequence of their sexualisation and objectification of the players. If officials – and fans – really want netball in Malawi to become a more gender-inclusive sport – as for example reflected in the recent name change of the sport – and if they do want to attract more women into sport, then it is of crucial importance to create an environment – on and off the playing field – where all players feel safe and included *as players*. Ensuring that the players are celebrated for their sporting successes – rather than being criticised for their physical appearance – and are safe from negative and derogatory portrayals as sexual objects of desire is an important aspect of this.

References

Adjepong, Anima. 2019. Are you a footballer? The radical potential of women's football at the national level. In Sybille N. Nyeck (ed.), *Routledge Handbook of Queer African Studies*, 76–89. Routledge.

Angouri, Jo, & Ruth Wodak. 2014. 'They became big in the shadow of the crisis' The Greek Success Story and the Rise of the Far Right. *Discourse & Society* 25 (4). 540–565.

Braumüller, Birgit, Tobias Menzel & Ilse Hartmann-Tews. 2020. Gender Identities in Organized Sports – Athletes' Experiences and Organizational Strategies of Inclusion. *Frontiers in Sociology* 5:578213.

Chappell, Robert. 2005. Sport in Namibia: Conflicts, negotiations and struggles since independence. *International Review for the Sociology of Sport* 40 (2). 241–254.

Chirwa, Garry. 2016. August 26. 'NAM outweighs FAM on funding.' *The Nation online.* https://mwnation.com/nam-outweighs-fam-on-funding/

Courtney, Michael, Michael Breen, Claire McGing, Iain McMenamin, Eoin O'Malley & Kevin Rafter. 2020. Underrepresenting reality? Media coverage of women in politics and sport. *Social Science Quarterly* 101(4). 1282–1302.

Devonport, Tracey J., Kate Russell, Kath Leflay & Jennifer Conway. 2019. Gendered performances and identity construction among UK female soccer players and netballers: A comparative study. *Sport in Society* 22 (7). 1131–1147.

English, Peter, Angela Calder, Simone Pearce & Katy Kirby. 2019. A new sporting horizon: a content analysis of Super Netball newspaper coverage. *Media International Australia* 171(1). 110–124.

Fairclough, Norman, &Ruth Wodak. 1997. Critical discourse analysis. In Teun A. van Dijk (ed.), *Discourse as Social Interaction*, 258–284. London: SAGE Publications Limited.

Fairclough, Norman. 2010 [1995]. *Critical discourse analysis: The critical study of language*, 2nd edn. Harlow: Longman group limited.

Fangen, Katrine. 2020 Gendered Images of us and Them in Anti-Islamic Facebook Groups. *Politics, Religion & Ideology* 21(4). 451–468, DOI: 10.1080/21567689.2020.1851872

Fasting, Kari, Diane Huffman & Trond Svela Sand. 2014. *Gender, Participation and Leadership in Sport in Southern Africa: A baseline study.* Norwegian Olympic and paralympic Committee and Confederation of Sports.

Fink, Janet S. 2015. Female athletes, women's sport, and the sport media commercial complex: Have we really "come a long way, baby"? *Sport management review* 18(3). 331–342.

Kasanda, Mathews. 2021. October 05. Patricia Kaliati bemoans sex for grades. *The Times.* https://times.mw/patricia-kaliati-bemoans-sex-for-grades/

Kelly, Laura. 2011. 'Social inclusion' through sports-based interventions? *Critical social policy* 31(1). 126–150.

Khamula, Owen. 2020. November 02. Polytechnic female students say enough on 'sex for grades'. Nyasa Times. https://www.nyasatimes.com/polytechnic-female-students-say-enough-on-sex-for-grades/

Leseth, Anne Birgitte. 2014. Experiences of moving: a history of women and sport in Tanzania. *Sport in Society* 17(4). 479–491, DOI: 10.1080/17430437.2013.815514

Lwanda, John Lloyd Chipembere & Michael Muti Phoya. 2019. Malawi at 50: Culture, Sport and Music. *The Society of Malawi Journal* 72(1). 35–58.

Machin, David & Andrea Mayr. 2012. *How to do Critical Discourse Analysis: A multimodal introduction.* Los Angeles: SAGE Publications limited.

Manning, Stephanie, Ho Fai Chan & David A. Savage. 2021. Discrimination, disequilibrium and disincentives: Behavioural economics in women's sport. In Hannah Josepha Rachel Altman, Morris Altman & Benno Torgler (eds.), *Behavioural Sports Economics*, 119–138. New York: Routledge.

Mansfield, Louise. 2014. Towards an understanding of netball in Malawi, international sport development and identification: theoretical and methodological sensitizing issues. *Sport in Society* 17(4). 492–506. DOI: 10.1080/17430437.2013.815515

Marfell, Amy. 2019. 'We wear dresses, we look pretty': The feminization and heterosexualization of netball spaces and bodies. International Review for the Sociology of Sport 54(5). 577–602.

Marfell, Amy. 2021. Netball and the (re) production of a dominant femininity: The good game for kiwi girls. In Damion Sturm & Roselyn Kerr (eds.), *Sport in Aotearoa New Zealand*, 42–52. New York: Routledge.

Mfune-Mwanjakwa, Damazio. 2022. Aesthetic and Functional Exploration of *Chitenje* as an African Cultural Icon. *Journal of Humanities* 29(1). 27–46.

Mlanjira, Duncan. 2020. December 10. NAM changes Chichewa name for netball to 'Mpira wa Manja'. *Maravi Express*. https://www.maraviexpress.com/nam-changes-chichewa-name-for-netball-to-mpira-wa-manja/

Mwale, Joseph. 2022. February 09. Kaliza has case to answer- Police Probe. *The Nation Online*. https://mwnation.com/kaliza-has-case-to-answer-police-probe/

Nogueira, Abel, Olga Molinero, Alfonso Salguero, Fabio Lucidi, & Sara Márquez. 2018. Identification of gender discrimination in sports: Training of agents of change. *Revista de Psicologia Del Deporte* 27(3). 43.

Peng, Altman Yuzhu; Wu,Chunyan and Chen, Meng 2022. Sportswomen under the Chinese male gaze: A feminist critical discourse analysis. Critical Discourse Studies, pp.1–18. DOI:10.1080/17405904.2022.2098150

Pigozzi, Fabio, Xavier Bigard, Juergen Steinacker, Bernd Wolfarth, Victoriya Badtieva, Christian Schneider, Jeroen Swart, James Lee John Bilzon, Demitri Constantinou, Michiko Dohi, Luigi Di Luigi, Chiara Fossati, Norbert Bach, Guoping Li, Theodora Papadopoulou, Maurizio Casasco, Dina Christina (Christa), Janse van Rensburg, Jean-François Kaux, Sandra Rozenstoka, Jose-Antonio Casajus, Irina Zelenkova, Emre Ak, Bulent Ulkar, Francisco Arroyo, Anca Ionescu, André Pedrinelli, Mike Miller, Patrick Singleton, Malav Shroff, Nick Webborn, James Barrett, Blair Hamilton, Michael Geistlinger, Gianfranco Beltrami, Sergio Migliorini, Lenka Dienstbach-Wech, Stéphane Bermon, Yannis P. Pitsiladis. 2022. Joint position statement of the International Federation of Sports Medicine (FIMS) and European Federation of Sports Medicine Associations (EFSMA) on the IOC framework on fairness, inclusion and non-discrimination based on gender identity and sex variations. *BMJ Open Sport & Exercise Medicine* 8(1). p.e001273.

Pulumutsa, Jossam. 2015. *A study to establish factors influencing the participation of women in netball in Macheke Zone after completion of secondary school education*. Zimbabwe: Bindura University of Science Education (BUSE) doctoral dissertation.

Rogers, Elizabeth. 2018. *Power, Paternalism, and Partnership: A postcolonial critique of the philosophies and practices of empowerment within a Sport for Development programme in Malawi*. Northern Ireland: University of Ulster Masters dissertation.

Schnurr, Stephanie. 2010. Humour. In Miriam Locher & Sage Graham (eds.), *Interpersonal Pragmatics*, 307–326. (Handbooks of Pragmatics 6). Berlin: De Gruyter Mouton.

Shifflett, Bethany, Daniel Murphy, Farzaneh Ghiasvand, Monica Carlton & Marisa Cuevas. 2016. Gender bias in sports-media analytics. *Journal of Sports Media* 11(2). 111–128.

Singh, Bal, Kanwaljeet Singh, & Narinder Sharma. 2010. Equality, equity and inclusion: transgender athletes' participation in competitive sports – a new era. *Physical Culture and Sport* 49. 85.

Tagg, Brendon. 2016. Men's netball or gender-neutral netball? *International Review for the Sociology of Sport* 51(3). 314–331.

Taylor, Tracy. 2001. A Compliant Femininity in Sport, Women and Netball. In *Proceedings and Newsletter-North American Society for Sport History*, 126–127.

Toffoletti, Kim, & Catherine Palmer. 2019. Women and Sport in Australia – New Times? *Journal of Australian Studies* 43(1). 1–6.

Trolan, Eoin. J. 2013. The impact of the media on gender inequality within sport. *Procedia-Social and Behavioral Sciences* 91. 215–227.

United Purpose. 2020. *Using netball to fight gender inequality*. Published report.

Van Leeuwen Theo, 2007. Legitimation in discourse and communication. *Discourse & communication* 1(1). 91–112.

Van Leeuwen, Theo. 2008. *Discourse and practice: New tools for critical discourse analysis*. Oxford: Oxford University Press.

Van Leeuwen, Theo. 2009 [2001]. Discourse as the recontextualisation of social practice: A guide. In Ruth Wodak & Michael Meyer (eds.), *Methods of critical discourse analysis*, 2nd edn. 144–161. London: SAGE Publications limited.

Vyas-Doorgapersad, Shikha. 2020. Gender equality in the sport sector: the case of selected Southern African Countries. *International Journal of Social Sciences and Humanity Studies* 12(1). 175–191.

Wodak, Ruth. 1997. Critical discourse analysis and the study of doctor-patient interaction. In Britt-Louise Gunnarsson, Per Linell & Bengt Nordberg (eds.), *The construction of professional discourse*, 173–200. New York: Addison Wesley Longman.

Wodak, Ruth. 2001. The discourse-historical approach. In Ruth Wodak & Michael Meyer (eds.), *Methods of Critical Discourse Analysis*, 87–122. London: Sage Publications.

Wodak, Ruth, & Norman Fairclough. 2010. Recontextualizing European higher education policies: The cases of Austria and Romania. *Critical discourse studies* 7(1). 19–4

Part II: **Inclusion/exclusion in the sports media. The representation of female and transgender athletes**

Melissa Kemble
Chapter 7
Good girls and bad boys? A corpus analysis of gendered discourses in Australian media coverage of "masculine" team sports

1 Introduction: Gender, sport, and the media

This chapter explores how issues of inclusion and exclusion related to gender bias and sexism in the professional sporting space are negotiated within the Australian print media. Women's sports have, historically, received very little routine media coverage compared to men's sports. Further, the existing media coverage has tended to focus on "gender appropriate" sports, such as tennis and swimming, and to portray women with respect to (binary) gender stereotypes rather than as serious athletes (Bruce 2016). Such media representations undermine the fact that these women are professional athletes (Duncan and Messner 1998; Shugart 2003), thereby constructing the sporting space as ideally and preferably male (Schirato 2013).

In Australia, the men's Australian Football League (AFLM) and men's National Rugby League (NLMM)[1] are two of the most widely consumed sports, with a national fanbase of all ages and genders. Both are high-contact team sports and thus fit the stereotype of a "masculine" sport. It is no surprise then that these sports have been male dominated at both the grassroots and elite levels for well over a century. In fact, the opportunity to become an elite female football player in one of these sports is relatively new. The AFL Women's (AFLW) launched its first season in 2017; the NRL Women's (NRLW) launched the following year.

---

[1] Australian Football League (AFL) and National Rugby League (NRL) are the official names used to refer to both the men's competitions as well as the sport more generally, with only the women's competitions gender marked (e.g., AFLW, NRLW). I argue that this asymmetrical marking contributes to the othering of female athletes. Thus, in this paper I purposefully use the gender marked abbreviations AFLM and NRLM to refer to the men's competitions and the unmarked versions AFL and NRL to collectively refer to the men's and women's competitions, along with the more colloquially used terms "footy" and "football" to collectively refer to both sports.

Melissa Kemble, The University of Sydney, Australia

https://doi.org/10.1515/9783110789829-008

As such, this research investigates how female and male athletes participating in the traditionally male-dominated and stereotypically masculine sports of AFL and NRL ("football") are represented in the Australian print media, with respect to gender stereotypes and biases. While there is a plethora of research into gender and sports news coverage, much of this sits outside the field of linguistics, with only a handful of studies taking a corpus linguistic approach (Aull and Brown 2013; Caple 2013; Kemble 2020; Ismail 2017). Studies focussing on gender biased language in AFLW media coverage are limited (see: Sherwood et al. 2019; Kemble 2020) with no known linguistic studies of NRLW media coverage. Further, there are no present linguistic studies that make comparisons between the media coverage afforded to men's and women's football with respect to gender bias.

This research, therefore, uses corpus-based discourse analysis to investigate whether salient lexical patterns contributing to the exclusion of female athletes are present in the OzFooty corpus, a corpus of Australian print news (see section 3). Specifically, I focus on the previously identified discursive practices of gender marking, infantilisation, sexualisation and trivialisation of athletic performance of female athletes. I consider whether current media coverage serves to counter instances of exclusion in this space or perpetuates traditional forms of hegemonic power. I discuss the potential impact the results may have not only for AFLW and NRLW but for women's sports more generally. Implications and practical considerations are also provided (section 5).

The following section (section 2) provides a brief review of the relevant literature on previously identified exclusionary discourses in sports media coverage, as relevant to this research. Section 3 outlines the corpus design and provides an overview of the analytical approach. Section 4 presents the findings according to the four exclusionary discourses which are the focus of this paper. Section 5 then provides a discussion of implications and practical considerations for sports media practitioners. Finally, section 6 makes conclusions and provides suggestions for further research.

1.1 A note on gender and sex

Before moving on, it is necessary to acknowledge that while gender and sex are different concepts, they are often conflated in common usage (see Baker 2014: 209). While I acknowledge that gender is not binary, in the domain of sport, specifically elite sport, this is not yet recognised. The historical binary of man/woman combined with the notion of team sport as inherently masculine has given us the current split of men's/male and women's/female sport and athletes. While some grassroots sports are making progress towards inclusion with respect to gender/sex, this is rarely addressed by the media with respect to elite sport. Instead, media representations of athletes have tended to draw heavily on binary and stereotypical representations of gender (e.g., Bruce 2016; see also Graf and Fleischhacker this volume; Jones and Bailey this volume). As such, this research follows the existing binary split of elite sport into the men's and the women's football competitions, while attempting to unpack some of the gender stereotypes that exist in this space.

2 Exclusionary discourses in media coverage of women's sport

Historically, both sport and the newsroom have been male-dominated domains (see also Chimbwete–Phiri and Schnurr this volume). As a result, women's sports and athletes are not only vastly underrepresented in the media, but also portrayed with respect to exclusionary stereotypes and biases. In fact, women's sports receive an estimated 5–15% of all coverage in Australia, a figure which has remained constant since the mid 1990's (Brown 1995; Toohey 1997; North 2012; Lumby, Caple and Greenwood 2014). This is despite continued growth in both female participation in sport as well as public interest in watching women's elite sport (Schirato 2013; Bolt 2017; Jenkins 2017). Further, existing media coverage has tended to portray women with respect to binary gender expectations, rather than as serious athletes, thus perpetuating the idea that sports are "by men and for men" (Schirato 2013: 78). While some recent studies have identified a potential shift in the way that sportswomen are represented in the media, these are often in the context of special international events where gender bias takes a backseat to fostering national pride (Toohey 1997; Kinnick 1998; Wensing and Bruce 2003; Jones 2004; Payne 2004; Ravel and Gareau 2016; Jaworska and Hunt 2017). Additionally, such gains have also been identified alongside existing or new biases (see Bruce 2016).

While much of the existing research has been undertaken outside the field of linguistics, there is no denying a clear pattern of exclusionary and biased coverage. A range of discursive practices have been identified in global sports media coverage which contribute to the patriarchal discourses of objectification, trivialisation, stereotyping and othering of female athletes and sports (Messner, Duncan and Jensen 1993; Aull and Brown 2013; Caple 2013; Bruce 2016; Ismail 2017; Kemble 2020). In this chapter, I focus on the discursive practices of gender marking, infantilisation, sexualisation, and trivialisation of performance, which I will now briefly explain in turn.

Asymmetrical gender marking of women's sporting leagues, tournaments, and players has a long-standing history which continues today. This discursive practice refers to affixing a gender label such as "lady/ladies", "female/s" or "women's" to sporting references, a practice which does not appear for men (Messner, Duncan and Jensen 1993; Duncan and Messner 1998; Billings 2007; Crolley and Teso 2007; Fink 2015). This includes both general references such as *the best female basketball player* or *the women's finals* (compared to *the best basketball player* or *the finals*) as well as official naming such as *Ladies PGA, Women's World Cup, AFL Women's* (compared to *PGA, World Cup* or *AFL*). In the more general marked references to female athletes and sports, such asymmetrical marking has been identified across "masculine", "feminine" and "neutral" sports (see Koivula 1995 for details on gender typing in sport) including, for example, basketball, tennis, gymnastics, and football/soccer (Messner, Duncan and Jensen 1993; Billings 2007; Ravel and Gareau 2016). Caple (2013: 278) argues that the use of such asymmetrical marking is "one of the simplest and most obvious ways of drawing attention to gender". This therefore positions men's sport as the "ideal" or "accepted" reference point and women's sports as an inferior "variation from the (male) norm" (Crolley and Teso 2007: 159).

Infantilisation refers to the linguistic positioning of adult females as children or childlike, where the equivalent is not found for adult males. This can occur through descriptions of childlike qualities, abundant references to youth, or via gendered terms such as "girls" or "ladies". Most of the existing research in sports media coverage shows that adult female athletes are disproportionally called "girls" compared to their male counterparts (Klein 1988; Sabo and Curry Jansen 1992; Messner, Duncan and Jensen 1993; Koivula 1999; Crolley and Teso 2007; Bruce 2016; Ravel and Gareau 2016), with scholars arguing that this undermines female athletes and their accomplishments (Jones 2004). However, much of this research takes a more quantitative approach, comparing only frequency of terms, which does not provide additional insight into how these terms are being used. For example, plural "girls" has been identified as a potential marker of in-group solidarity in sports media (Wensing and Bruce 2003; Ravel and Gareau 2016; Ismail 2017) including within AFLW (Sherwood et al. 2019; Kemble 2020). Other research has identified the use of alliterative effects, as in *golden girls* (Caple 2013), or fixed expressions as in *poster girl* (Ismail 2017), rather than deliberate attempts to infantilise female athletes. Thus, it is necessary to account for the co-text in which these terms occur, as well as understand the socio-cultural context in which these sports take place.

Sexualisation occurs when female athletes are presented as objects of (male) sexual desire, at the expense of their athleticism and sporting achievements (see also Chimbwete-Phiri and Schnurr this volume). The literature overwhelmingly points to a long-standing focus on the sexualised appearance of female athletes as compared to male athletes (Lee 1992; Kinnick 1998; Lenskyj 1998; Eastman and Billings 1999; Christopherson, Janning and McConnell 2002; Harris and Clayton 2002; Vincent 2004; Eagleman 2013; Ličen and Billings 2013; Ponterotto 2014). This includes both visual and verbal commentary on female athletes' body parts (lips, legs, breasts, etc.), body shape and weight, and aesthetic appearance or style (clothing, makeup, hairstyle, etc.). More recent research in Australia, however, suggests that sexualised depictions of female athletes in traditional media is on the wane (Caple 2013; Lumby, Caple, and Greenwood 2014; Sherwood et al. 2019; Kemble 2020).

Trivialisation of sporting performance occurs when female athletes are portrayed as less capable than their male counterparts. This is evident in descriptions of player abilities and achievements, where female athletes are presented as lacking experience, ability or composure (Duncan and Messner 1998; Billings et al. 2014). Additionally, successful performances may be attributed to luck, rather than hard work and skill as is done for male athletes (Billings, Angelini and Eastman 2005). Comparatively, when male athletes experience failures, "bad luck" is often attributed as the reason, rather than a poor performance (Billings et al. 2014; Duncan and Messner 1998). While some research suggests a shift towards female athletes represented as "legitimate sports players" in the media (Caple 2013: 289) these studies are often of special events such as the Olympic Games (e.g. Vincent et al. 2002), only focus on news headlines rather than full texts (Caple 2013), or do not include coverage of AFLW and NRLW (Lumby, Caple and Greenwood 2014).

Combined, such discursive practices perpetuate hegemonic masculinity, thereby contributing to the exclusion of elite sportswomen in the sports media space.

3 Methodology

This section presents an overview of the methodology used in this research, including a description of the corpus design, as well as the analytical approach.

3.1 The OzFooty corpus

To undertake this research a specialised corpus of print media coverage of AFL and NRL was constructed. The Factiva online database was used to collect relevant news items from the four most widely read metro newspapers – *The Sydney Morning Herald, The Daily Telegraph, The Age,* and *The Herald Sun* – along with the national newspaper, *The Australian,* for the period December 2017–2019.² Results were restricted to off-season coverage as previous research has indicated greater gender bias as compared to in-season coverage (Jaworska and Hunt 2017), which tends to focus on match outcomes (Caple 2016; English et al. 2019; Sherwood et al. 2019).

While an attempt has been made to collect all relevant news items, it is acknowledged that there may be some gaps where, for example, a news item only mentions a specific athlete's name.

In total, over 13,000 news items were collected comprising nearly six million tokens. The corpus includes two sub-corpora: OzFooty-W comprising the women's coverage and OzFooty-M comprising the men's coverage. While the focus of this chapter is on the *type* of coverage it is worth mentioning the vast discrepancy in the *amount* of coverage received. Coverage of men's football accounts for 92% of the total corpus whereas women's coverage is about 8% (see Table 1).

Table 1: News items in the OzFooty Corpus.

Corpus	The Age	The Australian	Daily Telegraph	Herald Sun	SMH	TOTAL news items
AFLW	190	47	60	450	39	786
NRLW	6	18	118	2	51	195
OzFooty-W	196	65	178	452	90	981 (7.5%)
AFLM	1316	506	625	3615	247	6309
NRLM	176	618	3316	359	1375	5844
OzFooty-M	1492	1124	3941	3974	1622	12,153 (92.5%)
OzFooty	1688	1189	4119	4426	1712	13,134

3.2 Analytical approach

This research uses corpus linguistic techniques to identify salient language patterns which are then further explored through qualitative text analysis. The corpus techniques used include frequency lists, keywords, semantic tags and concordances.

---

2 Data collection commenced with the announcement of NRLW and ended prior to the 2020 global pandemic.

Frequency[3] and keywords are two of the most commonly used methods in corpus-based discourse analysis as a way into the data. Keywords are words that are "typical of the corpus of interest compared to another corpus" and are "important when identifying key concepts in discourses" (Brezina 2018: 79–80). Semantic tags are used to identify groups of word senses, including multi-word units, that are related concepts. For example, words related to the discourse field of *the body and the individual* (Archer, Wilson and Rayson 2002) may potentially point to evidence of sexualisation. The concordance tool allows all identified words to be viewed in their co-text and sorted in different ways to help identify any patterns of language use. The corpus tools used here are AntConc (Anthony 2020) and the automated USAS tagger (Archer, Wilson, and Rayson 2002) in WMatrix (Rayson 2009). A subset of the News on the Web "NOW" corpus of general news coverage (Davies 2014) is also used as a reference corpus.

Words identified as potentially pointing to the four discursive patterns were explored via qualitative text analysis to investigate whether they contribute to inclusionary or exclusionary discourses. Section 4 provides the results for the four discursive practices addressed in this paper, including more detail regarding the specific corpus techniques used for each of the analyses.

4 Results

In this section, I present the findings for each of the four discursive practices described in section 2. I discuss key differences and/or similarities between the two OzFooty sub-corpora (women's/men's) as well as any notable trends across the whole corpus.

4.1 Gender marking

Targeted searches were undertaken in the OzFooty corpus for the gender identifiers *women's* (599), *men's* (168), *female* (759), and *male* (268). The concordance lines were then reviewed for instances where these words are followed by references to the sports or athletes (e.g., *afl, game, player, team*). For example, *female footballer* and *male footballer* would be included but "footballer" (indirectly referencing a male player) or "NRL Women's" (where the marker comes after the

---

[3] In the results (section 4), both absolute frequency (AF) and relative frequency (RF) are provided. Where relative frequency is used, this is per 10,000 words.

referent and is used in the official league name) would not. Where both female and male gender terms appear together as in *men's and women's football*, these are included in both lists. Table 2 presents a list of gender marked terms that appear 10 or more times in the corpus (both sub-corpora combined).

Table 2: Gender marked references (f ≥10) to AFL and NRL in the OzFooty corpus.

Gender marker (M)	References	Gender marker (F)	References
men's . . .	*game/s* (31)	*women's* . . .	*competition/s* (75)
	competition/s (15)		*football* (69)
	team/s (15)		*team/s* (46)
	season (11)		*game/s* (43)
			league/s (34)
			premiership (26)
			rugby league (25)
			footy (12)
male . . .	*player/s* (19)	*female* . . .	*player/s* (81)
	counterparts (10)		*athletes* (51)
			footballer/s (16)
			footy (14)
			team/s (8)

Overall, there are 634 instances of female marking (78%) in the OzFooty corpus, compared to 185 instances of male marking (22%). That is, female sport and athletes are marked 3.45 times more than males. The term *female player/s* has the highest frequency (81) followed by *women's competition/s* (75) and *women's football* (69). This is compared to the highest frequency male marked terms *men's game/s* (31) and *male player/s* (19).

When male marking does occur in the corpus, this is often alongside references to the women's game or players, either for reasons of clarity (see Figure 1) or comparison (see Figure 2). Comparisons include on-field topics such as game rules, injury, training and performance, as well as off-field topics such as sponsorship, salaries and pathways. Comparisons of performance include both positive and negative evaluation of female players' skills and performance. Previous research has shown that while female players are often compared to their male counterparts, the opposite does not occur (e.g., Eastman and Billings 2000). Based on the selection of texts analysed in this corpus thus far, it appears the same pattern occurs for media coverage of football.

When comparing the two sub-corpora, is it evident that female marking is more prevalent than male marking in both OzFooty-M and OzFooty-W (see

Rugby League will award the Golden Boot, in the	**men's**	and women's games, to the players adjudged to
women's NRL premiership to run in unison with the	**men's**	final series.
final could be played the week before the start of the	**men's**	finals (currently a bye weekend) to give it some
there will be several double-headers of AFLW and	**men's**	games in both the pre-season competition and
the effects of concussion in both the women's and	**men's**	leagues, including the annual surveillance of
earlier instead, so that it didn't overlap with the AFL	**men's**	season. "I was hoping for nine games,
the competition could not eventually overlap with the	**men's**	season. "So what if does?" she said.

Figure 1: Sample concordance lines showing male gender marking for clarity.

comparison is false and disingenuous. Today's median	male	AFL player earns nearly $400,000 a season. The
as lawn bowls. "But rugby league? No. I cannot see	male	and female professional athletes competing across
have the skills that are on a par with their highly paid	male	counterparts. It doesn't even matter that they may
the women play the equivalent of about four games of	men's	football. The women's pre-season training lasts
James Tedesco, having scooped the same awards in the	men's	game. But Sergis shrugs off the comparison.
it's true that congestion around the ball - an issue in the	men's	game - is worse in the developing women's league.
25 more tackles over 100 minutes of football than the	men's	game in 2018, while the women scored 25 points
game is slowly but surely improving compared to the	men's	game. "NRLW last year, for example, the game we
"What AFLW clubs look for is not dissimilar to the	men's	game - you need to be clean at ground level.
women's game is lesser, secondary to the main event: a	men's	version of a competition. As long as the men's

Figure 2: Sample concordance lines showing male gender marking for comparison.

Table 3). In OzFooty-M, female marking accounts for 66% male marking accounts 34%. That is, female marking occurs about two times more than male marking. In OzFooty-W, female marking accounts for 82% and male marking 18%. That is, female marking occurs about five times more than male marking. These results also show that female gender marking is more likely to occur in coverage focussing on women's sport than in coverage of men's sport.

Table 3: Number of gender-marked references found within OzFooty-M and OzFooty-W.

Marker	OzFooty-M				OzFooty-W		
	AF	RF			AF	RF	
men's . . .	31	0.06			85	1.87	
male . . .	27	0.05			41	0.9	
sub-total	58	0.11	34%		126	2.76	19%
women's . . .	63	0.12			335	7.35	
female . . .	47	0.09			190	4.17	
sub-total	110	0.21	66%		525	11.52	81%
TOTAL	168	0.32	100%		651	13.58	100%

These results clearly indicate a disproportionate tendency to gender mark female sport and athletes in the OzFooty corpus. Interestingly, there is a greater tendency to gender mark in coverage of women's sport, despite these news items already including the gender marked official league names (e.g., AFLW, NRLW) and focusing on the women's games. This overt and repetitive marking suggests that the news producers themselves view women's football as the Other to the default (and unmarked) men's version. This thus provides evidence of an ongoing exclusionary discourse which presumes AFL and NRL are masculine spaces, and that any deviation from this needs to be (repetitively) highlighted in the media.

4.2 Infantilisation

Targeted searches were undertaken to compare the frequency and use of the lemma GIRL (*girl, girls, girl's, girls'*) in OzFooty-W to that of BOY (*boy, boys, boy's boys'*) in OzFooty-M. Initially there appears to be strong evidence of infantilisation, as GIRL has a higher relative frequency (10.71) in the women's coverage than BOY (2.94) in the men's coverage. Table 4 provides further detail.

Table 4: BOY/GIRL frequency in the OzFooty sub-corpora.

OzFooty-W			OzFooty-M		
GIRL	AF	RF	BOY	AF	RF
girl	51	1.13	*boy*	443	0.73
girl's	3	0.07	*boy's*	4	0.01
girls	422	9.33	*boys*	1324	2.18
girls'	8	0.18	*boys'*	15	0.02
GIRL	484	10.71	BOY	1786	2.94

When examining referents, analysis of the concordance lines reveals that both GIRL and BOY are more likely to refer to an adult[4] than a child. In fact, BOY refers to adults in 75% of cases whereas GIRL refers to adults in only 47% of instances (see Table 5). This thus potentially points to a reversal of the existing discourse whereby males are being infantilised.

---

[4] The cut-off age used is the age at which players can be drafted. For AFLM, AFLW and NRLM this is 18+. For NRLW this is 17+.

Table 5: BOY/GIRL referents in the OzFooty sub-corpora.

	OzFooty-W			OzFooty-M		
	GIRL			BOY		
Reference to	AF	RF	Percent	AF	RF	Percent
children	190	4.2	40%	263	0.43	15%
adults	226	5.0	47%	1330	2.2	75%
unclear	34	0.75	7%	38	0.06	2%
n/a	34	0.75	6%	155	0.26	8%

As such, the co-text for all instances of adult referents was analysed to determine the specific person(s) being referenced i.e., players, coaches, etc. The results confirm that the majority of adult referents for both GIRL and BOY are the players (98% for women, 97% for men). Analysis of the source, that is, *who* is using these terms, shows that player referents for both BOY and GIRL are largely found in direct quotes or reported speech from other players, coaches, or team managers, rather than the journalists. For example:

(1) "We've had a few **boys** come into the squad with premiership experience and have played in big games, so it was great to hear them speak," [Harry Himmelberg, GWS] said. (AM_CA78E7B3)
(2) Fellow Cronulla prop Andree Fifita added: "He is a hardhead. A big **boy** who plays big minutes. I love the way he plays . . ." (LM_B340F2EF)
(3) "We've got a lot of new **girls** that have come to the club and they're excited to develop their skills." [Breann Moody, Carlton] (AW_25F825D7)
(4) "There's **girls** like the ones that played (in the Cup final) who have worked their backsides off for years to make sure they're strong enough, they don't get injured, they treat the game professionally. [Coach Brad Donald] (LW_18C3F726)

This therefore points to these terms being used as in-group identifiers by quoted sport participants, rather than as infantilising terms by journalists. These results align with recent findings into sports media discourse which suggest a shift away from infantilisation (Wensing and Bruce 2003; Ismail 2017; Sherwood et al. 2019; Kemble 2020). Instead, these terms are more likely being used to establish solidarity "according to their membership in a team" (Ismail 2016: 109), and thus help construct a sense of inclusion within the sporting space.

4.3 Sexualisation

Relevant words potentially pointing to sexualisation were identified via triangulation of keywords and semantic tagging. The keywords were generated by comparing OzFooty-W with a sub-set of the NOW corpus (Davies 2014) using a p-value of <.001 (Log Likelihood 10.83). The semantic tags were applied using the USAS semantic tagger in WMatrix (Rayson 2009). The semantic tags identified as potentially relevant to sexualisation include: B1 Anatomy and physiology, B5 Clothing and personal belongings, and O4.2 Judgement of appearance. Table 6 presents the words identified as potentially pointing to sexualisation.

Table 6: Semantically tagged keywords potentially pointing to sexualisation in OzFooty-W.

Semantic categories	Words	Frequency (AF)	Keyness
B1 Body	ankle	25	+23.17
	back	622	+99.37
	build	83	+12.76
	foot	52	+21.58
	head	198	+44.02
	knee	112	+242.74
	knees	13	+19.11
	leg	41	+14.74
	physically	24	+15.39
	physique	8	+30.9
	shoulder	30	+14.06
	squat	5	+13.97
	toe	13	+14.29
B5 Clothing	boot	23	+21.45
	boots	28	+51.91
	jumper	30	+85.19
	jumpers	8	+19.39
	outfit	22	+14.32
O4.2 Judgement of appearance	glammed	3	+18.66
	grotty	3	+18.66
	pretty	187	+128.54

Analysis of the co-text for the words identified in Table 6 reveals that there is no evidence of sexualisation. Most of the words in both the Body and Clothing categories are used in the context of gameplay, injury, and uniforms with no evidence of overt focus on players' physical appearance. In the Appearance category, the word *pretty* is used as an intensifier, often in player quotes talking about their experiences joining AFLW or NRLW. While *glammed* and *grotty* do refer to physical looks, they both appear in a single quote where a player talks about her experience at the awards night (*"I love getting glammed up, especially when you're normally grotty with hair up,"* she said) and thus does not provide evidence of sexualisation by the media.

The word *physique* shows no evidence of sexualisation. However, this word is used in relation to gender diversity policies in AFL and comes as a response to a VFLW (transgender) player wanting to play in the AFLW competition. Though outside the scope of this paper to do so, this coverage raises the question about if and how gender-diverse and transgender players are represented more widely in the corpus, and certainly warrants further analysis (see also Bailey and Jones this volume).

Overall, the analysis shows no overt evidence of sexualisation of female athletes by the media (but see Chimbwete-Phiri and Schnurr this volume). This aligns with previous research of AFLW coverage (Sherwood et al. 2019; Kemble 2020) as well as other recent studies of media coverage of female athletes in Australia (Caple 2013; Lumby, Caple and Greenwood 2014). This is a promising step forward towards a more inclusionary representation of female athletes.

4.4 Trivialisation of performance

Keyword lists were generated by comparing both OzFooty-W and OzFooty-M to the NOW corpus, using a p-value of <.001 (Log Likelihood 10.83). The lists were reviewed manually, and words pointing to player performance were identified and categorised as *Ability* (skills, capacity, blunders), *Achievement* (success, failure, awards) or *Luck* (for words attributing performance to hard work or luck/chance). Overall, a total of 114 keywords were identified in OzFooty-W and 221 keywords in OzFooty-M. The top 10 words by keyness for each of the three categories are shown in Table 7 below.

The keyword results from OzFooty-W are mostly neutral and positive keywords for ability and achievement, with only a handful of negative keywords (*missed, miss, amateur, wooden spoon*). Words for ability include both gameplay skills (e.g., *agility, kick, footwork*) as well as inherently evaluative words (e.g., *elite, skilful, talent*). Words for achievement include successful match outcomes (e.g., *championships, finals, premiership, title, undefeated, win*), awards (e.g., *best-and-fairest, crowned, mvp, gong, flag, title*) and related positive descriptors of the athletes (e.g., *champion/s, finalists, premiers, superstar/s*). The keywords for luck focus on players' thoughts and feelings about their involvement (e.g., *so grateful for the opportunity to play*).

Table 7: Top 10 keywords by keyness for performance.

Category	OzFooty-W		OzFooty-M	
	Keyword	Keyness	Keyword	Keyness
ABILITY	elite	+704.03	disposals	+2126.56
	talent	+377.55	kicked	+1597.67
	kick	+224.53	kick	+1410.24
	punt	+163.62	talent	+1405.16
	kicking	+156.15	elite	+1184.95
	goalkicker	+130.59	kicking	+1110.84
	marquee	+116.65	punt	+992.68
	level	+88.78	playmaker	+962.1
	disposals	+78.14	possessions	+820.72
	skills	+73.02	goalkicker	+815.73
ACHIEVEMENT	premiership	+1401.3	premiership	+16754.14
	fairest	+1053.88	last	+7234.33
	final	+619.37	final	+5831.89
	star	+598.83	finals	+4530.27
	finals	+569.19	won	+3887.9
	last	+538.27	star	+3416.36
	best	+300.14	fairest	+2999.2
	won	+278.85	gold	+2878.24
	first	+240.5	brownlow	+2524.11
	medal	+216.75	premierships	+2354.25
LUCK[5]	opportunity	+56.24	chance	+478.1
	chance	+19.84	opportunity	+211.03
	fortunate	+16.86	luckless	+62.59
	lucky	+12.68	deserves	+58.74
			earnt	+58.17
			deserved	+42.66
			blessed	+32.65
			unlucky	+30.64
			fated	+24.27
			lucky	+21.58
			luck	+20.95
			fortunate	+18.85

The keyword results from OzFooty-M also include mostly neutral and positive keywords for ability and achievement. There are some negative keywords for ability (e.g., *blunder, bumbled, inexperienced, missed*) as well as for failures/defeats (e.g.,

---

5 Note, only four keywords were identified in OzFooty-W as potentially pointing to LUCK.

beaten, blowout, conceded, lost, thumped) which are not prevalent in OzFooty-W. While some keywords for luck are related to gameplay, this is alongside a focus on criminal allegations and charges. Additionally, there is a notable pattern of violence keywords (e.g., *aggressive, barbarians, combative, strikepower, thrash, warhorse*) which is not present in OzFooty-W. This suggests a discourse drawing on more stereotypical descriptions of male athletes as strong or aggressive.

Overall, the keywords analysis indicates that the media coverage portrays both men's and women's players as capable and successful athletes. The lack of keywords for failures in OzFooty-W may be following a trend where women's sports are only deemed newsworthy when there is a top performance or success, though alternatively the lack of these negative keywords could also be a show of support for these new leagues. While there are some negative evaluations, this is to be expected in sport given the subjective nature of a given performance. Additionally, the pattern of violence keywords in the men's coverage is in line with previous research whereby men's sports tend to draw on stereotypical notions of masculinity through overt descriptions of violence and aggression, often through "power descriptors" and war metaphors (Vincent 2004: 448; Kinnick 1998).

4.5 Emerging discourses: "good girls" and "bad boys"

While undertaking the above analyses it became apparent that the corpus contains interesting patterns related to the construction of athlete identity and societal expectations. More precisely, the female athletes are trailblazers and positive role models for the younger generations, whereas the male athletes are involved in scandals relating to drugs, alcohol, sex, and violence. In the women's coverage, this is especially evident in the text analyses of *girls*, where a range of voices work to build this representation of these athletes as role models. For example:

(5) For girls, too, here at last were their role models. Here was something they could aspire to. For suddenly, the dream of a career path had opened up in a game they loved. (AW_61FB5972)
(6) "We've all got different stories but we're all speaking the same language to encourage young girls to play sport," [the cross-code Magpies star] said. (AW_8051C273)
(7) "Our players are so diverse and unique role models and heroes that girls can see and connect with and think, she's like me." [AFLW CEO Nicole Livingstone] (AW_7C1B163C)

In the men's coverage, the contrasting "bad boy" narrative is evident in the keywords list, with a range of words appearing related to scandal (e.g., *allegation/s, assault/ed, indiscretions, misbehaving, rape, scandal/s, snorting, substance/s*) as well as in the analysis of concordance lines for BOY (e.g., *bad boy/s, boys' club, party boy/s, boys being boys*). In some cases, the text analysis indicates that despite their off-field scandals, these male athletes are still upheld as elite players who are an integral part of the on-field game. For example:

(8) The disastrous 2012 supplements scandal and the resulting suspensions impeded on-field success. (AM_983C9624)
(9) NRL to take over punishment of footy's bad boys as clubs fail to act (LM_437C9D02)
(10) The birth of their son comes just three months after South Sydney star Sam, also 29, became embroiled in a "sexting" scandal. An internal club investigation into the claims cleared Burgess and other Rabbitohs players of "any actionable misconduct". (LM_568B5846)

This dichotomy of athlete identity and expectation of behaviour is not new in sports media coverage. A study of US newspaper coverage of on-court fights in basketball reveals different treatment of the WNBA and NBA players (Aull and Brown 2013). Coverage of the NBA fight is on the event itself and the individuals involved. Conversely, in coverage of the WNBA fight, the players are reprimanded by the media for acting like "boys" and setting bad examples as (female) "role models" by participating in the fight (Aull and Brown 2013). Such representations reinforce different expectations of athletes, with men's sport viewed with respect to the sporting game, and women's sport with respect to gendered expectations of "good girl" behaviour.

5 Implications and recommendations for practice

Sport is an integral part of Australian culture, and the way that sporting events and players are reported on in/by the media has great potential to influence the Australian public. Prejudices contributing to exclusionary discourses can be "reproduced, consciously or sub-consciously," therefore "constructing a sense of reality which is culturally encoded" and often based on patriarchal ideologies (Crolley and Teso 2007: 152). As such, the way that AFL, NRL, and other masculine team sports are covered by the media has the potential to either perpetuate or counter existing issues of exclusion/inclusion. Taking into consideration the findings from this study, along with the broader need to continue to actively support, promote and celebrate an inclusive sporting space in the media, a selection of themes is further discussed below with respect to more specific implications and recommendations for media practice.

5.1 Amount of coverage

The amount of off-season media coverage afforded to women's football is paltry in comparison to coverage of the men's games. Yes, the AFLW and NRLW are emerging competitions, with fewer teams and shorter seasons, but these factors do not make the women's games any less newsworthy than the men's. In fact, research has shown that many journalists hold – but do not acknowledge – the biased view that men's sport is more newsworthy simply because of the gender of the athletes playing. Instead, they cite other reasons of newsworthiness such as (perceived) audience interest, exceptional performance, and successfulness (Knoppers and Elling 2004; Gee and Leberman 2011). While it is acknowledged that the AFLW and NRLW are fledgling leagues, they will continue to grow with respect to both participation and viewership. This growth will ideally be reflected in the amount of future media coverage afforded to women's sport, not just football, so that coverage becomes the norm rather than the exception.

5.2 Gender marking

The continual marking of female football in coverage which specifically focuses on AFLW and/or NRLW is unnecessary. By drawing attention to gender this positions the marked (women's) as the anomaly, and the unmarked (men's) as the norm. Two potential courses of action are: i) reduce the general gender marking that occurs in the women's coverage to follow the current practice in men's coverage, or, ii) commence general gender marking in coverage of men's football as well as women's. Additionally, and perhaps more importantly, there is potential here for the media to initiate a larger cultural language change. In 2022, the Football Federation of Australia (which is the governing body for football/soccer) announced that the A-League (men's) and W-League (women's) would collectively be known as the A-League (women's or men's). As no such changes have been announced by the AFL or NRL, the media has the opportunity to initiate this change by purposely marking *AFL Men's* and *NRL Men's* in future coverage, as has been done in this chapter.

5.3 Comparisons

Previous research indicates that while top sportswomen are compared to male athletes, sportsmen are most often compared to other famous sportsmen, gods, or superheros (Billings and Eastman 2002; Vincent 2004). Continual comparisons of female athletes to their male counterparts, but not vice versa, perpetuates the belief that women must aspire to play as a male would in order to receive due recognition as athletes, or otherwise face harsh criticism. While women's and men's football have many similarities, there are also differences in rules, skill repertoire, and coaching and management styles, all of which will have an impact on how the games are played. Further, there is no denying that female athletes have had far less opportunity and access to resources than the 100-year-old versions of men's football being played today. However, these differences do not make women's football a lesser version. As such, AFLW and NRLW should be considered valuable and newsworthy sports in their own right, not in comparison to men's sport. Future coverage may benefit from including (female) comparisons to players from other teams or previous seasons, or successful elite athletes from other sports.

5.4 Celebrating women in sport

The text analyses illuminated a positive narrative of women's football growth and progress. Interestingly, these narratives are not confined to AFL/NRL. A study of the Australian press from 2015–17 found that various news sources pointed to this being a "boom time" for women's sport (McLachlan 2019). However, the same study also found evidence that this "celebratory discourse" of female involvement in sport has been present in the Australian press since the 1920s (McLachlan 2019: 9). It therefore must be considered whether this ongoing progress narrative in the media is indeed helping move towards a more inclusive sporting space, or if it "potentially constrains the possibilities for gender equality (in sport)" (McLachlan 2019: 20) by painting the picture that equality is just around the corner and no further action is required. Future coverage would benefit not only from celebrating the progress of women's sport, but also continuing to highlight the ongoing inequities in sport. Additionally, including a wide variety of women's sport as part of routine coverage will assist in moving towards a more inclusive space in the sports media.

6 Conclusion

This chapter used corpus-based discourse analysis to explore how issues of inclusion and exclusion related to gender bias and sexism in the professional sporting space are negotiated within the Australian print media. Specifically, I analysed a corpus of print news coverage of women's and men's AFL and NRL for the discursive patterns of gender marking, infantilisation, sexualisation, and trivialisation of performance.

In sum, the results point to a potential shift away from some of the historical exclusionary discourses of female athletes in the sports media. Positively, there is no evidence of sexualisation, with these women instead represented as skilful and successful athletes. Additionally, while the use of GIRL is prominent, the text analysis shows that the sources using these terms are mostly players and other in-group members, thus suggesting it is likely used for establishing solidarity and inclusion within the new competitions. There remains, however, strong evidence of asymmetrical gender marking. Most surprising was the prominence of this in the coverage of women's sport. Overt repetition of this exclusionary discourse thus has the potential to influence the readership to internalise the hegemonic ideology that the sporting space is "naturally" male.

The text analyses also revealed patterns relating to the construction of athlete identity and societal expectations with respect to gender stereotypes. The women are positioned as role models who are progressing women's sport. While this sets a positive example for younger generations, it can also be argued that the traditional role of females as domestic caretakers is being repurposed for a sporting context, a role that is not required of their male counterparts. In contrast, coverage of the men focuses on their "bad boy" behaviour. The notion of men as strong or aggressive is evident in the keywords, both in the context of gameplay as well as off-field antics. Involvement in scandal is prevalent, along with a seemingly lack of recourse handed down by clubs, therefore suggesting a "boys will be boys" attitude.

And finally, it is necessary to reiterate that the stark discrepancy in amount of coverage indicates that women's football is simply less important and newsworthy than the male versions.

Overall, the findings from this research provide valuable insight into how exclusion/inclusion in team sports are constructed and negotiated within the Australian print media. This is one of few corpus linguistic studies of gendered language with respect to inclusion/exclusion in sports media coverage, and thus provides a foundation for future research in this space. There is no doubt about the necessity for further research into intersectionality, with respect to gender diversity, sexuality, and ethnicity/race. Additionally, analysis of other news platforms would provide a more wholistic picture of inclusion/exclusion in the wider sports media community. Also necessary is a deeper exploration of how media structures, partnerships with sporting institutions, and individual sentiments in the sports newsroom may influence media coverage.

In conclusion, while gains have been made, there are still some clear (gendered) differences in the way that men's and women's football is covered by the media. Such differences construct the sporting space as ideally and preferably male, thereby perpetuating exclusionary discourses of women's sport and its athletes. The challenge now is to cast away patriarchal ideologies in order to view women's sport as legitimate and newsworthy in its own right, thereby constructing a more inclusionary sports media landscape.

References

Anthony, Laurence. 2020. AntConc (Version 3.5.9). [Computer software]. Tokyo: Waseda University. www.antlab.sci.waseda.ac.jp

Archer, Dawn, Andrew Wilson & Paul Rayson. 2002. "Introduction to the USAS Category System." https://ucrel.lancs.ac.uk/usas/usas_guide.pdf (accessed March 2021).

Aull, Laura L. & David West Brown. 2013. Fighting words: a corpus analysis of gender representations in sports reportage. *Corpora* 8(1). 27–52.

Baker, Paul. 2014. *Using corpora to analyze gender*. London; New York: Bloomsbury.

Billings, Andrew. 2007. From Diving Boards to Pole Vaults: Gendered Athlete Portrayals in the "Big Four" Sports at the 2004 Athens Summer Olympics. *Southern Communication Journal* 72(4). 329–44.

Billings, Andrew C., James R. Angelini & Susan T. Eastman. 2005. Diverging Discourses: Gender Differences in Televised Golf Announcing. *Mass Communication & Society* 8(2). 155–71.

Billings, Andrew C., James R. Angelini, Paul J. MacArthur, Kimberly Bissell, Lauren R. Smith & Natalie A. Brown. 2014. Where the Gender Differences *Really* Reside: The "Big Five" Sports Featured in NBC's 2012 London Primetime Olympic Broadcast. *Communication Research Reports* 31(2). 141–53.

Billings, Andrew C. & Susan T. Eastman. 2002. Selective Representations of Gender, Ethnicity, and Nationality in American Television Coverage of the 2000 Summer Olympics. *International Review for the Sociology of Sport* 37(3/4). 351–70.

Bolt, A. 2017. "AFLW late mail: It's a lockout at Ikon Park." www.afl.com.au/news/2017-02-03/aflw-late-mail-historic-round-set-to-explode (accessed May 2019)

Brezina, Vaclav. 2018. *Statistics in corpus linguistics: a practical guide*. Cambridge: Cambridge University Press.

Brown, Peter. 1995. Gender, The Press & History: Coverage of women's sport in the *Newcastle Herald*, 1890-1990. *Media Information Australia* 75. 24–34.

Bruce, Toni. 2016. New rules for new times: Sportswomen and media representation in the third wave. *Sex Roles* 74. 361–76.

Caple, Helen. 2013. Competing for Coverage: Exploring emerging discourses of female athletes in the Australian print media. *English Text Construction* 6(2). 271–94.
Caple, Helen. 2016. Results Resolve Reaction: Words, Images and the Functional Structure of Online Match Reports. In David Caldwell, Elaine Vne & Jon Jueidini (eds.), *The Discourse of Sport: Analyses from Social Linguistics*, 209–227. London/NewYork: Routledge.
Christopherson, Neal, Michelle Janning & Eileen Diaz McConnell. 2002. Two Kicks Forward, One Kick Back: A Content Analysis of Media Discourses on the 1999 Women's World Cup Soccer Championship. *Sociology of Sport Journal* 19. 170–88.
Crolley, Liz & Elena Teso. 2007. Gendered narratives in Spain: The Representation of Female Athletes in Marca and El País. *International Review for the Sociology of Sport* 42(2). 149–66.
Davies, Mark. 2014. Corpus of News on the Web (NOW):
 3+ billion words from 20 countries, updated every day. https://www.english-corpora.org/now/ (accessed March 2021)
Duncan, Mary Carlisle & Michael A. Messner. 1998. The media image of sport and gender. In Lawrence Wenner (ed.), *MediaSport*, 170–185. London/New York: Routledge.
Eagleman, Andrea N. 2013. Constructing gender differences: newspaper portrayals of male and female gymnasts at the 2012 Olympic Games. *Sport in Society* 18(2). 234–47. https://doi.org/10.1080/17430437.2013.854509
Eastman, Susan & Andrew Billings. 1999. Gender Parity in the Olympics: Hyping Women Athletes, Favoring Men Athletes. *Journal of Sport & Social Issues*, 23(2). 140–170.
Eastman, Susan & Andrew Billings. 2000. Sportscasting and sports reporting: the power of gender bias. *Journal of Sport and Social Issues* 24(4). 192–213.
English, Peter, Angela Calder, Simone Pearce & Katy Kirby. 2019. A content analysis of Super Netball newspaper coverage. *Media International Australia* 171(1). 110–24.
Fink, Janet S. 2015. Female athletes, women's sport, and the sport media commercial complex: Have we really "come a long way, baby"?. *Sports Management Review* 18. 331–42. dx.doi.org/ 10.1016/j.smr.2014.05.001
Gee, Bidget L. & Sarah I. Leberman. 2011. Sports Media Decision Making in France: How They Choose What We Get to See and Read. *International Journal of Sport Communication* 4. 321–43.
Harris, John & Ben Clayton. 2002. Feminity, Masculinity, Physicality and the English Tabloid Press. *International Review for the Sociology of Sport* 37. 397–413.
Ismail, Habibah. 2016. Of Cover Girls and Bad Boys: A Corpus Linguistic Analysis of Gendered Keywords in Malaysian Sports News Discourse. In David Caldwell, Elaine Vine & Jon Jueidini (eds.), *The Discourse of Sport: Analyses from Social Linguistics*, 161–176. Routledge.
Ismail, Habibah. 2017. *A Corpus-assisted Multimodal Discourse Analysis of Malaysian Sports News Discourse: Exploring the Representation of Female and Male Athletes*. The University of Sydney thesis.
Jaworska, Sylvia & Sally Hunt. 2017. Differentiations and intersections: a corpus-assisted discourse study of gender representations in the British press before, during and after the London Olympics 2012. *Gender and Language* 11(3). 336–64.
Jenkins, Kate. 2017. Football's new stars lead way to close gender gap. *Herald Sun*. www.heraldsun.com.au (accessed May 2019)
Jones, Dianne. 2004. Half the Story? Olympic Women on ABC News Online. *Media International Australia incorporating Culture and Policy* 110. 132–46.
Kemble, Melissa. 2020. As good as the men? A corpus analysis of evaluation in news articles about professional female athletes competing in 'masculine' sports. *CADAAD Journal*, 12(1). 87–111.

https://www.lancaster.ac.uk/fass/journals/cadaad/wp-content/uploads/2020/10/Vol12.1-5-Kemble.pdf

Kinnick, Katherine N. 1998. Gender Bias in Newspaper Profiles of 1996 Olympic Athletes: A Content Analysis of Five Major Dailies. *Women's Studies in Communication* 21(2). 212–37. https://doi.org/10.1080/07491409.1998.10162557

Klein, Marie-Luise. 1988. Women in the Discourse of Sport Reports. *International Review for the Sociology of Sport* 23(2). 139–52.

Knoppers, Annelies & Agnes Elling. 2004. 'We Do Dot Engage in Promotional Journalism': Discursive Strategies Used by Sport Journalists to Describe the Selection Process. *International Review for the Sociology of Sport* 39(1). 57–73.

Koivula, Nathalie. 1995. Ratings of Gender Approrpriateness of Sports Participation: Effects of Gender-Based Schematic Processing. *Sex Roles* 33(7/8). 543–57.

Koivula, Nathalie. 1999. Gender Stereotyping in Televised Media Sport Coverage. *Sex Roles*, 41(7–8). 589–604.

Lee, Judy. 1992. Media Portrayals of Male and Female Olympic Athletes: Analyses of Newspaper Accounts of the 1984 and the 1988 Summer Games. *International Review for the Sociology of Sport* 27(3). 197–219.

Lenskyj, Helen. 1998. 'Inside sport' or 'on the margins'? Australian Women and the Sport Media. *International Review for the Sociology of Sport* 33(1). 19–32.

Ličen, Simon & Andrew C. Billings. 2013. Cheering for 'our' champs by watching 'sexy' female throwers: Representation of nationality and gender in Slovenian 2008 Summer Olympic television coverage. *European journal of communication*, 28. 379–96.

Lumby, Catharine, Helen Caple & Kate Greenwood. 2014. *Towards a Level Playing Field: sport and gender in Australian media.* Commissioned by the Australian Sports Commission. Canberra, Australia. http://www.ausport.gov.au/__data/assets/pdf_file/0007/356209/Towards_a_Level_Playing_Field_LR.pdf

McLachlan, Fiona. 2019. It's Boom Time! (Again): Progress Narratives and Women's Sport in Australia. *Journal of Australian Studies* 43(1). 7–21. https://doi.org/10.1080/14443058.2019.1575262

Messner, Michael A., Margaret Carlisle Duncan & Kerry Jensen. 1993. Separating the Men from the Girls: The Gendered Language of Televised Sports. *Gender and Society* 7(1). 121–37.

North, Louise. 2012. The gendered world of sports reporting in the Australian print media. *Journalism, Media and Cultural Studies*. http://cf.ac.uk/jomec/jomecjournal/2-november2012/north_women sssport.pdf

Payne, Rachel. 2004. Rething the Status of Female Olympians in the Australian Press. *Media International Australia incorporating Culture and Policy* 100. 120–31.

Ponterotto, Diane. 2014. Trivializing the Female Body: A Cross-cultural Analysis of the Representation of Women in Sports Journalism. *Journal of International Women's Studies* 15(2). 94–111.

Ravel, Barbara & Marc Gareau. 2016. 'French football needs more women like Adriana'? Examining the media coverage of France's women's national football team for the 2011 World Cup and the 2012 Olympic Games. *International Review for the Sociology of Sport* 51(7). 833–47.

Rayson, Paul. 2009. Wmatrix: a web-based corpus processing environment. Computing Department, Lancaster University. http://ucrel.lancs.ac.uk/wmatrix/

Sabo, Don & Sue Curry Jansen. 1992. Images of men in sport media: The social reproduction of gender order. In Steve Craig (ed.), *Men, Masculinity and the Media*, 169–184. London: Sage.

Schirato, Tony. 2013. *Sports Discourse*. London/New York: Bloomsbury Publishing.

Sherwood, Merryn, Marissa Lordanic, Tharindu Bandaragoda, Emma Sherry & Damminda Alahakoon. 2019. A new league, new coverage? Comparing tweets and media coverage from the first season of AFLW. *Media International Australia* 172(1). 114–30.

Shugart, Helena A. 2003. She shoots, she scores: Mediated constructions of contemporary female athletes in coverage of the 1999 US women's soccer team. *Western Journal of Communication* 67. 1–31.

Toohey, Kristine. 1997. Australian Television, Gender and the Olympic Games. *International Review for the Sociology of Sport* 32(1). 19–29.

Vincent, John. 2004. Game, Sex, and Match: The Construction of Gender in British Newspaper Coverage of the 2000 Wimbledon Championships. *Sociology of Sport Journal* 21. 435–56.

Vincent, John, Charles Imwold, Vandra Masemann & James T. Johnson. 2002. A Comparison of Selected 'Serious' and 'Popular' British, Canadian, and United States Newspaper Coverage of Female and Male Athletes Competing in the Centennial Olympic Games: Did Female Athletes Receive Equitable Coverage in the 'Games of the Women'?, *International Review for the Sociology of Sport* 37(3–4). 319–35.

Wensing, Emma H. & Toni Bruce. 2003. Bending the Rules: Media Representations of Gender during an International Sporting Event. *International Review for the Sociology of Sport* 38(4). 387–96.

Yasemin Erdoğan-Öztürk, Esranur Efeoğlu-Özcan, and Hale Işık-Güler

Chapter 8
From "the National Pride" to "the Daughters": Media representations of Olympic sportswomen in Turkey

1 Introduction

"Turkish woman" makes history at Tokyo 2020[1] *("Türk kadını" Tokyo 2020'de tarihe geçti)* was the headline that the largest news agency outlet in Turkey, *Anadolu Ajansı*, used in its coverage to celebrate Turkish athletes in the 2020 Summer Olympic Games in Tokyo. With the start of the 2020 Tokyo Olympics, women's participation in several disciplines of professional sports have been covered more widely than ever in the Turkish media.[2] In contrast to their exclusion in routine media coverage of sports, women athletes participating in the Olympics were nationally celebrated with extensive coverage in televised, online and print media, during and after the Olympic Games. The public and media attention centred mainly on medal-winning women athletes in the branch of boxing and on the women's national volleyball team despite its elimination in the quarterfinals. The quoted headline at the beginning aptly illustrates the explicit attention that female athletes received from the media. The Olympic news not only focused on the performances of sportswomen representing Turkey but also opened up a gendered discursive ground on the inclusion and exclusion of sportswomen by the media outlets. Extensive inclusion of women athletes in the news revealed prob-

---

[1] "Turkish woman" is enclosed by single quotation marks by the news agency. No emphasis added. See the link for the original headline in Turkish: https://www.aa.com.tr/tr/spor/turk-kadini-tokyo-2020de-tarihe-gecti/2328685
[2] With 50 female and 54 male athletes, the Turkish team won 13 medals in Tokyo, which was a national Olympic record in Turkey's history. The women who participated in the Olympic games in Tokyo achieved a similar historic record by winning one golden (boxing), one silver (boxing) and three bronze medals (taekwondo, karate and wrestling).

Yasemin Erdoğan-Öztürk, Karabük University, Turkey
Esranur Efeoğlu-Özcan, Gazi University, Turkey
Hale Işık-Güler, Orta Doğu Teknik Üniversitesi (METU), Turkey

https://doi.org/10.1515/9783110789829-009

lematic portrayals of their bodies, identities and performances as controversial ideological symbols.

Our chapter aims to explore the discursive inclusion and exclusion practices by media outlets towards the sportswomen in Turkey, who participated in the 2020 Tokyo Summer Olympics. We explore the discursive strategies through which female athletes are represented and framed in newspapers. Drawing on a Feminist Critical Discourse Analytical approach (Lazar 2005, 2007, 2014), we critically seek to understand the ideological workings of the media in their power to construct sportswomen. More specifically, we engage in the question of how Turkish Olympic sportswomen are represented in newspapers in connection to nationalism and the ideological positions of media outlets: that is, (i) how newspapers perform inclusionary and exclusionary discursive strategies to portray them, (ii) what roles nationalism and ideological stances play in their inclusion/exclusion. To capture how media outlets create multiple, complex or conflicting representations based on their ideological and political stances, we expand our analytical lens beyond the sports pages of newspapers to see discussions around sportswomen outside the periphery of sports. Therefore, the data in our study involves news texts, opinion articles and columns published in all sections of 11 Turkish newspapers appealing to different audiences with different political alignments.

Our study contributes to the research on inclusion and exclusion of sportswomen in the media in a number of ways: It addresses an urgent need to explore an understudied issue within diverse geopolitical settings beyond the European and North American contexts. It also attempts to adopt an intersectional lens by integrating the analysis of nationalism and ideology to the analysis of gender in the representations of women athletes to gain a deeper insight into the linguistic operation of inclusivity and exclusivity in media texts.

In the rest of the chapter, we first present a brief overview of the literature regarding media representations of women athletes. This is followed by the section of methodological approach and analytical tools. Next, our data collection procedures and dataset are described. In section four, our analyses and main findings are presented. Lastly, we conclude our chapter with a discussion of our key findings and suggest practical implications for practitioners.

2 Media coverage and representation of women athletes

A substantial body of literature consistently documented that women's sports have long been excluded or marginalized in TV broadcasts and news media coverage (Duncan and Messner 1998; Billings and Eastman 2002; Messner, Duncan and Cooky 2003; Billings et al. 2008; Kane 2013; Billings; Cooky, Messner and Musto 2015; Fink 2015; Angelini and MacArthur 2018; Kemble, this volume). Sportswomen are globally reported to receive less than 10 percent of the routine sport coverage in comparison to men (Markula 2009; Markula, Bruce, and Hovden 2010). The "symbolic annihilation" and exclusion of women in routine sport media coverage not only erase women from the sports arena but also imply the false conclusion that women's sports do not exist (Markula, Bruce, and Hovden 2010), and women are not interested or skilled in sports (Kane 2013). In other words, media outlets "reaffirm *hegemonic masculinity* through the constant stream of content on male athletes and men's sports" (Cooky and Antunovic 2022: 3). Hegemonic masculinity is privileged, naturalized and perpetuated by the media through the attachments of cultural meanings associated with masculinity to the sports. In this way, media, as a powerful ideological site, constructs sports as a male domain built on the perspective of hegemonic masculinity (Trujillo 2000).

Major sport events, particularly the Olympic Games, are significant exceptions to the exclusion of women's sports in the media. Research shows that sportswomen receive notably increased and more equitable coverage during the Olympic Games (Billings et al. 2008; Markula, Bruce, and Hovden 2010). Although this increase might be interpreted as a development in terms of gender equality in the area of sport, most researchers cautiously problematize the assumption that representation in quantity will bring gender equality. An extensive body of research on the media representations of women athletes in the Olympic Games reveals that women are still marginalized in multiple ways despite their increased visibility and inclusion in media coverage (Duncan and Messner 1998; Birrell and McDonald 2000; Billings and Eastman 2002; Wensing and Bruce 2003; Markula 2009; Boykoff and Yasuoka 2015; Fink, 2015; Cooky and Antunovic 2022). As a powerful ideological tool, mass media include women in the Olympics in gendered ways through particular discursive strategies. Duncan and Messner (1998) identified four significant categories of exclusionary practices towards sportswomen: (i) production, (ii) athletic attribution, (iii) formulae of exclusion and (iv) symbolic dominance. In the domain of production, the authors highlight that the amount of coverage, technical quality and intentional audience building are arranged to trivialize women's games compared to men's. The domain of athletic attribution involves assigning symbolic superiority to male athletes through the adjectives of *big* and *strong* as opposed to female athletes who are labelled as *weak* and *small*. The domain of formulae of exclusion underlines that women's errors are overemphasized while men's are downplayed. Lastly, the domain of symbolic dominance emphasizes the differences between men and women through the strategies of asymmetrical gender marking, infantilization and sexualization.

Similarly, Wensing and Bruce (2003) and Fink (2015) list five key conventional "rules" of the mass media to frame female athletes: *gender marking, compulsory heterosexuality, appropriate femininity, infantilization* and *non-sport-related aspects*. Gender marking refers to identifying a sport event as a *women's* event. Compulsory heterosexuality includes presenting female athletes according to the male gaze as either sex objects or in heterosexual roles as mothers, wives etc. This strategy also contributes to the entire exclusion of LGBTIQ+ athletes or their biased inclusion as a problem or threat (Markula 2009). Appropriate femininity involves the emphasis on traditionally feminine physical appearance and behaviours. Infantalization refers to the portrayal of sportswomen as young girls. Emphasizing non-sport-related aspects is the presentation of female athletes' personal and family lives.

In their analysis of the media coverage of aboriginal athlete Cathy Freeman in the 2000 Sydney Olympic games, Wensing and Bruce (2003) observed how the intersection of nationalism and gender has led to an ambivalent representation of Freeman as a symbol of national reconciliation, with a marked absence of ethnic and gendered stereotypes. Discourses of nationalism in the media tend to erase gendered conventions to emphasize national glory and pride by including female athletes as model citizens and national heroes (Bruce 2016). Therefore, nationalism, especially in the case of the Olympic Games, functions as a substantial power dynamic to be considered in the media representations of sportswomen. Several studies on the media coverage of 2004 Athens Olympics in different parts of the world including Turkey, Korea, Canada and other national settings underlined the powerful effect of nationalism in media coverages of female athletes and discussed that athletes are not sexualized in any way, but instead presented as valuable national symbols for their countries (Koh 2009; Koh 2010; Koca and Arslan 2010; Wensing and Macneill 2010).

3 Methodological approach and analytical tools

In our study, we adopt a feminist critical discourse analysis (henceforth FCDA) approach, which combines insights from critical discourse analysis (henceforth CDA) and feminist theory. FCDA echoes Fairclough's (1992) argument that social practices are reflected and constituted by discourse. It also aligns with van Dijk's

(2001: 352) approach to discourse which aims to understand and expose the ways "social power abuse, dominance, and inequality are enacted, reproduced, and resisted by text and talk in the social and political context". Building on CDA, FCDA advocates for a feminist political critique of social practices. While CDA is concerned with all forms of power, dominance and inequality, FCDA has explicit feminist concerns within the intersection of gender, power, and ideology. As a result, the strand of research conducted within an FCDA perspective contributes to critical discourse studies by its nuanced understanding of gendered social practices.

Lazar (2005, 2007, 2014) articulates five key principles as the tenets of FCDA theory and research: (i) feminist analytical activism, (ii) conceptualization of gender as ideological structure and practice, (iii) complexity of gender and power relations in terms of intersectionality, (iv) a poststructuralist and dialectical view of discourse in the (de)construction of gender, and (v) critical reflexivity as praxis. FCDA utilizes various levels of analysis and benefits from the analytical tools provided in the paradigm of CDA. These tools include choices in lexis, clauses/sentences/utterances, conversational turns, structures of argument and genre, interdiscursivity etc. (Lazar 2007: 151).

Informed by the key principles of the FCDA approach, our study adopts "frame analysis" (Semino et al. 2018) and "perspectivation" (Wodak 2001) as its primary analytical tools. Frames[3] and perspectivation allow for a multilevel investigation of news texts. We explore (i) lexical choices and metaphorical expressions surrounding sportswomen by means of frames, and (ii) ideological representations and positionings of sportswomen by means of perspectivation.

Our study adopts Semino et al.'s (2018: 627) overarching definition in which a *frame* is specified as "a portion of background knowledge that (i) concerns a particular aspect of the world, (ii) generates expectations and inferences in communication and action, and (iii) tends to be associated with particular lexical and grammatical choices in language". In this perspective, lexical choices, metaphorically used expressions and their patterns correspond with the linguistic evidence regarding frames which reflect people's attitudes, values, reasoning regarding various issues. As for our understanding of *perspectivation*, we follow Wodak's (2001) definition which describes perspectivation as a set of discursive strategies helping to express and legitimize ideological distances or involvement on a social issue from certain ideological perspectives. The analytical framework of perspec-

---

[3] The concept of a "frame" has been used in a variety of different fields with different scopes. Among these fields, please refer to Goffman (1967) for detailed account of the notion of "frames" in sociology, Minsky (1975) for the field of artificial intelligence, and Fillmore (1985) for semantics, and Entman (1993) for communication studies.

tivation allow us to explore the ways of justifying certain social actions and actors while delegitimizing others by employing a certain ideological standpoint.

4 Data

The data used in this study consists of Turkish news articles collected from national newspapers published in Turkey. The timeframe set for the data collection was designed to compile data which encompasses pre-Olympics, Olympics, and post-Olympics news coverage. With this purpose, the starting point for the data collection was set as July 1st 2021 which corresponds to three weeks before the Tokyo Summer Olympics starts and the cut-off point was determined as September 30th 2021, which is seven weeks after the Olympic games were officially over.[4] The data source of this study are national newspapers which were selected based on the following inclusion criteria: (i) having a wide print circulation among all newspapers in the Turkish market, and (ii) representing different political alignments. Combining these two criteria, a total of 11 newspapers were identified for the purposes of this study. The selected newspapers were *Cumhuriyet, Evrensel, Hürriyet, Milliyet, Sabah, Sözcü, Takvim, Türkiye, Yeni Akit, Yeni Asya,* and *Yeni Şafak*. As a whole, the selected group of newspapers present a variety of political alignments within the spectrum of left to right ideological positioning. The newspapers differed in terms of the scope and type of content they presented in different modes of publication, namely the articles in print versions and their official online editions. As a result, the sampling procedure adopted a complementary approach to compile the data and used both print versions and online coverage of the selected newspapers as its data source. After the target newspapers were selected, the related news articles were gathered through a keyword search through the keywords *kadın* 'woman', *kız* 'girl', and *olimpiyat* 'olympics'.[5]

Within the designated timeframe and selected newspapers, the keyword search retrieved 395 results. Exclusion of duplications and content irrelevant to

---

[4] We started data collection three weeks before the Olympics and stopped collection seven weeks after the Olympics as this time period provided the most comprehensive news coverage regarding our focus of study.
[5] An initial study was conducted to identify these keywords through a close reading of cover stories published in the selected newspapers published on August 8th, 2021, which corresponds to the last day of the Olympics. The date was selected on the basis that the newspapers reported on the overall performance of the national athletes in the games. The results showed that the news articles which reported details about sportswomen had either *kadın* 'woman' or *kız* 'girl' intersecting with *olimpiyat* 'olympics' as keywords.

Tokyo Summer Olympics yielded a final dataset of 312 news pieces, which consisted of 272 articles and 40 opinion columns. Table 1 below presents the distribution of data tabulated by newspapers in the dataset.

Table 1: The overview of the dataset.

Newspaper*	Political alignment (2022)	No. of texts		Total
		Articles	Columns	
Cumhuriyet	left, secularism	37	12	49
Evrensel	left, socialism	7	2	9
Hürriyet	right	14	2	16
Milliyet	right	40	6	46
Sabah	right	27	9	36
Sözcü	nationalism, secularism	37	6	43
Takvim	right	41	1	42
Türkiye	conservatism	28	1	29
Yeni Akit	fundamentalist far-right	20	0	20
Yeni Asya	convervatism	13	1	14
Yeni Şafak	convervatism	8	0	8
Total		272	40	312

*In alphabetical order.

As illustrated above, the data of this study presents a comprehensive coverage of the representations of Turkish sportswomen within the discourses of the Olympic games constructed by and communicated through domestic newspapers with different political agendas and target audiences. In our data collection procedure, we did not limit our keyword search with the sports sections and expanded our search to all sections and pages of newspapers to capture the political discussions including Olympic sportswomen. As a result, the dataset ended up containing news about the Olympics from different sections of the newspapers, including sports, national news, local politics and columns.

5 Analysis

In this part, our analyses and main findings are presented under four sections: (i) the analysis of frames used to represent women athletes in the Olympics, (ii) representation of women athletes in connection to nationalism, (iii) the role of ideological positions embraced by the media outlets in the representations of women athletes, and (iv) coverage of marginalized gender identities in inclusion and exclusion of women athletes.

5.1 Frames used for the representation of Turkish sportswomen

this section, the analysis focuses on the frames used for constructing inclusionary representations of Turkish sportswomen in the Tokyo Olympics. The results are presented under two sub-sections: (i) frames used for all Turkish sportswomen in the Olympics and (ii) discipline-specific frames. For each sub-section, words or expressions used to construct specific frames are identified and the representations constructed by means of these frames are explained.

5.1.1 Common frames used for representations of Turkish sportswomen

The analysis shows that Turkish media outlets make use of the frames of *power, war, light, and kinship* to construct representations of Turkish sportswomen. While existing literature indicates that media representations of sportswomen are not promoted through qualities of strength and skill but rather their appearance (e.g., Bernstein 2002; Capranica and Aversa 2002), the representation of Turkish sportswomen frequently orients towards the power frame rather than their appearance as in excerpts (1) and (2) below.[6]

(1) Türk kadını, olimpiyatlardaki erkek egemenliğini artık **kıracak**.
    Turkish women will **demolish** (lit. to break) the male domination in the Olympics.
    (Sözcü_2021-08-13)

(2) Türk kadını, Tokyo 2020'ye **damga vurdu**.
    Turkish women **left a mark** (lit. stamp impression) on Tokyo 2020.
    (Takvim_2021-08-09_02)

In the examples above, the successful performances of Turkish sportswomen in the Olympics leads to the description of Turkish women as active agents who are

---

[6] The words and expressions used to construct these frames are indicated in **bold** within the excerpts.

powerful enough to demolish (literally "to break" in Turkish) the male hegemony in the Olympics as in (1) and demonstrating enough strength to leave a mark on the overall Olympic games as in (2). The frame of power is intertwined with another traditionally masculinized frame, war, as the media coverage for the games Turkish sportswomen won depicts them as 'heroines' *kahramanlar* who 'crush' *ezip geçmek* their opponents and 'make history' *tarih yazmak*. The power frame combined with elements from the war frame produces a nationalism-oriented discourse in which Turkish sportswomen contribute to the ideas of national belonging and pride by showing dominance over teams representing other nations. Evidently, these frames are discursive tools that help us trace the inclusionary practices used in the newspapers.

An additional frame used to highlight masculinized power is the frame of *light*. Rather than the widespread notion of light being associated with femininity through the characteristics of delicacy and appeal, the representations within the frame of *light* assign Turkish sportswomen agency, reinforcing discourses of hope as in (3) and (4) below.

(3) Ve o doğu başkentinde Türk sporunun ümit ışıkları doğdu, geride bıraktığımız iki haftada. [. . .] Bir şampiyon, bir başarı, bir ışık olur ülke gençlerine.
And in that eastern capital, a ray of hope for Turkish sports was born in the past two weeks. [. . .] A champion becomes a success, a light for the youth of the country.
(Sabah_2021-08-10)

(4) Bir meşale yakıldı ve arkasından niceleri gelecek belli.
A torch has been lit and it is certain that many more will follow.
(Sözcü_2021-08-13)

The representation of sportswomen as 'a source of light' in the examples above is used for constructing a promising and reassuring vision for both the overall Olympic performance of Turkey and the future of the country.

A final representation of Turkish sportswomen is manifested within the *kinship* frame. This frame produces a counter-representation of Turkish sportswomen compared to the representations present in the frames of power and light. While sportswomen were depicted as active and skilful agents in power and light frames, they are infantilised by using the referent *kızlarımız* 'our girls' in the kinship frame. The existing literature on the infantilised representations of sportswomen also shows the use of 'girls' in other languages and sports contexts (see also Borcila 2000; Bruce 2003; Messner, Duncan and Cooky 2003; Wensing and Bruce 2003; Chimbwete-Phiri and Schnurr this volume). However, Turkish data provides an additional facet to this representation by highlighting the dependency of women by means of lexically marking *kızlarımız* 'girls' with the first-person plural possessive suffix *–(I)mIz*, which corresponds to the first-person plural possessive pronoun 'our' in English. This representation, as exemplified in (5) below, trivializes the success of women by setting a hierarchy through kinship. The representation is not only overtly infantilised but also disempowers sportswomen as daughters who are in need of support by their senior family members, rather than self-sufficient individuals.

(5) Olimpiyatlarda özellikle de kızlarımızın başarıları öne çıktı, tüm dünyaya örnek Türk kadınını gösterdiler.
In the Olympics, especially the success of our girls came to the forefront, they demonstrated the exemplary Turkish women to the whole world.
(Cumhuriyet_2021-08-09_2)

It should be highlighted that in (5) above, an *ambivalent representation* (Wensing and Bruce 2003) of Turkish sportswomen is manifested through their portrayal as valued and exemplary women right after the infantilised image presented at the very beginning of the excerpt.

5.1.2 Discipline-specific frames used for representations of Turkish sportswomen

In addition to the frames used to create representations for the generic group of Turkish sportswomen, the results show that a number of frames are used exclusively for women's national volleyball team and national boxing athletes in the dataset. Within dualist feminine-masculine thinking, while volleyball is traditionally stereotyped as feminine, boxing is frequently treated as a masculine form of sports. Nevertheless, the analysis shows that the frames employed for the representations of volleyball players and boxing athletes are mainly the same in the Turkish newspaper dataset.

(6) Kadın voleybolcularımızı da baş tacı yaptık.
We also put our women volleyball players on a pedestal. (lit. we made our women volleyball players a crowning jewel)
(Sabah_2021-08-09_2)

These frames include *valuable assets* which involve the expressions such as *baş tacımız* 'our crown jewel' for the volleyball team and *altın kızlar* 'golden girls' for both volleyball players and boxing athletes; and the frame of *natural forces* which encompass metaphorically used words such as *fırtına* 'storm' for both the volleyball team and boxing athletes in addition to *şimşek* 'thunderbolt' used for volleyball players in the dataset.

Excerpt (6) above is an example for the frame of *valuable assets*. This representation shows that women's volleyball team is objectified as a jewel worn by the embodied nation. What should be noted regarding this conceptualization is that it bears assumption that sportswomen are not inherently of high value but rather the people of the nation bestow this value and high status to them.

The frame of *natural forces* again dehumanizes the sportswomen but elevates the characteristics of intimidating speed and uncontrollable force of a natural phenomenon such as in (7) below. In this excerpt, boxing athlete Buse Naz Sürmeneli is represented as *fırtına* 'storm' which emphasizes the unprecedented strength she showed against the rival she competed with.

(7) Buse Naz Sürmeneli fırtına gibi esti.
     Buse Naz Sürmeneli took it by storm.
     (Milliyet_05082021_2)

Overall, the results show that the frames of *valuable assets* and *natural forces* are adopted as inclusionary practices and achieved through non-human representations. Additionally, these inclusionary representations may be expressed through multiple facets. For example, power might be attributed to a sportswoman within the war frame in which she is a heroine or the frame of *natural forces* where the sportswoman is still a source of power, yet she is not affiliated with human-like attributes.

5.2 Nationalism and the representation of Turkish sportswomen

This section focuses on the exploration of the role of nationalism in the inclusion of Olympic sportswomen by media outlets. As hinted by the frames of *power* and *war* utilized for the representations of Turkish sportswomen, discourses of nationalism are recurring and are dominant in the dataset regardless of the disciplines of the sportswomen and the political alignments of the newspapers. Echoing Edensor's (2002: 78) argument that "sports is the most currently powerful form of national performance", the news concerning Turkish sportswomen's victories are deeply embedded in patriotic pride and national glory. This patriotism is discursively manifested by reinforcing a sense of national belonging through the historically coded narratives of notable national icons. The analysis shows that Turkish newspapers make use of a nationalist perspective when they represent sportswomen's achievements as exemplified in excerpt (8) below.

(8) Yürüyün kızlar!.. Türk önde, Türk ileri! [. . .] Çin gibi bir devden sonra, Rusya gibi bir başka devi daha deviren bu kızlar bizim. İnanın hayatımın en zor yazısını yazıyorum. Çünkü aklımda kelimeler değil, bizim kızların sevinç gözyaşları içinde birbirlerine sarılmış görüntülerini izlerken, ekrandan gelen mix edilmiş 10'uncu Yıl Marşı ve İzmir Marşı'nın sözleri var.
Go girls!. . . Turks ahead, Turks forward! [. . .] Our girls overthrew another giant like Russia after China. Believe me, I am writing the most difficult article of my life because all I have in mind are the words of the 10th Year Anthem and the Izmir Anthem played on the screen while I watch our girls hugging each other in tears of joy.
(Sabah_20210803_4)

In (8) above, the excerpt overtly illustrates how the success of Turkish volleyball players triggers sentiments regarding nationalist pride. The achievement of the team is contextualized within an atmosphere of historically coded anthems of the 10th Year Anthem and Izmir Anthem which are usually played on national victory days in Turkey. These anthems are about the glory of the republic and celebration of the establishment of the nation after the Turkish War of Independence. Shared knowledge of these anthems is discursively utilized by the newspaper columnist to evoke associations regarding the progress the volleyball team makes with the progress of the nation. As a result, the volleyball players are represented as part of the glorious and greater whole – the Turkish nation – with their athletic skills backgrounded. As the excerpt depicts, no information regarding the tactics or strategies used by the team to win the game is provided to the reader. Rather, national success and pride are highlighted.

Another aspect of nationalism-oriented discourses is what Bruce (2016) calls the representation of sportspeople as "model citizens" whose existence is acknowledged based on the exemplary citizenship they perform. Presenting sportswomen as model citizens to the Turkish readers is an example of a nationalist account of citizenship in which the success of the sportswomen contributes to the empowerment of their country against "the others" which is illustrated in excerpt (9) below.

(9) Olimpiyatlarda özellikle de kızlarımızın başarıları öne çıktı, tüm dünyaya örnek Türk kadınını gösterdiler.
In the Olympics, especially the success of our girls stood out, they showed the world the exemplary Turkish woman.
(Cumhuriyet_2021-08-09_2)

In the excerpt above, sportswomen who are model citizens are presented as representatives of all Turkish women. Turkey is discursively legitimized to be more powerful than the other countries thanks to its model citizens.

While some of the international studies repeatedly uncovered sexualised representations for sportswomen in other languages (English for Daniels & Wartena, 2011; Kane 2013, German for Weber & Barker-Ruchti, 2012), this study reveals that Turkish sportswomen were not depicted as the objects of male gaze. Rather in Turkish newspapers, the representation of sportswomen is intertwined with national success (Wensing and Bruce 2003; Quin, Wipf, and Ohl 2010; Bruce 2016). Discourses of nationalism outweigh discourses of sexualized femininity when sportswomen's Olympic achievements are covered. As a result, the celebration of the achievements of Turkish sportswomen leads to the downplaying of individuality as opposed to the overemphasis of the collective (the success of the individual versus the success of the nation) in the media.

5.3 Whose daughters? Olympic women as the sites of ideological controversy

This section investigates the ideological perspectivation strategies used by the newspapers for the inclusion and exclusion of Olympic sportswomen. We focus on the discursive area where sporting bodies of Olympic women are turned into a site of ideological struggle and controversy within the two ends of the political spectrum, between modernity and conservatism. To understand how traditional media outlets discursively frame Olympic women with respect to the political discussions around them, this section concentrates on a specific moment regarding female athletes in the Olympic Games, which sparked intense public attention and social media reaction. This moment was initiated with a tweet by a theologian, İhsan Şenocak, who criticized the uniforms worn by the women's volleyball team and made a contested religious call to Olympic sportswomen:

(10) *İSLAMIN KIZI! Sen OYUN ALANLARININ değil, imanın, iffetin, ahlakın, hayanın, edebin SUTANISIN; SEN "burnunu göstermekten utanan" ANALARIN EVLADISIN. Ekranlara ve sakallı ağabeylerinin popüler kültürün kurbanlarına "sultan" demesine aldanmayasın! Umudumuz da, duamız da SENSİN!*
DAUGHTER OF ISLAM! You are THE SULTAN of faith, chastity, morality, modesty, decency, not the PLAYGROUNDS; YOU are THE DAUGHTER OF MOTHERS who are "ashamed to show their noses". Don't be fooled by the screens and your bearded brothers calling the victims of popular culture "sultans"! YOU are our hope and our prayer![7]

The tweet targeting the Olympic athletes and volleyball team players who are referred to as *filenin sultanları* 'sultans of the net' received a very strong public and political backlash. It was collectively criticized both by the opposition and government party members. The tweet itself has significant ideological manoeuvres (Lazar 2021) around sportswomen, which discursively create alternative meanings attached to the metaphorical usage of 'sultan' and redefine the word with its imperial and Islamic connotations before the establishment of Turkey as a secular nation-state. Descriptions of professional volleyball players and other athletes as the 'daughters of Islam' function to take away the sportswomen's agency and reconstruct them as ideological objects subjected to a certain ideological position. Although this controversial tweet and the major backlash occupied the social media for a few days, it was not covered by the majority of the traditional media tools with the exceptions of the newspapers at the two extremes of the secularism-conservatism polarity. In our database, the incident was covered in three different newspapers, *Cumhuriyet*, a respectively niche newspaper with a secularist and social-democratic ideological position on the left; *Sözcü*, a more popular newspaper with a Kemalist and nationalist position; and lastly *Yeni Akit* which is placed at the radical conservative end of the spectrum.

(11) Kadın voleybolcularımızın olimpiyat başarısı böyle dedirtti: İşte Atatürk'ün kızları! [. . .] Sporcularımıza yönelik çirkin paylaşımlara sosyal medyada tepki yağdı. Duyarlı vatandaşlar Atatürk'ün kızlarına sahip çıktı.
The Olympic success of our women volleyball players: Here are Atatürk's daughters! [. . .] social media reacted to the ugly posts against our athletes. Sensitive citizens embraced Atatürk's daughters.
(Sözcü_2021-07-27)

---

[7] The tweet is verbatim translated to English. No emphasis added. Original tweet is accessible via https://twitter.com/ihsansenocak/status/1419296320267799187?s=20&t=Sqf07h4D_2cPGzsfN5mefQ

(12) Atatürk'ün kızları cehaleti yenecek. Filenin sultanlarına her kesimden büyük destek. İlahiyatçı Şenocak Olimpiyatlarda Çin'i yenerek gurur yaşatan Milli Voleybol Takımının formasını eleştirdi. Tepkiler çığ gibi yağdı.
Atatürk's daughters will defeat darkness. Great support for the sultans of the net from all walks of life. Theologian Şenocak criticized the jersey and shorts of the National Volleyball Team that defeated China in the Olympics. Reactions poured in like an avalanche.
(Sözcü_2021-07-27_2)

The headlines and subheadings in the excerpts reveal a sharp contrast to the singular tweet discussed above. The newspaper *Sözcü* on the nationalist and secularist end of the ideological polarization in the country uses a reversing framing strategy where they borrow the expression 'the daughters of Islam' and replace the ideological view of Islam with the name of Mustafa Kemal Atatürk, who is the founder of the Turkish republic and started the modernization and secularization process in the new-born nation-state. This intertextual move performed through the description 'Atatürk's daughters' is in line with the newspaper's nationalist and Kemalist position. As the headlines hint, in-text references to Atatürk as the source of light and modernity and as the creator of modern Turkish women are very frequent. The discursive approaches adopted by *Sözcü* is shared by *Cumhuriyet* to a certain extent. *Cumhuriyet* is one of the few newspapers addressing the event as a significant social problem in the country:

(13) Bir smaç da yobazlara. Dinciler yine şaşırtmadı. Cinsiyetçilik ve ayrımcılıkla "Filenin Sultanları'nı" hedef aldı.
Another slam-dunk for the religious bigots. Religionists did not surprise. They targeted the "Sultans of the Net" with sexism and discrimination.
(Cumhuriyet_2021-07-22)

Cumhuriyet's coverage emphasizes the contrast between secularists and religionists through its lexical choices. Using the word *yobaz* 'bigot' as a powerful and ideologically loaded word in the Turkish context helps the newspaper to position İhsan Şenocak and its supporters as sources of discrimination and sexism against women. While the words 'bigot' and 'religionists' create dangerous *others*, the word *smaç* 'slam-dunk' in volleyball jargon emphasizes the professional careers and achievements of the female players on the one hand, and strengthens their symbolic image as the faces of the modernity against the bigotry on the other. Lastly, *Yeni Akit*, which is positioned at the extreme end of right-wing politics with a focus on Islamism, covers the same news using a similar discursive structure yet in a quite contrasting way:

(14) Hakkı söyleyen İhsan Şenocak hoca efendiye laikçi linci! A Milli Kadın Voleybol Takımı'nın ortalıkta dolanan baldır bacak fotoğraflarının ardından, "İslamın kızı! Sen oyun alanlarının değil, imanın, iffetin, ahlakın, hayanın, edebin sultanısın" diyen Fıkıh Doktoru İhsan Şenocak, laikçiler tarafından sosyal medyada linç edildi.
Secularist lynching of İhsan Şenocak who speaks the truth! After the photos of the National Women's Volleyball Team' exposed calf and legs were circulated, he said, "Daughter of Islam! You are not the sultan of playgrounds, but of faith, chastity, morality, manners, decency", Dr. İhsan Şenocak, was lynched by secularists on social media.
(Yeni Akit_2021-07-26)

Yeni Akit's coverage of the tweet incident echoes Şenocak's voice in line with its own ideological alignment. As opposed to *Cumhuriyet* and *Sözcü*, *Yeni Akit*, in its coverage, reclaims the definition 'the daughters of Islam' to describe an idealized image of women within the codes of Islam. The excerpt invalidates professional sportswomen and their modern attire. The invalidation occurs by means of a typical old media framing technique, *sexualization* (Koh 2009; Bruce 2016) with the lexical choice *baldır bacak* 'exposed calf and legs' implying a disapproved sexuality and physicality. Although sportswomen are not provocatively visualized as sexual objects, sexualization is achieved by reducing the sporting bodies of professional women's volleyball team to body parts and by embracing a disapproving patriarchal voice intersecting with hegemonic masculinity and Islamism.

The examples suggest that Olympic women's sporting bodies are reconstructed as sites on which ideologies are built. We observe opposing representations of sportswomen by secular and religious newspapers. The discursive tactic which can be formulated as the 'daughter of x' within the axis of secularism and Islamism has significant functions and implications in the representation of female athletes. The newspapers as ideological apparatuses transform the sportswomen into ideological objects rather than agents. Media as an ideological apparatus might treat sportswomen as tools to validate any ideological perspective they support.

5.4 Gender identity as a discursive site of exclusion and inclusion

In this section, we analyse how gender identity of an Olympic athlete is framed by the newspapers by means of ideological perspectivation strategies. We discuss sexuality as a significant area for the discursive inclusion and exclusion of sportswomen by focusing on one particular moment. This moment concerns the trigger event initiating discussions around Ebrar Karakurt's sexuality, one of the players in the national volleyball team. The Olympic player has been subject to verbal abuse on social media after posting a photo with her girlfriend and felt compelled to delete the photo after homophobic reactions. She received great social media support from the public, her teammates and the Volleyball Federation. Ebrar's sexuality was first covered in the online website of Takvim, a newspaper with a highly right-wing position and a populist journalistic style:

(15) Ebrar Karakurt'un en büyük sırrı ifşa oldu. Herkes olimpiyatın yıldızı kimdir diye merak ederken skandal patlak verdi. Çıkanlar fena. [. . .] Ebrar Karakurt'un sevgilisinin yurtdışında yaşadığı ve kadın olduğu ortaya çıktı. Herkesi hayrete düşüren o fotoğraf, saatler içinde infial uyandırdı.
Ebrar Karakurt's biggest secret was revealed. While everyone was wondering who the Olympic star was, the scandal broke out. The revelations are bad. [. . .] It turned out that Ebrar Karakurt's lover lives abroad and is a woman. That photo, which shocked everyone, caused outrage within hours.
(Takvim_2021-08-17)

As Pirkko (2009) reminds us, the existence of the lesbian athlete is threatening since it challenges male hegemony in sports and power structures based on gender and femininity. The coverage above reaffirms the long-existing hypothesis that the media reacts negatively to nonconforming sexualities and gender identities. The excerpt above erases Ebrar Karakurt's professional sports career and presents her as a tabloid figure. The online news outlet describes her relationship as 'a scandal' which 'shocked' everyone. The use of lexical items like 'scandal', 'shock', 'revelation' and 'secret' builds a tabloid narrative with a clickbait expectation of tricking the audience into consuming the content. Yet, more interestingly, Ebrar Karakurt's LGBTQ+ identity and sexuality also serve as a base for political and ideological polarization as we have discussed before:

(16) Homofobik saldırıların hedefindeki voleybolcuya destek mesajı yağdı: 'Ebrar savaşçı sporcudur' [. . .] Federasyondan destek: Yürekli, cesur. . .
Support poured in for the volleyball player targeted by homophobic attacks: 'Ebrar is a warrior athlete' [. . .] Support from the federation: courageous, brave. . .
(Cumhuriyet, 2021-08-17)

(17) Yetkililere Ebrar Karakurt konusunda böyle seslendi! "LGBT'liden milli olmaz" Olimpiyat Oyunları'nda milli takım formasını giyen 21 yaşındaki Milli voleybolcu Ebrar Karakurt'a bir tepki de Mil-Diyanet Sen'den geldi.
This is how he addressed the authorities about Ebrar Karakurt! "LGBT people are not national" Another reaction to Ebrar Karakurt, the 21-year-old national volleyball player who wore the national team jersey in the Olympic Games, came from Mil-Diyanet Sen.
(Yeni Akit_2021-08-17)

Despite the notable silence of the traditional mainstream media tools, *Cumhuriyet* and *Yeni Akit*, covered the discussions around Ebrar Karakurt's sexuality in ways to reflect their own ideological standpoints. Both excerpts perform the discursive strategy of ideological perspectivation (Wodak 2001). While *Cumhuriyet* in excerpt (16) embraces an inclusive representation by marking the reactions as homophobic in parallel to its secularist approach, *Yeni Akit* in excerpt (17) attempts to exclude her as a professional national athlete by employing an Islamist perspective. Despite their contrasting ideologies, the discursive strategies they use are strikingly similar. Both newspapers resort to another voice or an authority through consistent use of direct quotations both in the headlines and in the text to validate their claims. *Cumhuriyet* quotes the president of the volleyball federation as the most powerful institutional authority in professional volleyball. The headline includes the quoted expressions 'Ebrar is a warrior athlete', 'courageous, brave...' with a more detailed testimonial speech in the news text. By presenting the federation's opinion, *Cumhuriyet* attempts to discursively reconstruct Ebrar Karakurt as a professional athlete with highlights on her courage and toughness as an athlete. In excerpt (18), *Yeni Akit* similarly uses a different quotation from the president of Milli-Diyanet Sen (National Religious-Affairs Union), who is presented as a religious authority. The quoted expression which declares that *LGBT people are not national,* – an expression very much in line with the governmental discourses of LGBTQ+ communities – function to exclude Ebrar Karakurt's professional identity as an athlete and reframe her as an immoral, threatening other. As the excerpts reveal, Ebrar's sexuality becomes a site of discursive war either to spread the recent pro-governmental discourses on LGBTQ+ people or to produce resistant discourses against the hegemonic political voice. This discursive war is performed in opposing directions to achieve either collective inclusion or exclusion of an LGBTQ+ athlete in the realm of sports and society.

6 Conclusion

This study focused on the representations of Turkish sportswomen in the 2020 Tokyo Summer Olympics covered by 11 newspapers with different political alignments in Turkey. The results of the frame analysis showed that Turkish newspapers build representations within the frames of *power, war, light, kinship, valuable assets* and *natural forces*. The results of perspectivation analysis revealed that nationalism and ideological positions in the axis of secularism versus conservatism play a major role to determine how sportswomen are presented and included in the news.

By taking a feminist critical discourse standpoint to the data, our analysis illustrated that the Turkish sportswomen are included as national prides, heroines and model citizens with a marked absence of sexualized representations. The inclusion of sportswomen in news texts are mainly performed by means of a nationalist ideology to celebrate national values and ideals. Competing and conflicting ideological positions were observed to be key elements which characterize the representation of Olympic sportswomen. Through the use of ideological perspectivation strategies employed by newspapers, Turkish sportswomen's sporting bodies and identities are instrumentalised as ideological symbols on which political ideologies are reaffirmed.

The analysis presented in this chapter highlights that discursive inclusion and exclusion of sportswomen have complex and multiple layers. An intersectional focus considering nationalism, ideology, socio-political dynamics of local settings in addition to gender can significantly change the ways of looking into sportswomen's media coverages. Such an intersectional lens can significantly contribute to the analyses on media texts for future research. The representation of Olympic athletes goes hand in hand with the broader and historically-constructed political standpoints and atmospheres, which also transform the ways exclusion and inclusion are linguistically and discursively built. In our context, linguistic and discursive choices of the media outlets are used as powerful tools in the instrumentalization of Olympic sportswomen to (in)validate ideological standpoints. Inclusion and exclusion of women athletes are fundamentally shaped by political ideologies and reflect the controversial political atmosphere in the country.

Our chapter also offers practical implications for practitioners and stakeholders. Given the scope of the research we have reported in this chapter, the main stakeholders for any plausible practical implication promoted would be geared towards the education and awareness raising of "the newsroom", i.e., journalists, sports writers and news editors. Undoubtedly, "the newsroom" and its members in any media outlet and their visual and linguistic preferences regarding the type of sports coverage they do is an immensely powerful tool in shaping norms and stereotypes about gender, and sportswomen, in particular. The media can construct, maintain and challenge norms and previous representations. The adoption of "gender mainstreaming" (Geertsema-Sligh 2014: 83) (i.e., the linguistic antithesis of gender marginalization) in newsrooms and media outlets could, in the long run, promote a more balanced and fair coverage and portrayal of sportspeople– irrespective of their genders. The most basic way forward would be the reversal of the ideation of a sportswoman as a "woman first and athlete second". The adoption of the principle as a working policy for media outlets could ultimately pave the way for the emergence of a less discriminatory, more inclusive and equitable society and media. This colossal task, however, would need to start with a reform of education programs and curricula for journalism at the design and implementation stages, following Josephi (2019: 47) who describes journalism education as a strong "agent of change". It would entail educating media professionals with a gender and critical media literacy perspective and transforming not the journalists/reporters of today but that of tomorrow.

References

Billings, Andrew. C. & Susan Tyler Eastman. 2002. Selective representation of gender, ethnicity, and nationality in American television coverage of the 2000 summer Olympics. *International Review for the Sociology of Sport* 37(3–4). 351–370. https://doi.org/10.1177/101269020203700302

Billings, Andrew C., Chelsea. L. Brown, James H. Crout, Kristen E. McKenna, Bethany A. Rice, Mary Elise Timanus & Jonathan Ziegler. 2008. The games through the NBC lens: Gender, ethnic, and national equity in the 2006 Torino Winter Olympics. *Journal of Broadcasting & Electronic Media* 52 (2). 215–230. https://doi.org/10.1080/08838150801992003

Billings, Andrew C., James R. Angelini & Paul J. MacArthur. 2018. Olympics Television: Broadcasting the Biggest Show on Earth. London: Routledge.

Birrell, Susan &Mary G. McDonald. 2000. Reading sport, articulating power lines: An introduction. In Susan Birrell & Mary G. McDonald (eds.), *Reading Sport: Critical Essays on Power and Representation*, 3–13. Boston: Northeastern University Press.

Borcila, Andaluna. 2000. Nationalizing the Olympics around and away from "vulnerable" bodies of women: The NBC coverage of the 1996 Olympics and some moments after. *Journal of Sport and Social Issues* 24(2). 118–147. https://doi.org/10.1177/0193723500242003

Boykoff, Jules & Matthew Yasuoka. 2015. Gender and politics at the 2012 Olympics: Media coverage and its implications. *Sport in Society* 18(2). 219–233. https://doi.org/10.1080/17430437.2013.854481

Bruce, Tony. 2016. New rules for new times: Sportswomen and media representation in the third wave. *Sex Roles* 74. 361–376. https://doi.org/10.1007/s11199-015-0497-6

Cooky, Cherly & Dunja Antunovic. 2022. Serving Equality: Feminism, Media, and Women's Sports. New York: Peter Lang.

Cooky, Cherly, Michael A. Messner & Michela Musto. 2015. "It's dude time!": A quarter century of excluding women's sports in televised news and highlight shows. *Communication & Sport* 3(3). 261–287. https://doi.org/10.1177/2167479515588761

Daniels, Elizabeth & Heidi Wartena. 2011. Athlete or sex symbol: What boys think of media Representations of Female Athletes. *Sex Roles* 65(7–8), 566–579. https://doi.org/10.1007/s11199-011-9959-7

Duncan, Margaret Carlisle & Michael A. Messner. 1998. The media image of sport and gender. In Lawrence A. Wenner (ed.), *MediaSport*, 170–185. London: Routledge.

Edensor, Tim. 2002. *National Identity, Popular Culture and Everyday Life*. Oxford: Berg.

Entman, Robert. 1993. Framing: Toward clarification of a fractured paradigm. *Journal of Communication* 43(4). 51–8. https://doi.org/10.1111/j.1460-2466.1993.tb01304.x

Fairclough, Norman. 1992. *Discourse and Social Change*. Cambridge: Polity Press.

Fillmore, Charles. 1985. Frames and the semantics of understanding. *Quaderni di Semantica* 6(2). 222–53.

Fink, Janet S. 2015. Female athletes, women's sport, and the sport media commercial complex: Have we really "come a long way, baby"?. *Sport Management Review* 18(3). 331–342. https://doi.org/10.1016/j.smr.2014.05.001

Geertsema-Sligh, Margaretha. 2014. Gender mainstreaming in journalism education. In. In Montiel, Aimée Vega (ed.), *Media and Gender: A Scholarly Agenda for Global Alliance for Media and Gender* 83–86. Paris: UNESCO.

Goffman, Erving. 1967. *Interaction Ritual: Essays in Face-to-Face Behaviour*. New Brunswick: Aldine Transaction Publishers.

Josephi, Beate. 2019. Journalism education. In Wahl-Jorgensen, Karin & Thomas Hanitzsch (eds.), *The Handbook of Journalism Studies*, 42–58. New York: Routledge.

Kane, Mary Jo. 2013. The better sportswomen get, the more the media ignore them. *Communication & Sport* 1(3). 231–236. https://doi.org/10.1177/2167479513484579

Koca, Canan &Bengu Arslan. 2010. Turkish media coverage of the 2004 Olympics. In Toni Bruce, Jorid Hovden & Pirkko Markula (eds.), *Sportswomen at the Olympics: A Global Content Analysis of Newspaper Coverage*, 195–208. Leiden: Brill.

Koh, Eunha. 2009. Heroes, sisters and beauties: Korean printed media representation of sport women in the 2004 Olympics. In Pirkko Markula (ed.), *Olympic Women and the Media: International Perspectives*, 168–184. New York: Palgrave Macmillan.

Koh, Eunha. 2010. Media portrayal of Olympic athletes: Korean printed media during the 2004 Athens Olympics. In Toni Bruce, Jorid Hovden, & Pirkko Markula (eds.), *Sportswomen at the Olympics: A Global Content Analysis of Newspaper Coverage*, 237–254. Leiden: Brill.

Lazar, Michelle M. (2005) Politicizing gender in discourse: feminist critical discourse analysis as political perspective and praxis. In Michelle Lazar (ed.), Feminist Critical Discourse Analysis: Gender, Power and Ideology in Discourse, 1–30. Hampshire: Palgrave MacMillan.

Lazar, Michelle. 2007. Feminist critical discourse analysis: Articulating a feminist discourse praxis. *Critical Discourse Studies* 4(2), 141–164. http://dx.doi.org/10.1080/17405900701464816

Lazar, Michelle. 2014. Feminist critical discourse analysis. In Susan Ehrlich, Miriam Meyerhoff & Janet Holmes (eds.), The Handbook of Language, Gender and Sexuality, 180–199. West Sussex: Wiley Blackwell.

Markula, Pirkko. 2009. Introduction. In Pirkko Markula (ed.), *Olympic Women and the Media: International Perspectives*, 1–29. Basingstone: Palgrave Macmillan.

Markula, Pirkko,Tony Bruce & Jorid Hovden. 2010. Key themes in the research on media coverage of women's sport. In Toni Bruce, Jorid Hovden & Pirkko Markula (eds.) *Sportswomen at the Olympics: A Global Content Analysis of Newspaper Coverage*, 1–18. Leiden: Brill.

Messner, Michael A., Margaret Carlisle Duncan & Cherly Cooky. 2003. Silence, sports bras, And wrestling porn: Women in televised sports news and highlights shows. *Journal of Sport and Social Issues* 27(1). 38–51. https://doi.org/10.1177/0193732502239583

Minsky, Marvin. 1975. A framework for representing knowledge. In Patrick H. Winston (ed.) *The Psychology of Computer Vision*, 201–310. New York: McGraw-Hill Book.

Quin, Grégory, Élodie Wipf & Fabien Ohl. 2010. Media coverage of the Athens Olympic Games by the French press: The Olympic Games effect in L'Équipe and Le Monde. In Toni Bruce, Jorid Hovden & Pirkko Markula (eds.), *Sportswomen at the Olympics: A Global Content Analysis of Newspaper Coverage*, 103–114. Leiden: Brill.

Semino, Elina, Zsófia Demjén & Jane Demmen. 2018. An integrated approach to metaphor and framing in cognition, discourse, and practice, with an application to metaphors for cancer. *Applied Linguistics* 39 (5). 625–645. https://doi.org/10.1093/applin/amw028

Trujillo, Nick. 2000. Hegemonic masculinity on the mound. Media representations of Nolan Ryan and American Sports Culture. In Susan Birrell & Mary G. McDonald (eds.) *Reading Sport: Critical Essays on Power and Representation*, 14–39. Boston: Northeastern University Press.

van Dijk, Teun. 2001. Critical discourse analysis. In Deborah Schiffrin, Deborah Tannen & Heidi E. Hamilton (eds.), *The Handbook of Discourse Analysis*, 352–371. Malden: Wiley Blackwell.

Weber, Julia & Natalie Barker-Ruchti. 2012. Bending, Flirting, floating, flying: A critical analysis of female figures in 1970s gymnastics photographs. *Sociology of Sport Journal*, 29(1). 22–41. https://doi.org/10.1123/ssj.29.1.22

Wensing, Emma H. & Toni Bruce. 2003. Bending the rules: Media representations of gender during the international sporting event. *International Review for the Sociology of Sport*, 38(4). 387–396. https://doi.org/10.1177/1012690203384001

Wensing, Emma & Margaret Macneill. 2010. Gender Differences in Canadian English-language Newspaper Coverage of the 2004 Olympic Games. In Toni Bruce, Jorid Hovden, & Pirkko Markula (eds.), *Sportswomen at the Olympics: A Global Content Analysis of Newspaper Coverage*, 167–182. Leiden: Brill.

Wodak, Ruth. 2001. The discourse historical approach. In Ruth Wodak and Michael Meyer (eds.) *Methods of Critical Discourse Analysis*, 63–94. London: Sage.

Aimee Bailey and Lucy Jones

Chapter 9
"Fairness versus inclusion": Representations of transgender athletes in British newspaper reports

1 Introduction

In June 2022, the Fédération Internationale de Natation (FINA) announced its new policy on the participation of transgender athletes in global aquatic events. While the policy specifies the eligibility criteria for men's *and* women's events, it received widespread media attention due to the restrictive criteria set out for transgender women participating in the women's category. The policy states that trans women may compete in the category "if they can establish to FINA's comfortable satisfaction that they have not experienced any part of male puberty beyond Tanner Stage 2^1 or before age 12, whichever is later" (FINA 2022). In other words, trans women must have recognised their trans identity and accessed trans-affirming healthcare (most notably "puberty blockers"[2]), at an early age if they are to have a chance of competing in the category that aligns with their gender identity. Given that this requires athletes to have experienced no barriers in accessing this healthcare at such a young age – which is unlikely, given that puberty blockers are either illegal or subject to controversy in many countries around the world – the policy effectively bans trans women from competing in elite women's events.

When FINA's policy was introduced, it impacted one high-profile athlete in particular, Lia Thomas. Only a few months before FINA's ruling, Thomas, representing the University of Pennsylvania, became the first trans athlete to win the

---

1 "Tanner Stage 2" refers to the stage of sexual maturity at which puberty begins.
2 "Puberty blockers" are the colloquial term for hormone suppressants which delay the bodily changes that otherwise occur in puberty, such as menstruation and genital growth.

Acknowledgements: The authors would like to thank Jai Mackenzie for her thoughtful and invaluable comments on an earlier draft of this chapter, and the editors of this volume for the invitation to make this contribution.

Aimee Bailey, De Montfort University, United Kingdom
Lucy Jones, University of Nottingham, United Kingdom

National Collegiate Athletic Association's Division I championship for the women's 500-yard freestyle event. Her success was picked up by the press and framed by many as unfair to the cisgender women (those assigned female at birth) she competed against. Indeed, it seems likely that Thomas's win informed FINA's policy, and – as we will show below – the ruling was often positioned in newspapers as a move which would ban her, in particular, from competing in the future. This story became newsworthy in part because the notion of trans inclusion in sport challenges the use of long-standing categories rooted in the concept of sex as a binary and immutable fact – something which has proven to be deeply controversial; this will be demonstrated in the data below. The issue also relates to broader discourse around the inclusion of trans women in female spaces more generally; this has become highly divisive, as "gender critical" voices argue that trans inclusion threatens women's "sex-based rights".

We therefore take the story of Lia Thomas's win and the subsequent FINA ruling as a case study in this chapter, one which offers a window into how news reporting has represented the question of trans inclusion in elite sport. We use corpus-assisted critical discourse analysis to unpack the discourses surrounding Thomas in the British press in the run-up to her championship win and FINA's landmark ruling on trans inclusion. Approaching the data from a queer, feminist, trans linguistic perspective, we examine the cisnormative basis of the data, with cisnormativity referring to the "idea that cisgender identities are 'normal,' 'natural,' and 'factual,' while transgender identities are 'abnormal,' 'unnatural,' and 'fictional.'" (Zimman 2018: 176).

2 Literature review

2.1 Queer and trans linguistics

As mentioned above, we take a critical approach in this chapter. Specifically, our analysis draws on both *queer linguistic* and *trans linguistic* perspectives. Queer approaches to linguistics have the explicit political aim of problematising heteronormative ideologies as they are reproduced in language (Motschenbacher and Stegu 2013). This means that queer linguists challenge discourses which, by reproducing normative expectations around gender and sexuality, position all subjects other than cisgender heterosexuals as "other". For example, queer linguists have found that implicit strategies are deployed by opponents of same-sex marriage to discursively position same–sex couples as a threat to heterosexuals and reproduce heteronormative ideology (Love and Baker 2015; Turner et al. 2017).

A trans linguistic approach follows the aims of queer linguistics but, in addition, has the explicit intention of amplifying trans people's perspectives and challenging transphobia. Although trans linguistics as an approach has only recently been defined and labelled (Zimman 2021), an established body of research which meets these aims has investigated the representation of trans people in contemporary media. For example, in Baker's (2014a) exploratory study of British newspaper coverage of trans people during 2012, he finds a pattern of trans people being painted as easily offended, and as "freakish objects" that were associated with sex scandals and jokes about genitalia (2014a: 223). Similarly, in the US context, Billard (2016) finds common use of misgendering through, for example, using a subject's birth name rather than their chosen name and the use of pronouns which conflict with an individual's identifying gender. Billard also found there to be a preoccupation with trans people's bodies and medical histories in US newspapers. Zottola's (2018) corpus study of British newspapers finds that trans people are typically portrayed as dangerous, with tabloids in particular aligning trans people with criminality.

Compared to his corpus of data from 2012 (Baker 2013), Baker (2019) finds approximately 3.5 times as many stories about trans people in the British press in 2018–2019, with a particular increase in stories about "the trans lobby" and articles which question the prevalence of British broadsheets, whereby "politically correct (PC) language and anti-discrimination policy, which is meant to prevent causing harm to marginalised groups, [is framed as] infringing on the human right to freedom of expression" (Montiel-McCann 2022: 9). It is evident from these analyses that' practices intended to create equality for trans people – and trans people themselves – are portrayed as dangerous, with the rights of the majority being framed as under threat. Although much of this representation is not explicit in discriminating against trans people, in that it does not typically articulate disgust or hatred towards them, sociolinguistic studies to date have found ample evidence of a more implicit form of transphobia in newspapers.

This coverage can be linked to the rise in "gender critical feminism", a political perspective within the UK context which seeks to "advance what its acolytes refer to as 'women's sex-based rights'" (Borba 2022: 74). Key to this perspective is the cisnormative stance that biological sex (particularly genitalia) determines whether somebody is a woman, not gender identity, which therefore means that trans women should not be allowed access to women-only spaces (Pearce et al. 2020). Clear similarities have been observed between the gender critical position and anti-genderism, a global movement characterised by a "far-right populist rhetoric" and an ultra-conservative stance towards topics such as homosexuality and reproductive rights (Borba 2022; Honkasalo 2022). The movement uses feminist rhetoric to advance anti-feminist agendas and relies on the concept of "gender ideology" to position traditionally privileged groups as under threat, and to "[shield] its users from being accused of bigotry" (Borba 2022: 59).

In this chapter, we follow a trans linguistic approach by investigating implicit transphobia and gender critical discourse in newspaper representations of the inclusion of trans women in sports. We endeavour to act here as trans allies, which includes acknowledging that our experience as cisgender researchers will lead to potential blind-spots in our analysis. We therefore cite wherever possible commentary from trans scholars and writers who, through their subjective experience of being trans, are best placed to comment on the potential impact of transphobic discourse (see Jones 2022).

2.2 Trans inclusion in sport

The gender critical discourse outlined above is particularly productive within the context of professional sports competition. As competitions typically rely on a strictly binary, sex-segregated system, it has been extremely difficult for trans athletes to take part. Elite sport's reliance on sex distinction has a long history, with "sex verification testing" (including gynaecological examinations and chromosomal tests) taking place since the 1960s; this "illustrates the extent to which sport organisations have invested in a segregated system organised around a binary understanding of sex" (Love 2014: 377). Key to this tradition are concerns around fairness; for athletes to be fairly matched in physical challenges, factors such as testosterone levels or stature (which are ideologically, but problematically, assumed to be consistent between the sexes) are required to be comparable.

Even in cases where policies have been developed with the apparent intention to *include* trans athletes, their requirements can actively *exclude* those without legal status of their identifying gender or a particular medical history. As Love (2014: 379) argues, this excludes intersex athletes (many of whom have been disqualified) and those without the means to engage in the specific type of transition required. Furthermore, many policies impacting trans women and intersex people insist on hormone treatment; the World Athletics federation, for example, requires all women (whether trans or cis) with testosterone levels classified as higher than average to either take medication to reduce the difference between them and other sportswomen or compete against men. From a queer theoretical perspective, however, such actions do not create fairness: they stigmatise and punish those who sit outside of a pre-defined norm which is determined by cis-normative ideology.

Unsurprisingly, the issue of trans inclusion in elite sports has been widely discussed in the media, but trans sportswriters have communicated their frustration at how the subject tends to be covered. Sports journalist Emma Smith argues that news coverage creates "an atmosphere of fear and prejudice" which ultimately frames trans inclusion as "toxic", while football blogger Grace Robertson describes coverage of trans people in sport as "viewing us as a problem to be solved rather than human beings with any kind of agency" (cited in Smith 2021). This is reflected in the findings of sports scholars Lucas and Newhall (2019), who comment on the relative invisibility of trans athletes within sports media websites and publications. Typically, they argue, stories about trans athletes attempting to access sporting domains are prioritised over stories of trans athletes being successful in their sporting endeavours, meaning that reports of contexts in which they are unwelcome gain hypervisibility. They find that trans sportspeople are most commonly discussed in terms of "the issue" of trans inclusion, with debates being constructed about the "fairness" of their participation in elite competitions and the need for an "equal playing field" (Lucas and Newhall 2019: 108); the prevalent discourse of fairness is often enabled by the framing of trans women athletes as cheating or having an unfair advantage due to the "residual benefit" of their hormonal past (Lucas and Newhall 2019: 113).

Trans author Julia Serano argues that this discourse stems from the cisnormative framing of a trans woman as "a man in a dress", a conservative position which fuels the notion of men "'invading' women's spaces" (cited in Webb, 2021). This is supported by the findings of Knott-Fayle et al.'s (2021) discursive psychology analysis of media texts concerning trans inclusion. They consider responses to tennis champion Martina Navratilova's 2018/2019 arguments against trans women's inclusion in female sports, finding cisgenderism – the process of delegitimizing trans people on the basis of cisnormativity – to be highly prevalent. For example, discourse positioning self-identification as absurd (by framing it in terms of a man "deciding to become female") facilitates the argument that trans women would essentially be cheating if they competed as female athletes, drawing links between this and the use of performance enhancing drugs. Again, then, "fairness" is a key theme in this discourse, as is suspicion and scepticism around the legitimacy of trans identity.

This review demonstrates that trans people are likely to face discriminatory coverage in the British press. Assumptions of binarity and cisnormativity underpin much of the representation found; trans people's existence is often reduced to their bodies, which are othered and problematised, and they are frequently treated with suspicion as potential threats. When trans people are discussed in the context of elite sports, their bodies become even more central to the narrative; the cisnormative assumption that male bodies are stronger and bigger than female bodies informs the rhetoric that any athlete assigned male at birth would have an unfair physiological advantage. The reliance on sex segregation by elite sport organisations has evidently made it extremely difficult for trans athletes to gain acceptance, and this may be exacerbated by a mainstream media which is apparently hostile to *all* trans people.

Below, we explore in more detail the themes of binarity, cisnormativity, implicit transphobia and the construction of trans people as a threat. We do this through our analysis of news coverage relating to the case study described above: swimmer Lia Thomas's win in a NCAA women's 500-yard freestyle event, and the FINA ban which followed. Firstly, however, we outline our methods of data collection and analysis.

3 Methodology

3.1 Corpus-assisted critical discourse analysis

To explore the representation of Thomas, we use a combination of corpus linguistics and critical discourse analysis (CDA). Corpus linguistics provides concepts and methods for investigating recurrent patterns of language through large electronic collections of text (corpora) (Baker 2014b). Critical discourse analysis is an issue-oriented approach, aiming to uncover ideologies in text and talk that work to reproduce or resist power, dominance and inequality in society (van Dijk 2015; see also Chimbwete-Phiri and Schnurr this volume). The combination of corpus linguistics and critical discourse analysis is believed to offer a "best-of-both-worlds scenario", where the addition of one approach remedies some of the limitations of the other (Mautner 2009: 125). Most notably, it facilitates the use of qualitative and quantitative procedures and captures both incremental and context-specific uses of discourse; this is well-established in queer linguistic research (e.g., Baker 2014a, 2019; Bailey 2019; Jones and Collins 2020).

As described above, our analytical approach is informed by queer and trans-perspectives, aiming to uncover the mechanisms of heteronormativity and cisnormativity in discourse. Our approach also draws on feminist CDA, which is aimed at "critiquing discourses which sustain a patriarchal social order: that is, relations of power that systematically [. . .] disadvantage, exclude and disempower women as a social group" (Lazar 2005: 6). As we are taking a trans linguistic perspective here, we are aligned with these goals, while recognising the specificities of trans women's experiences that cis women do not share (Faye 2021). These perspectives therefore help us to understand how media language reinforces, or in some cases challenges, trans women's exclusion from sex-segregated sport.

3.2 Building the corpus

A specialised corpus was built for the study by searching Nexis for UK newspaper articles containing the full term "Lia Thomas". Although Thomas' story has been reported on globally, we decided to focus on the UK context for two key reasons. Firstly, the story has implications for UK-specific policy: while international governing bodies such as FINA set standards, it is up to local governing bodies to accept them. At the time of data collection, FINA's decision was supported by then Prime Minister Boris Johnson and Secretary of State for Digital, Culture, Media and Sport Nadine Dorries, with other sports encouraged to follow suit. Secondly, as discussed above, there has been a rise in "gender critical feminism" within the UK, and sport is a key area of contention regarding trans rights. Focusing on the UK context also allows us to build on existing large-scale studies of trans representation, most of which have examined British newspapers (e.g., Baker 2014a, 2019; Zottola 2020). Like previous studies, we also restricted our corpus to print newspaper articles; this allowed us to avoid duplication, since many print articles were also published in online format. We collected articles published between 1 December 2021 and 30 June 2022. This timeframe encompasses Thomas' first publicised win at a women's event, her first mention in the British press (starting with a *Daily Mail* column by the journalist Piers Morgan), her success as the first trans NCAA Division I champion, and FINA's June 2022 ruling on trans athletes.

Our criteria resulted in a corpus of 225 articles totalling 162,936 words. It was compiled from ten national newspapers, including their Sunday editions: *The Independent* (53 articles), *The Telegraph* (45 articles), *The Mail* (38 articles), *The Times* (35 articles), *The Sun* (20 articles), *The Guardian* (15 articles), *The Express* (7 articles), *The Mirror* (4 articles), *The Evening Standard* (4 articles) and *The Star* (4 articles). A breakdown of the corpus is shown in Figure 1. We decided not to separate the newspapers into sub-corpora by type, due to the imperfect nature of the categories; for example, while *The Guardian* is generally considered a broadsheet in terms of content, it has been published in tabloid format since 2018. Metalinguistic tagging did, however, make it possible to identify any patterns specific to a particular publication.

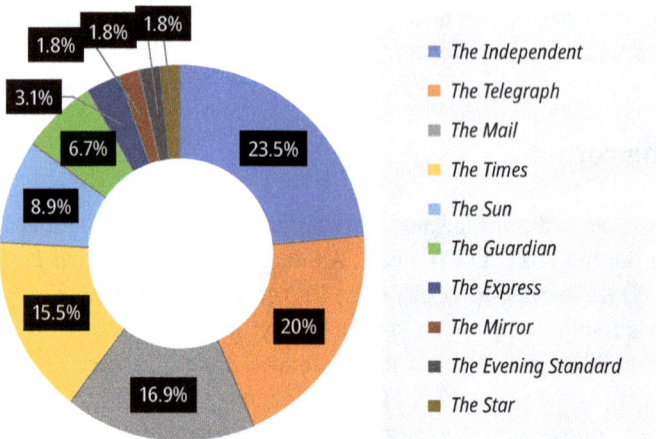

Figure 1: Breakdown of the Lia Thomas corpus by number of articles.

3.3 Analysing the corpus

Our analysis was conducted using the online corpus analysis interface Sketch Engine (Kilgarriff et al. 2014). An initial overview of the corpus, in the form of keywords, guided our analysis. The keyword procedure reveals words which are statistically more significant in one corpus (the focus corpus) compared to another (the reference corpus). We compared our corpus to The English Timestamped Monitor Corpus which, at over 60 billion words, is the largest corpus available on Sketch Engine. The corpus is made up of news articles collected between 2014 and 2021, and is therefore well-suited for comparison with our data. The results were ranked by Sketch Engine's default keyword statistic Simple Maths, and we narrowed down the results to focus on the top 50 keywords (Table 1). Although this cut-off point was arbitrary, we found it was sufficient to gain key entry points into the data. We then grouped the results into categories, two of which are analysed in this chapter: sex and gender, and inclusion and fairness. These categories point to the crux of the debate over trans women's inclusion in elite sport and therefore allow us to examine how constructions of sex and gender underpin the concepts of inclusion and fairness in this discourse.

From this point, we used collocation and concordance procedures to zoom in on our keywords. Collocation marks the statistically significant relationship between words, premised on the idea that a word's meaning is shaped by the company it typically keeps. Collocates are therefore words that "have a tendency to occur near or next to each other in naturally occurring language use" (Baker 2014b: 24). We

Table 1: Top 50 keywords in the "Lia Thomas" corpus.

	Item	Focus freq.	Ref freq.	Score
1	trans	956	635276	265.99
2	lia	414	32921	209.95
3	transgender	737	887220	172.68
4	swimmer	323	192347	134.82
5	testosterone	296	159706	128.29
6	fina	173	30952	88.524
7	athletes	530	2191749	68.298
8	uci	143	88501	68.01
9	puberty	141	79739	67.822
10	swimming	355	1348586	64.656
11	fairness	158	465142	50.864
12	thomas	645	4154454	49.505
13	compete	418	2629990	46.828
14	bridges	204	943102	46.485
15	sport	601	4189519	45.807
16	governing	201	945746	45.735
17	biological	187	899259	43.814
18	ncaa	246	1453182	42.731
19	freestyle	116	324914	42.616
20	swimmers	101	248639	40.174
21	cycling	159	831097	38.977
22	hormone	96	290822	36.6
23	athlete	164	1029984	35.577
24	coe	69	92403	33.113
25	female	470	4613038	32.998
26	male	342	3243419	32.392
27	ioc	71	182648	30.58
28	davies	101	550046	30.514
29	sharron	55	10666	29.615
30	competing	184	1669226	29.126
31	gender	255	2590379	28.994
32	inclusion	151	1270681	28.792
33	starmer	57	61918	28.603
34	keir	56	66233	27.96
35	athletics	107	791561	27.077
36	transitioning	68	265266	26.821
37	weyant	48	1640	26.303
38	olympic	186	1977407	26.055
39	unfair	103	901948	24.289
40	rowling	51	107528	24.245
41	elite	170	1981174	23.803
42	omnium	43	10720	23.367
43	transphobic	44	34024	23.132

Table 1 (continued)

	Item	Focus freq.	Ref freq.	Score
44	cyclist	57	244024	23.106
45	emily	99	927347	22.999
46	championships	145	1787940	21.919
47	biology	75	623644	21.539
48	transitioned	48	172219	21.18
49	jk	42	97316	20.376
50	males	68	602747	19.891

specified that collocates should occur within five words to the left and five words to the right of the search term and, to make the analysis manageable, they should have a minimum frequency of 5 and a minimum Mutual Information score of 6. Mutual Information is a statistic that compares the number of times words appear together (as collocates) to the number of times they appear separately. Concordancing provides a more detailed view of a word's *usage, by displaying* a concordance is a list of all the occurrences of a certain search term in a corpus, accompanied by their immediate co-text on the left and right. The concordance procedure enables close qualitative analysis of corpus results, making it possible to identify salient patterns in usage (Baker 2014b).

We focus below on the keywords from Table 1 which produce the two categories under consideration here: sex and gender, and inclusion and fairness. We examine frequent collocates of these keywords and provide concordance examples of their use in context, conducting qualitative analysis on selected extracts from the newspaper articles they appear in. We have chosen extracts for closer scrutiny which demonstrate the patterns identified in our quantitative analysis.

4 Analysis

4.1 Sex and gender

The most prominent theme within our keywords is sex and gender; 14 words out of 50 (28%) fit into this category. This encompasses words which refer to: trans identity or experience (*trans, transgender, transitioning, transphobic, transitioned*); sexual characteristics and processes (*testosterone, puberty, biological, hormone, biology*); binary categories (*female, male, males*) and *gender* itself. The two most frequent, and respectively the most and third-most key terms in the corpus, are *trans* (n = 956) and *transgender* (n = 737). The terms are both more frequent than Thomas' name (*Thomas* = 645, *Lia* = 414) – the search term used to build the corpus – which reflects Thomas' position within a wider debate based on a sexed and gendered category. *Trans* is 30% more frequent than *transgender* which, compared with previous studies, indicates a terminology shift in the British press. Baker (2014a) found that *transgender* was three times more common than *trans* in 2012 and that they were equally as common in 2018/2019. Other terms highlighted by previous studies are very infrequent in our corpus, including *transsexual* (n = 4), *tranny* (n = 1) and *transvestite* (n = 1). There is therefore a clear preference for *trans* and *transgender* in the representation of Lia Thomas.

As their collocations show (Table 2), there are differences in the way the two terms are used. *Trans* is used more in relation to social and political groups (*extremists, advocates, lobby, activist(s)*) and in relation to conflict (*anger, attacks, exclude*,*[3] *argue*). In comparison, *transgender* is used more in relation to official regulation (*bar*, ban*, participati*, eligibility, reviewing, document*) and institutions (*America's, collegiate*). The theme of novelty also occurs here, with collocates that refer to Thomas' status as the first trans woman to win a NCAA title (*became, openly, known, first*). In both sets of collocates, it is clear that the discourse extends far beyond Thomas' individual story, to include collectives (e.g., *activists, athletes*), other sports (*cycling's*) and broader contexts (e.g., *toilets*). These themes will be discussed further as we turn to look at the use of these collocations in context.

Table 2: Collocates of trans and transgender, listed in order of statistical significance.

Term	Collocates
trans	drops, younger, exclude, extremists, advocates, anger, attacks, lobby, excluded, argue, activists, toilets, retain, male-to-female, activist, person's, women
transgender	sport-by-sport, non-binary, student-athletes, bar, banning, male-to-female, became, athletes', banned, openly, participating, win, eligibility, known, backed, players, cyclist, participation, bans, major, America's, athletes, barred, athlete, cycling's, ban, reviewing, first, under, document, collegiate

The phrase *trans activist* (n = 24) is used to support explicitly negative stances towards trans inclusion in 96% of occurrences in the corpus. Trans activists are

---

[3] The asterisk denotes a wildcard to include any string of letters following those specified. For example, *exclude** includes *exclude* and *excluded*.

characterised as behaving in aggressive, confrontational and manipulative ways; a representative example is given below:

(1) The more the debate is so crudely warped, the more reluctant people are to venture even reasonable scepticism about a natal male becoming a female swimming champion. It is the same everywhere you look: whenever JK Rowling articulates her conviction that women's sex-based rights should be defended, she receives death threats or has her address published online by **trans activists** perversely masquerading as beacons of tolerance. (*The Daily Telegraph*)

Extract 1 sets up a binary opposition between sceptics of trans inclusion, whose concerns are labelled as "reasonable", and supporters of trans inclusion, who are by implication, unreasonable. The debate is described as "crudely warped", with the adjective "warped" presenting it as being twisted out of its normal shape and the adverb "crudely" connoting immorality and poor quality. Immorality is further emphasised through the adverb "perversely", with the supposed inclusivity of trans activists marked as artificial ("masquerading as beacons of tolerance") due to their aggressive behaviour. Those responsible for this are portrayed as the sum total of their politics through the noun "activists", while those trying to engage in "reasoned" debate are described simply through the generic noun "people". One example of the latter is given through the reference to JK Rowling, an author well-known for her "gender critical" views. Indeed, the term "women's sex-based rights" is used here; as argued by Borba (2022), this is representative of "gender critical feminist" discourse. Rowling is described as "defending" women's sex-based rights, which positions them as under attack. This is reflected in the preceding line which contrasts "natal male" with "female swimming champion". The use of sex-binary terms supports the proposition that Thomas' biology is incompatible with the sporting category. This is underscored by the use of the modifier "natal", which positions biological sex as being fixed at birth.

While the use of the phrase "trans activists" is predominantly limited to the right-leaning press, the use of the term "natal" is also found in the left-leaning press, as the following example demonstrates:

(2) In a notable intervention, the scientists warn that IOC's new guidance – which states there is no need for trans women to lower their testosterone to compete against **natal** women – ignores the science on sex, gender and performance and focuses mostly on inclusion. (*The Guardian*)

In Extract 2, "natal" is again used to mark a distinction between two groups of people. However, unlike Extract 1, which contrasts sex categories, the distinction is between two gendered categories: "trans women" and "natal women". The choice of the phrase "natal women", rather than cis women, is striking in its association with trans-exclusionary discourse; it is the semantic equivalent of the term "women-born-women", a term which is reminiscent of trans-exclusionary events such as the Michigan Women's Festival (Williams 2020). There is also a link with gender critical feminism within the same publication, as another article from *The Guardian* includes the term "natal" next to a quotation from a spokesperson for Fair Play for Women, a group who campaign for women's "sex-based rights" in the UK (Pearce et al. 2020). Thus, while the stance against trans inclusion is less explicit in Extract 2 than Extract 1, being constructed through the proxy of scientists' warnings, it is implicitly signalled through word choice.

As stated above, the use of the term *transgender* is more commonly used in the context of official regulation. It frequently collocates with the term *ban** (n = 69), referring to the decision of sporting bodies to ban trans women from competing in women's events. The below extract, written by celebrity businesswoman Karren Brady, offers an example of this:

(3) I'm sure I am not the only person out there who is relieved the swimming body FINA has **banned transgender** swimmers such as Lia Thomas from competing in elite women's races. (. . .) Before anyone reaches for their phone to troll me, I think I share the view of lots of women who are also not transphobic, but who are confused about where they should stand on this issue. It is so blatantly unfair that anyone who has gone through male puberty should compete on the same platform as someone born biologically female. To point that out is not being transphobic, and to suggest otherwise is no more than bullying. (*The Sun*)

Using the first person, Brady's opinion piece celebrates FINA's ban and presents a "common sense" argument against the inclusion of trans women in elite women's competitions. She uses two constructions to position her view as a common one ("I'm sure I am not the only person", "I think I share the views of lots of women"). The former expresses certainty, while the latter, through the verb "share", invokes a sense of solidarity with others. Those who share her views are labelled simply as "women", without premodifiers such as *cis*, indicating her discursive exclusion of trans women from the category.

Brady disavows the labelling of her views as transphobic. She claims that "to point that out" ("that" being her opinion that it is "blatantly unfair" to include trans women) is not transphobic, despite this being an evaluative judgement rather than a factual statement. Similar to Extract 1, she presents herself as the victim of aggressive behaviour, being on the receiving end of trolling and bullying. Importantly, Brady's determination of what is not transphobic is based on her own understanding of transphobia, an understanding commensurate with her privilege as a cis person (who cannot be subjected to transphobia) and reflective of a cisnormative worldview (where it is obvious that trans women's participation in women's sport is "unfair"). As in the previous extracts, biology is alluded to as justification for her stance; "biologically female" is juxtaposed with "male puberty". Again, sex differences are privileged over gender identity, and the cisnormative assumption that a trans woman would inevitably have a physical advantage over a cis woman is reified.

As the extracts above demonstrate, the focus on sex differences is fundamental to the representation of trans women in our corpus. This is most frequently seen through the deployment of the binary sex categories, *female** (n = 534) and *male** (n = 410). Female is the more frequent term of the two, which is to be expected given that participation in the female category is the subject of debate in relation to Thomas. However, *male* appears in the keyword list (Table 1) twice, in its singular and plural forms, and often reflects more contentious propositions towards trans inclusion, as illustrated below:

(4) TRANS swimmer Lia Thomas, who is said to still have **male** genitalia, apparently likes to wander naked around the ladies' changing rooms. As she's also sexually attracted to women, this understandably makes her teammates feel deeply uncomfortable. I'm starting to think that, **male** or **female**, Lia is at best a fool, at worst a thoroughly nasty piece of work. (*Mail on Sunday*)

This extract comprises the full text, part of a series of short opinion pieces by columnist Sarah Vine. Through the amplification of rumours ("who is said to", "apparently likes to"), Vine constructs Thomas as a threat to her (implicitly cis) teammates. As discussed above, the exclusion of trans women in women-only spaces is a key theme within gender critical discourse; through a combination of embodiment ("male genitalia") and behaviour ("wander naked"), we argue that Vine draws on transphobic discourse to frame Thomas as a potential predator. Furthermore, Thomas' sexual orientation ("sexually attracted to women") is linked to making her teammates feel "deeply uncomfortable", a sentiment with which the author sympathises ("understandably"). This implies that women-desiring women do not belong in women's changing rooms; this is, we argue, also an example of homophobic discourse due to its effect of "stereotyping, tabooing, punishing [and] stigmatizing homosexuality" (Baker and Ellece 2011: 56).

The attack continues by labelling Thomas as either a "fool" or as "nasty", implying that she is either unthinking or deliberately offensive. The premodification of "nasty" with "thoroughly" suggests Vine believes the latter because "fool" (a relatively inoffensive word) is comparatively backgrounded through its lack of modification. Furthermore, the idiom "piece of work" connotes unpleasantness and maliciousness, so in itself its use is damning. To premodify this with "thoroughly nasty" leaves no ambiguity as to the way that Vine means to frame Thomas: as a potential predator. That this evaluation is drawn in relation to the claim about Thomas's genitalia suggests that Baker's (2014a) finding that trans people are positioned as "freakish" through the objectification of their genitalia remains true a decade later and reflects the argument of trans writers that popular culture remains preoccupied with trans people's bodies (e.g., Lester 2017; Faye 2021). Indeed, by including it in this brief opinion piece, itself published in the best-selling print newspaper in the UK (Tobitt and Majid 2022), Vine makes the question of Thomas's genitalia newsworthy and increases the unwanted and intrusive attention trans people are subjected to. Furthermore, this transphobic and homophobic piece effectively frames Thomas – and, by extension, all trans people – as dangerous and abnormal.

Having looked at the way the debate is underpinned by limited and problematic conceptions of sex and gender, we now turn to examine the crux of the debate: the issues of inclusion and fairness.

4.2 Inclusion and fairness

As mentioned in section 3.3, inclusion is a marked theme in the corpus, relating to three words in the keyword list: *inclusion, fairness* and *unfair*. We now consider each of these in turn.

Inclusion is more than five times as likely to be mentioned than its direct antonym exclusion (*inclu** = 326, *exclu** = 62). Instead, inclusion is more commonly discussed in relation to fairness (*fair** = 298). *Fairness* is a top collocate of *inclu** with 36 co-occurrences. The terms are predominantly presented in opposition, linked by constructions such as *balance X and Y* (n = 17), *or* (n = 6) and *versus* (n = 3). An example of how the term interact is given below:

(5) It is as if the UCI know the reality, the parameters, of the **fairness versus inclusion** debate, but don't know how to acknowledge them. [. . .] Clearly, there must be a border where **fairness trumps inclusivity**. Bridges can compete as a women [sic] for her university, for her club, as the alternative is to deny her access to her sport; but is it right that she takes the place of a woman who has trained all her life with elite participation as the goal? Who has her sights on a professional career, maybe the Olympics? Who has trained and sacrificed with none of the advantages of a born male? (*Mail on Sunday*)

In this extract, Thomas is linked with Emily Bridges, a British trans cyclist who was prevented from competing in a women's race (the National Omnium Championships) by the international governing body for cycling (the UCI) during the period of our data collection. "Fairness" and "inclusion" are firstly positioned as competing priorities through the conjunction "versus", and secondly as hierarchical through the verb "trump", thus implying that fairness is more important. This is illustrated by comparing Bridges' participation in women's sport with a hypothetical cisgender competitor. Bridges represents the perils of inclusion, occupying a position unfairly due to having "the advantages of a born male". Through the determiner "the", it is presented as a simple fact that trans women have certain (unspecified) physical advantages over cis women. This reflects most concordances for the collocation, where fairness is configured to mean fairness towards cis women, rather than trans women.

The hypothetical cis athlete in this example represents the morality of fairness, signalled through the construction of the interrogative phrase "is it right". This argumentation strategy also paints her as more deserving of elite competition than a trans woman, not simply in terms of biology but an apparently greater dedication to her sport: Bridges is framed as an interloper who "takes the place of a woman who has trained all her life". This phrasing suggests that the place already belongs to the woman, that it is her "sex-based right" to have it. It implies that Bridges has not worked as hard as her cis opponents, and thus that she has an unfair advantage due to being trans; this reflects Lucas and Newhall's (2019) finding that trans athletes are often represented in the media as cheats. An unquestioned cisnormative assumption underpins this argument: that those assigned male at birth always have a physical advantage over those assigned female. The framing of Bridges as "a born male" transforms this assumption into fact and then uses it to justify the argument against trans inclusion.

In some extracts from the data, the creation of a new, open category is positioned as a way to navigate the problem of inclusion and fairness. The extract below, written by former Olympic swimmer, Sharron Davies, offers an example of this:

(6) We need reasonable discussion based on facts and science, not ideology and feelings that only one group in the debate is allowed to have. UK Sports Council policy says that "the inclusion of transgender people into female sport cannot be balanced regarding transgender **inclusion, fairness** and safety in gender-affected sport". [. . .] An open category is the **fairest** way of achieving trans **inclusion** and **fair play** and protection of the female classification. (*The Times*)

Echoing the phrasing used in Extract 1, there is an appeal to reason ("we need reasonable discussion"), which implicitly positions Davies' concerns as being fair. There is also an appeal to authority and objective reality ("facts and science") which is negatively contrasted with subjectivity ("ideology and feelings"). This, we argue, has traces of anti-genderism discourse, in which "ideology" is "used in the most Marxist fashion as distortions of a (biological God-driven) reality" against which opponents must work to reveal the truth (Borba 2022: 62). Extending upon the theme in the corpus whereby the social group *trans activists* are framed as manipulative, supporters of trans inclusion here are aligned with false beliefs and emotions. Their emotions are constructed as unfairly privileged through the phrase "allowed to have" although, in our corpus, it is actually the feelings of cisgender opponents who receive the most coverage. The inclusion of the direct quotation

Chapter 9 "Fairness versus inclusion" — **209**

from UK Sports Council, in which "inclusion", "fairness" and "safety" are presented as incompatible priorities, supports the proposition that one must choose between them. Davies avoids doing this directly as the open category is presented as "achieving trans inclusion and fair play". She thus represents herself as reasonable, having considered both "sides", whilst indicating via repetition ("fairest way", "fair play") and perspective ("protection of the female classification") that she favours fairness.

The construction of fairness can be further explored by looking at the concordances for the third and final keyword in this category, *unfair*. In line with the use of *fairness*, *unfair* typically reflects the view that trans women competing in female sports is unfair to cis women, although unfairness towards trans women is occasionally considered. The example below illustrates both:

(7) Before I go any further, I despise anti-trans bigotry. Indeed, I'd hope I would despise any prejudice shown towards any minority group but the way Thomas, with her residual masculine strength, beat her opponents at the recent NCAA championship seemed grossly **unfair**. On the podium her opponents cowered beneath her huge frame. Actually, I thought it **unfair** on Thomas, too, who was ridiculed and even ostracised following her wins. (*The Times*)

In a similar vein to Extract 3, the unnamed author of Extract 7 offers disclaimers that they are not transphobic nor discriminatory ("I despise anti-trans bigotry, I'd hope I would despise any prejudice"). The differences in epistemic modality between these two phrases weakens the disclaimer; while the first phrase is clear and certain, expressed in the simple present tense, the second is less certain, expressed hypothetically. This is further weakened by the contrasting conjunction "but", which distinguishes the author's general evaluation of themselves from their specific view of Thomas who is seemingly an exceptional case.

Thomas' exceptionality is reflected in the premodification of "unfair" with "grossly" to describe her winning while having an unfair advantage ("residual masculine strength"). Thomas is painted as menacing in her physical appearance ("her huge frame"), which makes her opponents afraid; the fact that they are depicted through shrinking posture ("cowering") creates an exaggerated picture of the size difference. The author goes on to argue that the competition is "unfair on Thomas too", though this is comparatively backgrounded due to the lack of premodification and the positioning as an afterthought through the discourse marker "actually". Thomas is depicted as being treated poorly ("ridiculed and even ostracised"), although the sincerity of the author's sympathy is undermined by the preceding line in which Thomas is ridiculed for her size. This therefore functions as an argumentative strategy, not to call out negative behaviour towards Thomas in order to stop it, but rather to argue that trans women should be excluded for their own good.

As seen from the extracts above, the idea of trans women having a biological advantage is widespread in the data. Indeed, 49% of occurrences for *unfair* (n = 103) collocate with *advantage* (n = 50), 84% of which are the direct expression *unfair advantage*. While many of these instances are reaffirming the idea or reporting on the opinions of policymakers and celebrities, several articles from *The Independent* contest the notion:

(8) The argument made by Ms Hartzler and other critics is that trans athletes – specifically men who have transitioned to women – have an **unfair advantage** over "biological" women due to their strength. Ms Hartzler was formerly a women's track runner and coach. (. . .) "Women's sports are for women, not men pretending to be women," she says in the video. (. . .) While it appears Ms Hartzler is just trying to exploit a new culture war issue to rile up voters, her position – if not the dehumanizing way she presents it – does have some support among Democrats. (*The Independent*)

Unlike the others included in our discourse analysis above, this article is critical of those claiming that trans women have an unfair advantage, with the argument framed in terms of the "dehumanizing" way in which opponents, such as American congresswoman Vicky Hartzler, talk about trans people. The author suggests that a campaign ad of Hartzler's deliberately engages with the ongoing debate around trans inclusion (referenced as "a new culture war") in order to engage in "fear-mongering", taking a negative evaluative stance against her behaviour. This is also evident from the use of quotation marks around "biological"; the author indicates their awareness that the framing of cis people in this way is problematic given that it prioritises sex-based characteristics over gender identity. Nonetheless, the author of this article also uses the potentially harmful phrase "men who have transitioned to women". Whilst this foregrounds the importance of the process of transition, the preposition *to* implies a straightforward swapping from male to female. In fact, transition concerns a gradual process of affirmation and public claiming – whether socially, bodily, or otherwise – of an existing gender identity, rather than a switch from one to another (Lester 2017). While the evaluative tone of this article is broadly supportive of trans inclusion, then, it nonetheless relies on a problematic framing of trans identity.

5 Discussion and implications for practice

We have considered here two of the thematic categories that we identified within our corpus of newspaper articles discussing Lia Thomas: sex and gender, and inclusion and fairness. We have demonstrated that a trend in the corpus is to construct an opposition between inclusion and fairness, concepts which are configured in limited ways. Fairness relates to biological factors and is taken to mean fairness towards cis women, while inclusion relates to social factors and is taken to mean the inclusion of trans women. This ideological binary positions the needs of two groups of women in opposition, eliminating any crossover between them; what is fair for trans women, and the benefits that the inclusion of trans women may have for cis women, are not considered. Our findings mirror those of Lucas and Newhall (2019) and Knott-Fayle et al. (2021), in that trans inclusion is typically represented as a threat to the fairness of sport. Although a more liberal stance *does* exist within the corpus, the most frequently invoked argument is that allowing trans women to participate in women's sport would be unfair on cisgender women due to biological sex differences.

The focus on sex differences and the body (including genitalia) enables the argument against the inclusion of trans athletes in elite sport to be framed as common-sensical. We argue that this reinforces and reproduces the "gender critical" position gaining prominence in UK reporting of trans issues. It also demonstrates the prevalence of cisnormative ideology, which relies on a conservative, binary understanding of sex (Love 2014). Within the context of our corpus, this ideology involves the taken-for-granted assumption that those assigned male at birth *always* have physical and biological advantages over those assigned female. While it is assumed on this basis that all women in a given sporting category may compete against one another on a "level playing field", the assumption itself relies on all women's bodies conforming to the norm. Indeed, the reliance on binary sex characteristics leads to any woman (whether cis or trans) having her legitimacy questioned if she is seen to be too strong, too powerful or too large – criteria which typically use white bodies as their normative yardstick (Erikainen et al. 2022). Furthermore, questioning based on a restrictive ideological norm ultimately suppresses the extent to which trans women's inclusion in elite sport can even be considered. An important theme within this data is the framing of social actors and groups. Supporters of trans inclusion are most frequently portrayed in negative terms, being characterised as aggressive and manipulative. Although our qualitative analysis reveals at least one instance where trans individuals themselves are framed in these terms (as "thoroughly nasty"), overall, it is *those supporting trans inclusion* – which may include both trans people and their cis allies – who are typically problematised in these data. This indicates that many of the writers focus their criticism on the *concept* of trans inclusion and the social movement in favour of it, rather than on the trans athletes mentioned in their articles. We argue that this strategy enables many authors to frame their argument against inclusiveness in less personal and therefore less hostile terms, reducing the degree to which they might be perceived as being transphobic.

In this way, we can identify a shift in representations of trans people from previous studies of British newspapers; although there *is* evidence of explicit transphobia using the strategies identified by Baker (2014a) and Zottola (2018), overwhelmingly what we find in this corpus is evidence of *implicit* transphobia. There are similarities here with previous sociolinguistic research into discourses around the rights of same-sex couples. In the context of same-sex marriage, Turner et al. (2017) found a dominant pattern in newspapers of Christians being constructed as the passive victims of an overbearing government and gay rights activists, while Love and Baker's (2015) analysis of parliamentary discourse found that heterosexuals were positioned as the victims of equality legislation. In our data, we see cis women athletes being constructed as the potential victims of trans athletes who will inevitably be stronger and faster than them in competitions, and the potential victims of predatory trans women in their changing rooms. The inclusion of trans athletes in sport is thus constructed as straightforwardly unfair to cis women, a position which is enabled by dominant cisnormative ideology.

Given that this position is shared by the majority of newspapers in our corpus, little space is provided for counter-argument. This means that there are few opportunities for readers to consider the possibility of ways that fairness for *all* athletes could be ensured – such as by rethinking the categories within which groups of athletes compete – other than by banning trans women from elite sport altogether. We therefore suggest that newspaper reporting on this issue in the future should make room for those advocating for trans athletes. With a topic as divisive as trans inclusion in sport, it is particularly important that both sides of the argument are heard; without balanced coverage, the nuances and complexities of this issue are easily overlooked. The dominant view shown in our corpus is likely to influence popular opinion, which may ultimately lead to reduced access to sport – and therefore its health benefits – at grassroots and local levels, including for gender non-conforming and non-binary children (already a potentially very vulnerable group). The exclusion of trans people from any social space should be carefully explored by sports journalists and those with editorial responsibility within the mainstream press, given that this is an already highly marginalised group; whilst the competitive nature of elite sport makes inclusion here more controversial, it should not be portrayed as impossible or nonsensical. As sports journalist and trans man Lee Hurley argues, many stories about trans people in sport are misleading and reinforce problematic and restrictive interpretations. To change the narrative, he argues, media organisations should "hire trans people, look for different perspectives, challenge preconceived notions" (cited in Smith 2021). Based on the dominance of the "fairness versus inclusion" discourse demonstrated in our data, we enthusiastically endorse these recommendations.

References

Bailey, Aimee. 2019. 'Girl-on-girl culture': Normative discourses in a corpus of lesbian sex advice, *Journal of Language and Sexuality* 8(2). 195–220.

Baker, Paul & Sibonile Ellece. 2011. *Key Terms in Discourse Analysis*. London: Continuum.

Baker, Paul. 2014a. "Bad wigs and screaming mimis": Using corpus-assisted techniques to carry out critical discourse analysis of the representation of trans people in the British press. In Christopher Hart & Pitor Cap (eds.) *Contemporary Critical Discourse Studies*, 211–236. London: Bloomsbury.

Baker, Paul. 2014b. *Using corpora to analyze gender*. London: Bloomsbury.

Baker, Paul. 2019. November 2019. Comparison of the coverage of stories about trans people in 2012 and 2018–19. *Mermaids Press* https://mermaidsuk.org.uk/news/exclusive-mermaids-research-into-newspaper-coverage-on-trans-issues/

Billard, Thomas J. 2016. Writing in the Margins: Mainstream News Media Representations of Transgenderism, *International Journal of Communication* 10. 4193–4218.

Borba, Rodrigo. 2022. 'Enregistering "Gender Ideology": The Emergence and Circulation of a Transnational Anti-Gender Language'. *Journal of Language and Sexuality* 11(1). 57–79.

Erikainen, Sonja, Ben Vincent, & Al Hopkins. 2022. Specific Detriment: Barriers and Opportunities for Non-Binary Inclusive Sports in Scotland. *Journal of Sport and Social Issues* 46(1). 75–102.

Faye, Shon. 2021. *The Transgender Issue: An Argument for Justice*. Milton Keynes: Penguin.

FINA. 2022. Policy on eligibility for the men's and women's competition categories. https://resources.fina.org/fina/document/2022/06/19/525de003-51f4-47d3-8d5a-716dac5f77c7/FINA-INCLUSION-POLICY-AND-APPENDICES-FINAL-.pdf (accessed 6 October 2022)

Honkasalo, Julian. 2022. 'Revitalizing Feminist Politics of Solidarity in the Age of Anti-Genderism'. *European Journal of Women's Studies* 29(1_suppl). 139S–150S.

Jones, Lucy. 2022. 'I'm a boy, can't you see that?': Dialogic embodiment and the construction of agency in trans youth discourse. *Language in Society*. 1–22. Online First article https://doi.org/10.1017/S0047404522000252

Jones, Lucy & Luke Collins. 2020. PrEP in the press: A corpus-assisted discourse analysis of how users of HIV-prevention treatment are represented in British newspapers. *Journal of Language and Sexuality* 9(2). 202–225.

Kilgarriff, Adam, Vít Baisa, Jan Bušta, Miloš Jakubíček, Vojtěch Kovář, Jan Michelfeit, Pavel Rychlý & Vít Suchomel. 2014. The Sketch Engine: Ten years on. *Lexicography* 1(7). 7–36.

Knott-Fayle, Gabriel, Elizabeth Peel & Gemma Witcomb. 2021. '(Anti-)Feminism and Cisgenderism in Sports Media'. *Feminist Media Studies*. 1–18. Online First article https://www.tandfonline.com/doi/full/10.1080/14680777.2021.1992644

Lazar, Michelle. 2005. *Feminist critical discourse analysis*. Basingstoke: Palgrave Macmillan.

Love, Adam. 2014. *Transgender Exclusion and Inclusion in Sport*. Routledge Handbooks Online.

Love, Robbie & Paul Baker. 2015. The hate that dare not speak its name? *Journal of Language Aggression and Conflict* 3(1). 57–86.

Lucas, Cathryn B. & Kristine E. Newhall. 2019. Out of the Frame: How Sports Media Shapes Trans Narratives. In Rory Magrath (ed.), *LGBT Athletes in the Sports Media*, 99–124. Cham: Palgrave Macmillan.

Mautner, Gerlinde 2009. Checks and balances: How corpus linguistics can contribute to CDA. In Ruth Wodak & Michael Meyer (eds.) *Methods of Critical Discourse Analysis* (2nd edn.), 122–143. London: Sage.

Montiel-McCann, Camila Soledad. 2022. '"It's like We Are Not Human": Discourses of Humanisation and Otherness in the Representation of Trans Identity in British Broadsheet Newspapers'. *Feminist Media Studies*. 1–17. Online First article: 10.1080/14680777.2022.2097727.

Motschenbacher, Heiko & Martin Stegu. 2013. Introduction: Queer linguistic approaches to discourse. *Discourse and Society* 24(5). 519–35.

Parsons, Vic. 2021. October 8. Protesters demand the Guardian 'stop platforming transphobia' outside newspaper's HQ. *Pink News*. https://www.pinknews.co.uk/2021/10/08/guardian-transphobia-protest-london/

Pearce, Ruth, Sonja Erikainen & Ben Vincent. 2020. TERF wars: An introduction, *The Sociological Review Monographs* 68(4). 677–698.

Smith, Emma. 2021. March 24. The Truth about Being Trans in Football Journalism. *Sports Media LGBT+*. https://sportsmedialgbt.com/the-truth-about-being-trans-in-football-journalism

Tobitt, Charlotte & Aisha Majid. 2022. August 22. National Press ABCs: Every newspaper records annual decline in July 2022. *Press Gazette*. https://pressgazette.co.uk/most-popular-newspapers-uk-abc-monthly-circulation-figures/

Turner, Georgina, Sara Mills, Isabelle van der Bom, Laura Coffey-Glover, Laura Paterson & Lucy Jones. 2017. Opposition as victimhood in newspaper debates about same-sex marriage. *Discourse and Society*. 29(2). 180–97.

van Dijk, Teun. 2015. Critical discourse analysis. In Deborah Tannen, Heidi Hamilton, & Deborah Schiffrin (eds.), *Handbook of Discourse Analysis* (2nd edn.), 466–485. Oxford: Wiley.

Webb, Karleigh. 2021. April 30. Author Julia Serano counters anti-trans backlash with cautious optimism. *Outsports*. https://www.outsports.com/2021/4/30/22410730/julia-serano-trans-athletes-backlash-whipping-girl-transphobia-biden-levine

Zimman, Lal. 2018. Pronouns and possibilities: Transgender language activism and reform. In Netta Avineri, Robin Conley, Laura R. Graham, Eric Johnson & Jonathan Rosa (eds.), *Language and Social Justice: Case Studies on Communication and the Creation of Just Societies*, 176–183. New York: Routledge.

Zimman, Lal. 2021. Beyond the cis gays' cis gaze: The need for a trans linguistics. *Gender and Language* 15(3). 423–29.

Zottola, Angela. 2018. Transgender identity labels in the British press: A corpus-based discourse analysis. *Journal of Language and Sexuality* 7(2). 237–262.

Part III: **Reflecting on the language of inclusion and exclusion by athletes and coaches**

Eva-Maria Graf and Melanie Fleischhacker

Chapter 10
Within binaries instead of beyond? The discursive (self-)exclusion of young female football players from football as a male and masculine space

1 Introduction

> *The future seems bright for women who want to play football. Yet . . . sexism, exclusion, and discrimination remain ever present within the game* (Drury et al. 2022: 2).

Practices of inclusion and exclusion continue to characterize grassroot and associate football in the 21st century: players' age functions as a defining, i.e., including or excluding, factor for organizing teams and leagues below the seniors, players' biological sex decides on their inclusion in male or female squads, and a team's rank in the national league includes or excludes them from participating in international tournaments. Beyond such formal institutional and organizational practices of inclusion and exclusion, football as amateur and professional sport of near-global importance predisposes hegemonically masculine core discourses, values, imperatives, and categories that (still) ideologically exclude women in their playing and non-playing roles as footballers, managers, referees, or CEOs of clubs. Irrespective of recent inclusive tendencies as regards the representation and equality of women (e.g., closing the gender pay gap for US Soccer women), overall, women continue to be organizationally and socio-culturally excluded as "the other" in more or less subtle ways from football. As indicated by Bryan et al. (2021), football continues to represent a sport dominated by men on and off the pitch, governed by norms, values, and discourses of hegemonic masculinity that prioritize men's bodies and masculine sportsmanship and that naturalize men's entitlement to football. As a result, women's overall participation in football is (still) marked and women continue to feel the need to make an extra effort to find acceptance and earn their place in playing and non-playing roles as their athletic, professional and leadership identities remain the target of male acts of (micro-)aggressions (Drury et al. 2022). Disfavorable and harmful gender dynamics thus continue to

Eva-Maria Graf, Melanie Fleischhacker, Department of English and American Studies, University of Klagenfurt

https://doi.org/10.1515/9783110789829-011

exist for women on and off the pitch. The origins and manifestations of these diverse forms of excluding and othering women in football as a male-dominated and masculine space are closely tied to "'common sense' beliefs and taken-for-granted assumptions which influence the entitlement of football, present obdurate, and often impenetrable, barriers that women and girls continually negotiate in their quest to be actively involved" (Caudwell 2012: 1). Football remains organizationally and ideologically organized around two biologically defined categories with an uncontested and legitimated male and masculine dominance as regards embodiment and physical attributes as well as frameworks, practices, and governance (Welford and Kay 2007; Norman et al. 2018; Pfister and Bandy 2018; Caudwell 2019; Bryan et al. 2021). In this vein, Dunn and Welford claim that "[. . .] women's football cannot be understood away from men's football: it has developed within its shadow, and men's football continues to be the benchmark against which women's football is judged" (2019: 140).

Given its near-global socio-cultural significance and prominence, football represents a promising epistemological site to (linguistically) explore how a contested cultural space is discursively negotiated in the first quarter of the 21st century and how gender (ideology) – as one of its key social constructs – is implicitly and explicitly (re-)produced and organized, but also challenged by people involved (Mean 2001; Fielding-Lloyd and Mean 2016; Caldwell et al. 2017). Following Francombe-Webb and Palmer's (2018: 180) call that there is need to "focus on the day-to-day, lived experiences of adolescent girls as they become involved in football" to better understand the "becoming" of female footballing identities, this chapter documents and critically analyzes how young female players experience, negotiate, and criticize exclusion from football as a male and masculine space, but also how they (re-)produce forms of (self-)exclusion in their own discourses. To this end, and as part of a larger research project on female football in Austria, we conducted two in-depth focus-group interviews with young players from a Viennese U16 girls' team in 2018. The interviews are analyzed in two steps, via Thematic Analysis (Braun et al. 2019) followed by a critical interpretation of the findings using Critical Discursive Psychology (Wiggins 2017). Considering recent egalitarian developments in female football (in the Western hemisphere) as regards its prominence, visibility and organizational advancements, our analysis (re-)addresses the following questions:

RQ1: How do female football players experience and make sense of their (excluded) status? What forms and instances of (self-)exclusion emerge in the interviews?

RQ2: How do they discursively (re-)produce and maintain, but also challenge and possibly overcome exclusion on the basis of gendered (football) discourses? What ideological dilemmas emerge?

We first discuss football as an "(extremely) gendered organization" (Bryan et al.2021), and "cultural field" (Schirato 2013), as both concepts allow for specifying what exclusion means for women in football and what constitutive roles language and discourse(s) play therein. This is followed by a literature review that summarizes the most relevant research on the lived experiences of (young) females on the pitch. Next, data and methodology are described, and our findings are presented in the final Section, followed by a critical interpretation and a conclusion, which includes possible practical implications of our research.

1.1 Football as an "extremely gendered organization" and "cultural field"

In socio-cultural approaches to football, football is discussed as an "extremely gendered organization" (Bryan et al. 2021), as a "distinctly male-dominated profession" (Drury et al. 2022), as a "cultural field" (Schirato 2013) and as a "naturally male-only space" (Bryan et al. 2021). In what follows, we will elaborate on football as an "extremely gendered organization" and "cultural field" as we interpret reported instances and practices of female exclusion from football in our data against these two notions. Although our analysis focuses on ideological rather than structural forms of exclusion, both are inextricably linked, and their intertwined discursive influence emerges in the participants' exclusion accounts and practices.

The concept of an "extremely gendered organization" was introduced by Sasson-Levy (2011) for the military. According to Sasson-Levy (2011: 393), "(t)he gendering of organizations occurs at several levels: structural (policies, divisions of labor, formal or informal practices), cultural (pervasive images, symbols and ideologies about femininity and masculinity) and interactional (which includes both individual identity and interpersonal relations and focuses on participants' agency), in which 'doing gender' is often performed". These three dimensions "interact continuously and operate simultaneously. It is their concurrence that produces and reproduces the 'gender regime'" (Sasson-Levy 2011: 393). Such organizations are not only "closely bound up with essentialist and hierarchical conceptions of gender" (Sasson-Levy 2011: 392), but they entail a robust cultural association with hegemonic masculinity surrounding exclusion and oppression of women based on e.g., male bodies characterized by strength, robustness, and sturdiness. A high degree of legitimacy for gender inequality thereby functions as a necessary precondition for the existence of extremely gendered organizations.

Extremely gendered organizations, too, encounter social and political pressure to actively reduce gender inequalities in times of advancing gender equality. Acker (2006) suggests that organizations are more prone to change if their inequality regimes have high visibility, are not perceived as legitimate, and are situated within a social and political environment promoting change. Yet, extremely gendered organizations face the challenge to integrate women without endangering and sacrificing their overall (socio-cultural) masculine character (Sasson-Levy 2011; Tyler et al. 2019). As a consequence, there is a *degendering* on the structural level, yet a *regendering* on the cultural level via (re-)activating gendered discourses that help to maintain and recreate the organization's gender hierarchy.

While Sasson-Levy (2011) claims that the military holds a unique status as an extremely gendered organization, Bryan et al. (2021), in turn, extend the concept to other male-dominated contexts such as men's club football. Characteristic of this "broader category of atypical organizations" as extremely gendered is said centralizing of men's bodies in their reading as sites of strength, skills, and power and, more generally, the retaining of heteronormative and hegemonically masculine and male-dominated cultural norms and values despite an ongoing wider social shift towards equality (Bryan et al. 2021: 947). Football, in particular, continues to function as a leading definer of masculinity in contemporary society, both in and through its organizational and discursive practices.

The second relevant notion for this analysis is Schirato's (2013) concept of sport as a "cultural field", which is founded on larger socio-cultural practices and discourses that surround its social actors and their position, habitus and capital. It contextualizes the structural, cultural and agentive dimensions of extremely gendered organizations and accounts for their continuing legitimacy: football exerts and naturalizes its hegemonic power due to the ongoing existence of football as a male- and masculine-dominated cultural field. At the core of the cultural field "football" are specific discourses and discursive practices (in Fairclough's (1991) sense) on e.g., sportsmanship, competition, or male bodies, which function as ideological building blocks and concurrently as lenses through which this sport is seen (Schirato 2013: 2). These discourses and discursive practices entail norms and prescriptions that create the standards against which male and female performance, legitimacy, belonging, and more generally, inclusion and exclusion from the field of football, is judged (Schirato 2013: 4).

The social actors on a cultural field are "shaped, constrained and disposed towards thoughts and actions through their immersion in, and their incorporation of, the discourse of a cultural field" (Schirato 2013: 2). Additionally, the sharing of dominant beliefs and rules centering on e.g., masculine strength, perseverance and agentiveness as expressed in these discursive practices unites social actors into imagined communities and underlies their identity construction and communal identification. This, in turn, creates a sense of "us" against "them", an originally ideological inclusion and exclusion (in/from this cultural field) which is naturalized, perpetuated, and taken over – as will be shown in our data – by all involved social actors, to varying degrees. Simultaneously, these essentialist discourses of male and masculine legitimacy and dominance on the cultural field "football" underline and promote structural inclusion and exclusion in football as extremely gendered organization.

Next, we turn to prior research on the lived experiences of inclusion and exclusion of girls and women when playing football. Our own research presented in Section 5 builds on and further elaborates existing findings.

2 Prior research on female footballers' experiences on the pitch: Literature review

The following summary of (discourse-oriented, qualitative) research on women playing football spans the last 20 years and allows to sketch developments or stagnancy as regards female exclusion from football. As argued by Caudwell (2007) and reiterated recently by Francombe-Webb and Palmer (2018), in-depth analyses of football's gendered power relations and the regulations of women's footballing bodies as experienced and discursively framed by female participants themselves are indispensable to assess the wider socio-cultural significance of increasing numbers and growing visibility of women in football and its possible challenge to male supremacy.

Prior research by e.g., Scraton et al. (1999), Cox and Thompson (2000), Harris (2007), Jeanes and Kay (2007), Clark and Paechter (2007), Jeanes (2012), and Francombe-Webb and Palmer (2018) on the everyday lived experiences of girls and women with football, document an ongoing, excluding, and impeding binarism – often perpetuated by the female participants themselves – with female football as the marked format that deviates from, and is inferior to, football as a male and masculine space, both on the institutional and the ideological level. These studies also report an incompatibility and friction of the (young) female players' feminine, athletic (and sexual) identities that often play out in a "multiplicity of corporeal tensions" (Cox and Thompson 2001: 17), due to the pressures arising between normative notions of femininity and physicality (Drury et al. 2022). In what follows, we briefly summarize the most relevant aspects of this research.

The interview studies by Scraton et al. (1999), Cox and Thompson (2000) and Harris (2007) focus on adult women and their gendered experiences with becoming and being (semi-)professional players. Football was experienced as a male and masculine dominated space from very early on: as girls in school, they were organizationally excluded as football was exclusively offered for boys; this institutional "division of girls and boys into 'sex-appropriate' activities" (Scraton et al. 1999: 103–104) and an attitude that football is not appropriate for girls socialized many of them. Once they did enter the male world of football, football allowed the girls to act outside the feminine "girlie" norm. Displaying masculine attributes such as competitiveness or active physicality in the context of a "soccer body" (Cox and Thompson 2000) fit in well with a sporting identity for the girls and was experienced as powerful. Yet, all players reported that as they matured the mismatch between their "masculine" physicality, athleticism and strength and their (developing) femininity and feminine body became more challenging and more negatively evaluated by themselves and others. For all interviewees, their gendered footballing identities represented a core (discursive) dilemma due to constant, but changing, frictions between their "soccer bodies" and their "feminine bodies". Being accepted and taken seriously as a female football player meant a continuous and tiresome struggle as well as a conscious and careful gender and identity management, in which their physical appearance and, later, their (hetero-)sexuality, remained a prominent matter of concern. The interviewees agreed in their assessment of female football as second best, yet also as a shared feminine space based on joint values of taking pleasure in being active and being together as women / team.

The studies by Clark and Paeachter (2007), Jeanes and Key (2007), Jeanes (2012) and Francombe-Webb and Palmer (2018), focus on girls' (aged between 10 and 13) developing (gendered) identities and their involvement in football in playground and school activities. They all investigate the girls' active participation in football as a possibility to overcome the girls' perception of football as male-owned space and non-feminine physical activity, as an opportunity to raise the girls' acceptance on the field and as a possible way to create "alternative female gender identities" (Jeanes and Kay 2007: 105–6). To this end, all but the study by Clark and Paeachter (2007) worked with girls, who started to play football as part of these investigations. Prior, these girls had all disliked football and had evinced an essentialist understanding of female participation, yet they also had critically pointed out structural inequalities e.g., not offering football for girls in PE. Once the girls started to actively play football (in all-female teams) in the context of organized workshops and after-school activities, they very much enjoyed the joint physical activity. Playing football also offered them the opportunity to try out different facets of their developing gendered identities. However, they only "allowed" themselves and others to perform those alternative feminine identities as long as an ideal (visual and physical) feminine identity (Jeanes 2012) drawing on "feminine looks and appearance", "niceness", "gentleness" and "supportiveness" was cultivated. Such gender-constricting bodily behaviour by girls, often in the form of "holding something back" is also reported in Clark and Paechter's (2007) study on ownership, permission, and marginalization in theoretically "open-to-all" playground football in schools. "Playing like a girl" meant being excluded from full physical freedom on the pitch, while at the same time being included in the "girl culture", based on a policing of niceness when playing football. Girls and their football thereby remained excluded and removed from "real" football in its traditional hegemonically male reading. In its status as alternative activity, girls' football was constantly devaluated, discredited, and othered by the boys (Jeanes and Kay 2007).

Overall, all studies revealed girls' mere involvement with football did neither challenge their largely traditional feminine identities nor football as a male-dominated space. These findings illustrate how continuing gendered expectations and norms of appropriate feminine behavior and physicality (still) hinder girls to participate "fully" on the pitch. Redefining their own football along feminine norms positioned their play on the margins of a sport owned and dominated by men.

3 Data and methodology

Our data stem from a larger exploratory linguistic research project on female football in Austria (Graf and Fleischhacker in press). Between April and August 2018, various data sets were collected from a U16 girls' team (and its closest external influences such as parents or trainer) of a renowned Viennese club with a long tradition of female football. The two in-depth focus-group interviews, analyzed for the current purpose, form part of this data set. They were conducted with thirteen (four and nine randomly grouped) players of the entire squad. The participants were between 14 and 16 and had been playing football for four to 12 years. They come from different social, cultural, and national backgrounds; some of them speak German as their second language.[1] The participants represent an age group and a player status that have so far received very little linguistic or discourse-oriented attention.

---

[1] While these backgrounds play an important role in the girls' overall identity constructions, intersectional aspects will not be considered for the current purpose.

The interview guideline was developed around questions and hypotheses about the importance of football as an identity-defining activity as well as the experience of football as a gendered social practice. After a short warm-up, participants were asked general questions about the relevance of football in their daily lives, followed by enquiries into football as a (possibly) gendered space. The final thematic block addressed a possible future as professional players. The participants were also invited to formulate wishes to important stakeholders in football. The interviews were conducted in German, relevant passages were translated into English for the current purpose. Interviews were moderated by one of the authors, lasted between one and two hours each and were audio- and video-recorded and subsequently transcribed (and anonymized using pseudonyms for the girls' names) following a verbatim transcription system. The girls and their caretakers had given their written consent to use the interviews for research purposes.

The overall benefits of using qualitative accounts that allow women to articulate their lived experiences as female footballers are frequently stressed (e.g., Francombe-Webb and Palmer 2018). Focus groups, in particular, provide access to (collective, but group-specific) perceptions, ideologies, or interpretations of a particular topic and help gain insights into individual meaning-making patterns and diverse social experiences (Bohnsack 2010). The "multivocality of participants' attitudes, experiences, and beliefs" (Madriz 2003: 364) can be juxtaposed with the collective "product" of the group interaction. While the interactional process and the micro-level co-construction of opinions, arguments etc. are not addressed, we still adopt a constructivist viewpoint using Critical Discursive Psychology to explore the different and opposing discourses (or interpretative repertoires, see below) and positions (or subject positions, see below) (co-)produced by the participants in their complex and dynamic processes of (re-)negotiating and co-constructing, meaning(s) in the context of ideological dilemmas (see below).

Our analysis consists of two steps: First, as a thematic pre-structuring of the interviews, we carry out a thematic analysis that focuses on the girls' accounts of (self-)exclusion as female footballers from football. We then form higher-level themes to establish different forms of "exclusion". Second, we carry out a critical analysis of the recurring topics within those higher-level themes to carve out positions and repertoires. Finally, as we are particularly interested in the girls' own discursive contributions to female exclusion from football, we further analyze higher-level themes that entail the players' practices of excluding others and of self-excluding in the context of emerging ideological dilemmas. An interpretation of our findings against football as "cultural field" and "extremely gendered organization" completes the analysis.

3.1 First analytic step: Thematic analysis and coding

The interviews were first analyzed via Thematic Analysis (Braun et al. 2019) using Atlas.ti to identify themes and to organize them into a coding system in accordance with the research questions. The themes were developed by both researchers in a recursive and reflective process, oscillating between data-exploration, focused immersion into the data and (further) theme-development. The process was both inductive – as themes emerged from the engagement with the data itself – and deductive – using "(self-)exclusion" as a sensitizing concept to identify possibly relevant passages and themes to operationalize our research question. Provisional higher-level themes were tested whether they fit the data and captured the essence of the female footballer's (self-)exclusion experiences, to ensure "systematic, coherent and robust set of codes" (Braun et al. 201: 196). Afterwards, the interviews were coded individually by two coders. All coded segments and assigned themes were compared and critically discussed by both coders and the first author. In case of missing themes or mismatches, agreement was reached in a critical dialogue.

3.2 Second analytic step: Discursive analysis and critical interpretation

Secondly, the relevant text passages that emerged from the higher-level themes were analyzed using Critical Discursive Psychology (CDP) (Wetherell 1998; Edley 2001; Wiggins 2017) with the help of the three concepts "interpretative repertoires", "subject positions" and "ideological dilemmas".

Interpretive repertoires (IR) (see Wetherell 1998; Edley 2001; Wiggins 2017) are recurrent (but flexible) discursive patterns to talk about a particular issue, such as football, in different ways. As conversational building blocks, they help create a shared cultural understanding to be referenced or evoked in different contexts. Such cultural anchoring means that fragments are sufficient to invoke a particular IR among participants. It also means that they are ideological in nature mirroring participant's social and political standpoints. IR develop strong social dynamics that naturalize them until they become dominant and hegemonic categories of thought, perception, and argumentation. They are central components of discursive identity construction that form the background or "argumentative texture" (Wetherell 1998: 294) for gender, sexual, athletic etc. identities.

Subject positions (SP) (see Edley and Wetherell 2008; Wiggins 2017) connect "the wider notions of discourses and interpretative repertoires to the social construction of particular selves" (Edley 2001: 209) and allow speakers to flexibly position themselves or others in conversation. SP are closely related to the various, context-dependent identities of speakers; speakers can thereby actively switch between different positions within the same interaction, though dominant discourses as well as rigid institutional and social structures influence positionings.

Ideological dilemmas (ID) (see Edley 2001; Edley and Wetherell 2008) are contradictory and competitive argumentative lines that develop and consolidate over time in a specific culture and are embodied and expressed by different interpretative repertoires. Opposing perspectives within a society are essential to discuss divergent values and norms as well as social dilemmas; ID thus function as rich and flexible resources in interactions that can (co-)initiate social change. In their contradiction, they enable divergent SP and (other-)positionings, which can lead to troublesome identity constructions or pose dilemmas for speakers as they try to negotiate between IRs.

CDP is a fitting method as its primary goal is "to identify the culturally available repertoires that shape our understanding of a particular topic" (Wiggins 2017: 33). It is concerned with analyzing hegemonic or culturally dominant discourses as well as normalization and naturalization processes (Edley 2001). The concrete observable linguistic micro-level in the interviews, i.e., the emerging higher-level themes, can thus be connected to the socially constructed macro-level (Wetherell 1998). Critically interpretating the lived and reported experiences of the young female football players with the help of CDP allows for relating and contextualizing the subjective and individual discourse with the larger socio-cultural discourses of football (see also Bryan et al. 2021).

4 Findings

In what follows we will present our findings of both analytic steps.

4.1 Thematic analysis

Concerning **RQ 1**, four higher-level themes have emerged. These refer to exclusion from football as "extremely gendered organization" and as "cultural field". A clear pattern emerges regarding the frequency of occurrence of these four higher-level themes. While themes 1, 2 and 3 occur equally often in the data set, theme 4, i.e., the socio-cultural self-exclusion by the players, is used nearly twice as often as the others.

– Higher-level theme 1: Structural-organizational exclusion *of* the players
This theme includes external exclusion by various (official) institutions and organizations (e.g., football organizations, schools, academies, or the media) as reported by the players. While these gate-keeping practices are structural in football as "extremely gendered organization", they are also based on dominant gender-differentiating discourses. Gate-keeping practices refer to club fees, equipment, pitch allocation, or the gender pay gap in football which limits career possibilities. Girls also topicalize a lack of leagues, academies, and educational institutions and the resulting shortage of training and playing options, career opportunities for female players as well as official professional trainer education for female coaches. Inadequate representation of women in the media is addressed, too.

– Higher-level theme 2: Socio-cultural exclusion and othering *of* the players
Here, the players describe ideological gate-keeping practices by various social actors (trainers, teachers, male players, acquaintances etc.) based on dominant (hegemonic) discourses, stereotypes, and role expectations. These discourses construct football as a men's game and women as inferior players since they lack "natural" talent and the appropriate physicality. Women are thus underestimated (in terms of footballing skills and expertise), not taken seriously, having to prove themselves to be allowed to play and earn (some) respect. The girls are excluded from participating in football and usually start playing football outside of institutional structures. However, this not-belonging is also manifested in "marked inclusion", in which male allies introduce girls to (organized) football. Socio-cultural exclusion leads to women operating on the margins of football (despite good performances and continuous efforts), lacking recognition, popularity, and visibility.

– Higher-level theme 3: Socio-cultural exclusion and distancing *by* players
Players (in various constellations and roles) form different in- and out-groups ("us" vs. "them") in which others such as other (girly) girls, and boys, who are not sportive of female trainers, are degraded, judged, or (more neutrally) excluded based on different, football-, team- or gender-related criteria (also based on hegemonic discourses of gender differences) in the interviews. The players thereby assume various positions (as a football team, as football playing girls and as social actors in football) from which to (include some and) exclude others such as girls / women and boys / men.

– Higher-level theme 4: Socio-cultural self-exclusion *by* players
This theme contains practices of (internal) (self-)exclusion of the athletes themselves (and of other female actors) from football by perpetuating dominant discourses and gender-differentiating practices. These claim that men and boys are indeed (or should be) superior players so that women / girls cannot compete against

them. The men's game as well as men's bodies are described as the norm. Concurrently, women in football are "located" at the periphery of the sport perpetuating their supportive roles in football (as physiotherapists etc.). Self-excluding discourses are also based on ideas of female communality policing competitiveness, self-confidence, or aggressive play. There are also practices that represent "second order" gendered discourses promoting a mindset that (partly) lacks agency (e.g., to change the situation of women's football in general) and commitment or seeks stability and (financial) security.

In higher-level themes 1 and 2 the players merely report on how they are excluded (by others) based on existing structural and socio-cultural circumstances, a focus that has already received substantial scholarly attention. Without going into further detail, the forms and instances of (self-)exclusion in themes 1 and 2 evince an overall critical stance of the participants with regards to existing structural disadvantages for female footballers as well as their marked status as "the other" in football. Young women in 2018 faced an unchanged situation when compared to the experiences by female footballers in prior studies (see Section 3).

Higher-level codes 3 and 4, in turn, entail the young footballers' own discursive constructions of (gender) hierarchies / regimes in football, which resulted in practices of (self-)exclusion, a so-far less researched perspective. In what follows, we critically analyze and interpret these discursive (re-)productions of gendered (football) discourses in more detail.

4.2 Critical analysis

With regards to **RQ 2**, we address the players' various positionings, interpretative repertoires and, if present, ideological dilemmas regarding practices and strategies of (self-) exclusion.

4.2.1 Practices of socio-cultural exclusion and distancing by the players

A more thorough analysis of the higher-level theme "Socio-cultural exclusion and distancing *by* the players" evinces how the interviewees discursively engage in building and assessing in- and outgroups based on their status as (empowered) athletes, girls, football players, team members and more generally as social actors in football. In so doing, they stage themselves as a homogenous in-group by coinciding in their (explicit) evaluation of themselves and of others as outgroup, i.e., by mostly supporting each other's positioning and drawing on the same interpretative repertoires. They discursively build these in- and outgroups primarily, but not exclusively,[2] by recurring to hegemonic gendered discourses (Sunderland 2004) such as "male agentiveness and female communality", "gender binaries and differences" or "biological essentialism". Considering football as a gendered space, these are the focus of our analysis.

In what follows, we first present various groups the participants exclude (i.e., boys (Table 1), the male trainer (Table 2), other girls (Table 3) and women in general (Table 4)) on the basis of gendered discourses by listing the emerging repertoires, dominant positionings and instances taken directly from the interviews.

Table 1: Excluding boys.

Repertoires	Most Relevant Positionings	Instances from Interviews
Boys are less team-oriented	– Boys are not as much of a team as girls – Boys would not accept girls as part of their team	– 'I can imagine that in boys' teams they aren't that much of a team.'
Boys are more competitive	– Boys' teams are about competition – Boys fight on and off the pitch	– 'They are more competitive.' – 'Boys, they fight with each other in the locker rooms.'
Boys are aggressive, reckless, and dangerous	– Playing against boys is a battle (not football) due to aggressive play/fouls – Boys are unaware of their own strength and other's (physical) limits – They pose a threat to girls (i.e., a risk of injury) – Boys are physically / verbally aggressive, insensitive, and reckless	– 'Sometimes it's just more of a battle and you actually just want it to be over.' – 'Then it's dangerous because you know boys at that age just have . . . Just do not know how far they can go.'
Boys are overly self-confident	– Boys have more self-confidence and brag about their own abilities (because they are boys) – Girls are more modest and never brag or invite others to games	– 'So many have simply so much more self-confidence because they are a boy.' – '"Come watch me at a match, I'm really good." I have never heard girls [saying] something like that.'

---

[2] Other criteria include performance, participation in football, athleticism, or level of commitment.

Table 1 (continued)

Repertoires	Most Relevant Positionings	Instances from Interviews
Boys should be better at sports than girls	– Girls being better than boys in sports is embarrassing (for boys) – Boys, who lose against girls' teams, should stop playing football	– I'm sorry for the boys because in the past, we often won against boys, and then I think to myself "Yeah, they should all stop playing football."'

Table 2: Excluding the male trainer.

Repertoires	Most Relevant Positionings	Instances from Interviews
Trainer lacks communicative and emotional skills	– One cannot talk with a male trainer as with a female (co-)trainer – Men are not good to confide in or trust with problems	– 'I don't think I can talk to a trainer the way I could talk to a female trainer. [. . .] 'I couldn't say that openly to my trainer.'
Trainer shouldn't be caring	– Being consoled by the trainer is unpleasant	– 'If the coach comes and says: "But you played well anyway." Then it's just worse, no not worse, just more unpleasant.'
Trainer cannot understand girls' problems	– Trainer does cannot understand women's problems (i.e., menstrual pain) – Male trainer is relentless and wants them to just deal with pain	– 'He just doesn't understand.' – 'Because he doesn't have such pain.' – 'He always says, "It's not that bad . . ."'

Table 3: Excluding other girls.

Repertoires	Most Relevant Positionings	Instances from Interviews
Girls do not like and understand football	– Girls do not even try to play football – Girls hate football and do not want to play it in school – Most girls do not understand football at all	– 'I'm in a girls-only class and they all hate football' – 'Like 90% of all girls and they don't understand this at all.'
Girls are less athletic and afraid of ballgames	– Girls at school lack ability to play football or catch a ball – Girls at school are hysterically afraid of balls	– 'You throw a ball with 2km/h and . . . And they get out of the way. . . . And scream, yeah.'
Girls who only play against girls do not play good football	– Playing against girls is no real competition or challenge – Playing against girls is no fun – Winning against girls is not exciting – We play faster / perform much better than other girls	– 'It's really not as much fun against the girls, because we are quite bored, because we are simply much faster, . . . because we play against the boys.' – 'We have no competition among the girls' teams.'

Table 4: Excluding women.

Repertoires	Most Relevant Positionings	Instances from Interviews
Female footballers are less interesting and visible	– Female footballers aren't role models and mostly unknown – Men's football is interesting because of its popularity/visibility – W lack knowledge about female football	– 'But due to the fact that women are never mentioned, I personally don't know any women football players myself.' – 'I just don't know anything about women's football.'
Women are secondary in football	– Female trainers are rare and have less expertise – Women work rather in secondary / feminine professions in football	– 'There aren't many female trainers.' – 'Rather masseuses or . . . physiotherapists . . . but not really trainers. Because they are rather rather secondary'

Table 4 (continued)

Repertoires	Most Relevant Positionings	Instances from Interviews
Women should serve as co-trainers	– It would be good and practical to have a female co-trainer – Female co-trainers are much more understanding, easier to talk to and to confide in – Women can understand women's issues and (menstrual) pain	– 'I think it's kind of convenient to have, for example, a female co-trainer.' – 'I do think that some are more open towards women than towards men.' – 'She understands us better.'

Next, we analyze one telling example and thereby document the shared positionings of the interviewees as regards their practices of excluding girls/women and boys/men. No major ideological dilemmas emerged in these cases.

Excerpt 1: Excluding girls (and boys)

Context: The girls discuss how they deal with losing a match and whether negative emotions accompany them afterwards.

1 Valentina: *With us it's the case that if I take it to school, the others in my form also play football and with them it's the same.*

IR "People who play football / do sports understand them" (other-positioning classmates)

2 Lena: *Yes, but sometimes there are kind of dumb comments, like "It's only a game".*

IR "People who do not play football / do sports don't understand them" (other-positioning)

3 Several girls: *Yeah*
4 Manuela: *But it's a game that you didn't win. That's just a phrase: "It's only a game."*

IR "People who do not play football /do sports don't understand them" (self-positioning)

5 Sophia: *Especially when you say something like this, I mean the ones from my class don't understand this at all . . .*

IR "People who do not play football /do sports don't understand them" (other-positioning classmates)

6 Lena: *Yeah.*
7 Sophia: *I'm in a girls-only class and they all hate football.*

IR "Girls do not like and understand football" (other-positioning girls)

8 Lena: *That's terrible, yeah.* Anna: *Yes*
9 Mirlinda: *Same.*

IR "Girls do not like and understand football" (other-positioning girls)

10 Sophia: *Just like 90% of all girls and they don't understand it at all. So . . .*

IR "Girls do not like and understand football" (other-positioning girls)

11 Manuela: *In my class, it's partly also the boys, they don't understand it at all because they aren't really athletic or something like that. Some of them at least and the rest . . .*
IR "Girls do not like or understand football", "People (i.e., boys) who do not play football/do sports do not understand them" (other-positioning girls/boys)
12 Anna: *Yes, and I hate it.*
13 Anna: *But it's also really sa, well, I'm sorry for the boys because in the past we often won high against boys, then I think to myself "Yeah, they could all stop playing football." (laughter)*
IR "Boys should be better at sports than girls" (self- and other-positioning boys)

In this excerpt, the girls form in- and out-groups based on who can and cannot play or understand football. While boys (and people in general) are positioned as not understanding football when they do not engage in the sport themselves, girls at their respective schools are excluded and positioned as rejecting football and lacking knowledge, simply because they are girls. This way, they tap into the same repertoire men and other social actors employ (as reported in the higher-level theme 2), i.e., that football is essentially a sport *for* boys (and only *some* girls) thus excluding other girls from the activity. An unanimous voice emerges that supports, adds to, and similarly evaluates each other's positionings. Towards the end, girls also engage in excluding boys based on a lack of athleticism and performance in sports. While most girls are considered unathletic, boys are expected to outperform girls (recurring to an IR of male athletic superiority) and – if they fail to do so – considered ultimate losers. The laughter (line 13) underlines how embarrassing boys' loss against girls is perceived.

4.2.2 Practices of socio-cultural self-exclusion by the players

With regards to the higher-level theme "socio-cultural self-exclusion *by* the players", the interviewees negotiate their own, but also women's belonging to the cultural field of football as a male and masculine space. In these negotiations, the young footballers oscillate between explicit and implicit self-exclusion, but also self-inclusion, and reiteration of their status as "the other" in football. While they position themselves as a (more or less) homogenous group when it comes to out-grouping others, here we witness a more fragile group formation due to individually conflicting, but also intra-individually troubled, positionings. The following main ideological dilemmas emerge in the form of competing IR:
1. Male vs. female football
2. Male vs. female performance and physicality
3. External change vs. individual agency
4. Individual ambitions vs. team cohesion

5. A future in football vs. (financial) security and stability
6. Playing "professional" football vs. playing football as a hobby and having fun

In the following, we further analyze only the first four dilemmas focusing on their competing IR (see Tables 5–8) and the players' various (troubled) positionings via four examples. While these four dilemmas have emerged in both interviews, the other two are more prominent in only one interview and are thus considered less representative. One IR can be opposed by several other / different IR.

Male vs. female football

Table 5: Competing IR for dilemma 1.

COMPETING REPERTOIRES	
MALE FOOTBALL/FOOTBALLERS IS/ARE THE NORM / STANDARD	FEMALE FOOTBALL/FOOTBALLERS IS/ARE OUT OF THE NORM
FOOTBALL IS A SPORT DOMINATED *BY* AND (NATURALLY) *FOR* MEN	FOOTBALL IS A SPORT ALSO *FOR* WOMEN
MALE FOOTBALL IS PRIVILEGED, MORE POPULAR, AND VISIBLE	FEMALE FOOTBALL IS LESS POPULAR, VISIBLE, AND DEVELOPED
MALE FOOTBALL IS SUPERIOR (I.E., FEMALE FOOTBALL IS INFERIOR)	FEMALE FOOTBALL IS NOT INFERIOR (ONLY IN COMPARISON TO MEN)
MALE AND FEMALE FOOTBALL MUST NOT / CANNOT BE COMPARED	FEMALE FOOTBALL IS DIFFERENT FROM MEN'S FOOTBALL
MALE FOOTBALL IS (TOO) AGGRESSIVE (I.E., NOT GOOD FOOTBALL)	FEMALE FOOTBALL IS MORALLY SUPERIOR
MALE FOOTBALL IS COMPETITIVE AND LESS TEAM-ORIENTED	FEMALE FOOTBALL IS TEAM-ORIENTED AND LESS COMPETITIVE
MALE FOOTBALLERS RECEIVE BETTER PAY (I.E., CAN LIVE JUST FROM FOOTBALL)	FEMALE FOOTBALLERS AREN'T PAID ENOUGH (I.E., CANNOT LIVE JUST FROM FOOTBALL)
MALE FOOTBALLERS CAN SECURE THEIR FUTURE	FEMALE FOOTBALLERS CANNOT SECURE THEIR FUTURE
FEMALE FOOTBALL IS GAINING POPULARITY / IS DEVELOPING	FEMALE FOOTBALL IS NOT DEVELOPING FAST ENOUGH
MALE FOOTBALLERS ARE ROLE MODELS	FEMALE FOOTBALLERS ARE ROLE MODELS

Male vs. female performance and physicality

Table 6: Competing IR for dilemma 2.

COMPETING REPERTOIRES	
MEN'S/BOYS' PERFORMANCE IS SUPERIOR	MEN'S/BOYS' PERFORMANCE IS NOT NECESSARILY SUPERIOR
	WOMEN'S/GIRLS' PERFORMANCE IS EQUAL TO MEN'S
	U16 GIRLS PERFORM AT HIGH(EST) LEVEL
WOMEN'S/GIRLS' PERFORMANCE IS INFERIOR / PLAYING AGAINST GIRLS IS LESS CHALLENGING AND FUN	WOMEN'S/GIRLS' PERFORMANCE IS EQUAL TO MEN'S
PLAYING AGAINST BOYS IS BETTER / MORE CHALLENGING	GIRLS (CAN) OUTPERFORM BOYS
PLAYING AGAINST BOYS IMPROVES PERFORMANCE / GIRLS WHO PLAY AGAINST BOYS HAVE AN ADVANTAGE	
MEN AND WOMEN'S PERFORMANCE / STRENGTH/SKILLS CANNOT/MUST NOT BE COMPARED	MALE AND FEMALE BODIES AND PERFORMANCE ARE DIFFERENT
MEN'S SKILLS ARE SUPERIOR	WOMEN'S SKILLS ARE SUPERIOR/NOT INFERIOR
	WOMEN'S SKILLS ARE EQUAL TO MEN'S
MEN/BOYS ARE PHYSICALLY STRONGER AND FASTER	WOMEN/GIRLS ARE EQUALLY OR ALSO STRONG AND FAST
MALE BODIES ARE SUPERIOR	MALE BODIES ARE NOT GENERALLY SUPERIOR
FEMALE BODIES ARE VULNERABLE	
GENDERED TEAMS ARE NECESSARY (FROM A CERTAIN AGE) / MALE AND FEMALE BODIES MUST BE SEPARATED	MIXED TEAMS WORK (UP UNTIL A CERTAIN AGE)
BOYS/MEN ARE (PHYSICALLY/VERBALLY) AGGRESSIVE AND DANGEROUS	GIRLS/WOMEN ARE (PHYSICALLY/VERBALLY) LESS AGGRESSIVE AND DANGEROUS

External change vs. individual agency

Table 7: Competing IR for dilemma 3.

COMPETING REPERTOIRES	
FEMALE FOOTBALL IS LESS POPULAR/VISIBLE (EXCLUDED FROM THE MEDIA)	FEMALE FOOTBALL IS GAINING POPULARITY / IS DEVELOPING
FEMALE FOOTBALL IS GAINING POPULARITY / IS DEVELOPING	FEMALE FOOTBALL IS NOT DEVELOPING FAST ENOUGH
FEMALE FOOTBALL IS LESS INTERESTING / ENGAGING / RELEVANT	FEMALE FOOTBALL IS ALSO INTERESTING / ENGAGING / RELEVANT
MALE FOOTBALL IS INTERESTING	FEMALE FOOTBALL IS INTERESTING
CHANGE MUST COME FROM OTHERS	CHANGE CAN COME FROM THEM / CHANGE STARTS SMALL
CHANGE CANNOT COME FROM THEM	
CHANGE COMES FROM NUMBERS / POPULARITY IS A PREREQUISITE FOR CHANGE	

Individual ambitions vs. team cohesion

Table 8: Competing IR for dilemma 4.

COMPETING REPERTOIRES	
GOOD PERFORMANCE IS BASED ON TEAM COHESION/ WORK, TRUST, AND FRIENDSHIP	TEAM CONSISTS OF SUB-GROUPS / SOME ARE CLOSER FRIENDS
BEING A TEAM MEANS BEING FRIENDS / HAVING A GOOD RELATIONSHIP	
BEING A TEAM MEANS TAKING CARE OF/LOOKING OUT FOR EACH OTHER	
THERE IS NO REAL DIVISION DESPITE SUB-GROUPS	
TEAMS CONSIST OF SUB-GROUPS	TEAM COHESION HAS IMPROVED
BEING A TEAM MEANS SPENDING TIME TOGETHER (*ON* AND *OFF* THE PITCH)	LEISURE TIME IS SPENT WITH CLOSEST FRIENDS FRIENDS SHARE THE SAME INTERESTS

Table 8 (continued)

COMPETING REPERTOIRES	
GIRLS' TEAMS ARE NOT COMPETITIVE	COMPETITION AS BAD RELATIONSHIP
	COMPETITION AS TRAINER PRIVILEGE
FOOTBALL IS A TEAM SPORT / NOT AN INDIVIDUAL ACTIVITY	FOOTBALLERS ALSO HAVE INDIVIDUAL AMBITIONS/ INTERESTS
FOOTBALL IS A TEAM PERFORMANCE / TEAM IS RESPONSIBLE FOR SUCCESS	FOOTBALL IS AN INDIVIDUAL PERFORMANCE /INDIVIDUALS ARE RESPONSIBLE FOR FAILURE

After listing the relevant competing IR of the four ID considered, we will now zoom in on how these IR emerge in the interview, how the speakers position themselves and others with respect to these repertoires and whether these positionings are individually or collectively troubled or untroubled, i.e., represent different/competing IR or not. In the excerpts, lines taken from the interviews are followed by the IR involved therein and an indication of (un-)troubled positionings.

Excerpt 2: Male vs. female football (dilemma 1)

1   Valentina: *Yes, but this is then again the problem that men think women simply don't belong on the sports field. And this way you can't form a team . . . women's team.*

IR "Football is a sport dominated by and for men" (other-positioning men, criticized), "Male football/footballers is / are the norm" (self-positioning)

P   Internally troubled position, interactionally untroubled/supported positioning

2   Sophia: *At least not on the football field. But somehow always when men say that "Yeah, women can't play football" it's because they compare women's football with men's football.*

IR "Football is a sport dominated by and for men" (other-positioning men, criticized), "Male and female football must not/cannot be compared" (self-positioning)

P   Internally troubled positioning, interactionally untroubled/supported positioning

3   Lena: *Yes, yes.*
4   Sophia: *That can't be compared with each other.*

IR "Male and female football must not/cannot be compared" (self-positioning)

P   Internally untroubled, interactionally troubled positioning

5   Anna: *It's different. It's simply different.*

IR "Female football is different from men's football" (self-positioning)

P   Internally untroubled, interactionally troubled positioning

6	Sophia: *It is, I admit it. Women's football isn't as good as men's football. It won't ever be as good.*
IR	"Male football is superior" (self-positioning, evaluated as confessing an unspoken truth)
P	Internally untroubled, interactionally untroubled/supported positioning
7	Anna: *Yes, yes.*
8	Lena: *Men's football is definitely more high class.*
IR	"Male football is superior" (self-positioning)
P	Internally untroubled, interactionally untroubled positioning
9	Anna: *Men are faster* (Sophia: *One can*) *and physically stronger. That's simply the case. It is, it is, it doesn't mean that we as women are worse or anything like that, but it's different.*
IR	"Men are physically stronger and faster" (other-positioning men, evaluated as natural/evident), "Female football is not inferior", "Female football is different from men's football" (self-positioning as woman)
P	Internally troubled positioning, interactionally troubled positioning
10	Sophia: *It's simply a different level.*
IR	"Male football is superior" (self-positioning)
P	Internally untroubled, interactionally troubled positioning
11	Lena: *Women then also solve it completely differently with with with other with other*
IR	"Female football is different from men's football" (self-positioning women)
P	Internally untroubled, interactionally troubled positioning
12	Sophia: *It's a different level one cannot women's football with men's football, one can compare women with women and men with men, but men with women, one can't say women can't play football, just because they are worse than men, it's also the physique is just completely different.*
IR	"Male football is superior", "Male and female football must not/cannot be compared" (self-positioning), "Female football is not inferior", "Male and female bodies and performance are different" (self-positioning women, positioning men vs. women)
P	Internally troubled positioning, interactionally untroubled positioning
13	Anna: *It's . . . . The bodies yes, the body . . . the body proportions*
IR	"Male and female bodies and performance are different" (positioning men vs. women)
P	Internally untroubled, interactionally untroubled
14	Lena: *And then one thinks women don't give it all. Yes, but when a a a I don't know a woman rams another woman, who both weigh 70 kilos, then it's something different than two men with 90 kilograms throw themselves against each other.*
IR	"Women's performance/skills are inferior" (other-positioning, criticized), "Men and women's performance / strength cannot be compared" (positioning men vs. women)
P	Internally troubled, interactionally untroubled / supported (evaluated as true/evident)
15	Sophia: *Yes, that's true.*
16	Sophia: *Men train everything, they can do everything, it's the physique and speed. It's simply something different.*

IR	"Men's bodies are superior", "Men are physically stronger and faster", "Male and female bodies and performance are different" (other-positioning men, self-positioning)
P	Internally troubled positioning, interactionally untroubled positioning
17 Anna:	*They also have more muscles. They generally have more muscles.*
IR	"Men's bodies are superior" (other-positioning men)
P	Internally untroubled positioning, interactionally untroubled positioning

Here the female players discuss the dilemma of women's vs. men's football. They thereby continuously (explicitly or implicitly) position (themselves as) women in contrast to the dominant group "men" in an "us" vs. "them" manner.

Men are portrayed as faster, better footballers and physically superior, but are also criticized for employing the IR "Football is a sport for and by men" (see 1 and 2). The girls are torn between the dilemma of how others perceive their role and abilities in football and how they perceive themselves and make sense of such an excluded or inferior status. They do this mainly by recurring to biological essentialism (see 12ff), which supports their viewpoint that men and women cannot / must not be compared, as this will "naturally" lead to women's bodies and athleticism being seen as inferior. Alternatively, they construct women's football as different and apart from men's football (i.e., as a possible second cultural field). However, they reinforce their dilemma by repeatedly describing men's football and physicality as superior and orienting to male football as the norm, while at the same time trying to argue for and defend women's football as worthwhile and women's bodies and performance (as different though) not inferior. The dilemmatic nature of their argumentation becomes observable in troubled positionings within single speakers (e.g., see 12) and between speakers as different or alternative repertoires to other speaker's contributions are added, while there is no overt contradiction (e.g., see 5 and 6). The girls engage in self-exclusion by employing and thereby reinforcing repertoires such as "Male football is the norm" or "Male bodies are superior". The status of women's football as "the other" is also marked linguistically (team vs. women's team, see 1) and highlighted primarily in the context of football (sports field vs. football field, see 2). The socio-culturally pervasive perception of male superiority in football remains largely unchallenged, but is rather actively re-produced and justified by recurring to biological differences in body proportions, physique, speed etc.

Excerpt 3: Male vs. female performance and physicality (dilemma 2)

1	Elena: *I don't think so, I think no sport is only for men or for women. It's simply the case that men are better.*
IR	"Sports are not gendered" (self-positioning), "Men's performance is superior" (other-positioning men)
P	Internally troubled positioning, interactionally troubled positioning
2	Marija: *Not always.*
IR	"Men's performance is not necessarily superior" (other-positioning men)
P	Internally untroubled positioning, interactionally untroubled positioning
3	Cornelia: *No, they are not. They are not better, they are just physically stronger.*
IR	"Men's performance is not necessarily superior", "Men are physically stronger and faster" (other-positioning men)
P	Internally troubled positioning, interactionally troubled positioning
4	Marija: *No no*
IR	"Men are not necessarily stronger and faster" (other-positioning men)
P	Internally untroubled positioning, interactionally troubled positioning
5	Elena: *Okay, so you want to tell me that Neymar isn't better than some female player?*
IR	"Men's performance is superior" (positioning men vs. women)
P	Internally untroubled positioning interactionally troubled positioning
6	Cornelia: *Chill, you can't make this comparison. It's something different.*
IR	"Men's and women's performance must not/cannot be compared" (other-positioning interactional partner/self-positioning)
P	Internally untroubled positioning, interactionally troubled positioning
7	Elena: *Oh yes you can.*
IR	"Men's performance is superior" ("Men's and women's performance can be compared") (self-positioning, other-positioning interactional partner)
P	Internally untroubled positioning, interactionally possibly troubled positioning
8	Cornelia: *There are . . .*
9	Elena: *Men simply have a better technique.*
IR	"Men's skills are superior" (other-positioning men)
P	Internally untroubled positioning, interactionally untroubled positioning
10	Cornelia: *They are faster.*
IR	"Men are physically stronger and faster" (other-positioning men)
P	Internally untroubled positioning, interactionally troubled positioning
11	Mathilda: *And women aren't as famous as men.*

IR	"Female football is less popular/visible/developed" (self-positioning women)
P	Internally untroubled, interactionally untroubled (not taken up by others)
12	Marija: *You can train everything.*
IR	"Women's skills are not inferior" (referring to skills) or "Female bodies are not generally inferior" (referring to speed) (self-positioning women)
P	Internally untroubled positioning, interactionally untroubled positioning
13	Cornelia: *Look at videos of the world's best women. Okay, it is, one can't compare them to Neymar. But still.*
IR	"Women's skills are equal to men's" or "Women's performance is equal to men's," "Men and women's performance, strength and skills cannot be compared" (other-positioning women/best players, positioning men vs women)
P	Internally troubled positioning, interactionally untroubled positioning

This excerpt succinctly illustrates another dilemma in the interviews between "Male and female performance and physicality", already partly addressed in excerpt 2. Here, we find overt counter-positions between speakers alongside troubled positionings within single speakers (e.g., see 3). The girls (Elena, Marija, and Cornelia) (though sometimes internally conflicted) quite consistently use different repertoires ("Men's performance is superior" and "Men are physically stronger and faster" vs. "Men's performance is not necessarily superior" and "Men are not necessarily stronger and faster"). They oppose each other's positionings and illustrate the existing dilemma between men's perceived superior performance (e.g., see 1 or 5), skills (see 9) and especially physicality (e.g., see 3 or 10) in contrast to women's performance / bodies and their ability to reach equal athletic standards via training (see 12 or 13). Again, male performance and superiority are connected to "natural" (and thus unsurmountable) differences. The supposed superiority, however, might also be rooted in a lacking awareness of internationally successful and skilled female football players illustrated in the comparison between "Neymar" and "some female player" or "the world's best women", who remain anonymous. The girls predominantly other-position men and although Marija consistently counterargues, the dominant group position is tilted towards women's performance as inferior whenever compared to (biologically advantaged) men, who socio-culturally and in the girls' perception represent the norm against which all athletic achievements are measured. Interestingly, we find one of the rare instances in which a potential single cultural field "football" for both men and women is addressed (see 1). However, Elena immediately positions men as superior in sports thus retreating from the idea that men and women could co-inhabit one field.

Excerpt 4: (External) change vs. individual agency (dilemma 3)

1 Interviewer: *And what would you, or what can you do yourself to make changes happen?*
2 Mirlinda: *Nothing.*

IR	"Change canncannot come from them" (self-positioning)
P	Internally untroubled positioning, interactionally untroubled positioning

3 Sophia: *Nothing really.*

IR	"Change cannot come from them" (self-positioning)
P	Internally untroubled positioning, interactionally untroubled positioning

4 Anna: *Nothing, we can't do anything about it.*

IR	"Change cannot come from them" (self-positioning as group)
P	Internally untroubled positioning, interactionally untroubled positioning

5 Pauline: *You can't do anything.*

IR	"Change cannot come from them" (self-positioning)
P	Internally untroubled positioning, interactionally troubled positioning (speaker breaks off)

6 Lena: *Well, we could . . .*

IR	"Change can come from them" (self-positioning as group)
P	Internally untroubled positioning, interactionally untroubled positioning

7 Valentina: *Maybe we could demonstrate, maybe that might help.*

IR	"Change can come from them" (self-positioning as group, collaborative completion)
P	Internally untroubled positioning, interactionally untroubled/supported positioning

8 Sophia: *Yes, with posters*
9 Lena: *Exactly.* [. . .]

IR	"Change can come from them" (self-positioning)
P	Internally untroubled positioning, interactionally untroubled positioning

10 Interviewer: *But in general, what what could you do to, because you said general equality also beyond the sport, what what what can one do? What can we all do?*
11 Anna: *As a woman one simply has to well, more women ought to play football.*

IR	"Change must come from others" (other-positioning women, who do not play football)
P	Internally untroubled positioning, interactionally untroubled/supported positioning

12 Lena: *Yeah* Sophia: *Yeah*
13 Lena: *More women simply have to speak up about what they don't like. And unfortunately, only very few do that.*

IR	"Change must come from others", "Change comes from numbers" (other-positioning women)
P	Internally untroubled positioning, interactionally untroubled/supported positioning

14 Several girls: *Yeah*

15	Manuela: *For example, in every, every historic event, also many people protested and there were, well, a big crowd protested and then change took place, if this happens again, it could come to change. And one also has to, I think, when the results are partly there, and in the sense of, I don't know, more fans coming to the games and so on, then it would, then great changes would be possible. I really believe that.*
IR	"Change comes from numbers/Popularity is a prerequisite for change", "Change can come from them", "Change must come from others", "Change comes from numbers" (self-positioning and other-positioning fans)
P	Internally troubled positioning, interactionally troubled positioning
16	Bea: *Yes. But for this to happen it would have to be promoted and supported much more.*
IR	"Change must come from others" (self-positioning)
P	Internally untroubled positioning, interactionally untroubled/supported positioning
17	Manuela: *Yes, exactly.*
18	Sophia: *This has to be done in any case.*
IR	"Change must come from others" (self-positioning)
P	Internally untroubled positioning, interactionally possibly troubled positioning
19	Manuela: *But that then has to, but . . .*
20	Sophia: *Without any support, like fundings with, I don't know, financial support or like.*
IR	"Change must come from others" (self-positioning)
P	Internally untroubled positioning, interactionally troubled positioning
21	Manuela: *But when you look at it, social media, for example, through social media you can promote this as well, we partly do this already, too, and I believe, even if it's something very small, it already helps a bit. Because people are made aware of it, and this is already something good. I believe so.*
IR	"Change can come from them", "Change starts small" "Popularity is a prerequisite for change" (self-/other-positioning interactional partner)
P	Internally untroubled positioning, interactionally troubled positioning
22	Sophia: *But you also see it on social media, when you visit pages about football, there are only men.*
IR	"Female football is less visible/popular", "Change must come from others" (self- and other-positioning interactional partner)
P	Internally untroubled positioning, interactionally untroubled positioning

Excerpt 4 illustrates a dilemma between the decried socio-cultural and structural conditions of women in football and the power structures and possible motors involved to bring about change. At first, the girls unanimously adhere to the IR "Change cannot come from them", categorically negating their own opportunity to spark change (see 2–5). Further on, the interviewees alternate between "Change can come from them" and "Change must come from others" more forcefully illustrating the dilemma between external socio-cultural and structural changes (coming from, e.g., media) and their personal agency in contributing to change (e.g., via increasing women's visibility on social media). They also address other women as potential change-inducing entities (see 11 and 13) and the power of numbers (e.g., see 15), without explicit self-inclusion. While especially Manuela voices possibilities for the girls to have an impact, her contributions are accompanied by low epistemic or no access status and down-toning particles.

The girls sometimes argue as a group, but explicit positionings are rare as they more often recur to indefinite pronouns, never employing the first-person pronoun to talk about their individual agency. They repeatedly trouble each other's positioning, shifting between repertoires but mostly attributing power to others instead of themselves. Using social media to increase visibility and awareness, for instance, is troubled by framing media's focus on men as obstacle (see 22). Yet, there are instances where they collaboratively complete each other's attempts to articulate possibilities for interventions (see 6 to 8). Overall, the players present themselves as powerless and incapable of advancing their own and women's situation in football; responsibility is mostly attributed to others and the motor for change is located outside of their control. They not only downgrade their own agency but exclude themselves from efforts to change the status quo.

Excerpt 5: Individual ambitions vs. team cohesion (dilemma 4)

1	Sophia: *There are still groups within the team, it is always like this, there will never be one united group*
IR	"Team coconsists of sub-groups" (self-positioning, evaluation as evident/unchangeable)
P	Internally untroubled positioning, interactionally troubled positioning
2	Manuela: *Although I think at the moment it isn't as extreme as in the beginning of the season, but it is always like this.*
IR	"Team cohesion has improved", "Team consists of sub-groups" (self-positioning, evaluation as unchangeable)
P	Internally troubled positioning, interactionally slightly troubled positioning
3	Anna: *Although it has really become much better.*
IR	"Team cohesion has improved" (self-positioning)
P	Internally untroubled positioning, interactionally untroubled/supported positioning
4	Bea: *Yes, at the moment it isn't that bad.*
IR	"Team cohesion has improved" (self-positioning)
P	Internally untroubled positioning, interactionally troubled positioning
5	Sophia: *But the groups still get along well. Totally.*
IR	"No division despite sub-groups" (self-positioning as sub-groups)
P	Internally untroubled positioning, interactionally untroubled positioning
6	Anna: *For example, with Soph, I don't spend my free time with her, but I would do it.*

IR	"Team consists of sub-groups", "No real division despite sub-groups", "Being a team means spending time together on and off the pitch" (self-positioning)
P	Internally troubled positioning, interactionally possibly troubled positioning
7	Lena: *There were times . . .*
8	Sophia: *Yes, we get along well. So . . .*
IR	"No division despite sub-groups" (self-positioning as team)
P	Internally untroubled positioning, interactionally untroubled/supported positioning
9	Anna: *Yes. I have known her for 9 years? And now it is [. . .]*
IR	"No division despite sub-groups", "Knowing each other for long unites" (self-positioning)
P	Internally untroubled positioning, interactionally troubled positioning
10	Lena: *There are definitely people with whom one (Sophia: spends more time) spends more time, but simply because . . .*
IR	"Team consists of sub-groups", "Free time is spent with closest friends" (self-positioning)
P	Internally troubled positioning, interactionally (slightly) troubled positioning
11	Anna: *But also because we have the same interests.*
IR	"Team consists of sub-groups", "Friends share the same interests" (self-positioning as sub-groups)
P	Internally troubled positioning, interactionally untroubled/supported positioning
12	Sophia: *Yes, exactly.*
13	Anna: *Still, the reason is just that I don't like . . . I don't know . . . meeting up with boys or something like this*
IR	"Team consists of sub-groups", "Friends share the same interests" (self-positioning)
P	Internally troubled positioning, interactionally untroubled positioning
14	Lena: *Yeah*
15	Anna: *It is simply, she is interested in this, I'm interested in that . . .*
IR	"Team consists of sub-groups", "Friends share the same interests" (self- and other positioning of team member)
P	Internally troubled positioning, interactionally untroubled then troubled positioning
16	Sophia: *Yes, it's simply*
17	Anna: *But we still like each other and we would hang out together.*
IR	"No division despite sub-groups", "Being a team means spending time together on and off the pitch" (self-positioning as team)
P	Internally untroubled positioning, interactionally untroubled/supported positioning
18	Lena: *Yeah* Manuela: *Yeah*
19	Anna: *We would do it voluntarily, too.*
IR	"No division despite sub-groups", "Being a team means spending time together on and off the pitch" (self-positioning as team)

P	Internally untroubled positioning, interactionally troubled positioning
20	Sophia: *It also depends on the circle of friends.*
IR	"Team consists of sub-groups", "Free time is spent with closest friends"
P	Internally troubled positioning, interactionally untroubled/supported positioning
21	Anna: *Yeah* Lena: *Yeah*
22	Sophia: *I have a completely different circle than, for example, Anna or for example, Marija or Cornelia, are totally part of my circle of friends.*
IR	"Team consists of sub-groups", "Free time is spent with closest friends"
P	Internally troubled positioning, interactionally untroubled/supported positioning
23	Anna: *Yes*
24	Sophia: *That's why I often hang out with them in my free time.*
IR	"Free time is spent with closest friends"
P	Internally untroubled positioning, interactionally untroubled positioning
25	Lena: *This then happens automatically, when she is there, the others come along as well.*
IR	"Team consists of sub-groups, "Free time is spent with closest friends"
P	Internally troubled positioning, interactionally troubled positioning
26	Anna: *But this doesn't mean that we don't like each other.*
IR	"No real division despite sub-groups"
P	Internally untroubled positioning, interactionally untroubled/supported positioning
27	Lena: *Yes, that's not at all the case.*
IR	"No real division despite sub-groups"
P	Internally untroubled positioning, interactionally untroubled positioning

The final dilemma between individual ambition and upholding team cohesion is not exclusive to girls' teams but is a phenomenon of team sports in general. However, the dilemma seems intensified against ideas of female communality and relationship- and friendship-based team concepts. The players are torn between the existence of sub-groups within the team (a fact that cannot be negated yet requires mitigation) and arguing that these sub-groups are not formed on individual sympathies but aspects such as shared interests or circles of friends (e.g., see 15 and 20). This tension emerges on the language level in adversative particles at the beginning of (but also within) several contributions (see 5, 11, 13, 17, 26), as well as in modal particles such as "simply" (e.g., see 15 or 16).

The predicament of (a lack of) team cohesion and its need to be carefully negotiated is also visible (see 2, 3 and 4): an improved team cohesion ("not as extreme", "really become much better", "not as bad") is discussed that mitigates an inadequate previous (and to some extent also present) situation. The group interview situation might influence what can and cannot be uttered freely here more than in other thematic contexts. The speakers are thus not exactly troubling each other, but they seem to be struggling with this dilemma as a group.

The dilemma does not only exist between the IR explicitly addressed, but also in relation to prevailing team repertoires (e.g., "Good performance is based on team cohesion" or "Being a team means being friends"), which is why spending time together and expressions of sympathies for each other are stressed continuously. In terms of self-exclusion, such strong orientation towards friendship and team cohesion (i.e., female communality) impedes individual ambitions and professional (self-)development.

5 Interpretation of findings

The gender regime in football is firmly in place in the interviewees' accounts. Their explanations very much replicate the picture that has emerged in research over the last 20 years as players continue to experience football as a male and masculine space. Despite their (self-)inclusion in football, having played (semi-professional) associate football for many years in a successful girls' team, the girls report and criticize continuous disadvantages regarding education / training, money, opportunities, infrastructures etc. This attests to a lack of true change in football as "extremely gendered organization": while their own play as well as more generally rising numbers of female footballers document some positive development (Bryan et al. 2021; Drury et al. 2022), these changes represent an *accommodation* of women rather than a true *transformation* of the organization's gendered logic (Pape 2020: 82; Drury et al. 2022 for a critical assessment). The adolescent players' current status quo in their club affirms rather than challenges the binary and hierarchical notions of gender differences. As was argued by Acker (2006), successful change in (extremely) gendered organizations necessitates a low legitimacy of gender inequalities. Our data suggests otherwise. What is more, the girls themselves contribute to a continuing legitimization of male and masculine entitlement to football by arguing within binaries instead of beyond: While they construct themselves as athletically able footballers, they unanimously reconfirm the status of male football and footballers as the norm, perpetuating the association of masculinity and football regarding physique/physicality, dynamics, athleticism and prestige; their own and women's play in general are discursively framed as inferior to male superiority on all these levels. The girls also centralize male bodies and attest to a dilemma between female and male sporting bodies or embodiment on the field. Yet, on the other hand, they attribute specific feminine values such as caring for each other and greater fairness to their own game that morally elevates them and their play – again in opposition to boys/ men's game. A cultural field "female football" is discursively created, which exists as a secondary space alongside the cultural field "football" in its original "hereditary" and natural reading as "male football". The girls engage in practices of self-exclusion and contribute from "the inside" of this secondary cultural field also more generally to women's continuing (self-)exclusion. Concurrently, despite their own troubled minority status, the young female footballers engage in shared acts of discursive exclusion and othering of other social actors on the basis of gender(ed) expectations and ascriptions.

All in all, the girls both actively and passively support the binary system in football and add to their own as well as other female footballers' socio-cultural, and thus also practical, exclusion as the legitimacy of the extremely gendered organization football remains unchallenged. Against this overall picture, it is interesting to observe that we find less interactionally and individually troubled positions regarding the theme "Socio-cultural exclusion and distancing *by* players" (and in their account of socio-cultural and structural exclusion) than in the theme "Socio-cultural self-exclusion *by* players". It seems that the girls' discursive position both as an in-group and out-group is stronger than their discursive positions as individuals, where greater conflicts within the group, but also within the players themselves emerge. Such inconsistencies arise – following Stride et al.'s (2019: 773) argumentation that draws on Archer's (2004) notion of "fr/agility" – as girls or women are placed in particular discursive configurations imbued with relations of power, whilst also being active agents in challenging dominant discourses. In combining notions of power and weakness with agency and action (conveyed through agility), "fr/agility" recognizes the enduring nature of power relations and inequalities alongside the emerging of resilience and resistance. While we maintain a critical stance towards the girls' lack of agency and their explicit acts of self-exclusion, most visible in their direct negation of any possibility to change the situation attributing responsibility to the others, we also want to relativize this critique to some extent. According to Drury et al. (2022) and Francombe-Webb and Palmer (2018), our critique can also be interpreted as symptomatic of an increasingly postfeminist discourse seeing women as responsible for their own representation and integration in football and society at large, instead of attributing their continuous exclusion to a political and socio-cultural reality and – in our case – to their age and developmental stage as teenagers. The participants' age more generally must be raised as a caveat as their IR and SP may be more influenced by their caretakers and other social actors of importance than is the case with adult interviewees. While we are all influenced by larger socio-cultural discourses and ideologies, adolescents are particularly liable to either taking over or resisting adults' stances.

6 Conclusion and practical implications

Drury et al. (2022: 4) recently argued that "(w)hilst advances have been made toward eradicating essentialist myths about women's biological inadequacy for playing football, progress has been comparatively slower in terms of challenging unfounded assumptions about women's alleged incapability to fulfil leadership or decision-making roles". Our findings of women in playing roles tell a somewhat different story. The players who participated in our study adhere to existing hegemonic discourses of (biological) gender differences, (implicitly) perpetuate and reproduce the gender regime in football and collaboratively display strategies of (self-)exclusion and a lack of agency *in* and *through* their negotiations of football as a cultural field. In more detail, the girls sketch two cultural fields, each based on the inclusion of some social actors and the exclusion of "others". While the cultural field "male football" occupies the uppermost position in the ideological football hierarchy with an uncontested superiority, their football is positioned as second-best on the socio-cultural ladder, yet as a separate field "own" by them and imbued with female and feminine characteristics and values. Language and discourse in the form of repertoires, positionings and dilemmas have been (re-)established as vital tools to include and exclude social actors from football as "cultural field" and "extremely gendered organization".

We would like to end with elaborating on the **practical implications** of our research. Our findings have once again corroborated that a mere participation of females in football as players is not enough to truly and positively shake up the deeply and historically rooted conceptualization of football as an exclusively male space. As linguists and discourse analysts, we consider the empowering potential of language and discourse a particularly promising venue for lasting changes in the sense of Pape's (2020) and Bryan et al.'s (2021) *transformation*. The gendered behavioral, biological, and social expectations as regards the connection between football and masculinity of all social actors invested in the game must therefore be understood in all their complexities, nuances, and changing forms. More critical in-depth research as regards this (discursive) interplay of ideology and organization is needed. On this basis, it will become possible to raise the critical awareness of all stakeholders in football, including the female players themselves, and how they, in and through their linguistic and discursive practices of (self-)exclusion, contribute to a continuous legitimization of the association of football and masculinity in its derogatory and limiting consequences for everybody involved. In return, the constructive power of language and discourse as an emancipatory tool to make gender binarism visible and to narrate new *de*-gendering football narratives must be promoted. Delegitimizing boys' and men's entitlement to football should happen in private contexts, i.e., children's homes, in educational contexts such as schools, but also in organizational contexts such as football clubs and associations. Moreover, the players themselves – in addition to a more sensitive, i.e., *de*-gendering, use of interpretative repertoires and subject positions when talking about football as (male- and masculine dominated) sport – should be motivated to linguistically and discursively do "being a footballer" instead of doing "being a female footballer". By promoting their professional identity as footballer instead of their gendered identity, the players could thus actively help to shift the perspective "away from the stereotypical gendered manner in which society expects them to behave and enable them to perform by accommodating to the requirements of their jobs" (McDowell 2021: 7).

References

Acker, Joan. 2006. Inequality Regimes: Gender, Class, and Race in Organizations. *Gender & Society* 20(4). 441–64.
Bohnsack, Ralf. 2010. Gruppendiskussion. In Uwe Flick, Ernst von Kardorff & Ines Steinke (eds.), *Qualitative Forschung. Ein Handbuch*, 369–384. Hamburg: Rowohlt.
Braun, Virginia, Victoria Clarke & Paul Weate. 2019. Using Thematic Analysis in Sport and Exercise Research. In Brett Smith & Andrew Sparkes (eds.), *Routledge Handbook of Qualitative Research in Sport and Exercise*, 191–202. Abingdon: Routledge.
Bryan, Amée, Stacey Pope & Alexandra Rankin-Wright. 2021. On the Periphery. Examining Women's Exclusion from Core Leadership Roles in the "Extremely Gendered" Organization of Men's Club Football in England. *Gender & Society* 35(6). 940–970.
Caldwell, David, John Walsh, Elaine Vine & Jon Jureidini (eds.). 2017. *The Discourse of Sports: Analysis from Social Linguistics*. London: Routledge.
Caudwell, Jayne. 2011. Gender, Feminism and Football Studies. *Soccer & Society* 12(3). 330–344.
Caudwell, Jayne. 2019. Football and Misogyny. In John Hughson, Kevin Moore, Ramón Spaaji, & Joseph Maguire (eds.), *Routledge Handbook of Football Studie*s, 204–314. Abingdon: Routledge.
Clark, Sheryl. 2021. *Sporty Girls. Gender, Health and Achievement in a Postfeminist Era*. Cham: Sprinter Nature.
Clark, Sheryl & Carrie Paechter. 2007. 'Why Can't Girls Play Football?' Gender Dynamics and the Playground. *Sport, Education and Society* 12(3). 261–276.
Cox, Barbara & Shona Thompson. 2000. Multiple Bodies: Sportswomen, Soccer and Sexuality. *International Review for the Sociology of Sports* 35(1). 5–20.
Drury, Scarlett, Annette Stride, Hayley Fitzgerald, Nia Hyett-Allen, Laura Pylypiuk, & Jodie Whitford-Stark. 2022. "I'm a Referee, not a Female Referee": The Experiences of Women Involved in Football as Coaches and Referees. *Frontiers in Sports and Active Living* 3. 1–15.
Dunn, Carrie &Joanna Welford. 2019. Women's Elite Football. In John Hughson, Kevin Moore, Ramón Spaaij & Joseph Maguire (eds.), *Routledge Handbook of Football Studies*, 138–150. Abingdon: Routledge.
Edley, Nigel. 2001. Analysing Masculinity: Interpretative Repertoires, Ideological Dilemmas and Subject Positions. In Margaret Wetherell, Stephanie Taylor & Simeon J. Yates (eds.), *Discourse as Data: A Guide for Analysis*, 189–228. London: SAGE.

Edley, Nigel &Margaret Wetherell. 2008. Discursive Psychology and the Study of Gender: A Contested Space. In Kate Harrington, Lia Litosseliti, Helen Sauntson, & Jane Sunderland (eds.), *Gender and Language Research Methodologies*, 161–173. Basingstoke: Palgrave Macmillan.
Fairclough, Norman. 1992. *Discourse and Social Change*. Cambridge: Polity Press.
Fielding-Lloyd, Beth & Lindsey Meân. 2011. "I Don't Think I Can Catch It": Women, Confidence and Responsibility in Football Coach Education. *Soccer & Society* 12(3). 345–64.
Fielding-Lloyd, Beth & Lindsey Meân. 2016. Women Training to Coach a Men's Sport: Managing Gendered Identities and Masculinist Discourses. *Communication & Sport* 4(4). 401–423.
Fleischhacker, Melanie. 2019. *Multimodal Discourses of Gender and Sexuality in Austrian EFL Textbooks*. Klagenfurt: University of Klagenfurt (unpublished) MA Thesis.
Francombe-Webb, Jessica &Laura Palmer. 2018. Footballing Femininities: The Lived Experiences of Young Females Negotiating "The Beautiful Game"". In Kim Toffoletti, Holly Thorpe & Jessica Francombe-Webb (eds.), *New Sporting Femininities. Embodied Politics in Postfeminist Times*, 179–205. Cham: Palgrave-Macmillan.
Graf, Eva-Maria & Melanie Fleischhacker (in press). Football as opportunity! Exploring and transforming gender inequalities via inter- and transdisciplinary football research with a special focus on qualitative linguistic discourse analysis. *Soccer & Society* (special issue).
Graf, Eva-Maria & Melanie Fleischhacker. 2020. „Wenn ich es nicht schaffe, liegt es an meiner Person und nicht an meiner Leistung". Die Individualisierung struktureller Probleme im Coaching weiblicher Führungskräfte. *Coaching | Theorie & Praxis* 6. 111–133.
Harris, John. 2007. Doing Gender on and off the Pitch: The World of Female Football Players. *Sociological Research Online* 12(1). Np.
Jeanes, Ruth. 2012. 'I'm into High Heels and Make up but I Still Love Football': Exploring Gender Identity and Football Participation with Preadolescent Girls. In Jayne Caudwell (ed.), *Women's Football in the UK*, 80–98. London: Routledge.
Jeanes, Ruth &Tess Kay. 2007. Can Football be a Female Game? An Examination of Girls' Perceptions of Football and Gender Identity. In Jonathan Magee, Jayne Caudwell, Katie Liston & Sheila Scraton (eds.), *Women, Football and Europe: Histories, Equity and Experiences*, 105–129. Oxford: Meyer & Meyer Sport.
Madriz, Esther. 2003. Focus Groups in Feminist Research. In Norman Denzin & Yvonna Lincoln (eds.), *Collecting and Interpreting Qualitative Materials*, 363–388. London: Sage.
McDowell, Joanne (ed.). 2021. *De-Gendering Gendered Professions. Analysing Professional Discourse*. New York: Routledge.
Meân, Lindsey. 2001. Identity and Discursive Practice: Doing Gender on the Football Pitch. *Discourse & Society* 12(6). 789–815.
Norman, Leanne, Alexandra Rankin-Wright & Wayne Allison. 2018. "It's a Concrete Ceiling; It's not even Glass": Understanding Tenets of Organizational Culture that Supports the Progression of Women as Coaches and Coach Developers. *Journal of Sport and Social Issues*, 42(5). 393–414.
Pape, Madeleine. 2020. Gender Segregation and Trajectories of Organizational Change: The Underrepresentation of Women in Sports Leadership. *Gender & Society* 34(1). 81–105.
Pielichaty, Hanya. 201. 'It's Like Equality Now; It's not as if It's the Old Days': An Investigation into Gender Identity Development and Football Participation of Adolescent Girls. *Soccer & Society* 16(4). 493–507.
Pope, Stacey. 2017. *The Feminization of Sports Fandom: A Sociological Study*. London: Routledge.
Pfister, Gertrud & Susan J. Bandy. 2018. Gender and Sport. In Richard Giulianotti (ed), *Routledge Handbook of the Sociology of Sport*, 220–231. Abingdon: Routledge.

Pfister, Gertrud & Stacey Pope (eds.). *Female Football Players and Fans. Intruding into a Man's World*. London: Palgrave Macmillan.

Sasson-Levy, Orna. 2011. The Military in a Globalized Environment: Perpetuating an 'Extremely Gendered' Organization. In Emma Jeanes, David Knights & Patricia Yancey Martin (eds.), *Handbook of Gender, Work, and Organization*, 391–410. Chichester: Wiley.

Schirato, Tony 2013. *Sports Discourse*. London: Bloomsbury.

Scraton, Sheila, Kari Fastin, Gertrud Pfister & Ana Bunuel. 2018 [1999]. It's Still a Man's Game? The Experiences of Top-Level European Women Footballers. In Gertrud Pfister, Stacey Pope (eds.), *Female Football Players and Fans. Football Research in an Enlarged Europe*, 19–37. Palgrave Macmillan: London.

Stride, Anette, Scarlett Drury & Hayley Fitzgerald. 2019. 'Last Goal Wins': Re/engaging Women of a 'Forgotten' Age through Football? *Sport Education Sociology* 24. 770–783.

Sunderland, Jane. 2004. *Gendered Discourses*. New York: Palgrave.

Tyler, Meagan, Lisa Carson & Benjamin Reynolds. 2019. Are Fire Services "Extremely Gendered" Organizations? Examining the Country Fire Authority (CFA) in Australia. *Gender, Work & Organization* 26(9). 1304–23.

Welford, Joanna & Tess Kay. 2007. Negotiating Barriers to Entering and Participating in Football: Strategies Employed by Female Footballers in the United Kingdom. In Jonathan Magee, Jayne Caudwell, Katie Liston, & Sheila Scraton (eds.), *Women, Football and Europe. Histories, Equity and Experience*, 151–173. Oxford: Meyer & Meyer Sport.

Wetherell, Margaret. 1998. Positioning and Interpretative Repertoires: Conversation Analysis and Post-structuralism in Dialogue. *Discourse & Society*, 9(3). 387–412.

Wiggins, Sally. 2017. *Discursive Psychology. Theory, Method and Applications*. London: Sage.

Richard Pringle and Erik Denison
Chapter 11
A critical examination of homo-negative language use and the pragmatics of inclusion and exclusion of gay rugby players

1 Introduction

Sport participation can increase feelings of happiness, well-being and inclusion (Wilson et al. 2022). Yet for some, participation can produce feelings of social exclusion, incompetence, physical pain and can even be a cause of poor self–esteem and depression. These negative experiences within sport are connected to the somewhat dramatic youth sport withdrawal rates (Gardener, Magee, and Valla 2017). Survey results reveal that sporting participation rates for youth aged 15–19 years are 50% lower compared with 11–14 years (Eime, Harvey, and Charity 2019).

One such group that has been deterred from participating in sport are gay and bisexual males. Gay and bisexual youth have been found to play team sports at half the rate of their straight peers (Center for Disease Control and Prevention 2020; Doull et al. 2018). Moreover, there is evidence to suggest that discrimination and the use of homophobic banter are factors that actively discourage many gay teenagers from participation (Denison, Bevan and Jeanes 2021). Greenspan, Griffith and Watson (2019: 169) report that LGBTQ+ youth tend to avoid "physical activity settings (e.g., physical education classes, locker rooms, and sport fields) due to feeling both unsafe and uncomfortable. These feelings and experiences might deter LGBTQ+ youth from achieving well-documented physical, cognitive, and social-emotional benefits that are often associated with physical activity and sport involvement."

In this chapter we draw on Foucauldian theorising to examine how homo-negative language use in rugby teams can work to exclude the participation and acceptance of male players who identify as gay or bisexual. We draw on results from eight focus group interviews with gay and straight rugby players from Britain in order to explore the intent and impact of the ongoing use of homophobic language. We begin by reviewing relevant literature associated with sport, masculinity and sexualities, followed by a section that introduces our research method

Richard Pringle, Erik Denison, Monash University, Australia and Foucauldian theoretical lens for understanding how language can act as a dividing practice to exclude and include. We then present our results.

2 Sport, masculinity, diverse sexualities and homophobia: A contextual overview

Until the 1970s the sporting world was primarily deemed to be a masculine domain (Dunning 1986). Females were sanctioned to participate in a narrow range of sports, such as tennis, gymnastics, netball and swimming yet were often viewed as "athletic intruders" in the football codes, combat sports or sports that involved displays of strength (Bolin and Granskog 2003). Whereas males were typically encouraged to play one of the dominant winter sporting codes, such as rugby union, ice hockey, soccer or Aussie Rules. Although since the 1970s there has been tremendous growth in female sport participation (Cooky and Messner 2018), sport is still regarded as vitally important in influencing how men and boys understand and practice masculinities. Indeed, the truism that sport involvement "turns boys into men", with reference to masculine men, still exerts considerable influence. Relatedly, critical sport scholars have emphasised how a dominant form of masculinity is performed and reproduced within male sporting contexts that broadly privilege males over females, and orthodox masculinities over males who are judged as effeminate, unmanly, epicene or as homosexual (McKay, Messner and Sabo 2000).

The recognition of the close relationship between sport and masculinities has been both a cause of celebration and concern. Male sporting achievements are disproportionately celebrated within the media, yet critical voices have tended to be marginalised. Indeed, the critical sport scholar may be viewed as a "killjoy" (see Ahmed 2010), as they are viewed as critiquing a seemingly morally sound and healthy leisure pursuit. Many critical commentators throughout the 1980s and 90s, nevertheless, illustrated that sport, particularly the dominant winter football codes, problematically linked physical skill, competition, aggression, pain tolerance and sexism with a dominant but problematic form of masculinity (e.g., Pringle and Markula 2005; Magrath, Cleland, and Anderson 2020; Stick 2021). This hegemonic form of masculinity has been associated with higher rates violence, injury, abuse, suicide, drug and alcohol problems and poor health (Sabo and Gordon 1995). Hickey and Fitzclarence (1999: 52), relatedly, worried that the central "masculinity" lesson that boys gained within sport settings was unhealthy, as they primarily learnt "how to get back up after being knocked down, how to express themselves physically, how to impose themselves forcefully, how to mask pain and how to release anxiety".

Although these critical researchers from the 1990s acknowledged that the hegemonic form of sporting masculinity reinforced male dominance over females, relatively few, with the prime exception of Pronger (1992), examined how male sporting participation adversely shaped relationships between straight and gay males. This was despite the fact that the dominant theorising of the time drew on Connell's (1995) concept of hegemonic masculinity and the associated notion that heteronormativity was a key structuring principle for performances of masculinity. This theoretical lens asserted that the dominant form of masculinity produced within sporting contexts acted to subjugate "softer" forms of masculinities. Of which, the most subjugated form was understood to be linked to gay men (Connell 1995).

Messner (1996: 225) acknowledged the social significance of heteronormativity and argued that sport participation was typically viewed as offering a "normalising equation" for men: "Athleticism = masculinity = heterosexuality". This seemingly simple equation reflected the broad view that team sports, particularly the heavy-contact high-speed collision sports, "have been considered a key vehicle for the production of a socially valued archetype of heteromasculinity, based upon men being aggressive, stoic and homophobic" (Murray and White 2017: 536). Messner's equation highlights how sport reinforces a "normal" form of masculinity that is assumed to be heterosexual. Yet, of course, not all men who play or enjoy sport are heterosexual.

Throughout the first decade of the new millennium, a growing body of evidence revealed that homophobic attitudes within sporting contexts caused anxiety for gay men and acted as a strong deterrent for participating in sport (e.g., Anderson, 2002; Demers, 2006; Plummer, 2006; Brackenridge et al. 2007; Osborne and Wagner, 2007). Plummer (2006: 122) found that within Australian sporting contexts, homophobic language (using terms such as "poofter" and "faggot") were "used to police the boundary between 'successful manhood' and those who, according to their peers, fail to 'measure up'". He concluded by asking rhetorically: "Is it really so surprising that physical peer-based activities such as tough team sports are so problematic for boys who feel different?" (Plummer 2006: 136). Sporting contexts, however, were not simply places within which homophobic language occurred but were also viewed as breeding grounds for homonegativism. Osborne and Wagner (2007) reported that men who participated in the popular sporting codes were three times more likely to hold homophobic attitudes in comparison to those who did not participate in these sports. And these attitudes were found, at times, to manifest in acts of homophobic abuse and violence.

In the last decade there is, however, evidence to suggest that a progressive shift in the performance of sporting masculinities is occurring. This evidence reveals that many young straight men are performing a more respectful or inclusive form of masculinity that rejects violence and bullying while also being pro-feminist and gay friendly (McCormack and Anderson 2014; Magrath, Anderson and Roberts 2015). The proponents of inclusive masculinity theory (see Anderson and McCormack 2018) have, correspondingly, suggested that the apparent softening in contemporary masculinities is tied to a progressive shift in the acceptance of diverse sexualities; of which there is accumulating evidence. A recent major survey of 30,000 Americans found, for example, that 49% believe that same-sex sexual activity was "not wrong at all", which was up from only 11% in 1973 and 13% in 1990 (Twenge, Sherman and Wells 2016: 1713). Although a positive shift, we note that the majority were still not convinced that same-sex sexual activity was not "wrong at all".

Caudwell (2015) recognised that there is a progressive shift away from homonegativism yet suggested that the narrative of progress and equality is somewhat problematic as it acts to conceal a host of problems still tied to homosexual prejudice. Although signs of greater acceptance of diverse sexualities amongst heterosexual athletes are apparent (see Magrath, Anderson and Roberts 2015), conflicting evidence still reveals that sporting contexts remain a challenging context for LGBTIQ+ athletes (Denison, Bevan and Jeanes 2021; Hartmann-Tews, Menzel and Braumüller 2021). Hartmann-Tews et al.'s (2021: 1009) large scale survey (N = 5524) of LGBTIQ+ sporting individuals aged over 16 years revealed "that homo- and transnegativity are still present in sport in Europe and are potent problematic influences on the sporting experiences of LGBT+ people" with approximately 50% of the respondents having experienced homo or trans negative language in the last 12 months. They concluded "that competitive and team sports continue to privilege male hegemony and encourage language that polices masculinity" (Hartmann-Tews et al. 2021: 1010).

Of significance, we suggest that the undercurrent of homonegativism, as reflected in the continued use of homophobic language in sporting clubs (Denison, Bevan and Jeanes 2021), may still have harmful impact. We are particularly concerned that the problematic rates of self-harm and suicide amongst LGBTIQ+ people have not changed in over three decades and, importantly, these rates have been linked to damaging life experiences associated with homonegativism (DeFoor, Stepleman and Mann 2018; Painter et al. 2018).

2.1 Debates concerning the use of homophobic language

One area of contention within examinations of homosexualities and sport relates to the ongoing use of "potentially" homophobic language within the context of sporting clubs. Evidence clearly illustrates that the use of phrases such as "that's so gay" or "fag" are still relatively common within sport (Greenspan, Griffith and Watson 2019; Denison, Bevan and Jeanes 2021; Hartmann-Tews, Menzel and Braumüller 2021). Yet those who draw on inclusive masculinity theory (e.g., Anderson and McCormack 2018) contend that the use of this seemingly homonegative language is not underpinned by homophobic intent. Anderson and McCormack (2018), for example, argue that some straight men use phrases such as "that's so gay" but that they are supportive of same-sex sex. They accordingly argue that the interpretation of such language needs to understand the context and intent of the speaker. McCormack, Wignal and Morris (2016) relatedly devised an intent–context–effect matrix to explain how different people interpreted phrases like "that's so gay". They argued that shared norms within specific groups shaped how different individuals judged phrases as acceptable or not dependent on the context. Within this framework of thinking they argued that the on-going use of seemingly homophobic slurs, such as "faggot" and "that's so gay", are not necessarily worthy of critical concern, as the intent is not to denigrate LGBTIQ+ people.

Yet we are troubled that the uncritical acceptance of language, that was once unquestionably deemed homophobic – and in the ongoing light of disparate rates of self-harm and suicide amongst the LGBTIQ+ population – is deemed no longer worthy of critical concern by some scholars. It is our concern with the potential negative health and wellbeing effects of homophobic banter that we have undertaken this examination. In light of the divergent research findings surrounding the use of seemingly homophobic language in sport, we present the results of a study that drew on mixed methods to examine the apparent disconnect between the expression of inclusive attitudes towards queer people and the continued usage of homophobic language that can act to exclude and denigrate. Before we introduce our research methods, we detail our Foucauldian theoretical lens for understanding the use of language and its connections to power relations and the production of differing subjectivities, social exclusions and inclusions.

3 Foucauldian theory: Discourse/language and identity

Foucault's writings were concerned with how the workings of discourse, as linked to the workings of language, played a significant role in the constitution of identities or "subjectivities" and the associated power relations between differing people. Foucault (1972: 49) considered that discourses were more than linguistic phenomena as they could be circulated in numerous non-verbal ways such as via postures, expressions, clothing and various social interactions. In this manner, he argued that discourses could be regarded broadly as social "practices that systematically form the objects of which they speak" (ibid.). In simplistic terms, he understood that discourses shape how humans understand *or* know particular objects, ideas or people. For example, an observer watching a game of rugby union may come to understand rugby players as strong, competitive, aggressive and tough: from a discursive position the observer may come to know rugby as a "masculine sport". Foucault (1978: 100) further argued that "it is in discourse that power and knowledge are joined together". As an example, the discursive knowledge that has historically positioned rugby as a masculine or man's game, underpinned the exclusion of women from participating in rugby until the early 1970s. This discursive knowledge still exerts contemporary influence as some people still view female rugby players as intruders within rugby contexts (Bolin and Granskog 2003). The circulation of gendered, sexist or homophobic discourses, which is often performed verbally, can therefore act to encourage inclusion or exclusion of particular identities within certain contexts.

Language is clearly important in the circulation of discourses and researchers who undertake discourse analysis typically analyse interview transcripts to identify the underpinning discourses. In the following section we discuss how we conducted and analysed our interviews to examine how the use of "homophobic" banter contributes to the divisions between straight and gay rugby players and the associated relations of power.

4 Methods

The data we report on was collected using surveys and focus group interviews with rugby players from amateur rugby clubs in the UK. We surveyed players to find out about the usage of homophobic language within their clubs, their perceptions of this language, and their attitudes towards gay people. Players completed a paper and pen 10-minute survey prior to their normal team practise. The surveys were completed with 139 players aged between16 to 60 years, with a median age of 25 years. Nearly all (95.9%) identified as being Anglo-European.

We also conducted focus group interviews with rugby players from mainstream clubs and an openly gay and inclusive rugby club – the Kings Cross Steelers – who were founded in 1995 and were proud of being known as the world's first gay inclusive rugby club. None of the players from the mainstream clubs identified as queer during the focus group interviews. The interviews lasted between 40 and 80 minutes and were conducted in club settings. The heterosexual players came from two Colts teams (ages 18 to 20) from different clubs, and we conducted individual interviews with a senior player, a female coach, and a fitness coach. The survey results suggested that players recalled using homonegative language but suggested that they were not homophobic. Given these results, we undertook the interviews to understand why the players frequently used "homonegative" language but did not typically appear overtly homophobic. In addition, we examined, in more depth, the culture of the teams in relationship to issues concerned with pain, injury, alcohol, feminism and diverse sexualities, which was a focus of our broader research project but not specific to the results we present in this chapter. With respect to the gay rugby players, we sought to understand their experiences and perceptions concerning the use of homophobic language in their sport, the associated impact of this language and, more broadly, their motivations for playing.

The interview transcripts were read and re-read, and written comments were made in the margins of the transcripts with respects to the broad themes of the conversation, such as, rugby injury, alcohol use, competition outcomes, friendships, gender relations, female players and sexualities. We then re-read the transcripts associated with various themes to identify the discourses that the rugby players talked of in referring to various social practices, such as, getting on the beers, competing for victory, managing injuries or trying to score with women. For example, when the players talked of a "big night on the turps" and "getting up to trouble cos of the beers" it was apparent that these were joyous occasions talked of with a degree of reverence. In this respect, we interpreted that alcohol consumption was discursively "known" as a positive socially bonding experience. Relatedly, we attempted to examine and identify the discourses that propped up the interview conversations to understand the meanings associated with playing rugby and, importantly, the "homophobic" language that occurred within rugby contexts. We wanted to know what purpose this language served and how it acted to include or exclude diverse sexualities.

5 Results and discussion

The results from our surveys (n =139) revealed that 37% of the players had self-reportedly used homophobic slurs in the two weeks prior to the survey being conducted. Moreover, 62% reported that they had heard their teammates use homophobic language (i.e., "that's so gay") within the same time period. These results supported previous findings that homophobic language remains commonplace within various sporting contexts (see Denison et al. 2021a; Hartmann-Tews, Menzel and Braumüller 2021). Of the 139 players who completed the anonymous surveys across all mainstream clubs only one player identified as gay and one as bisexual. These two players equate to 1.4% of our total rugby sample: a percentage lower than the estimated population mean of 3.6% for adult men who identify as gay or bisexual men (Wilson et al. 2020) and the 9% of teenage men who identify as gay, bisexual, or not exclusively heterosexual (Shanklin et al. 2020). Moreover, none of the players who participated in the focus group interviews, from the mainstream clubs, could identify any of their teammates as gay or bisexual. Although Eddy (a colt's player) remembered that a previous player "for our team came out as bi". He added, "but he obviously didn't want to play rugby at that point anymore (as) he left shortly after." The players acknowledged that there could be gay players in their teams but, if so, "they're not open about it" (Mick – senior player). These results suggest that exclusionary forces were at work to either dissuade queer men from participating in rugby and/or to prevent them from coming out within their rugby clubs.

Although our survey data suggested that 94% of the players would welcome gay players into their club, the focus group conversations revealed that it could be difficult to be an openly gay rugby player in their clubs: as indicated in the following interview excerpts:

Excerpt 1:

Richard (lead author): "do you have any gay players in the team?"
Kev: Not that I know of.
Luca: Not that we know of. No.
Thomas: No.
Richard: Do you think there might be some that just haven't come out?
Kev: I don't know.
Luca: I think you never really know, do you?
Kev: No not necessarily.
Thomas: There could be.
Luca: Yes, there could be definitely.
Thomas: Who's everyone thinking of? Sort of like, who could it be?

Thomas' question prompted the team mates to look at each other, with a degree of speculative intrigue. The coach said, "I could probably name him in three guesses". Although this conversation did not reveal overt homophobia, the notion of "naming" or "outing" a gay player in the team appeared to be of great interest to the players. This interest in naming a potentially gay player then prompted an immediate discussion of the masculine culture of the club, as evidenced by talk of heterosexuality:

Excerpt 2:

Kev: Yeah, it's a very masculine environment innit?
Luca; There's always a lot, on. A Saturday night whenever we go out, there's a lot of talk about girls and . . . recent successes. So I imagine in that environment you'd be quite loathed to (come out) . . . but I don't think people would be ok . . . I think it would be an intimidating environment to come out in.
Kev: Yeah, I could understand why someone wouldn't want to come out.

Discursively the players identified the team culture as masculine and heterosexual, a culture that they identified could act to exclude gay players from belonging. They elaborated on this culture by talking of a recent team trip, and how they entertained each other in their shared search for meeting local women on dating apps and their competitive interest to see who had "success" or "failure". Kev noted "I think just throughout the whole week there's a lot of friendly banter about the issue." Thomas acknowledged that the heterosexual language was an aspect of the team culture and "everyone gets a piece taken out of them for anything here". Thomas illustrated, "We've got a boy, he's a priest". And Luca affirmed: "Yep, he gets shit for it, but he loves it". The intimation of this conversation was that if there was an openly gay player in the team, he would face "friendly teasing" about his sexuality. More broadly, although the players suggested that they would welcome a gay player they nevertheless recognised that the dominating culture of hetero-masculinity could be off–putting for a gay player.

Younger players from a colts' team (aged 16–18), similarly affirmed that they would welcome gay players into the team. Trent believed that gay players "would maybe be comfortable enough to be out (in his team) but there doesn't appear to be any". Trent was so confident that the team culture would be welcoming of gay players that he suggested "maybe it is a stereotype of gay men that they do not want to play sport, rather than people who play sport saying they are not accepting of gay people". Yet Mal immediately countered:

Excerpt 3:

In school, I have seen that gay people have come out and then a couple of weeks after, you can see the change in the whole team . . . they will start to mock him, or they will start to move away from him or not talk to him as often or just say a slur or gay reference. Whereas if they never knew about this, they would never have said anything like this.

Two of the other colts suggested that they had not witnessed such behaviour. Trent affirmed that he had a queer friend, yet the ensuing conversation revealed a mixture of feelings towards sexual diversities:

Excerpt 4:

Trent: Personally, me and James have one friend who is bi.
James: Which one is that?
Trent: Sam
James: Oh yeah (laughs)
Trent: And Mal also.
Richard (Author): Mal are you bi?
Mal: No! No. No. No. No! (others laugh in the background)
Richard (author): Why the laughter?
Michael, "I just thought it was fun" (more laughter occurs).

It was apparent within this team banter that the questioning of a team member's sexuality was a source of humour and that the attention was not welcomed by Mal, as evidenced by his drawn-out denial (i.e. "No! No. No. No. No!"). It was also evident that some teenagers who come out can be excluded within schools. Yet, on the other hand, both Trent and James asserted that their friend's bisexuality was not a problem for them and that they would even physically defend them: "If someone were to be homophobic towards him, and I saw it, I would probably get into a fight with them because "I don't take that stuff" (Trent). In this manner, it was apparent that the rugby players were aware of the problem of homophobia yet their laughter towards the questioning of Mal's sexuality suggested that a gay player within their team could still be subject to exclusionary practices.

Additional interview data revealed that discourses of homonegativism were clearly present within the club cultures. The colt's players from both teams, as examples, talked about the fact that the team does not shower naked with each other to avoid allegations of being gay. Instead, they shower with their boxers/undies on and then get changed privately in a toilet cubicle. The players explained:

Excerpt 5:

Mat (Colt's player): I think it's just insecurity.
Al: Don't want to be different . . . you pop in the shower naked here, and everyone else walks in in their boxers.
Len: You get mocked if you shower naked here.

The other colts' players similarly suggested that they showered with their undies on "as people like to shower in their privacy" (James). He added: "Whatever people are comfortable with. I don't particularly want to see 'it' (laughing) you know. Frankly, I don't need to see 'it' (laughing)." The 'it' referred to a penis. Den added: "I've just never done that so I wouldn't start doing it." Mal asserted: "with private schools many of them still do it but after a match now, people think it's weird, people make fun of people who shower together, I've seen it happen." James confirmed Mal's perspective: "Yeah! The private school culture. Yeah. Yeah."

Excerpt 6:

Richard (author): what kind of comments do they make?
Mal: now that I look back it would be homophobic comments.
Richard: Like that's a bit gay?
Mal: Yeah (nodding) that's a bit gay that they are all showering together.

Others in the team affirmed Mal's perspective that showering together naked would be assumed to be akin to being "gay" and that players would not want others to potentially consider that they were gay or become the subject of gay taunts. Richard (author) sought clarification: "is that part of the concern, that if you are showering with your underwear off with other guys that it is a bit gay?" Trent affirmed that players might become the subject of homophobic banter but stipulated: "although they might use homophobic language, I don't think any of them would be homophobic towards a gay person."

The players clearly affirmed that they were aware that homophobic taunts to a gay person were wrong. Moreover, many of the players declared that terms or phrases such as –– "poofta", "fag", "bender", "that's so gay" or "no homo" –– were terms of an older generation and they claimed that they did not use them or very rarely heard them: as the following assertions from various members of different clubs reveal:

Excerpt 7:

Rob (seniors): Personally, I haven't heard derogatory almost slating of homosexuals in the way of, "Come on you faggots, come on you gays" in a long time – I don't think people use that as a phrasing anymore.
Den (Colts team 1): we don't use them.
Len (Colts team 2): I personally haven't.
Matt (Colts team 2): I don't use those phrases.
Trent (Colts team 2): that is not something I would say to someone.
Jake (Fitness trainer for a colts team): For me it's an absolute non-issue . . . I can't recall it (homophobic language), I can't recall it going on within any of my sessions.
A female coach of a colt's team reported that she had heard sexist language but not homophobic:

Excerpt 8:

Alley: I have heard 'man up' or 'stop being a girl's blouse'.
Richard: What's your reaction to that?

Alley: I've checked them a few times when I hear and then I say 'who is your coach?'. And then, 'Oh, sorry Miss' or 'Sorry coach.'
Richard: What about language like: "You're a bit gay?"
Alley: Genuinely, I have not heard the boys saying that. I can't remember an incident of any of the lads that I've coached, or I can't remember hearing any of the boys that I coach saying that. Around me anyway.

In this respect there appeared to be very little use of homophobic banter. Yet these comments countered the results from our anonymous surveys of language use. Our survey results illustrated that homophobic language was seemingly relatively common within the teams, with 29% of the players even reporting that they had also been a target of homophobic slurs. When Richard (author) raised this issue within the focus group interviews, there was reluctant acknowledgement that such language did still occur, but the players defended this language use by suggesting that it was not used with homophobic intent and/or not directed to LGBTIQ+ people, as the following conversation with senior players reveals:

Excerpt 8:

Rob: I've been of the opinion for quite a while now that the word gay no longer is associated with homosexuality in throw off comments. I hear my students say it quite a lot, "That's gay", you know what I mean? They're talking about their phone not working properly, in no way can it be – and I know necessarily it's not the right usage of word, but I just don't think they associate it with that anymore . . . it does still hold a negative undertone to the idea of what they're using it for, but I don't think they intend to link it to homosexuality.
Mick: I doubt – I wouldn't use just that (language) by itself to say that somebody is homophobic as a result of it.
Luigi: It's context –
Bryan: It could be a really stupid mistake, or it could be a stupid use of words, not thinking about it.
Rob: That's the thing though, I know people that would call things gay just in passing and they are in no way homophobic. I know that because I've known them for a long time or whatever, and like I say I don't think that usage of the word now has the connotation that links to homosexuality.
Bryan: With the wrong individual in the wrong situation, it's definitely insensitive, but
Luigi: It's not malicious.
Mick: Yeah, wouldn't allude to prejudice of any kind.

After the players had defended particular sayings – such as "that's so gay" with the belief that it can be used in a non-homophobic manner – some were then willing to acknowledge that they used such words or phrases:

Excerpt 9:

Richard: so you guys use those words?
Mark (colts): I personally say yes, I'll be honest . . . I'll be like, 'oh this is so gay to mean it's shit (it's just like a word you use).
Den: I think people just use it in the wrong way.
Mark: now that I say it in comparison to that is shit it make me sound homophobic (laughing) but I am not homophobic. Disclaimer (others laugh) that's not how I want it to come across, it's not my intention because I have gay uncles and I'm friends with gay people and I have no problem with gay people.
James: I remember in primary school when we didn't really understand, and we used to say that's gay all the time.
Alan: We learned it from others, we just feel comfortable saying it.
Mal: I have been in class where we were doing group work and there were gay people there and someone said 'that's gay' and we all just laughed.
Richard (author): how do you think the gay guys would have felt?
Mal: we asked them afterwards because we knew that they were gay and the teacher asked and I think it's the tone of how you use it, we are all laughing and stuff, it's the tone that you use it in.
James: it's quite silly and sad that it has been normalised so much, I don't know they said it was okay (the guys in Mal's story) but if I was in their shoes I would say it is okay too -- even if it wasn't because everyone was laughing. So, if I said it's not okay then I am inconveniencing everyone.

James' comment was intuitive as the players in the King's Cross Steelers (a gay and inclusive rugby team) were clear that the language, whether intended to be homophobic or not, hurts and is damaging. The Steelers' acknowledged that they heard such language on the pitch, such as "fairy" and "gay", but that it was not overly common, but they were still concerned about it:

Excerpt 10:

Tom: So, I guess we are sort of used to it but putting the club hat on, as I say, we have more concerns now about this use of language and what the impact is on the next generation going forward.
Bill: Particularly younger guys.
Tom: Yeah. So those 13, 14s, who are starting to identify as LGBT, are they going to feel welcome if they hear their coaches, even if they are going around using it in what they think is non-homophobic way? . . . And is that putting off good potential players from playing the sport?
Richard: Well, what do you think? You think it would?
Tom: I think it does. I think it does. I think it puts people off. I think you need visible, you need role models, but you also need to feel safe. At that age and as you're coming to terms with your sexuality is such a delicate time for people. You want to surround yourself with... You don't want to feel any more uncomfortable than you already do feel. So if you have it there, then it's really tough.

The Steelers revealed that the homophobic language was damaging when they were young and it put them off playing as teenagers, as they did not feel safe being in a team that used homophobic slurs.

6 Concluding thoughts and implications

We draw this chapter to a close by reflecting on the discourses that underpinned our interviewees' views on homonegativism and their use of language that would historically be defined as "homophobic" in the same way as the "N" word would be defined to be a "racist" term. We suggest that competing discourses surrounded the multiple understandings of homosexuality. Homonegative practices and overt language appeared to be publicly known as problematic and unacceptable. In this discursive context, players did not want to appear homophobic. Some of the straight players even discussed that if they heard homophobic language that they would call it out and potentially defend their gay friends. More broadly, the interviewees did not want to disclose that they used words or phrases that could implicate them as being homophobic, which is an identity they publicly rejected, despite engaging in language that would be considered to be homophobic by many. This points to a disconnect between attitudes and behaviours found in other research conducted in rugby union (Denison et al. 2021b). Furthermore, if the players acknowledged that they used words, such as "gay" or "bender", they wanted it known that they were using such terms in a non-homophobic manner. They also wanted it known that they had gay friends or uncles, as if this would prove that they were not homophobic. They also understood that if they used such language in front of people who identified as queer, that this was problematic. Nevertheless, many acknowledged that they used such language in their rugby clubs, as they believed (rightly or wrongly) that there were no gay players in the team and, therefore, they erroneously believed that their language use was not problematic.

Although homophobic language and practices were deemed to be socially unacceptable in public contexts (particularly if there might be gay people present), the straight players were deeply offended if others judged that they were gay. Homosexuality, in this discursive light, was still viewed as "odd", "abnormal" or potentially "deviant". The colt's players, correspondingly, would not shower in the nude, as they were concerned that this could be interpreted as gay behaviour. And if a player was judged as "gay" this accusation had to be clearly refuted (e.g., Mal's response "No! no, no, no, no!"). The straight players still believed that it was appropriate to publicly show, or prove, that they were straight. Indeed, a key form of entertainment of one of the senior teams, while on tour, was to demonstrate that you were trying to connect with women (via dating apps) and were hopefully having success. Dating is normally a relatively private activity, so we argue that the point of publicly attempting to meet or have success (i.e., sex) with girls is likely to indicate that someone is heterosexual and, correspondingly, a normal male. Heteronormativity was still very much expected within mainstream rugby clubs.

Finally, the players who identified as gay from the Steeler's acknowledged that they heard homonegative language on the field and on the sidelines. Importantly, they indicated that this language, regardless of intent, was damaging and considered this language to be homophobic, regardless of motivation. They were particularly concerned about the impact this language might have on younger players in acting to exclude them from participating. They further acknowledged that publicly identifying as gay was difficult and that language, that was potentially homophobic, made players feel unsafe and encouraged players to quit. In this discursive light, language such as "bender" or "gay", can be understood as *always* problematic. They advocated that this type of language – like the racist and offensive term "nigger" – should *never* be used. In this light, we are broadly critical of conclusions drawn from inclusive masculinity researchers (e.g., McCormack and Anderson, 2014; Magrath, Anderson and Roberts 2015; Anderson and McCormack 2018; Magrath, Cleland and Anderson 2020) that suggest slurs such as "that's so gay" can be deemed inconsequential.

Our results highlight the importance of language for acting to include and exclude members of sport teams. Although the heterosexual players argued that "homophobic" language was not intended to act in a derogatory manner, there appears a clear disconnect between how such language was used and how some (i.e., particularly gay players) interpreted its use. The heterosexual players appeared naïve in their use of such language as they were unaware of the harm that such language use still perpetuated. Yet we do not believe that their intention in using such language was to cause harm. In contrast, we argue that the intended usage was to indicate their normality: in this sense they were using this language for their own purposes of feeling including as part of the team and more broadly, to feel like a normal male.

Our results have important implications for rugby club leaders, coaches, captains and players. Firstly, there is a need for education within clubs to inform of the damage that homophobic language can still have. We suggest that messages at rainbow-themed pride games, should not simply be "everyone is welcome" or "celebrating" the LGBTQ+ community, but should instead be used as opportunities to convey clear messages that usage of phrases such as "that's so gay" is never okay and it is very harmful. Secondly, training courses for rugby coaches and captains need to include information on how homophobic language can be linked to higher rates of suicide, self-harm and drug/alcohol addiction amongst LGBTIQ+ people. Thirdly, given the harms of homophobic language, rugby club members, particularly those who are respected (e.g., captains) should be encouraged to intervene when others use homophobic slurs. This act of intervening is, however, challenging to undertake, particularly with individuals who desire to feel accepted or normal within a group. Although bystander interventions

(Gidycz, Orchowski and Berkowitz 2011; McMahon and Banyard, 2012) and ally programmes are now relatively common in post-secondary educational institutions, they are still uncommon in sporting clubs. Correspondingly, there are opportunities for coach/captain training programmes to include instruction on how to implement bystander interventions and peer-to-peer education.

We recognise that it is relatively easy to make these pro-active suggestions moving forward but that the realities of putting these inclusive strategies into practice to create transformational change, particularly in the contexts of sporting clubs, can be difficult to achieve (Sharp, Forrester and Mandingo, 2011). Nevertheless, there is a growing research agenda examining how sporting clubs can foster diversity and inclusivity that focus on practical solutions associated with policy, funding and education (e.g., Cunningham 2015).

In conclusion, we encourage anyone who uses homophobic language or hears it, irrespective of context, to have the strength to not use or call it out. Indeed, to not do so, is to be complicit with an exclusionary practice that can encourage depression, self–harm and suicide.

References

Ahmed, Sara. 2010. Killing joy: Feminism and the history of happiness. *Signs: Journal of women in culture and society* 35(3). 571–594.

Anderson, Eric. 2002. Openly gay athletes: Contesting hegemonic masculinity in a homophobic environment. *Gender & Society* 16(6). 860–877.

Anderson, Eric & Mark McCormack. 2018. Inclusive masculinity theory: Overview, reflection and refinement. *Journal of Gender Studies* 27(5). 547–561.

Bolin, Anne & Jane Granskog (eds.). 2003. *Athletic intruders: Ethnographic research on women, culture, and exercise*. New York: SUNY Press.

Brackenridge, Celia, Ian Rivers, Brendan Gough, Karen Llewellyn & Cara Aitchison. 2007. Driving down participation: Homophobic bullying as a deterrent to doing sport. In Cara Aitchison (ed.), *Sport and Gender Identities: Masculinities, Femininities and Sexualities* 122–139. London: Routledge.

Caudwell, Jayne. 2018. Configuring human rights at EuroPride 2015. *Leisure Studies* 37(1). 49–63.

Centers for Disease Control and Prevention (CDC). 2020. 1991–2019 High school youth risk behavior survey data. *Centers for Disease Control and Prevention (CDC)*.

Coalter, Fred. 2007. *A Wider Social Role for Sport: Who's Keeping the Score?*. London: Routledge.

Connell, Raewyn. 1995. *Masculinities*. New York, NY; Routledge.

Cooky, Cheryl & Michael Messner. 2018. *No Slam Dunk*. Rutgers University Press.

Cunningham, George. 2015. *Diversity & inclusion in sport organizations: A multilevel perspective*. London: Routledge.

DeFoor, Mikalyn, Lara Stepleman & Paul Mann. 2018. Improving wellness for LGB collegiate student-athletes through sports medicine: a narrative review. *Sports Medicine-open* 4(1). 1–10.

Denison, Erik, Nadia Bevan & Ruth Jeanes. 2021a. Reviewing Evidence of LGBTQ+ Discrimination and Exclusion in Sport. *Sport Management Review*, 24(3). 389–409.

Denison, Erik, Nick Faulkner, Ruth Jeanes & Daniel Toole. 2021b. Relationships between Attitudes and Norms with Homophobic Language Use in Male Team Sports. *Journal of Science and Medicine in Sport* 24(5). 499–504.

Demers, Guylaine. 2006. Homophobia in sport—fact of life, taboo subject. *Canadian Journal for Women in Coaching* 6(2). Retrieved from http://www.coach.ca/files/CJWC_APRIL2006_EN.pdf

Doull, Marion, Ryan J. Watson, Annie Smith, Yuko Homma & Elizabeth Saewyc. 2018. Are we levelling the playing field? Trends and disparities in sports participation among sexual minority youth in Canada'. *Journal of Sport and Health Science* 7(2). 218–26.

Dunning, Eric. 1986. Sport as a male preserve: Notes on the social sources of masculine identity and its transformations. *Theory, Culture & Society* 3(1). 79–90.

Eime, Rochelle, John Harvey & Melanie Charity. 2019. Sport drop-out during adolescence: is it real, or an artefact of sampling behaviour? *International Journal of Sport Policy and Politics* 11(4). 715–726.

Foucault, Michel. 1972. *The archaeology of knowledge*. London: Tavistock. (Original work published in 1969)

Foucault, Michel. 1978. *The history of sexuality, Volume 1: An introduction* (R. Hurley, Trans.). New York, NY: Random House. (Original work published 1976)

Gardner, Lauren, Chris Magee & Stewart Vella. 2017. Enjoyment and behavioral intention predict organized youth sport participation and dropout. *Journal of Physical Activity and Health* 14(11). 861–865.

Gidycz, Christine, Lindsay Orchowski & Alan Berkowitz. 2011. Preventing sexual aggression among college men: An evaluation of a social norms and bystander intervention program. *Violence against women* 17(6). 720–742.

Greenspan, Scott, Catherine Griffith & Ryan Watson. 2019. LGBTQ+ youth's experiences and engagement in physical activity: A comprehensive content analysis. *Adolescent Research Review* 4(2). 169–185.

Hartmann-Tews, Ilse, Tobias Menze & Birgit Braumüller. 2021. Homo-and transnegativity in sport in Europe: Experiences of LGBT+ individuals in various sport settings. *International Review for the Sociology of Sport* 56(7). 997–1016.

Hickey, Chris & Lindsay Fitzclarence. 1999. Educating boys in sport and physical education: Using narrative methods to develop pedagogies of responsibility. *Sport, Education and Society* 4(1). 51–62.

Magrath, Rory, Eric Anderson & Steve Roberts. 2015. On the door-step of equality. *International Review for the Sociology of Sport* 50(4). 804–821.

Magrath, Rory, Jamie Cleland & Eric Anderson. 2020. Introducing the Palgrave handbook of masculinity and sport. In *The Palgrave Handbook of Masculinity and Sport*, 1–16. Palgrave Macmillan, Cham.

McCormack, Mark & Eric Anderson. 2014. Homohysteria: Definitions, context and intersectionality. *Sex Roles* 71(3). 152–158

McCormack, Mark, Liam Wignall & Max Morris. 2016. Gay guys using gay discourse: Friendship, shared values and the intentcontext-effect matrix. *British Journal of Sociology* 1–14. doi:10.1111/1468-4446.12203

McKay, Jim, Michael Messner & Don Sabo (eds). 2000. *Masculinities, gender relations, and sport* (Vol. 13). Thousand Oaks, CA: Sage.

McMahon, Sarah & Victoria Banyard. 2012. When can I help? A conceptual framework for the prevention of sexual violence through bystander intervention. *Trauma, Violence, & Abuse* 13(1). 3–14.

Messner, Michael. 1996. Studying up on sex. *Sociology of Sport Journal* 13(3). 221–237.

Muir, Kenneth, Eric Anderson, Keith Parry & David Letts. 2021. The changing nature of gay rugby clubs in the United Kingdom. *Sociology of Sport Journal* 39(2). 178–185.
Murray, Ashnil & Adam White. 2017. Twelve not so angry men: Inclusive masculinities in Australian contact sports. *International Review for the Sociology of Sport* 52(5). 536–550.
Osborne, Danny & William Wagner III. 2007. Exploring the relationship between homophobia and participation in core sports among high school students. *Sociological Perspectives* 50(4). 597–613.
Painter, Kirsten, Maria Scannapieco, Gary Blau, Amy Andre & Kris Kohn. 2018. Improving the mental health outcomes of LGBTQ youth and young adults: A longitudinal study. *Journal of Social Service Research* 44(2). 223–235.
Plummer, David. 2006. Sportophobia: Why do some men avoid sport? *Journal of Sport and Social Issues* 30(2). 122–137.
Pronger, Brian. 1992. *The arena of masculinity: Sports, homosexuality, and the meaning of sex*. New York: Macmillan.
Pringle, Richard, Jayne Caudwell & Robert Rinehart. 2015. *Sport and the social significance of pleasure*. Routledge: London.
Pringle, Richard & Pirkko Markula. 2005. No pain is sane after all: A Foucauldian analysis of masculinities and men's rugby experiences of fear, pain, and pleasure. *Sociology of sport journal* 22(4). 472–497.
Rail, Geneviève. 1998. Introduction. In Geneviève Rail (ed.), *Sport and postmodern times*, ix–xxi. Albany, NY: State University of New York Press.
Sabo, Don & David Gordon (eds.). 1995. *Men's health and illness* (Vol. 8). Thousand Oaks: Sage.
Shanklin, Nicholas, Alice Roberts, Barbara Queen, David Chyen, Lisa Whittle, Connie Lim, Yoshimi Yamakawa, Michelle Leon-Nguyen, Greta Kilmer, Jennifer Smith-Grant, Zewditu Demissie, Sherry Everett Jones, Heather Clayton & Patricia Dittus. 2020. 'Youth Risk Behavior Surveillance Survey – 2019'. *Morbidity and Mortality Weekly Report* 69(1). doi: 10.15585/mmwr.su6901a1
Sharpe, Erin, Scott Forrester & James Mandigo. 2011. Engaging community providers to create more active after-school environments: results from the Ontario CATCH kids club implementation project. *Journal of Physical Activity and Health* 8(1). 26–31.
Stick, Max. 2021. Conflicts in sporting masculinity: The beliefs and behaviors of Canadian male athletes. *The Journal of Men's Studies* 29(3). 315–334.
Twenge, Jean, Ryne Sherman & Brokke Wells. 2016. Changes in American adults' reported same-sex sexual experiences and attitudes, 1973–2014. *Archives of Sexual Behavior* 45(7). 1713–1730.
Wilson, Oliver, Chris Whatman, Simon Walters, Sierra Keung, Dion Enari, Andy Rogers & Justin Richards. 2022. The value of sport: Wellbeing benefits of sport participation during Adolescence. *International Journal of Environmental Research and Public Health* 19(14). 8579.
Wilson, Tom, Jeromey Temple, Anthony Lyons & Fiona Shalley. 2020. What is the size of Australia's sexual minority population? *BMC Research Notes* 13(1). 1–6.

Farhana Abdul Fatah
Chapter 12
"*Ha ha ha you don't cover you aurat*": Exploring modesty, prayer, and Malaysian Muslim women gymnasts' experience of inclusion and/or exclusion

1 Introduction

This chapter addresses the issue of religious diversity in sports pertaining to Islam and Muslim women athletes. Specifically, it investigates how the interrelated Islamic concepts of modesty and *aurat* (referring to parts of the female body from the hair to the bottom of the feet that should be covered) are entangled with issues concerning Muslim women's participation in competitive gymnastics, particularly in a Muslim-majority setting like Malaysia. Moreover, this study found that the issue concerning the performance of the *solat* 'ritual daily prayers', is also a significant factor of inclusion and exclusion. I apply inclusion to refer to the individual's right to participate – in this context, in women's gymnastics – under circumstances that are of quality, just, and equitable (Haug 2016) and that also involve positive interpersonal relationships in shared spaces (Felder 2018) with relevant parties such as coaches, fellow teammates, and family. Exclusion is understood in opposition to this. The terms inclusive and exclusive are not used as these apply to broader, systematic, and institutionalised concerns on achieving inclusion (Coady, Harper, and De Jong 2016; Haug 2016). Building upon an emerging and dynamic body of work of Feminist Poststructuralist Discourse Analysis (FPDA) (Baxter 2003; Castañeda Peña 2008; Glapka 2018; Kamada 2009) and the "doing of intersectionality" (Staunæs 2006), this paper thus examines the ways that Muslim women gymnasts in Malaysia occupy and negotiate their troubled and untroubled subject positions (Widding 2015; Glapka 2018) as Muslim women and professional gymnasts, specifically within the religious and/or gendered "aurat Discourse" and "solat Discourse".

Farhana Abdul Fatah, Universiti Sains Malaysia, Malaysia

2 Muslim women in sports

Abdul Rahim, Mohd Jani and Mohamad Diah (2019) argue that sports and physical activities are acts of *ibadah* 'worship' in Islam, apart from the specific ones outlined in the five pillars (including daily prayers, fasting during Ramadhan, among others). Citing Ibn Taimiyah, a thirteenth century Islamic scholar, the authors emphasise, "Islam encourages its followers to become active and healthy. Keeping our body in good shape is essential," (Abdul Rahim et al. 2019: 92; see also Walseth 2006; Kızar 2018). Since the time of the Prophet Muhammad, Muslims have historically practiced athletics, weightlifting, and wrestling (Kızar 2018), and the Prophet's wife, Aisha, was also noted to have participated in horseracing (Abdul Razak, Omar-Fauzee and Abd-Latif 2010).

Although the common consensus dictates that physical activity and sports are permissible and promoted in Islam (Winter and Shavit 2011; Kızar 2018; Abdul Rahim et al. 2019), it remains an issue that is constantly up for debate among Islamic jurists who have issued *fatwas*, 'legal ruling and opinion', on the matter of which sports are permissible and the conditions under which Muslim athletes are allowed to compete (see Winter and Shavit 2011 for an overview of these developments). Such debates inevitably bring to the fore issues of inclusion and exclusion, as although sports are permissible for Muslims, they must be performed in line with Quranic precepts (Abdul Rahim et al. 2019).

For Muslim women athletes, this issue is particularly striking, as it involves the notion of *aurat*. Aurat refers to parts of the body that the Quran dictates should be covered. For men, these concealed areas are commonly prescribed to be between the navel and the knees; and for women, they are to conceal the areas from the top of their head and hair, all the way down to their feet (with only the face and hands being visible). Although the injunction applies to both men and women, it is women's dress that has received unequivocal focus in the sporting arena (Benn and Dagkas 2013) and is one of the main factors impacting upon their involvement in sports (Hamzeh and Oliver 2012; Khoo and Nor Eeza 2021).

When it comes to Muslim women, conversations surrounding the aurat typically revolve around the issue of veiling/non-veiling. In the context of participation in sports and physical activity, Hamzeh and Oliver (2012: 330) found the hijab is at the core of "veiling-off opportunities for physical activity" in the Muslim girls' negotiation with their parents. Walseth (2006), on the other hand, found that some women in her study in Norway utilised the veil as a symbol of loyalty to their Muslim community. As the veil signifies loyalty to their community, these women believe that wearing the veil has, in turn, led to more freedom for them to be physically active.

Professional women gymnasts are bound to a strict dress code following international gymnastics standard, which typically involves wearing tight-fitting leotards or fitted tank tops. Safety has been used to justify such attire for professional women gymnasts and is thus a prerequisite for participation in competitive events. However, Muslim gymnasts and athletes can find themselves wrestling to reconcile this aspect of their athletic professionalism, with their gendered and religious identities as Muslim women (Kavasoğlu and Koca 2020).

Increasing scrutiny and criticism of women athletes' attire have been observed in Malaysia, a Muslim-majority country that has been undergoing Islamisation since the late 1970s (Barr and Govindasamy 2010). Such criticisms were brought to global attention in 2015, when Malaysian Muslim gymnast Farah Ann Abdul Hadi received international coverage not because of her double gold-medal performance in the 2015 Southeast Asian Games, but for the nationwide backlash over her revealing uniform (O'Neill 2015; FitzSimons 2016). Elsewhere, in 2017, a 10-year-old Iranian female gymnast came under fire from the Iran Gymnastics Federation for competing in an international gymnastics competition in Malaysia not wearing the hijab (Center for Human Rights in Iran 2017). These examples show that Muslim women gymnasts not only experience criticism for their appearance, but they may also be excluded from the dominant religious and gendered ideal of a "good Muslim woman" (Hamzeh and Oliver 2012). Debates concerning Muslim women athletes' dress have continued, and in light of worldwide praise on European women athletes' reclamation of their bodily autonomy (Tétrault-Farber 2021), the issue has also raised concerns of racism and double standard (Mir 2021).

3 Methodology

3.1 Analytical framework

In this study, I attempt to see how three former gymnasts positioned themselves as (un)troubled subjects in relation to dominant religious and gendered Discourses in the context of professional gymnastics. Widding's (2015) study on Swedish parenthood operationalised "untroubled subject position" to refer to participants being "good" parents; inversely, a "troubled subject position" is one whereby they grapple with the notion of "bad" parenting. Borrowing from that study, I applied "troubled subject position" as moments in the interviews wherein the participants wrestle with the self-perceived notion of being bad Muslims or bad gymnasts. In contrast, "untroubled subject position" here refers to moments where the participants speak of themselves as good Muslims and/or good gymnasts. In assuming either a troubled or an untroubled position, the participants are in effect talking of experiences of exclusion and/or inclusion, respectively. Their personal narratives highlight the discursive processes of their identity construction – specifically the intersections between their athletic, religious, and gender identities – and how these contribute to the participants' experiences of inclusion and exclusion. This study adopts a social constructionist understanding of identity. Informed by social constructionism's call to question essentialist and binary assumptions about the world (Burr 2015), this study therefore views identity as multiple, fluid, and fragmented, and is constructed in and through discourses (De Fina and Georgakopoulou 2015).

Feminist Poststructuralist Discourse Analysis (FPDA) is defined as "an approach to analysing intertextualised discourses in spoken interaction and other types of text. It draws upon the poststructuralist principles of complexity, plurality, ambiguity, connection, recognition, diversity, textual playfulness, functionality and transformation," (Baxter 2010: 130). It was proposed by Baxter as a supplementary theoretical and analytical approach, alongside other established frameworks such as Conversation Analysis (CA) and Critical Discourse Analysis (CDA). Over a decade since its inception, however, FPDA is still largely under-utilised in discourse-based research (Kamada 2009; Glapka 2018; Abdul Fatah 2019).

I used FPDA as it can identify and represent "sites of struggle", or a discursive location – e.g., religion, family, among others – wherein dominant discourses compete for dominance (Baxter 2003). Baxter (2003: 187) further argues that "on a micro-analytical level, sites of struggle also mean significant moments in spoken discourse where meanings are negotiated and contested, manifested by differences of viewpoint, clashes of opinions, or conflicting readings." Therefore, examining specific and different discourses that emerge from the narratives of these former gymnasts reveals the struggle for dominance and that the "disagreement among Muslims about what it implies for women to be good Muslims can be seen as an example of such a struggle for hegemonic positions within a religious collective identity" (Walseth 2006: 78).

This study is driven by FPDA's transformative quest, "to represent the complexities and ambiguities of female experience, and within this to give space to female voices that are being silenced or marginalised by dominant discourses," (Baxter 2003: 59). Furthermore, through a detailed micro-analysis of discourse, FPDA demonstrates how "speakers are able to take up, accommodate or resist relatively powerful or powerless subject positions made available within competing discourses at work within any given moment" (Baxter 2003: 59).

In applying FPDA, this study is concerned with the religious and gendered Discourses within which hegemonic ideologies concerning Muslim women's bodies in the context of religion and sport position women in agentic and/or submissive roles. I supplement FPDA with Staunæs' (2003: 101) reworking of intersectionality as "the concept can be a useful analytical tool in tracing how certain people seem to get positioned as not only different but also troublesome and, in some instances, marginalised." She foregrounds the notion of the "doing of intersectionality", which, due to its focus on the in-situ and interactional processes of subjectification, I provisionally rename as "discursive intersectionality". Specifically, it refers to "the doing of the relation between categories, the outcome of this doing and how this doing results in either troubled or untroubled subject positions" (Staunæs 2003: 105). Though the participants talk into being numerous social categories in their narratives, I anchor the analysis by focusing on three, which are their gender, religious, and athlete identities as Muslim women gymnasts.

3.2 Denotative-connotative interpretation of discourse

"Discourse" here is operationalised following Gee's (2014: 34) conceptualisation of big "D" discourse as "socially accepted associations among ways of using language, of thinking, valuing, acting, and interacting, in the 'right' places and at the 'right' times with the 'right' objects." Henceforth, capital D "Discourse" is used when specifically referring to and discussing the emergent religious and gendered Discourses. The microanalysis of the interview data revealed textual evidence of discourses or "linguistic repertoires" (Baxter 2010: 126) that point to hegemonic ideologies pertaining to Muslim women's participation in sports. I provisionally named the Discourses following Sunderland's (2004) convention, in particular her use of "scare quotes" to indicate the interpretive nature of such Discourses. Further, in identifying and naming the Discourses, I combined a denotative approach based on specific lexes that signified these Discourses with a connotative approach based on my own informed subjectivities as a researcher and a cultural insider, supplemented with findings from literature (Castañeda Peña 2008).

Two Discourses emerged as the most prominent in the women's talk on experiencing inclusion/exclusion – the "aurat Discourse" and the "solat Discourse". Abundant literature on Muslim women's participation in sports attest to the prevalence of the "aurat Discourse" as Muslim women are expected to cover their body parts to be deemed "permissible" to participate in physical activity (Hamzeh and Oliver 2012; Khoo and Nor Eeza 2021). In this sense, this Discourse is inherently religious and gendered. The "solat Discourse", on the other hand, is more explicitly religious, and points to the religious duty of Muslims to perform the obligatory five-a-day prayers, or *"solat"* in Malay. As the prayers take place at dawn, at noon, afternoon, at sundown, and lastly, at night, the participants spoke about how this impacted their gymnastics training and competitions. Emergence of the "solat

Discourse" in the participants' talk is evidence of its intertextuality with the "aurat Discourse", and more significantly draws attention to an oft-dismissed factor in debates concerning Muslim women's participation in sports, which are inundated with focus on their bodies.

3.3 Participants

Purposive and snowball sampling were employed to recruit via social media three Muslim women who are former members of the Malaysian gymnastics team. Although no official number has been recorded, my inquiries revealed the total number of Muslim women gymnasts to have represented Malaysia at international competitions to be less than a dozen. Repeated attempts to contact and recruit more than this number from the target purposive sample were conducted; however, they were unsuccessful. Former Muslim women gymnasts were recruited, instead of current members, to avoid any professional and ethical conflicts with the national Malaysian gymnastics body. All of the participants – whose pseudonyms are Ella, Gina, and Sara – are currently gymnastics coaches. They are all married women in their thirties who began their foray into professional gymnastics as young school aged girls in the 90s, reaching their competitive prime in the 2000s, between them having represented Malaysia at regional Southeast Asian (SEA) Games and/or the bigger stage of the Commonwealth Games. They were non-veiled Muslim women as competitive gymnasts; but Sara currently wears the hijab, whereas Ella and Gina do not.

3.4 Interview procedure

The women were each interviewed following a life history approach, as "the method calls on interview respondents to provide a subjective account of their life over a certain period" (Davies et al. 2018: 5). This study aimed to explore the relationship between their identity work (religious, gender, and professional) with their involvement in competitive gymnastics (Walseth 2006), and this focus on temporality is deemed apt to help reveal the specific moments whereby participants found themselves either excluded or included by fellow athletes, coaches, as well as their own families.

The interviews each lasted between 60–90 minutes and were conducted and recorded online via the video conferencing platform Webex, with Malay and English being the language medium. The interviews were only conducted once I had received a signed informed consent from each of the participant.

3.4.1 Transcription and coding

The interviews were later transcribed using the software Otter.ai. Translation of Malay portions of the interviews into English was conducted by me, a native Malay speaker. The transcriptions followed an adapted version of Jefferson's (2004) notation (Appendix), and were carefully reviewed to identify and extract interview portions that addressed the following research concerns:
1. In which instances do participants speak of experiencing inclusion and/or exclusion? (Discursive sites of struggle)
2. How do the participants discursively construct their gender, religious, and athlete identities in these instances?
3. How do the participants' identities impact on their negotiation of (un)troubled subject positions in these instances?

These selected extracts were then organised in a table and coded following Saldana's (2019) qualitative coding guidelines. The initial coding of the three transcripts garnered 48 codes that were later reduced to 47 upon subsequent reading and checking. As the interviews are not meant to be representative of the participants' respective experiences, the codes generated intended to show me the range of topics and concerns that were brought about by the participants. Therefore, although some codes emerged more prominently in one participant's interview, this was not necessarily the case for others. Nonetheless, when taken together, the five most prominent codes generated from the interviews are prayers (26), aurat (20), attire (14), temporality (13), and unitard[1] (12). Though useful, these numbers would not be used to identify the excerpts that would be used for analysis, as they do not adequately convey instances of inclusion/exclusion in Malaysian gymnastics for these former Muslim women gymnasts. However, they are able to highlight those matters concerning performing the obligatory *solat*, as well as concerns regarding the exposure of *aurat* in wearing the compulsory attire of professional gymnasts. Additionally, participants spoke about a notion of "being gymnasts while they still can" with regards to their age and physical (hence, implied sexual) and spiritual maturity, besides talking about the unitard as an accepted – though still problematic – alternative to Muslim women gymnasts' attire.

---

[1] Different than the leotard which exposes the legs, the unitard is a one-piece skintight body garment that covers the legs and arms.

4 Negotiating being "good Muslim women" and "good gymnasts"

The choice of excerpts to conduct analyses of the linguistic processes of inclusion/exclusion among these former Muslim women gymnasts was directed by specific instances wherein they spoke about being included/excluded on account of them being Muslim, women, and gymnasts. The specific instances of inclusion/exclusion – and the actors purportedly involved in them – take place outside of and/or within the gymnastics arena among the participants' own families, coaches, and fellow athletes and teammates. The interview extracts below predominantly feature code-switching and code-mixing in Malay and English. The original Malay transcript is provided above the English translation (italicised) where applicable.

4.1 Family

The extracts below highlight narratives from Ella and Sara as they recall experiencing criticism from their own families, in particular from their extended relatives like aunts and uncles, over their participation in gymnastics as Muslim girls. In their interviews, they noted that at least one parent – typically the father – would express reluctance to allow their daughter to participate in gymnastics in the beginning, but these concerns would eventually be allayed and turned to support. Gina also spoke about issues she faced with her own family but only with regard to their lack of support for her professional career, and not about the *aurat*. Overall, the participants noted that such incidents would typically occur in the *kampung* 'rural countryside' setting, where there is a general conservative attitude among Muslims concerning gymnastics for Muslim women and its revealing attire.

Extract 1 – Ella

1   bila balik kampung tu macam orang (.) ((bounces head))
    When [I] go back kampung people would be like
2   tak suka sangat lah kan sukan ni ((bounces head animatedly))
    not like this sport so much lah
3   *revealing the aurat lah*
4   *but (.) like, we just keep quiet only lah*
5   *but I just keep going anyway ((laughs))*

Extract 2 – Ella

1	Ada jugak lah ((nods head))
	There would be lah
2	like uh (.) someone would say like (.)
3	"Eleh! (.) Uh menang tu…kalau menang uhhh apa al-Quran punya hafazan boleh lah jugak di – dibanggakan."
	"Eleh! (.) Uh [if you'd] won. . .if [you'd won] al-Quran recitation then that would be something to be proud of lah."
4	Ha I just ((feigns smiling)) smile.
5	*Yeah, no problem*

Extract 3 – Sara

Below, Sara talks about her response in the face of criticism from relatives:

Maybe they don't, they're not like exposed to more of the reason um maybe the objective of the sports and all that. So they're just looking at, you know, teaching girls to expose their skin, expose the aurat and all that. But I know that, but for me, itself (.) I'm, I'm not so (.) um take that um (.) that comments, you know, to, to make me sad or that or what? I'm uh I'm not like that. I just hear and I just say okay, soon, soon, okay. Like that. And I'm just (.) relaxed. I don't like (.) argue with them. Ummm cry or what like that ((giggles)) because I know what I'm doing. And (.) not and… I I'm [a] practicing Muslim, I pray five times a week.[2]

Within the religious and gendered "aurat Discourse" Ella and Sara both assume a troubled subject position, as their choice to participate in an aurat-revealing sport such as gymnastics clash with the traditional feminine ideals of a good Muslim woman, which is amplified in a conservative *kampung* setting. Abdul Razak et al. (2010) also found that cultural and ethnic ideals on femininity – espoused by family – often underlie the resistance to Muslim women's participation in sports and physical activity. Here, power and hegemony relating to religious and gendered ideals on women's bodies work in covert and invisible means under the guise of family. Ella draws explicit attention to this troubled positioning when she uses the Malay exclamative *"Eleh"* (which connotes a sneering remark) in an indirect quote by a relative that diminishes her professional accomplishments and argues that if Ella had won a Quranic recital competition "then that would be something to be proud of *lah*" (extract 2). Ella and Sara attempt to subvert this troubled positioning in markedly differing ways. Ella does this by supposed nonchalance via feigned smiles (extract 2), a strategy which other non-veiled Muslim women have been noted to adopt in the face of criticism (see Abdul Fatah 2019). Sara, on the other hand, uses the contrastive conjunction "but" and her pacifying

---

[2] Upon subsequent clarification, Sara noted that she meant to say five-a-day prayers. This also applies to Extract 4.

claims of "okay, soon, soon, okay". She also resists the troubled position by drawing upon the "solat Discourse", within which she assumes the untroubled subject position of a practicing Muslim who regularly performs the mandated daily prayers.

4.2 Coaches

Sara and Gina recall instances whereby their respective coaches – in particular foreigners who are non-Muslims with limited cultural knowledge about Islam and its rituals – deterred the participants (then young school-aged gymnasts) from performing their obligatory daily prayers. Interestingly, the domain of coaches and institution is the only site whereby the "aurat Discourse" is not prevalent, and where "solat Discourse" instead takes precedence. The prevalence of this Discourse within this domain could be because as it is already an institutionalised requirement for women gymnasts to wear leotards as their standard uniform, exposed skin is therefore not a concern. Hence, within this domain the participants assume an untroubled subject position within the "aurat Discourse".

Extract 4 – Sara

I'm [a] practicing Muslim, I pray five times a week,[3] even um when [I] uh started national team my mom already told the coach that in between of the training I need to pray but there's there's one time that my mom needs to take me out from the training when the coach said no cannot cannot pray in the between so... that's where my mom wanted to take me out but after that the coaches uh let me do it so I started to continue.

Extract 5 – Gina

But of course our coaches don't really understand that because our coach is not from Malaysia and then they don't they are not well aware that we are Muslim and how we are doing our like daily things and everything. so the first time that I got to the national team so my parents and my teammates' parent just go to say to the coach that you know, they willing to come and training with you guys but they do have to do their prayers like in the middle of a training and they have to take like five to 10 minutes break just to pray is that okay or not? Does that interrupt um um the training process and everything. sometimes our coaches like try not to get us to pray because it's like it's disrupting the training you know, the training capacity and the training tempo or something like that.

Although their religious identities as practicing Muslims place them in untroubled subject positions within the "solat Discourse", Sara and Gina are inadvertently positioned as troubled within the professional domain as their religious identities conflict with their athlete identities as gymnasts. This demonstrates the overt

---

3 See Footnote 2.

workings of institutionalised power (Castañeda Peña 2008). They thus experience marginalisation and allegedly overt discrimination as their respective coaches deny them their right to perform their religious obligations and justify the action as "disrupting the training" (extract 5). Unable to take up resistance and subvert this powerless and marginalised position due to their young age, this action instead was assumed by their respective parents who intervened on their behalf. Although Gina's parents appear to have presented the demand as a reasonable request, "they have to take like five to ten minutes break to pray is that okay or not?" (extract 5), Sara's mother allegedly threatened to remove her from the training unless her coach relented to the demand, "my mom wanted to take me out" (extract 4). Their anecdotes point to the need for an elder figure to represent the best interests of these young gymnasts, and the need for institutions to be more religiously inclusive and accommodating (Khoo and Nor Eeza 2021).

Below, Ella responds to a question I posed on whether her being a Muslim had ever impacted on her performance as a gymnast:

Extract 6 – Ella

1 Oh, of course training lah sebab kadang kadang kita tak tu kan tapi... gantilah! ((laughs))
   Oh, of course training lah because sometimes we don't you know but. . .[I'll] replace lah!
2 Solat tetap solat.
   Solat is still solat
3 Yeah, and I am I am I am glad that because my coach is also a Muslim.
4 So she understands me so sometimes she will give time for me to go and pray.
5 Yes. And during fasting month also. Yeah.
6 Either our training load will go down a bit.
7 Yeah, she --- cuz I That's why I said I'm glad my coach is someone who is very important to me
8 supported me and she's as a Muslim we are supporting each other.

Unlike Sara and Gina, Ella's religious and athlete identities do not position her in competing and troubled positions within the "solat Discourse". Rather, she finds ways to compromise between the demands of her training and religious obligations, empathetically stressing the Malay particle *-lah*, that she'll "replace" her missed prayers (extract 6, line 1). In Islam, such an approach is called "qada" and is permitted to be done in circumstances where adherents find difficulty to perform their daily obligations under, for instance, strict and unaccommodating work conditions. Here, Ella further reiterates the untroubled subject position she assumes by emphasising that "solat is still solat", implying that religious duties should not be abandoned even amid unrelenting training regimes. In their respective interviews, Gina and Sara have also spoken about performing "qada" of their prayers following training and competitions. It is notable that Ella's ability to assume this untroubled subject position amid overtly competing religious and professional demands is aided by her coach, a fellow Muslim who understands the need for and the importance of both demands to be met. This therefore points to a need whereby more Muslim coaches should be trained and/or intercultural and interfaith sensitivity training is needed for professional coaches working in diverse contexts.

4.3 Fellow athletes and teammates

Gina recalled an especially confrontational incident that took place at the Malaysian national sporting academy, whereby a fellow Muslim athlete questioned her decision to continue with gymnastics upon reaching puberty.

Extract 7 – Gina

Like "[Gina] do you still want to do gymnastics at the age of 18? You know, 18 at that time, you should be wearing a tudung already, you know, you have to close up and it's not a sport that you supposed to do at the age of 18. Or after you reach your you know, you have your period, you know, it's different". I'm like, but I love gymnastics. It's my choice. You know? maybe now, there's one friend that I confronted, like, she's asking me this question. And I said, but you can't judge me like that, you know, maybe in five years, I'm gonna wear tudung faster than you I'm gonna be a better human for Allah, you know.

Gina mobilises the "aurat Discourse" indirectly with the mention of "tudung" – the Malay word for the headscarf worn by Muslim women typically at the onset of puberty – and its association with the notions of covering the body ("close up"), as well as temporality. The latter is especially striking, and is a notion spoken about by all three participants concerning a suitable timeframe before Muslim girls reach their physical and sexual maturity, during which it is most acceptable for them to do professional gymnastics (see also Abdul Razak et al. 2010). Gina explicitly comments upon this notion by reporting what her fellow colleague (an athlete of a different sport) says, "it's not a sport that you supposed to do at the age of 18" or after she starts having her period.

Within this Discourse, Gina's religious, gender, and athlete identities intersect to place her in a troubled and marginalised subject position. She seems to be fully aware of such positioning yet attempts to challenge this by taking up an untroubled subject position through asserting her agency. She does this by first emphasising her athlete identity, "I love gymnastics" and iterating the notion of personal choice (Abdul Razak et al. 2010; Glapka 2018). Further, although she is positioned as troubled within the "aurat Discourse" – and thus the implication that she is a "bad Muslim" – Gina attempts to shift to an untroubled position by drawing upon a hypothetical religious and gendered version of herself, specifically one who will be veiled and thus will be "a better human for Allah." Although Gina and her colleague relatively share the same power differential, I argue that Gina has been victimised by her colleague via the dominant religious and gendered "aurat Discourse" as Gina is accused of deviating against traditional notions of Islamic femininity (see Volk and Lagzdins' 2009 study on Canadian female athletes in a majority-Christian setting).

Whereas Gina was subjected to criticism, Sara experienced the opposite from her teammates:

Extract 8 – Sara

1	*So they, they really understand sometimes we will make it as a joke.*
2	*"Hey ha ha you tak tutup aurat, you tak pakai tudung"*
	"Hey ha ha you don't cover your aurat, you don't wear tudung"
3	*Aaa something like that ((laughs)).*
4	*They make fun of us, but we know (.)*
5	*we know that they are just joking.*
6	*You know what something like that.*
7	*For me, alhamdulillah, I had very good experience with my friends and all that*

Unlike Gina, Sara's religious, gender, and athlete identities do not position her as troubled and marginalised within the "aurat Discourse". Instead, Sara is able to assume a relatively untroubled position as a gymnast and a Muslim among her fellow gymnasts. In contrast with Gina who was clearly positioned on opposing sides with her judgmental Muslim colleague, Sara discursively positions herself to be on the same side as her fellow gymnasts – most of whom were non-Muslims – via the latter's use of sarcastic humour. Although Sara is seemingly positioned as troubled within the "aurat Discourse" ("you don't cover your aurat, you don't wear tudung"), she frames such comments as a joke ("haha"). Furthermore, this sarcastic jab arguably loses its bite as Sara's colleagues neither hold overt institutional power (by being merely colleagues) nor covert hegemonic religious power (by being non-Muslims) to reprimand her for being a non-veiled gymnast. Because of the absence of such covert and overt hegemony, Sara's non-Muslim teammates legitimately utilised humour to help "neutralise difficult topics" (Ronglan and Aggerholm 2014: 40) that would otherwise serve to marginalise Sara.

Extract 9 – Ella

Below, Ella recalls a moment of support she experienced from her fellow athletes:

1	*Like (0.2) I remember in Commonwealth Games (.)*
2	*when I arrived then the ---*
3	*because when we when the gymnastics team arrived*
4	*the the athletics team would go because they just finished their competition.*
5	*So we are changed like, like, changing house lah!*

6	Then the kakak *will say to me*
7	"okay ni kiblat ya"
	"okay this is the kiblat ya"
8	"oh, terima kasih akak!"
	"oh, thank you akak!"
9	Like, okay, all the kakak kakak *all support also lah...*

Instead of the "aurat Discourse" Ella draws upon the "solat Discourse". Here, Ella's religious, gender, and athlete identities intersect to position her in a relatively untroubled position as she recalls enjoying the support of fellow *kakak kakak* 'older female' athletes who would point to Ella the direction of the kiblat. The kiblat (or qibla) points to the direction of the Kaabah in Mecca, to which all Muslims turn in ritual prayers. An intertextual look by linking Ella's anecdote here to extract 6 shows how she has been consistently positioned as untroubled within the "solat Discourse" (Baxter 2003) in two different domains (coaches and fellow athletes), which further reveals the actors who have aided in making her religious and athletic identity as a Muslim gymnast unproblematic. Specifically, in extract 6, an authoritative figure, a coach, who is also a Muslim woman ("she") makes way for Ella to perform her solat; and here, her fellow Muslim and female athletes ("*kakak kakak*") are showing Ella the direction for ritual prayers.

5 Addressing inclusion/exclusion within the "aurat Discourse" and "solat Discourse"

By examining the ways in which participants negotiated between their religious, gender, and athlete identities as Muslim women gymnasts, this paper has highlighted the need for promoting inclusion for Muslim athletes to participate in competitive gymnastics without undermining their religious and cultural values. Specifically, by paying close attention to prominent linguistic features, this paper noted the emergence of the "solat Discourse" and the "aurat Discourse" as prominent sites wherein identity contestations between being "good, practicing Muslims" and "good gymnasts" are talked about by the participants, besides drawing further attention to specific discursive "sites of struggle" (i.e., the family, coaches, and fellow athletes) wherein these Discourses operate to position these Muslim women gymnasts as troubled and/or untroubled subjects.

This study corroborated findings on Muslim women's participation in sports by foregrounding the prominence of aurat and modesty (see Walseth 2006; Hamzeh and Oliver 2012), and it offers new insights by highlighting the importance of the ritual daily prayers, solat. In efforts to promote inclusion and address exclusion there is therefore a need for education to promote heightened awareness among coaches and gymnasts on these two significant religious aspects. As Muslim women gymnasts and athletes continue to negotiate between the conflicting demands of religion to "cover up" and abiding with the rules of attire for certain sports (Walseth 2006; Abdul Rahim et al. 2019), highlighting that performing the ritual solat is crucial to push for a "transformative quest".

Together with the workings of discursive intersectionality, FPDA's locus of "transformative quest" has highlighted moments of critical awareness by the participants with regards to their exposing their aurat and their commitment to gymnastics, and how resistance/subversion can be done in light of this (Glapka 2018). Here, I extend Glapka's (2018) call to challenge the feminist notion that resistance *should* be done by troubled subjects, and instead highlights how it *can* be done. To do so is to highlight the institutional hegemony wielded by majority professional sporting bodies that are overtly Anglo-European, and whose secular foundations have restricted or even "punished" athletes whose faith and religiosity are core aspects that impact upon their involvement in sports (Abdul Rahim et al. 2019). This hegemony further manifests in the form of double standard and hypocrisy revealed from the West's critique of Muslim women's bodies and modest dress (Abu-Lughod 2002; Mir 2021), and also in their overt praise of Anglo-European women "reclaiming" their bodies in sports such as gymnastics (Tétrault-Farber 2021).

Both covert and overt workings of religious and gendered hegemonic ideals have been shown to operate differently within these Discourses within different discursive sites of struggles. Furthermore, the data reveal how one Discourse offers more opportunities for subversion compared to the other, especially when rigid institutional requirements are considered. Specifically, participants drew upon the "solat Discourse" to either challenge their troubled subject positions as "bad Muslim women" within the "aurat Discourse" (extract 3), or to position themselves as untroubled "good Muslim women" and "good gymnasts" (extracts 4, 6, 9).

On how resistance and subversion *can* be done, the findings reveal several pragmatic and discursive approaches that can be taken by female athletes under marginalising conditions. For instance, the identification of the family, coaches, and fellow athletes as discursive sites of struggle wherein contention exists offers practitioners insights on the domains of concern that require attention. When it comes to the gymnasts' family, coaches or the local gymnastics association could organise a briefing or an onboarding session to help explain the expectations and demands of the sport and the arrangements that could be done to respect any specific religious and/or cultural needs. This is important because as the interview findings highlighted, parents have had to intervene on behalf of their young children when it came to advocating for the child's right to perform their prayers during training.

Within the domain of coaches, the findings also indicate the need for intercultural or interfaith training among coaches who do not share the same religious background as their Muslim trainees. The participants noted feeling supported and understood when coached by those who understood their religious beliefs and requirements, and thus were able to make the necessary arrangements in training. In their interviews, Ella, Sara, and Gina also offered several inclusive and accommodating practices that they have adopted as coaches to tailor to the needs of their young Muslim trainees, which could be similarly adapted by other gymnastics practitioners. These practices include designing a flexible coaching regime for Muslim trainees who attend religious after-school programmes, giving them adequate time to perform solat, reducing the training load during the Ramadhan fasting month, as well as giving them the option to wear the more modest unitard instead of the leotard.

Finally, the findings show the need for a solid peer support system among fellow gymnasts and other athletes, Muslim or otherwise. Intercultural and interfaith training among peers is beneficial, particularly in highlighting the sensitivity of certain topics such as aurat and solat. In cases whereby a gymnast faces abuse or harassment relating to these matters (extract 7), the gymnastics association must then take the necessary steps to address and resolve them.

6 Conclusion

This paper offers insightful contributions to sports research that look at religiosity, especially in Muslim-majority contexts (Abdul Razak et al. 2010) as a large body of work have focused on Anglo-European contexts (Abdul Rahim et al. 2019; see also Proios 2017). Abdul Rahim et al. (2019: 96) argue that "war and conflict" have been waged between practicing Muslims and non-Muslims, further claiming that the latter have stigmatised the former's religiosity to the point of restricting their participation in certain sports under the guise of institutional rules and regulation. Sports practitioners and policymakers should take heed, as it is important that communities and sporting institutions work together to foster inclusive and accommodating environments for sports participation (Abdul Razak et al. 2010; Hamzeh and Oliver 2012). This research was limited to only Muslim women who are former national gymnasts. Future research should include insights from current competitive gymnasts, their coaches, fellow peers, parents, as well as other relevant authorities to further explore the athletes' lived experiences of inclusion/

exclusion, and the approaches which could be taken by all parties to address these concerns. Though this study has demonstrated how "transformative" actions can be taken at the smaller-scale, local level, a more impactful undertaking demands the cooperation and collaboration between Muslim-majority countries such as Malaysia, which has the cultural awareness and knowledge to help Muslim gymnasts navigate such issues, with official governing bodies like the international gymnastics' federation.

Appendix

yes?	A question mark indicates rising intonation at turn completion.
yes.	A period after a word indicates falling intonation at turn completion.
((hand clap))	Double parentheses indicate transcriber's comments, including description of non-verbal behaviour.
(.)	A full stop inside brackets denotes a micro pause, a notable pause but of no significant length.
"xxx"	in-text quotation
xxx	non-English words
. . .	lengthened and hanging pause
[xxx]	input of own word/phrase

References

Abdul Fatah, Farhana. 2019. Discourses of the Non-Veiled: Exploring Discursive Identity Constructions Among Malaysian Muslim Women Who Do Not Veil. Warwick: University of Warwick thesis.

Abdul Fatah, Farhana & Stephanie Schnurr. 2020. Negotiating gender, religious and professional identities. Exploring some of the challenges of non-veiled Muslim women at work. *Yearbook of the Poznań Linguistic Meeting* 6(1). 243–267. https://doi.org/10.2478/yplm-2020-0012

Abdul Rahim, Baidruel Hairiel, Haizuran Mohd Jani & Nurazzura Mohamad Diah. 2019. Sports and Physical Activities in Islam: Reflections of Muslim Participation. *Journal al-Sirat* 18(1). 88–99.

Abdul Razak, Maesam T., Mohd Sofian Omar-Fauzee & Rozita Abd-Latif. 2010. The perspective of Arabic Muslim women toward sport participation. *Journal of Asia Pacific Studies* 1(2). 364–377.

Abu-Lughod, Lila. 2002. Do Muslim women really need saving? Anthropological reflections on cultural relativism and its others. *American Anthropologist* 104(3). 783–790. https://doi.org/10.1525/aa.2002.104.3.783

De Fina, Anna & Alexandra Georgakopoulou (eds). 2015. *The Handbook of Narrative Analysis*. West Sussex: Wiley & Sons.

Barr, Michael D. & Anantha Raman Govindasamy. 2010. The Islamisation of Malaysia: Religious nationalism in the service of ethnonationalism. *Australian Journal of International Affairs*. 64(3) https://doi.org/10.1080/10357711003736469

Baxter, Judith. 2003. *Positioning Gender in Discourse: A Feminist Methodology*. London/NewYork: Palgrave MacMillan.

Baxter, Judith. 2010. Discourse-analytic approaches to text and talk. In Lia Litosseliti (ed.), *Research Methods in Linguistics*, 117–137. London/New York: Continuum.

Benn, Tansin & Symeon Dagkas. 2013. The Olympic Movement and Islamic culture: conflict or compromise for Muslim women? *International Journal of Sport Policy and Politics* 5(2). 281–294. https://doi.org/10.1080/19406940.2012.656677

Benn, Tansin & Gertrud Pfister. 2013. Meeting needs of Muslim girls in school sport: Case studies exploring cultural and religious diversity. *European Journal of Sport Science* 13(5). 567–574. https://doi.org/10.1080/17461391.2012.757808

Burr, Vivien. 2015 [1995]. *Social constructionism*, 3rd edn. East Sussex/New York: Routledge.

Peña, Castañeda & Harold Andrés. 2008. 'I said it!' 'I'm first!': Gender and language-learner identities. *Colombian Applied Linguistics Journal* 10(1). 112–125. http://www.scielo.org.co/pdf/calj/n10/n10a06.pdf

Center for Human Rights in Iran. 2017. 10-year-old Iranian gymnast caught up in hijab controversy. *Center for Human Rights in Iran*. https://iranhumanrights.org/2017/12/10-year-old-iranian-gymnast-caught-up-in-hijab-controversy/

Cook, Kristen J. 2018. Uncovering the Evolution of Hijabs in Women's Sports. *The Graduate Review* 3(1). 62–67. http://vc.bridgew.edu/grad_rev/vol3/iss1/13

Coady, Maria R., Candace Harper & Ester J. De Jong. 2016. Aiming for equity: Preparing mainstream teachers for inclusion or inclusive classrooms? *Tesol Quarterly* 50(2). 340–368. https://doi.org/10.1002/tesq.223

Davies, Julia, Chandni Singh, Mark Tebboth, Dian Spear, Adelina Mensah & Prince Ansah. 2018. Conducting life history interviews. https://idl-bnc-idrc.dspacedirect.org/bitstream/handle/10625/58642/IDL-58642.pdf?sequence=2

De Fina, Anna & Alexandra Georgakopoulou (eds.). 2015. *The Handbook of Narrative Analysis*. New Jersey: John Wiley & Sons.

Felder, Franziska. 2018. The value of inclusion. *Journal of Philosophy of Education* 52(1). 54–70. https://doi.org/10.1111/1467-9752.12280

FitzSimons, Peter. 2016. January 15. Malaysian decision on Farah Ann Abdul Hadi showed no respect for women or common sense. *The Sydney Morning Herald*. https://www.smh.com.au/sport/malaysian-decision-on-farah-ann-abdul-hadi-showed-no-respect-for-women-or-common-sense-20160115-gm6mqa.html

Gee, James Paul. 2014 [1999]. *An introduction to discourse analysis: theory and method*, 4th edn. New York: Routledge.

Glapka, Ewa. 2018. 'If you look at me like at a piece of meat, then that's a problem' – women in the center of the male gaze. Feminist Poststructuralist Discourse Analysis as a tool of critique. *Critical Discourse Studies* 15(1). 87–103 https://doi.org/10.1080/17405904.2017.1390480

Goddard, Cliff. 1994. The meaning of lah: Understanding "emphasis" in Malay (Bahasa Melayu). *Oceanic Linguistics* 33(1). 145–165.

Hamzeh, Manal & Kimberly L. Oliver. 2012. "Because I Am Muslim, I Cannot Wear a Swimsuit". *Research Quarterly for Exercise and Sport* 83(2). 330–339. https://doi.org/10.1080/02701367.2012.10599864

Haug, Peder. 2016. Understanding inclusive education: ideals and reality. *Scandinavian Journal of Disability Research* 19(3). 206–217. http://dx.doi.org/10.1080/15017419.2016.1224778

Jefferson, Gail. 2004. Glossary of transcript symbols with an introduction. In Gene H. Lerner (ed.), *Conversation analysis: studies from the first* generation, 13–31. Philadelphia: John Benjamins Publishing Company.

Kamada, Laurel D. 2009. Mixed-ethnic girls and boys as similarly powerless and powerful: embodiment of attractiveness and grotesqueness. *Discourse Studies* 11(3). 329–352. https://doi.org/10.1177%2F1461445609102447

Kavasoğlu, Irem & Canan Koca. 2021. Gendered Body of Turkish Bikini Fitness Athletes on Instagram. *Communication & Sport* 10(4). 685–707. https://doi.org/10.1177%2F2167479520961370

Khoo, Selina & Nor Eeza Zainal Abidin. 2021. Sport in Malaysia: Towards gender equality. In Rosa Lopez De D'Amico, Maryam Koushkie Jahromi, & Maria Luisa M. Guinto (eds.), *Women and Sport in Asia*, 124–135. Oxford/New York: Routledge.

Kızar, Oktay. 2018. The Place of Sports in the Light of Quran, Hadiths and the Opinions of the Muslim Scholar in Islam. *Universal Journal of Educational Research* 6(11). 2663–2668. https://files.eric.ed.gov/fulltext/EJ1195716.pdf

Mir, Shabana. 2021. August 13. While German gymnasts are praised, Muslim women are scorned for modest dress. *Middle East Eye*. https://www.middleeasteye.net/opinion/german-gymnasts-praised-muslim-women-scorned-modest-dress

O'Neill, Marnie. 2015. June 18. Muslim gymnast Farah Ann Abdul Hadi offends Islamists with 'revealing' leotard. *News.com.au*. https://www.news.com.au/lifestyle/real-life/muslim-gymnast-farah-ann-abdul-hadi-offends-islamists-with-revealingleotard/newsstory/8383ccdf6519ed607b2ea83a3a95fb53

Proios, Miltiadis. 2017. Exploring the relationship between athletic and religious identities. *Trends in Sport Sciences* 3(24). 117–122.

Ronglan, Lars Tore & Kenneth Aggerholm. 2014. 'Humour helps': Elite sports coaching as a balancing act. *Sports Coaching Review* 3(1). 33–45. https://doi.org/10.1080/21640629.2014.885776

Staunæs, Dorthe. 2003. Where have all the subjects gone? Bringing together the concepts of intersectionality and subjectification. *Nora: Nordic Journal of Women's Studies* 11(2). 101–110. https://doi.org/10.1080/08038740310002950

Sunderland, Jane. 2004. *Gendered Discourses*. Hampshire/New York: Palgrave MacMillan.

Tétrault-Farber, Gabrielle. 2021. July 23. Gymnastics-German women take a stand in full-body suits in Tokyo. *Reuters*. https://www.reuters.com/lifestyle/sports/gymnastics-german-women-take-stand-full-body-suits-tokyo-2021-07-23/

Thimm, Viola (ed.). 2021. *Introduction: (Re-)Claiming Bodies Through Fashion and Style – Gendered Configurations in Muslim Contexts*. London/New York: Palgrave MacMillan.

Volk, Anthony A. & Larissa Lagzdins. 2009. Bullying and victimisation among adolescent girl athletes. *Athletic Insight* 11(2009). 15–33.

Walseth, Kristin. 2006. Young Muslim Women and Sport: The Impact of Identity Work. *Leisure Studies* 25(1). 75–94. https://doi.org/10.1080/02614360500200722

Widding, Ulrika. 2015. Parenting ideals and (un-)troubled parent positions. *Pedagogy, Culture & Society* 23(1). 45–64. https://doi.org/10.1080/14681366.2014.919955

Winter, Ofir & Uriya Shavit. 2011. Sports in contemporary Islamic law. *Islamic Law and Society* 18(2). 250–280. https://www.jstor.org/stable/23034925

Kieran File, Stephanie Schnurr, and Stuart Cain
Chapter 13
Putting inclusion into practice: A sociolinguistic lens on institutional practices for establishing an inclusive sports organisation

1 Introduction

In this chapter, we discuss six institutional practices sports organisations can deploy to foster inclusivity, particularly in relation to creating a welcoming stadium environment for all fans. To do this, we have drawn on data from an interview and guided reflection episode with an experienced leader and sports CEO – Stuart Cain (one of the authors of this chapter) – who was asked to reflect on experiences, successes and challenges when attempting to lead on establishing an inclusive sports organisation. From this interview, we extracted six practices or practical actions that demonstrate how Stuart and his sports organisation, Warwickshire County Cricket Club in the UK, went about the complex task of putting inclusion into practice.

The goals, process and analytical agenda of this chapter are deliberately different to the other chapters in this volume. In previous chapters, we have been more concerned with analysing language and illustrating how language is actually used by coaches and players in sports teams or by athletes, fans and media practitioners in the sports media or on social media to reflect or construct inclusive or exclusive social practices. Here we concern ourselves with locating wider institutional practices for promoting inclusion, in this case when strategizing and leading efforts to make a sports organisation a welcoming place for all.

However, despite presenting a wider angle in this chapter, we are still concerned with language and its role in the process of fostering inclusion. Our disciplinary interests in language and communication were influential when deciding which practices to highlight from the interview data and how to formulate the six practices as clear statements of institutional intent. Additionally, all of the practices we discuss below involve the organisation engaged in some form of communication

Kieran File, University of Warwick, United Kingdom
Stephanie Schnurr, University of Warwick
Stuart Cain, CEO Warwickshire County Cricket Club

with stakeholders of the professional sporting environment and can therefore be construed as sociolinguistic in nature. In the process of presenting the six practices discussed within, we draw attention to the broader, taken-for-granted sociolinguistic features and processes implicated in the enactment of each of these practices.

By considering these more sociolinguistic and communicative matters embedded in our six concrete practices, we continue to foreground discussion of *how* inclusion can be accomplished even as we offer a broader account of inclusion in a sporting context. While we hope our academic readership find these discussions interesting, our primary audience for this chapter is sports practitioners, particularly those who are themselves strategizing, leading or involved in working through their own organisational efforts to establish a culture of inclusion in their sports organisation.

In the next section we begin by briefly introducing our context – both the interviewee and the organisation he currently leads – mainly to justify why eliciting insights from this particular CEO can be considered valuable in relation to the mission of this chapter. We then highlight some of the key challenges that sports organisations often face when it comes to establishing a culture that foregrounds inclusion. The bulk of the chapter, though, will be concerned with introducing and discussing six institutional practices that appear to have been central to our CEO's successful efforts to establish an inclusive sports organisation and sociolinguistic or communicative actions implicated and/or intertwined with these practices. When doing this, we will make reference to the findings and observations regarding similar discursive practices aimed at increasing inclusion reported in some of the previous chapters.

2 Setting the scene: Warwickshire County Cricket Club as inclusivity champions

There are potentially a number of sports CEOs that we could have approached to help with the wider mission of this chapter. However, the decision to work together with Stuart Cain and mine his experiences leading inclusion efforts at Warwickshire County Cricket Club (WCCC) was deliberate. Firstly, the University of Warwick (where the other two authors are based) and WCCC are organisations from within the same Midlands community in the United Kingdom. As two local institutions aiming to help make this community that we cohabit a more inclusive and welcoming place to live, the chance to work together was one driver for this partnership.

However, perhaps more significant, certainly for the two academic partners in this chapter, was the clear evidence of an orientation to inclusion by WCCC in many of its initiatives and community engagement efforts. As an organisation, in the last year alone, WCCC have engaged in a number of initiatives that have put their commitment to greater inclusivity in the sport of cricket on show. For example, they became one of the first UK sporting organisations to announce a Multifaith charter, pledging their commitment to engage with religions across the West Midlands (Howson 2022). At the heart of this charter, which was created together with representatives from Islamic, Christian, Hindu, Buddhist, Jewish, Jain and Sikh communities from the West Midlands area, is a pledge by WCCC to learn the needs of those practicing these different faiths so they can ensure that the club is a safe, welcoming environment for all (players, fans and staff).

The club also engaged further with the Muslim community in the local area, running another iteration of the Ramadan Cricket League at Edgbaston (Maghribi 2022a). The Ramadan League is a cricket league Edgbaston has put on for the Muslim community during the holy month where they extend opening times of the stadium for the purposes of playing cricket and blowing off steam after iftar (the evening breaking of fast). WCCC also opened their grounds to the community for Eid al Fitr at the end of Ramadan where they accommodated over 2,000 people for the prayers and celebrations (Maghribi 2022b) and they hosted a panel on Islamophobia and racism which included guests like Baroness Sayeeda Warsi. WCCC also fronted up to and took action against members of the crowd who racially abused Indian fans during a test match at Edgbaston (ESPNcricinfo 2022). Their CEO went on live television to speak directly about the circumstances of the event and issued an apology to those affected, supported a criminal investigation of the offenders and took steps as a venue to weed out racist behaviour in the future by implementing undercover crowd spotters.

WCCC has also made a commitment to support the Birmingham Unicorns, the city's first LGBTQ+ inclusive cricket team, by, for example, offering coaching sessions led by first-team coach Mark Robinson and the club's director of cricket Paul Farbrace (Kotecha 2022). WCCC have also used the club's profile and social media channels to help promote the team and raise awareness about its existence in the club cricket landscape and provided cricket kit to get the team started. They have also implemented a similarly supportive initiative to help Birmingham's disability cricket team (Clarke 2022) and an over-50s senior team, all wearing the Warwickshire crest. Further initiatives have included the creation of sensory rooms to support neuro-diversity and a video based trials system to reduce class bias in the traditional selection processes.

These efforts suggest that WCCC is an organisation that is actively taking steps to promote their own organisation as inclusively minded, engage with the diverse communities that make up the local area and help under-represented and potentially invisible cricket loving communities access the sport. Such a backdrop offered a potentially rich site to mine important practices and actions sports organisations and their leadership need to take when leading a drive for inclusion in a sports organisation.

3 Being an inclusive sports organisation: Key challenges

However, despite the progressive picture presented above, sports organisations face a number of challenges that they need to navigate when trying to put inclusion into practice. On the surface, sport is often referred to as a largely inclusive activity. It involves or encourages (or needs) people to come together, whether that is to play or to support a team they have an affiliation with, and sports grounds and stadiums offer the physical space for these groups to come together. However, while there, groups and organisations need to support social inclusion, defined more in terms of bringing together multiple peoples of different ethnicities, faiths, genders etc., so they can all play and/or enjoy a sporting spectacle and feel safe and be part of a welcoming environment. This is a more complex achievement and one where sports organisations often encounter a series of challenges.

One of the most obvious challenges concerns the resources that are needed to conceptualise, administer, drive and evaluate efforts for more inclusion in sports organisations. Despite their status as posterchildren for inclusion, many sports organisations, even some of the larger ones (in the UK context), are under-resourced with most being classified as small or medium enterprises (SMEs). Edgbaston turns over roughly 20 to 25 million pounds and employs roughly 170 personnel to run its entire sporting organisation, classifying it well within the confines of a SME under UK tax law. Yet the expectation on sports organisations to operate as beacons of social inclusion is disproportionate with this resource. Meeting these demands, both in terms of the huge expectation and the limited resource, then becomes a key challenge for sports organisations.

However, beyond resource constraints, there are also additional challenges, some that are perhaps even harder to control. Cultural associations with particular sports can be unhelpful barriers to increasing efforts to welcome a more diverse population to engage with the sport. With specific respect to cricket, certain class and colonial associations have perhaps narrowly defined cricket as being more for a middle-to-upper class audience or group and, in some countries, ethnically delineated. Whether true or not, such associations may prevent people from communities outside of perceived cultural archetypes from wanting to join in. Depending on how strong these associations are, they can render even the best thought-out solutions or initiatives ineffective on arrival.

Additionally, some sports stadiums can have thousands of attendees at a sporting event. Edgbaston, for example, can attract over 100,000 people across the week when a test match is played. This is the size of a small town and within any small town there are bound to be a share of racist, sexist or bigoted individuals who will attend sports matches. Sports organisations can find themselves suddenly needing to deal with wider societal tensions playing out in the behaviour of sports fans in a stadium environment.

With specific reference to putting on a sporting event, different communities or groups of fans who attend are likely to have very different tastes or even expectations that can make establishing a shared space a complex accomplishment. One simple example concerns alcohol with many sports fans wanting to consume alcohol while watching sport while others do not. Striking a balance so that these different sport-goers can find a space to enjoy the match in ways that are in line with their expectations is, amongst others, a logistical challenge. It can also require delicate negotiation and articulation as inclusion is not about excluding one group of people (and their interests or expectations) in order to make another group of people more welcome.

Sports organisations clearly face a number of challenges, not just in terms of limitations on resources but also in terms of the complexity of trying to meet the needs of a diverse community of sports fans and maintaining an organisational reputation as a place that is progressive and taking inclusivity seriously. How they can navigate this challenging landscape and put inclusion into practice is what we elaborate on in the next section.

4 Locating institutional practices for supporting inclusion: A sociolinguistic lens

Our goal in the remainder of this chapter is to present and discuss six institutional practices that can help organisations to establish and communicate their identity as an inclusive sporting organisation. These six practices emerged from narratives of experience elicited from an in-depth interview with one of the authors of this chapter – Stuart Cain, the CEO of the WCCC. From these experiences, we were able to locate and reimagine several concrete practices that appeared to underlie efforts and successes in establishing Edgbaston as a welcoming place for staff, coaches, players and sports fans from the diverse Birmingham area. We might consider these practices as statements of intent for a sports organisation geared towards promoting and communicating greater inclusion. The bulk of the practices we present and discuss below concern how organisations can seek and support efforts to create a welcoming environment for sports fans coming to the stadium to enjoy sports matches, with several addressing some of the challenges highlighted immediately above.

However, as well as presenting these six practices, where relevant, and given the wider focus of this book, we have also highlighted several of the taken-for-granted sociolinguistic or communicative actions that underlie or are implicated in the enactment of these practices. This includes sociolinguistic or communicative actions like initiating conversations with key stakeholders, ensuring important institutional interactions take place between the members of a diverse group of people, inviting and being open to critical self-reflection in organisational interactions and clearly communicating the consequences for those who do not align with institutional policies on inclusion.

5 Findings: Successfully putting inclusion into practice

From our analysis of the interview, six key practices appeared to underlie the actions of WCCC as the club strove to make their organisation and particularly their stadium a welcoming place for all. These six practices are:
1. commit to reaching out and serving fan communities, particularly the local communities that the organisation is physically embedded within,
2. establish diversity of thinking at every level of the organisation and in every process of the organisation's business,
3. promote and encourage a "think differently" mentality to promoting inclusivity across the organisation, especially with respect to working around resource constraints,
4. frequently audit current and taken-for-granted processes for promoting inclusion to assess the extent to which they work,
5. have clearly communicated and non-negotiable consequences for offenders who exercise exclusionary attitudes,
6. adopt the mindset that achieving greater inclusion is an ongoing and never-ending race.

Each of these institutional practices is now discussed with help from excerpts from our interview, and links are made to some of the previous chapters where relevant.

5.1 Commit to reaching out and serving your fan communities, particularly the local communities that the organisation is physically embedded within

One of things that we're trying to do is say that Edgbaston isn't just about cricket, it has to reflect the communities that we serve and to be an impactful community hub. What can we do to help in those communities not just through the cricket but through the bricks and mortar of Edgbaston stadium on a day-to-day basis?

One of the more overarching practices that emerged in the interview as significant to inclusion efforts at WCCC was the importance of engaging with, reaching out and finding ways to ultimately serve the local community, particularly those sections a sports organisation is looking to directly engage.

For WCCC, the area immediately surrounding Edgbaston is over 40% South Asian and attracting a representative group of this community has proven over the years to be a difficult prospect. However, what has helped has been efforts led by WCCC to directly engage with the South Asian community and offer the bricks and mortar of Edgbaston for community events. Examples of this were cited above where cultural events like Eid and Ramadan celebrations, which typically require a significant amount of space to accommodate large-scale activities, were hosted by Edgbaston. In showing a willingness to engage with the cultural rituals and events of significance to this community, WCCC has been able to open channels of communication between the organisation and the South Asian community and correct or shift attitudes and unhelpful cultural associations about cricket and Edgbaston that were preventing this section of the local community from engaging. They have also been able to build relationships with key stakeholders within this community who they have been able to engage with on further efforts to promote the stadium and game to the South Asian community.

While there are several practices highlighted above, perhaps the most taken-for-granted sociolinguistic one is the active and leading role WCCC has played in reaching out to and initiating interactions with the community they wish to build closer ties. In many of the experiences reflected on in our interview, it was WCCC that actively sought and enthusiastically and open-mindedly initiated conversations with a pocket of their wider community in a direct effort to build closer ties.

An organisation in WCCC's position might ordinarily consider the non-attendance of large sections of the local community as evidence that they are not interested in cricket. Alternatively, they might be content with the idea that it is the South Asian community's responsibility and/or choice to decide whether or not to engage with WCCC. However, instead, as an organisational practice, the WCCC reached out and actively established a dialogue to better understand and collaborate with them on community events. As an organisational practice, this sociolinguistic action of reaching out to otherwise overlooked and marginalised groups shows a proactive approach to increasing the involvement of underrepresented communities in the club. In the process, the WCCC create the potential for meaningful and honest feedback from this community which can, in turn, develop trust.

5.2 Establish diversity of thinking at every level of the organisation and in every process of the organisation's business

> We've tried to do a lot more than just change the way we think about what inclusivity means and tried to make sure that we've got people that represent different faith groups as well as gender groups and feel empowered to challenge and be part of the debate as well as the solution. We need to ensure that we don't just reinforce some of the stereotypes that we'd have as a white middle class leadership team. We've created an Inclusion Advisory Board, which meets bi-monthly, and has representatives from a number of different communities that cover all nine of the protected characteristics as well as additional local needs. That's become a really important sounding board for floating ideas and saying "we are thinking about doing this". This encourages feedback and debate from those on the Board and I have to admit that when people often say "have you thought of this" I have to be honest and say that I haven't. So that's been a really useful sounding board for me and the Club and helped us confront a number of prejudices and cultural misunderstandings or knowledge gaps.

Another key practice that appeared to be significant across the interview was efforts to establish diversity of thinking at every level and in every process of the organisation's business, particularly when diagnosing and talking about issues and making decisions about *how* to be a more inclusive organisation (see also Rock, this volume). At the heart of this practice is ensuring that potential barriers to achieving greater or more successful inclusion, or issues with the implementation of specific initiatives, can be accurately assessed by those with appropriate cultural and/or contextual knowledge to be able to do so (see also Ozinanir and Mullany this volume).

The above excerpt from our interview refers to a very specific and overarching mechanism the club has established in this regard: the Inclusion Advisory Board. Through this board, the organisation can discuss and leverage people's knowledge of their own cultures and communities vis-à-vis key decisions the organisation is taking (sometimes on behalf of particular groups or peoples) in a safe environment. As the excerpt illustrates, organisations, while acting in good faith, may overlook issues with implementation or wider concerns that might damage a particular outlook or strategic initiative's chances of success. As a practice, establishing diversity of thinking into the organisational decision-making process operates as an auditing process, ensuring efforts to, for example, generate strategy for making the stadium a more welcoming place for a diverse group of fans can be scrutinised by members of those communities before action is taken (see also Chimbwete-Phiri this volume, for an example of a context that would benefit from such auditing processes).

From a sociolinguistic perspective, the Inclusion Advisory Board and the wider practice of welcoming or bringing a diverse array of individuals into consequential conversations for the organisation is a strategic way to orient towards a culture of inclusion. Obviously, just assembling a diverse group of people and giving them the mission and the authority to shape the organisation's direction does not guarantee an institutional culture of inclusion; a lot will depend on how the conversations (in the boardroom and beyond) actually unfold between the individuals present, particularly regarding the way power works in these interactions and the degree to which people feel encouraged to contribute (see also Pringle and Denison; Graf and Fleischhacker both this volume). However, by diversifying the makeup of boardroom conversations, the organisation can seek to include and ultimately benefit from the lived experiences of a more representative cross-section of society.

For a sports organisation, achieving diversity of thinking can be complex given the various strands of professional activity encompassed in a sports organisation. However, ideally, sports organisations should ensure there is a diverse leadership group which actively encourages and seeks ongoing conversations and consultations with stakeholders, including informing action and decision making at all levels of the organisation, from the offices or administrative wings of the company, within the professional and academy coaching and support teams and in the stadium when putting on the matches.

5.3 Promote and encourage a "think differently" mentality to promoting inclusivity across the organisation, especially with respect to resource constraints

> This is one of the biggest things sport needs to get its head around. Promoting inclusivity doesn't always require more money. It just requires a different mindset and being flexible. Like I said there's things coming out of the woodwork all the time now. Things we would have never thought about based on traditional thinking, until we started on this journey.
>
> You do need some resource to drive administration as there has to be some structure to inclusivity, but it's one person that also looks after other areas of governance. It's not their job to drive EDI. It's every manager's job to take ownership and drive change.
>
> Changing how leaders think doesn't necessarily cost a lot. Me reaching out to a Mosque and having coffee with an Iman only costs my time, but I've done this a number of times and always come back thinking differently about an opportunity and also developed a relationship that allows me to ask difficult questions and have tricky conversations without fear. This 'safe space' mentality is crucial in driving change.
>
> We haven't employed a whole lot more people. We've only spent a small amount of money and that's mainly on educating leaders and creating the interventions that challenge their perceptions and more importantly, motivate them to think differently.

Earlier in this chapter, we noted that a key challenge facing sporting organisations when it comes to nurturing greater inclusion is limited resources. A key practice that emerged in discussions about resources was the need for sports organisations to encourage employees and leadership to "think differently" or think outside the box when it comes to seeking greater inclusivity on what can be wafer-thin or non-existent budgets.

Many of the underlying practices and strategic initiatives discussed throughout the interview (several of which are presented in this chapter) are born out of the need to navigate constraints on resource. The Inclusion Advisory Board, discussed immediately above, is one such example where impactful action can be achieved through little cost. Building relationships with key figures in the community, also cited immediately above, and meeting them for a coffee for an open dialogue to directly discuss potential barriers to involving different community groups has the potential to foster stronger ties and feed strategic insights into the work of the organisation. These specific examples present as less-costly alternatives to hiring external consultants to advise on or drive inclusion efforts.

Another example of thinking differently was cited in relation to hiring and embedding a person responsible for EDI in the organisation. WCCC do not have an EDI role in their organisation and instead conceptualise EDI as everyone's responsibility. They do this through educating their staff on matters of inclusion, sending the signal that upholding values of inclusion is not just the responsibility of a single individual within the organisation. Whole-staff meetings held monthly are used by WCCC to bring in speakers to lead discussions about various topics often geared towards raising awareness about issues or barriers to inclusion. Specific examples include people coming in to speak about different religions (Judaism, Islam, Christianity), neurodiversity, from LGBTQ+ charities and/or experts coming in to speak about language and cultural behaviours. As well as signalling to the organisation that EDI is everyone's responsibility, this action saves money on salary for an EDI individual.

The organisation has also reinvented some of their reporting processes to help perform data collection and data presentation purposes for the wider organisation. The more traditional annual report, for example, now includes much more than just the financial figures and a statement from the chair of the organisation. It includes reporting on, for example, the percentage ethnicity within the team's academy groups and how that changed over four or five years, the gender mix of the people working in the offices, pay parity between male and female and the offices or sexuality, wherever they have the data. This simple communicative action arguably helps to ensure regular internal research, reporting and transparency on areas of progress (or lack of progress) that can be made visible and become part of the organisation's joint conversations.

In the context of both resource constraints and an increasing expectation on sports organisations to promote inclusion, it appears one of the key tasks for an organisation's leadership is to foster a "think differently" mentality that not only guides their own decision making as leaders but also encourages ownership of efforts for increasing and living values of inclusion by all members of the business. From a sociolinguistic perspective, fostering this "think differently" mentality can involve leaders modelling inclusion as a central value for the organisation perhaps by making inclusivity events (like guest speaker talks on inclusion) whole-staff events and part of whole-staff meetings, rethinking how traditional genres of business communication (like the annual report) might be repurposed to communicate the organisation's commitment to inclusion, and encouraging employee dialogue on ways to meet the challenge of increasing inclusion under sometimes severe resource constraints.

Resource is certainly needed to administer efforts to promote inclusion and it may be needed to fund high-tech tools that are increasingly being used to police efforts to make stadiums safe spaces for everyone (a topic we discuss further below in point 5). However, the idea that resource constraints needed to be addressed or dealt with fully *before* progress towards greater inclusion can be made perhaps shows limited initiative. Fostering a mentality of thinking differently, with respect to establishing greater inclusion, can drive success in this area.

5.4 Frequently audit current and taken-for-granted processes for promoting inclusion to assess the extent to which they work

Can you imagine a young woman who's been subject to sexist or misogynistic behaviour and already feels scared having to take action by walking up to a highly visible, potentially intimidating man in a hi-viz jacket and telling him there's a problem and then being asked to visibly point them out before heading back to her seat, potentially in the vicinity of those just visibly identified.

It isn't going to work, is it? We've had to find ways of making it easy to quietly report issues without making yourself open to more abuse and facilitating a quick response that puts the women's mind at rest and allows her to enjoy the rest of the day feeling safe and welcome. That response also has to demonstrate to others that there's a real consequence to unacceptable behaviour, that's the best deterrent there is. We've invested a significant amount in developing app-based reporting and a high definition camera system that makes it easy to identify, track and report issues to internal stewards and the police if necessary.

What was also clear in the experiences reflected on in this interview was the relative success that came from auditing and critically assessing inclusion initiatives and processes the organisation has put in place to ensure they are working as intended. This theme emerged particularly in discussions about enforcing an inclusion policy during sporting events and the mechanisms that were in place to help those subjected to abuse to come forward and report it (for a critical discussion of the role of the media in some of these discussions, see Bailey and Jones this volume).

The excerpt presented above provides an illustration of one such process being worked through and assessed. In this instance, the Edgbaston app is being spoken about as an important resource added to the armoury designed to help get around issues with reporting abuse in the stadium. Traditionally, stewards are present in stadiums to be a point of call for those subjected to abuse during sports matches. However, approaching a steward to report abuse – going to a (likely male) steward and admitting having been victim of abuse, and locating the abusers – can in its own right be a daunting prospect. The app is spoken about here in relation to these issues. It has helped create conditions for a more anonymous reporting experience, foregoing the need to approach a steward and possibly point offenders out in full view.

What lies below the surface of the above excerpt and discussion is a deeper commitment to auditing and critically reflecting on the initiatives and processes in play that are designed to help create a safe environment for sports fans. Simply releasing or implementing initiatives for supporting inclusion work is not enough. It is important to collect evidence that they are working, and/or to critically reflect on barriers to their use. An obvious sociolinguistic account of this practice, then, is the need to locate and assess the interactional dynamics that underlie or are required for the successful use of or engagement with inclusion initiatives or mechanisms. Regardless of how good in theory an inclusion initiative might be, assuming humans will use it without critical thought as to interpersonal realities that underlie its use, may limit their effectiveness (see also File and Schnurr this volume). A commitment, therefore, to auditing the interpersonal dynamics that underlie inclusion initiatives, in order to diagnose or assess barriers to their use, is an important practice if an organisation is to ensure the effectiveness of their efforts to promote or support inclusion.

5.5 Have clearly communicated and non-negotiable consequences for offenders who exercise exclusionary attitudes

We had an issue last year where there were two young women sitting watching one of the England games, and there was some kind of sexist abuse by a bunch of men behind them. Within 5 minutes of the women pressing the button on the app to report the issue, we reviewed the footage and sent stewards and a Police Officer in to the stand to eject those responsible. There's real consequence there. Hopefully that gave those young women the confidence to enjoy the rest of their day knowing that they were safe and welcome..

[. . .]

We also had an issue with racism last year. It wasn't reported on the day, which was unfortunate, but through social media after the game. It blew up, but we could pinpoint those responsible using the HD cameras and hand over footage to the police which allowed them to prosecute those involved for a racially aggravated public order offence. Again, real consequence for unacceptable behaviour and the only real way to deter those intent on causing problems – as well as showing that Edgbaston is safe and welcome for all.

Connected to the above point is the importance for sports organisations to have clearly communicated and non-negotiable consequences for perpetrators – *that are acted upon.* This is not only important for the actual act of removing those who are preventing others from feeling safe and secure as they enjoy a sports match, but also for gaining the trust of those who may be feeling reticent about attending sports stadiums due to being historically subjected to abuse.

Steps taken by WCCC in this regard included clearly communicating to sports fans coming to the stadium that the organisation had expectations about behaviour. Pre-communication materials were an important resource in laying out these expectations, as was ensuring stadium goers sign up to these expectations when buying tickets. Efforts to make these resources inclusive, primarily by presenting them as visual resources, were also noted here so as to make them accessible and easy to process. This was important in WCCC's context as there are a number of fans coming who may not speak English as a first language.

However, it is the effective policing of these policies where trust with the wider community is likely to be garnered and an organisation is able to develop a reputation for practicing what it preaches. In short, organisations cannot talk a good game and then have it fail at the point of execution. While we noted constraints on resource above, methods for managing issues of intolerance in the stadium was an area where the WCCC has invested heavily. An array of technological tools from the Edgbaston app through to high-definition camera systems capable of pinpointing individuals in the stadium and identifying what they have said or done are now in place and part of the everyday running of a sporting event. Not every sports organisation is going to have the money to be able to fund the implementation of high-definition cameras, but for sporting bodies serious about giving the sports and stadiums they oversee the tools to be effective upholders of inclusive values, such an investment offers great potential. Both excerpts presented above illustrate this policing in action and show a non-negotiable approach to abuse being taken by the organisation. However, such an approach appears to be somewhat dependent on undeniable forms of evidence being collected and assessed to help inform policing efforts.

Sports organisations can only go so far in trying to predict who is going to cause them trouble before they enter their stadiums. All they can do is communicate their expectations, construct an environment that shows an orientation to ensuring people are able to feel safe and welcome regardless of their backgrounds, and police these expectations rigorously in a no-tolerance fashion. Language is obviously implicated in all of these actions and organisations face choices with respect to how to use language to appropriately and clearly encode or index their organisation's expectations in pre-communication materials, through to how they report on instances where they have removed offenders from their stadiums. Choices in how language is used to communicate expectations and consequences help to send the message that exclusionary behaviour will not be tolerated.

5.6 Adopt the mindset that achieving greater inclusion is an ongoing and never-ending race

> Inclusivity is a race that we will never stop running. It's not something you do once and then sit back and relax. You have to keep talking, listening, challenging, learning and reviewing how you do things. That's the only way to drive meaningful cultural change that leads to inclusivity being part of our DNA. It's the only way to ensure that people from all communities look back and recognise that things have really changed at Edgbaston.

Finally, it was apparent across the interview that organisational efforts to promote inclusion needed to be construed and approached as a never-ending race and that accepting this was an important step for a sports organisation. Efforts to be inclusive were recognised as needing to be built into day-to-day thinking and working processes. In the above excerpt, the foundational and ongoing thinking and constant dialogue around the nature of inclusion work is construed in this way by referring to it as being part of the organisation's DNA. One of the ways this mindset can help a sports organisation is to ensure they have the ethos and language that supports them to consolidate inclusion efforts already underway, meet new challenges that are on the horizon, and be open to new issues of inclusion that have yet to emerge. During the interview, it was clear that WCCC felt like they were starting to get their heads around challenges in relation to ethnicity and in getting more women into sport and along to stadiums to watch sport. However, new issues surrounding gender and transgenderism (see also Bailey and Jones this volume), for example, were not well understood, especially in relation to sports organisation's efforts to be welcoming places for academy athletes coming into pathways and whether they play for boys or girls teams (see also Graf and Fleischhacker this volume).

Calls for greater inclusion can mushroom as society becomes increasingly aware of the various challenges people face when attempting to enter sports, as players, employees or fans (see also Abdul Fatah this volume). As sports organisations are, at their core, places where large and sometimes diverse groups of people congregate to play or enjoy sport, they need to have the right mindset and culture to be able to address emerging challenges. Overlay pressure to be inclusive with increasing calls to be sustainable and it becomes clear how important it is for sports organisations to be flexible and embrace the complexity that comes with running a modern-day sports organisation. Embracing this complexity and seeking ways to establish a culture which has at its heart the drive to create a welcoming space to play, work and watch sport is an essential point of departure. This ultimately means making inclusion a regular part of the everyday conversations with a sporting organisation, in the ways we have highlighted throughout this chapter.

6 Doing being an inclusive sports organisation

In this chapter, we have provided a brief account of how a sports organisation can put inclusion into practice. We have done this by highlighting six key practices or practical actions that we argue can support the accomplishment of inclusion, particularly in relation to creating a welcoming sporting environment in which to watch sport. This list of practices was certainly not intended as an exhaustive list, but they present themselves as significant underlying themes that emerged in and across our interview data and some of the previous chapters and were therefore deemed worthy of discussion here.

We also made the choice to highlight these six practices based partially on several important sociolinguistic implications that are perhaps taken for granted but that are essential for enacting these institutional practices of inclusion. This involved showing how underlying institutional strategy and efforts to be inclusive are sociolinguistic and communicative actions like:

- communicating directly to a range of communities and taking responsibility for driving interaction with these communities, in order to create 'safe space' environments that allow for the honest conversations that are needed to drive change.
- ensuring consequential institutional conversations are made up of people from a diverse array of backgrounds,
- modelling and communicating (directly or indirectly) to employees an institutional culture whereby inclusion is seen as everyone's responsibility and that it requires a "think differently" mentality,
- interrogating the interpersonal dynamics that lie at the heart of the various initiatives and practices a sports organisation has in place to support inclusion to ensure they work as intended,
- ensuring that a no-tolerance position is adopted, policed and enacted by the organisation in pre-match and during match encounters with fans.

What we have hopefully highlighted through this more explicit attention to the sociolinguistic aspects of these six practices is how embedded and central language is to the accomplishment of inclusion in a sports organisation. In many regards, inclusion is an interactional accomplishment, one that relies on multiple communicative processes and actions. Seen from this perspective, we could argue that the success of an organisation's efforts to be inclusive lies in its ability to successfully mobilise language and foster conversations or interactions in various stakeholder dynamics in order to locate barriers to inclusion, communicate initiatives for inclusion and uphold or police efforts to be inclusive.

This chapter was aimed particularly at a non-academic audience, one that might include a readership of sports leaders responsible for or struggling to manage increased calls for sports organisations to strive to be inclusive. As argued above, sports organisations face many challenges in this regard, and we hope that seeing how others have practically approached these challenges can provide sports leaders and practitioners with a point of departure for considering strategy and principles of practice in their own context.

References

Clarke, Nathan. 2022. December 3. Birmingham's disability cricket team want to make sport open for all. *BirminghamLive*. https://www.birminghammail.co.uk/news/midlands-news/birminghams-trailblazing-disability-cricket-team-25648216

ESPNcricinfo. 2022. July 7. Edgbaston to deploy undercover crowd spotters following racist abuse during India Test. *ESPNcricinfo*. https://www.espncricinfo.com/story/england-vs-india-t20i-series-edgbaston-to-deploy-undercover-crowd-spotters-following-racist-abuse-during-india-test-1323539

Howson, Nick. 2022. February 17. Warwickshire unveil "ground-breaking" multifaith charter as Edgbaston changes are introduced. *The Cricketer*. https://www.thecricketer.com/Topics/county cricket/warwickshire_multifaith_charter_edegbaston_changes.html

Kotecha, Tejas. 2022. February 23. Birmingham Unicorns: Trailblazing LGBT+ inclusive cricket club who want to make sport open for all. *Sky Sports*. https://www.skysports.com/cricket/news/12123/12547976/birmingham-unicorns-trailblazing-lgbt-inclusive-cricket-club-who-want-to-make-sport-open-for-all

Maghribi, Layla. 2022a. April 7. How British sports clubs are embracing Muslim athletes during Ramadan. *The National*. https://www.thenationalnews.com/world/uk-news/2022/04/07/how-british-sports-clubs-are-embracing-muslim-athletes-during-ramadan/

Maghribi, Layla. 2022b. April 25. Eid Al Fitr celebrations to make debut at UK's Edgbaston cricket stadium. *The National*. https://www.thenationalnews.com/world/uk-news/2022/04/25/eid-al-fitr-celebrations-to-make-debut-at-uks-edgbaston-cricket-stadium/

Kieran File and Stephanie Schnurr
Chapter 14
Bringing everything together: Considering the role of language in effecting inclusion and exclusion in sport

1 Introduction

Our aim in this volume was to add linguistic insights to wider debates about inclusion and exclusion in sport. Across the fourteen chapters presented in this book, authors shone a light on how issues of inclusion and exclusion manifest themselves in the language used by coaches, fans, athletes and the (sports) media. Using a range of authentic, naturally occurring interactions as data – in written, spoken and multimodal form – from a range of different sporting contexts, authors have located and unpacked issues of inclusion and exclusion in action in the domain of sport.

In this final chapter, we take a broader look across the chapters collected in this volume and consider what, collectively, we have contributed – through our linguistic lens on language – to wider discussions about inclusion/exclusion in sport. To do this, we revisit some of the key questions we raised in the introduction and reimagine these with help from the conclusions drawn by chapter authors. We also take stock of the applications for practice discussed in the previous chapters and reflect more broadly on how sports practitioners can mobilise the power of language to instigate and drive efforts to promote inclusion and reduce exclusion in the sports domain. We close this chapter and volume by noting how future research might build on insights generated by the studies presented here.

2 Looking at inclusion/exclusion in action in sporting contexts

In compiling this volume, the key questions we wanted to address were where and how inclusion is relevant in the wider sporting ecosystem, and where exclusion occurs. The previous chapters have convincingly demonstrated that

Kieran File, Stephanie Schnurr, The University of Warwick

https://doi.org/10.1515/9783110789829-015

inclusion and exclusion are ubiquitous issues which surface before, during and after the sporting event itself and emerge in a wide range of different contexts where sport is performed or consumed. Issues of inclusion and exclusion are relevant during interactions between players on the playing field (Stavridou and File) and after matches and training (O'Dwyer), as well as between coaches and athletes during training and competition (Rock; File et al.); they also emerge in online interactions among fans before and after sporting events (Chimbwete-Phiri and Schnurr), as well as on Instagram postings by athletes (Ozinanir and Mullany), and in media reports (Kemble, Erdoğan-Öztürk et al.; Bailey and Jones). The chapters have shown that questions around how to prevent exclusion and achieve greater inclusion in their sports are topics about which athletes (e.g., Ozinanir and Mullany; Pringle and Denison), coaches (e.g., Rock; File et al.) and other stakeholders (e.g., Graf and Fleischhacker) constantly reflect, and where they often see a concrete need for change (e.g., Abdul Fatah; Ozinanir and Mullany; File et al.).

As the various studies throughout this volume have illustrated, in many instances it was the athletes and coaches themselves who not only identified important issues of inclusion and exclusion, but who also took on the role of agents of change attempting to tackle these issues. In some cases, athletes used their own celebrity identity and status to make exclusion issues public – as was shown, for example in Ozinanir and Mullany's analysis of the Instagram posts of the F1 driver Lewis Hamilton who flagged up racial discrimination in F1. In other cases, it was the coaches rather than the athletes who understood it as their responsibility to create a more inclusive environment in which athletes would feel integrated and appreciated – such as the grassroots level football team researched by Rock, and the boxing coaches analysed by File et al. However, in several other cases, concrete issues of inclusion and exclusion were brought to light by the researchers – such as the issues around the representation of the netball players in the online fan groups researched by Chimbwete-Phiri and Schnurr, and the gendered portrayal of female athletes in the media coverage discussed by Kemble and Erdoğan-Öztürk et al.

But in spite of these different roles and responsibilities taken on by different agents, language always plays a particularly crucial role – not just in identifying and bringing these issues to the fore. As the previous chapters have demonstrated, focusing on language, and identifying and describing the specific pragmatic and discursive processes and strategies through which inclusion was achieved and celebrated (e.g., O'Dwyer) or through which exclusion was created – even if potentially unintended (e.g., Abdul Fatah; Chimbwete-Phiri and Schnurr) – enables researchers (and practitioners) to make practices and processes of inclusion and exclusion visible and subsequently develop concrete intervention measures to address them. We elaborate these observations in the next section.

3 Foregrounding the role of language in promoting or threatening inclusion

A central concern for the editors and authors of the chapters in this volume was to understand the role language played in threatening or helping to accomplish inclusion in sporting contexts. Authors of most chapters in this volume adopted a pragmatic or discourse view of language, seeking to understand meanings of inclusion or exclusion that were being signalled or constructed by language choices as they were being used in actual sporting contexts. In other cases, the language being studied was in the form of reflections by social groups and research participants as they reflected on their experience in sport. However, central to all chapters was a concern with locating specific practices of or reflections on language use in sporting contexts that could be identified as promoting or threatening inclusion.

Observing the training of a grassroots football team in Wales, Rock found that the coach successfully achieved inclusion by doing translanguaging and employing a range of multilingual practices, in combination with gesture and movement. In particular, by using repetition at various levels, as well as regularly drawing on sporting lexis, displaying linguistic accommodation, and using phrases and actions to establish an analogy with elite football, he managed to create an inclusive environment for his young players. In the other study on coaches' language in this volume, File et al. found that the boxing coaches' use of the ambiguous and highly complex pronoun "we" sometimes created inclusion but at other times had the opposite effect.

Focusing on the language of inclusion used by athletes rather than coaches, Stavridou and File observed that the inclusive leadership philosophy of the basketball team in the UK that they researched was reflected – and to some extent reinforced and created – through the players' tendency to interactionally distribute rights to govern the team in their team huddles. Patterns in the interaction analysed showed a distributed approach to tasks like identifying problems, developing solutions, evaluating performance, managing the emotional pulse of the team and leading the team's solidarity rituals, whereby multiple individuals could step up and lead these tasks. In a similar vein, O'Dwyer's chapter showed how the members of a Gaelic football and hurling club in Ireland regularly used collaborative humour and banter as a ritual to signal inclusion in the team and the club more widely.

However, many of these strategies – just like the use of the personal pronoun "we" researched by File et al. – are ambiguous and perform many functions, sometimes creating and fostering inclusion, while at other times contributing to exclusion. Banter is a very good example of this, as the chapters by O'Dwyer and Pringle and Denison have shown. While the former study emphasises the positive, team building and inclusion and solidarity creating functions of humour and banter, the latter reminds us of the discriminatory and exclusionary potential of humour against minority group members. Exploring how the use of homo-negative language may contribute to the exclusion of gay and bisexual male rugby players in the UK and Australia, Pringle and Denison found that although the participants in their focus groups generally agreed that homophobic language – such as the use of homophobic slurs and taunts – was not used in their club, anonymous surveys provided evidence of the opposite. Their findings illustrate that homophobic language – especially when disguised as banter and intended in "a non-homophobic way" – was often perceived and interpreted by the players as non-problematic, while still functioning to exclude gay and bisexual players.

In a similar reflective study to Pringle and Denison, issues around the exclusion of particular groups of athletes were identified in the research on female footballers in Austria presented in the chapter by Graf and Fleischhacker. Findings of this study showed that in the focus group discussions around their experiences, the players' language largely contributed to – rather than challenged and resisted – the cultural field which discursively creates football as a masculine space. Through describing themselves and other female players as "others" and through arguing within rather than beyond binaries (i.e., men against women), the women excluded themselves and normalised the marginalisation of women in this sport more widely.

A more critical stance towards excluding certain minority groups from professional sports – in this case Muslim gymnasts in Malaysia who wear the veil – was displayed by the women who participated in Abdul Fatah's study. Analysing the language used by these gymnasts in research interviews when recalling their difficulties of combining being a good gymnast with being a good Muslim, Abdul Fatah observed the emergence of what she refers to as the "solat Discourse" and the "aurat Discourse" as prominent sites where struggles around inclusion and exclusion took place.

However, while the chapters in this book provide ample evidence of the athlete's awareness of issues around inclusion and exclusion, the chapter by Chimbwete-Phiri and Schnurr on fan groups is testament to the lack of such an awareness among the fans of the National netball team of Malawi. Through their analysis of posts in different online fan fora, the authors identify and describe how through their use of language (and emoticons) the members of online fan groups contribute – even if potentially unknowingly – to the objectification and sexualisation of the players, thereby denying them their professional identity and marginalising them.

This relevance of language as an important site – as well as means – through which issues of inclusion and exclusion can be expressed, and in some cases made public, is also demonstrated by Ozinanir and Mullany's study on the Instagram posts of F1 driver Lewis Hamilton. Instagram provides a prime site for Hamilton to express his discontent and criticism over the existence of racism, discrimination and exclusion to a wider public audience. He achieves this by using an argumentative rhetorical style characterised by multimodal discourse and sociolinguistic features, including intertextuality and synthetic personalisation. Through these strategies Hamilton is able to portray himself as an activist and advocate for Black inclusion and social justice in F1 as well as more widely.

Another important site to observe the language of exclusion is the sports media. As the chapters by Kemble, Erdoğan-Öztürk et al., as well as Bailey and Jones have demonstrated, the language used to portray female and transgender athletes in the media plays an important role and considerably shapes public perception and Discourses around inclusion and exclusion. For example, analysing a corpus of British newspapers, Bailey and Jones found evidence of implicit transphobia against transgender athletes. The language used by the newspapers to largely argue for an exclusion of these athletes from competing against cisgender women relied largely on two thematic categories – sex and gender; and inclusion and fairness – which were used to frame the discussion around the potential inclusion of a transgender swimmer as unfair. This framing together with the negative portrayal of supporters of trans inclusion as aggressive and manipulative are characteristic of the language of exclusion observed in this chapter.

Similarly, Kemble observed and critically discussed the effects of gender marking, infantilisation, sexualisation and trivialisation in media reports about Australian women's football and rugby. Additionally, in their study of media representations of Turkish sports women during the 2020 Olympic games in Tokyo, Erdoğan-Öztürk et al. found that by using the frames of *war, power, light* and *kinship*, newspapers employed ideological perspectivation strategies to portray these athletes, through language, as ideological symbols and to instrumentalise their success to confirm political ideologies.

4 Widening the lens: From micro linguistic practices to macro ideological understanding of inclusion/exclusion in sport

Taken together, the studies in this volume provide empirical evidence that illustrates how issues and practices of inclusion and exclusion play out in various sporting contexts. However, through these empirical accounts, the authors have also been able to access and build claims about deeper levels of meaning – underlying ideologies about inclusion and exclusion in sports – that might help to explain the practices and issues discussed in their chapters. Understanding ideologies that might help to explain inclusive or exclusive practices in sporting contexts was another key question we sought to address in this volume.

In spite of the openly inclusive agenda that many sports organisations propagate, several of the routine language practices of athletes, coaches, fans, stakeholders, and the media located by authors in this volume highlight ideas and ideologies that feed into and in many cases normalise exclusionary practices, at the grassroots level (Rock) or at the international sports level (Bailey and Jones). In particular, ideologies around who and what constitutes an ideal athlete and who should have access to – and be included in – a particular sport or team, feature strongly in the work presented in the chapters of this volume. While some chapters provide evidence of successful attempts to turn these ideologies into concrete inclusionary actions and practices, thereby creating and shaping inclusive environments in which athletes can flourish (e.g., Rock, File et al., Stavridou and File), other chapters paint a bleaker picture and provide examples of where these ideologies gave rise to and supported exclusionary policies and practices. For example, for the female football players researched by Graf and Fleischhacker, the gay rugby players analysed by Pringle and Denison, as well as the transgender swimmer in Bailey and Jones' chapter, these ideas and ideologies often translated into very concrete consequences, such as a lack of access to training and funding, and even being excluded from competitions. Moreover, as the chapters by Chimbwete-Phiri, Kemble, Erdoğan-Öztürk et al. have shown, gender ideologies – which draw on a very limiting and stereotypical role set available to women and cater for and perpetuate a male gaze – prevail in many sports and characterise not only media portrayals of athletes but also surface in fan fora.

Moreover, as the previous chapters have demonstrated, these ideologies do not stand alone but are closely related and often intersect with each other, as well as with other ideologies and ideas – for example around race (Ozinanir and Mullany) and religion (Abdul Fatah). This intersectionality of underlying ideologies is one aspect of what makes challenging them – and thereby addressing their exclusionary effects – so complex and complicated. And yet, addressing these exclusionary effects and the underlying ideologies that feed into them is an important endeavour – especially since many of the ideologies and issues identified and discussed here, go beyond the concrete context of the specific sport and teams outlined in the chapters. Ideologies around gender stereotypes (Graf and Fleischhacker; Kemble; Chimbwete-Phiri and Schnurr; Erdoğan-Öztürk et al.), fairness (Bailey and Jones), race (Ozinanir and Mullany), religious freedom (Abdul Fatah), sexual orientation (Pringle and Denison), as well as leadership and teamwork (Stavridou and File; File et al.) are not just typical for the sports domain but characterise social life more generally.

5 Promoting inclusion in sport: Summarising the implications of our linguistic lens

Another key question we set out to explore in this volume was: how can we translate the theoretical findings of our linguistic research for sports practitioners? In the process of compiling their chapters, authors were asked to explicitly consider the role language could play in driving change and improving current practices within the sporting context they were exploring. In the process, a range of valuable insights were generated for various practitioners in the sporting ecosystem, including athletes (Ozinanir and Mullany), coaches and/or team managers (Rock; File et al; Stavridou and File; O'Dwyer; Abdul Fatah), sports associations (Chimbwete-Phiri; Graf and Fleischhacker; Pringle and Denison), leaders of sports organisations (File, Schnurr and Cain) and the Fourth Estate (Kemble; Erdoğan-Öztürk et al; Bailey and Jones).

In reflecting on these implications raised by authors, broader themes emerged that highlight how linguistic insights can be translated for practical use by these various practitioners in an effort to promote greater inclusion in sport. We unpack three of these themes below.

5.1 Using language to shape inclusive sporting environments

One of the more obvious themes, seen particularly across the chapters in Part One of the book, concerned the location and illustration of specific linguistic, interactional or multimodal practices used in the actual act of coaching and playing sport that can help to shape inclusive sports team environments or talk them into being.

Rock, for example, showed how a wide array of linguistic and multimodal practices used by a football coach in a multicultural, grassroots coaching environment established a welcoming and inclusive environment for the players in this environment. Stavridou and File provided an empirical illustration of a basketball team interactionally distributing responsibility for the management of the team across a wider array of individuals in ways that constructed what might be referred to as an inclusionary team management structure. O'Dwyer showed how the encouragement of light-hearted interactions and an appreciation of humour or banter can foster feelings of enjoyment and closeness between the players in a team, citing such exchanges, particularly cooperative humour exchanges, as helping to bond the group and engage everyone in the interactional construction of their togetherness. Shifting to the social media domain, and to promoting messages of inclusion in sport, Ozinanir and Mullany provide an empirical illustration of how athletes can construct and enact an activist identity, one that champions the causes of greater inclusion in their sport. Through their chapter, they offer other athletes a detailed example of how they might mobilise a range of linguistic and multimodal communicative affordances of social media communication platforms to both construct an identity as an inclusion activist and promote and engage audiences in messages of inclusion.

As well as highlighting for practitioners how specific linguistic, interactional or multimodal practices can foster inclusion, authors also modelled the need to more critically assess the potential for linguistic forms to promote inclusion by considering the meaning they are making in context. One chapter where this is particularly evident is File et al, who demonstrate this more critical thinking process in reference to collective pronouns. On the surface, collective pronouns (like "we") present a valuable resource in promoting inclusion. However, as demonstrated in Chapter 4, the context is a central component for encoding the meaning of linguistic forms. As the authors suggested, the meaning of "we" in some interactional contexts can be complex and may not encode meanings of inclusion between the speakers. A key implication here for practitioners is to realise that linguistic forms, even those that appear to be potentially useful resources for accomplishing inclusion, only make meaning when used in context. Therefore, any linguistic strategising by sports coaches, teams or organisations to foster greater inclusion needs to more critically assess the meaning potential of language choices within their context of use.

Still geared towards creating inclusive environments but taking a broader view of potential barriers to inclusion, Abdul Fatah indicates the potential benefits of intercultural or interfaith training for coaches who are coaching Muslim athletes, particularly in settings where the coach does not share the same religious background as their Muslim trainees. Through her study, Abdul Fatah notes that players felt supported and understood when coached by those who understood their religious beliefs and requirements, and thus were able to make the necessary arrangements in training.

Taken together, these chapters offered practitioners a range of illustrative examples of how specific linguistic, interactional and multimodal choices and practices function to establish inclusive team environments. While the specific features highlighted in the chapters may not be immediately transferrable or relevant in all contexts, the process of linking language to the construction of various forms of inclusion was modelled throughout the book in ways that will hopefully help practitioners consider links between language practice and inclusion in their own sporting environments.

5.2 Raising awareness of exclusionary language in sporting contexts

Approached from the other direction, several authors also raised awareness for practitioners of specific linguistic practices in sporting contexts that were functioning to exclude. As a set of practical insights, these chapters provided sports organisations, teams and institutions with specific illustrations of how taken-for-granted and normalised linguistic practices in sport create various forms of exclusion. They also discussed what was needed to redress these forms of exclusion and what is at stake if these practices are not addressed.

Chimbwete-Phiri and Schnurr showed this by drawing attention to sexualisation practices in the language of some netball fans in official fan fora on social media sites. They suggest that without intervention from officials from the Netball Association of Malawi, fan club representatives, media practitioners and marketers of netball sports competitions, such sexualisation practices could continue to trivialise these professional athletes and undermine the sport of netball in Malawi. The theme of exclusion and gender was also raised by Graf and Fleischhacker who suggest that a sport wide approach is needed to de-gender the language of football and raise critical awareness of how football belongs to all and not just male players. They suggest a coordinated effort by administrators, coaches, players and fans is needed to mobilise the empowering potential of language, particularly with respect to de-gendering any normalised terminology in the game that is male in form. Without such action, female players may continue to internalise exclusionary narratives that the game is not for them.

Pringle and Denison also argue for the need to change exclusionary linguistic practices in sport, with specific reference to language that normalises homophobic attitudes. Homophobic language has frequently been found to be prevalent in a sports team context (Plummer, 2006; Osborne and Wagner, 2007) and can have devastating consequences with such practices being linked to higher rates of suicide, self-harm and drug/alcohol addiction amongst LGBTIQ+ people (Sabo and Gordon 1995). Pringle and Denison argue for better and more direct education or training for rugby club leaders, coaches, captains and players that clearly and unequivocally conveys how exclusionary tropes heard in sports teams, like "that's so gay", are never okay.

What this collection of chapters demonstrates for practitioners is how, alarmingly, language can create meanings that can convey the idea that sport does not belong to everyone and that these practices can have devastating effects on those being excluded. These authors have given examples of specific linguistic practices that can cause exclusion and illustrated how such practices construct exclusionary ideas about who is or is not welcome in sport. While the evidence presented here is particularly relevant for those working towards creating a more inclusionary sports space and/or attitude towards female and homosexual athletes – social groups that have been traditionally excluded – they demonstrate the need for sports practitioners more generally to scrutinise taken-for-granted linguistic practices for their potential to exclude.

5.3 Representing sport as inclusive in the sports media

Finally, several authors raised implications directly for the Fourth Estate who reflect and reconstruct the Discourses (Gee 2014) of sport on a massive scale in and through their broadcast and media reporting on sports matches and sports issues. In this collection of papers, authors drew attention to a range of reporting patterns and practices utilised by sport journalists, editors and editorial boards that can be seen to reinforce exclusionary Discourses of sport. These authors argue that greater critical awareness by journalists of the way unchecked sports reporting practices influence the construction of sport as an unequal space for different social groups presents as a significant way to address issues on inclusion/exclusion in sport on a large scale.

Kemble, for example, argued that journalists and editors need to be critically aware of the way distinctions and disparities in coverage of men's and women's sport in the media are reinforcing the hegemonic ideology that sport is a male domain. These disparities occur not only in terms of the amount of coverage afforded to both men's and women's sport but also in terms of the distinct identities constructed for male and female athletes in sports reporting, with male athletes being more regularly constructed in line with culturally understood sporting values like being competitive and aggressive on the pitch. Addressing such distinctions in sports media coverage, through more critical writing and editorial processes, could help drive more inclusive attitudes in the public to women's sport.

The chapter by Erdoğan-Öztürk et al. also discusses similar implications on the issue of representing women's sport in the media. They argue that gender and critical media literacy education for journalists and editors could be a game changer in the fight to make sports reporting more gender neutral. As others have claimed, the media play a central role in shaping societal norms and attitudes to various issues making journalistic education programmes a particularly significant agent for change (Josephi 2019: 47). Aiming for balanced and fair coverage and portrayal of sportspeople irrespective of their gender and developing journalists' critical capacity to consider whether storylines unhelpfully undermine claims to a female athlete's athletic identity would be good places to start.

On the divisive issue of transgender athletes competing in high-performance sport, Bailey and Jones argue that the media debate needs to be fairer in order to consider both sides of the issue, especially with an issue as divisive as this one is. Their analysis suggests that the debate is dominated by the implicitly presented view that transgender involvement in high-performance sporting contexts is unfair, impossible or nonsensical which could be particularly damming for what is already a vulnerable group. Bailey and Jones suggest that such an almost exclusively exclusionary view of transgender athletes' involvement in high performance sport may also negatively impact access to grassroots sport and its health benefits by gender non-conforming and non-binary children. They recommend greater care be exercised by sports journalists and editors so as to better inform the public of the nuances and complexities of the issue of transgender involvement in sport.

Through this collection of chapters, the authors have provided research informed insights for media practitioners as to the various ways linguistic and/or reporting practices can (perhaps indirectly) create or reinforce meanings of exclusion, or unfairly represent issues alive in the sports domain, contrary to wider ideological media values of fairness and balance (Cotter 2010). As language both reflects and (re)constructs context, these patterns and practices raised by authors shine a light on deeper underlying bias and exclusionary attitudes that may give rise to and explain these practices and that are reinforced in press reports. The media, due to their reach, have both a responsibility and an opportunity to help society strive towards an understanding of sport that is more inclusive. Critically reviewing reporting practices presents as a key point of departure for achieving this mission.

6 Concluding thoughts and looking forward

In concluding this chapter, and with it the volume, we wish to consider where researchers could go from here with this research agenda. Many authors of the individual chapters have considered potential future research directions for continuing exploration within their specific sporting contexts or in relation to the specific issue of inclusion/exclusion they examined. However, there are some broader points that can be made about a future research agenda into inclusion/exclusion in sport that involves or is driven by linguistics and social interaction researchers.

The first point to make emerges from what we hope is the now demonstrated value of a linguistic lens on issues of inclusion and exclusion in sport. At a higher level, the chapters of this volume illustrate the applicability and power of linguistics (in sociolinguistic, discourse analytical, multimodal and critical forms) for unpacking and theorizing issues of inclusion/exclusion in sport. Through contextualised analyses of language use in real sporting contexts where people perform, support and/or write/speak about sport, we were able to highlight how people actively seek to accomplish inclusion and lay bare some of the linguistic practices that contribute to exclusion in a range of sporting contexts. We hope that, as a result of the work presented in this book, researchers from within or outside of linguistics will now be aware of the power of linguistic analysis tools and consider them in future research that seeks to better understand inclusion/exclusion in sporting contexts.

The second point to make concerns the broader but burgeoning field of sports discourse (Caldwell 2017; File 2022; Schnurr et al Wolfers 2017; Wilson 2011) and what we hope this volume encourages in terms of future research within this community. By drawing attention to the role of language in constructing inclusion or exclusion in a range of sporting contexts, this edited volume has made a number of important contributions to this subfield. In particular, we have widened the conversation on language use in sport by sourcing a more diverse collection of sports and socio-cultural contexts in an effort to contribute new insights to discussions on language and sport that have been dominated by work on football and rugby in Western contexts. We hope that this trend continues, and research in language and sport in a broader array of sociocultural contexts is brought forward.

Finally, we hope that future research will explore new issues of inclusion and exclusion in sport that we have not been able to address here. While there is a comprehensive collection of issues examined within the pages of this volume, we feel that we have barely scratched the surface. The volume should certainly not be viewed as exhaustive, either in terms of issues of inclusion/exclusion that we have covered (and that play out or are addressed in language) or in terms of the communities and social groups that engage in sport and may find themselves subject to exclusionary attitudes and actions. For example, one community we were regrettably unable to source a chapter for was athletes and fans with disabilities. With disabled athletes – professional or not – still facing severe barriers to involvement in sport (e.g., Di Palma et al. 2016; Kiuppis 2018), this is an obvious limitation of the volume. However, there are likely to be other communities and social groups who would benefit from having their access to or experiences in sport closely explored through a linguistic lens, and we call for more empirical studies in this space.

References

Caldwell, David, John Walsh, Elaine Vine & Jon Jureidini (eds.). 2017. *The Discourse of Sports: Analysis from Social Linguistics*. London: Routledge.

Cotter, C. (2010). *News talk: Investigating the language of journalism*. Cambridge University Press.

Di Palma, Davide, Gaetano Raiola & Domenico Tafuri. 2016. Disability and Sport Management: a systematic review of the literature. *Journal of Physical Education and Sport* 16(3). 785.

File, Kieran. A. 2022. *How Language Shapes Relationships in Professional Sports Teams: Power and Solidarity Dynamics in a New Zealand Rugby Team*. Bloomsbury Academic.

Gee, James Paul. 2014 [1999]. *An introduction to discourse analysis: theory and method*, 4th edn. New York: Routledge.

Josephi, Beate. 2019. Journalism education. In Karin Wahl-Jorgensen & Thomas Hanitzsch (eds.), *The Handbook of Journalism Studies*, 42–58. New York: Routledge.

Kiuppis, Florian. 2018. Inclusion in sport: Disability and participation. *Sport in society* 21(1). 4–21.

Osborne, Danny & William Wagner III. 2007. Exploring the relationship between homophobia and participation in core sports among high school students. *Sociological Perspectives* 50(4). 597–613.

Plummer, David. 2006. Sportophobia: Why do some men avoid sport? *Journal of Sport and Social Issues* 30(2). 122–137.

Sabo, Don & David Gordon (eds.). 1995. *Men's health and illness* (Vol. 8). Thousand Oaks: Sage.

Schnurr, Stephanie, Kieran A. File, Daniel Clayton, Solvejg Wolfers & Anastasia Stavridou. 2020. Exploring the processes of emergent leadership in a netball team: Providing empirical evidence through discourse analysis. *Discourse & Communication* 15(1). 98–116.

Wolfers, Solvejg, Kieran File & Stephanie Schnurr. 2017. "Just because he's black": Identity construction and racial humour in a German U-19 football team. *Journal of Pragmatics* 112. 83–96. https://doi.org/10.1016/j.pragma.2017.02.003.

Wilson, Nick. 2011. *Leadership as communicative practice: The discursive construction of leadership and team identity in a New Zealand rugby team*. Wellington: Victoria University of Wellington.

List of contributors

Farhana Abdul Fatah
Univesiti Sains Malaysia, Malaysia
Farhana Abdul Fatah is a Senior Lecturer at the School of Languages, Literacies, and Translation, Universiti Sains Malaysia, Penang. Her primary research interests revolve around discourse analysis, with a keen focus on the intersections between gender, religion, and race. She currently heads a research project examining the representations of Muslim women in Malaysian media.

Aimee Bailey
De Montfort University, United Kingdom
Aimee Bailey is Lecturer in English Language at De Montfort University. She is a queer feminist linguist, primarily interested in the study of gender and sexual discrimination in mediated contexts using corpus linguistic and discourse analytic approaches. Her PhD research examined the construction of normative discourses in online media for lesbian and bisexual women, and her current projects explore how transgender athletes and charities are represented in the news media.

Stuart Cain
Warwickshire Country Cricket Club, United Kingdom
Stuart Cain is the Chief Executive of Warwickshire County Cricket Club and Edgbaston Stadium, as well as a Director of Birmingham Phoenix and Central Sparks. He sits on the ECB's Professional Game Group and has also been on the Board of UK Athletics, Swim England and the Rugby League World Cup. Stuart was previously Chief Executive at Wasps/Ricoh Arena and Managing Director of Commercial Media at the NEC Group where he ran a national ticketing agency. Prior to that he was Global Managing Partner of Sport & Entertainment at Mindshare and Commercial Director at Rangers FC and Wolverhampton Wanderers FC. He also Chaired the London 2012 Data Legacy Committee and was previously an Independent Director of Swim England.

Rachel Chimbwete-Phiri
University of Malawi, Malawi
Rachel Chimbwete-Phiri is a senior lecturer in Media and Communication Studies at the University of Malawi. She holds a PhD in Applied Linguistics from University of Warwick, UK. Her research interests include, media discourse, professional discourse, and social and behaviour change communication. Rachel has co-authored book chapters and academic articles on communication in HIV/AIDS consultations and health education discourse in Malawi.

Amanda Coulson
England Boxing, United Kingdom
Amanda Coulson is the Lead National Coach for England Boxing. A previous trailblazing women boxer who competed for England and Great Britain between 1999 and 2012. Amanda now leads the coaching team of the performance pathway within England Boxing across the different age categories of school, junior, youth and senior – both men and women. She is responsible for talent identification, development and progression of boxers climbing the pathway towards the World Class Programme and one day becoming our future Olympians.

Erik Denison
Monash University, Australia
Dr. Erik Denison is a research fellow with Monash University's behavioural science institute, BehaviourWorks, and with the Faculty of Education. He has conducted multiple studies examining the drivers of homophobic and sexist behaviours in sport settings and other male-dominated environments.

Yasemin Erdoğan-Öztürk
Karabük Üniversity, Turkey
Yasemin Erdoğan-Öztürk is a doctoral candidate in Language Studies at Middle East Technical University (METU) and works as a research assistant at Karabuk University, Turkey. She is the founding co-convenor of Discourse and Corpus Research Group (DISCORE). Her works broadly focus on women's representation in the media and politics, gender and language, new media discourses, sociolinguistics of globalization, multilingualism in transnational contexts.

Esranur Efeoğlu-Özcan
Gazi University, Turkey
Esranur Efeoğlu-Özcan holds a PhD in Language Studies at Middle East Technical University (METU), Turkey. She compiled the Corpus of Turkish Youth Language (CoTY) to document the linguistic architecture of language used by young speakers of Turkish and explore how they co-create discourses for various interactional purposes. She is the co-founder and coordinator of Discourse and Corpus Research Group at METU.

Kieran File
University of Warwick, UK
Kieran File is an Associate Professor in the Department of Applied Linguistics at the University of Warwick, UK. His research explores issues related to language use in high-performance sporting contexts. His current research interests are in the areas of managing professional relationships in sports teams, building empowering team environments, and communicating effectively under pressure during live sporting events. He also applies this research findings and has helped some of the world's biggest sporting teams and organisations consider the role and impact of language choices in their high-performance sporting contexts.

Melanie Fleischhacker
University of Klagenfurt, Austria
Melanie Fleischhacker is a PhD student and project member. In her PhD, she is focussing on questioning sequences in coaching. As an applied linguist, her research focus to this date has been on professional (helping) interactions, i.e., (business and writing) coaching, as well as identity construction and gender ideologies in the context of (female) football or EFL textbooks.

Eva-Maria Graf
University of Klagenfurt, Austria
Eva-Maria Graf is an Associated Professor in Applied and English Linguistics at the University of Klagenfurt (Austria). She received her PhD from Ludwig-Maximilians-Universität, Munich. In her research she focuses on helping professions, particularly on coaching and psychotherapy, and on gender ideologies in language and social interactions such as football or leadership contexts.

Hale Işık-Güler
Orta Doğu Teknik Üniversitesi (METU), Turkey
Dr. Işık-Güler works as an Associate Professor of Linguistics at the Department of Foreign Language Education, Middle East Technical University (METU), Ankara. Her work over the last 20 years can be best described as being at the intersection of discourse analysis, socio-pragmatics and corpus linguistics. She is currently interested in corpus-assisted critical discourse analysis and online discourses and gender, identity and facework. She has worked on the compilation project of the first *Spoken Turkish Corpus* and has published in the *Journal of Pragmatics, Intercultural Pragmatics, Dilbilim Araştırmaları* and *Discourse, Context and Media, Linguistics and Education* among others. She is the research group leader of the Discourse and Corpus Research Group (DISCORE) at METU.

Lucy Jones
University of Nottingham, United Kingdom
Dr Lucy Jones is Associate Professor in Sociolinguistics at the University of Nottingham. She is a discourse analyst and linguistic ethnographer working on a range of topics relevant to language, gender and sexuality. Her published research includes normativity and identity construction amongst LGBTQ+ youth, homophobic discourse in relation to same-sex marriage and HIV prevention, analysis of YouTube videos by trans vloggers, and older lesbians' identity construction. Her current projects include a study of identity and intersectionality in British LGBTQ+ youth groups and critical discourse analysis of how trans athletes in elite sport are represented within the news media.

Melissa Kemble
University of Sydney, Australia
Melissa Kemble is currently a PhD Candidate in Linguistics at the University of Sydney, Australia. Her research interests include corpus linguistics, discourse analysis, news discourse, evaluation, and language, gender and identity.

Louise Mullany
University of Nottingham, United Kingdom
Louise Mullany is Professor of Sociolinguistics at the University of Nottingham UK. She has researched language and inequality for the last 25 years and published a number of books, articles and chapters in this area with international publishing houses. Her most recent book publication is *Globalisation, Geopolitics and Gender in Professional Communication*, co-edited with Stephanie Schnurr (Routledge). She is founder and director of Linguistic Profiling for Professionals, a research centre and business unit based at the University. She was winner of a Times Higher Education Award for Outstanding Contribution to the Local Community in 2021 for her joint work on gender-based violence and hate crime. She has presented her research in a number of global locations including Argentina, Brazil, Canada, China, Hong Kong, Kenya, New Zealand, Poland, Spain and Uganda.

Fergus O'Dwyer
Marino Institute of Education, Ireland
Fergus O'Dwyer is based at the Marino Institute of Education (an associated college of Trinity College Dublin, Ireland). Language use in sport and coaching make up some of his current interests. Previous research includes the project analyzed in this volume, which focused on the role of language in negotiating identities in a sports club.

Ozde Ozinanir
University of Warwick, United Kingdom
Ozde Ozinanir is a researcher of (critical) discourse analysis and sociolinguistics based at the University of Warwick, whose current research interests include language, identity construction, and social justice in sports and media discourse. Alongside teaching at the university, Oz is currently working on an AHRC-funded PhD thesis researching identity construction in women's football online news and social media.

Richard Pringle
Monash University, Australia
Professor **Richard Pringle** is a critical qualitative researcher who examines sporting and educational issues associated with genders, sexualities, power relations and emotions.

Alan Rapley
OLY; UK Coaching, United Kingdom
Alan Rapley is Coach Programme and Pathway Manager. He currently manages Coach Development programmes which have over 175 coaches, from over 35 sports, being supported on them annually. He has personally Coach Developed over 300 coaches in his career, the majority of which are GB international level or professional. He is the Olympic swimming captain from 1996 and has worked alongside many international squads and professional teams from multiple sports, supporting their development and growth.

Frances Rock
University of Cardiff, United Kingdom
Frances Rock is Reader in the Centre for Language and Communication Research at Cardiff University, Wales, UK. She investigates the mediation of experiences in social worlds by analysing how people make multimodal meaning alone and together. Her research has examined contexts including policing, workplaces and multilingual cities. Her work is published but also applied in forensic and other contexts.

Stephanie Schnurr
University of Warwick, United Kingdom
Stephanie Schnurr is Professor in Sociolinguistics. She has published widely on various aspects of professional communication, leadership discourse and gender in different professional contexts. Stephanie is the author of *Leadership Discourse at Work* (2009, Palgrave), *Exploring Professional Communication* (2013, Routledge), and the co-author of *Language and Culture at Work* (2017, Routledge) and *The Language of Leadership Narratives* (2020, Routledge).

Anastasia Stavridou
University of Manchester, United Kingdom
Dr Anastasia Stavridou is a Lecturer in the Centre for Translation & Intercultural Studies at the University of Manchester. Her research interests include discourse analysis and intercultural communication with particular applications in leadership-followership, identity construction and the media. Previously, she has also conducted research on COVID-19 narratives and identity construction on Instagram as well as on othering in stories of anti-Chinese racism.

Index

Analogy 18, 39, 311
Athlete activism 44, 46, 52, 55, 58–9, 61

Banter 9, 15, 112–9, 253, 257–8, 261–4, 311–2, 315
Belonging 17, 19, 39, 105, 108, 114, 119, 179, 182, 220, 227, 233, 261
Black Lives Matter (BLM) 43, 46–8, 52–6, 59

Children 4, 17–8, 27, 38, 67, 150, 157, 212, 249, 286, 319
Coaching 2, 18, 22, 28, 33, 65–6, 75–9, 109, 114–5, 117, 121, 164, 286, 293, 299, 315–6
Concordances 152–3, 155–6, 162, 200, 202, 208–9
Corpus linguistics 47, 198
Corpus-based discourse analysis 6, 148, 165
COVID-19 43, 47
Critical Discourse Analysis (CDA) 6, 49, 130, 172, 174–5, 189, 194, 196, 198, 206, 274
Critical discursive psychology 6, 218, 224–5
Critical feminism 195, 199, 205
Cultural field 219–2, 224, 226, 233, 239, 241, 248–9, 312

Discourse analysis 6, 48, 66, 68–9, 84, 86, 90, 210, 258
Discursive space 118, 120–1
Discursive strategies 10, 67, 80, 130–1, 139, 172–3, 175, 188
Diversity 2, 7, 20, 38, 55, 77, 100, 125, 159, 165, 168, 271, 274, 293, 296, 298–9, 301

Emotional intelligence 219–20
Ethnography 9, 17, 21–2, 105, 108–9, 111

Face-threatening act (FTA) 95, 106–7, 118–9, 121
Female footballers 221, 224, 228, 231, 247–8, 312
Feminist Critical Discourse Analysis (FCDA) 6, 172, 175, 189
Feminist Poststructuralist Discourse Analysis (FPDA) 271, 274–5, 285
Focus group 11, 224, 253, 258, 260, 264, 312

Foucault 253–4, 257–8

Gender marking 10, 148–50, 153, 155, 163, 165, 174, 313
Gender stereotypes 10, 125, 129–31, 137–8, 147–9, 165, 314
Gendered organisation 219–21, 224, 227, 247–9
Gendering 11, 125, 127, 195, 219–30, 249–50, 317
Gesture 18, 22, 27, 30–1, 36, 39, 48, 52–3, 55, 58, 96, 115, 311

Heteronormativity 2, 194, 198, 220, 266
Homonegativism 12, 253, 255–7, 259, 262, 266–7
Homosexuality 12, 195, 206, 254, 256, 263–4, 266, 318

Ideological dilemmas 219, 224–6, 228, 232–3
Ideology 11, 27, 52, 101, 130, 165, 172, 175, 189, 194, 196, 208, 211–2, 218, 249, 318
Indexicality 17, 24, 35, 48–9, 51, 53–6, 58–61, 66, 85, 94, 107, 110, 113, 115, 117, 119, 304
Infantilisation 10, 137, 148–50, 156–7, 165, 174, 179–80, 313
Instagram 9, 43–4, 47–50, 55, 58–61, 310, 312
Integration 17–9, 30, 36, 38, 248
Interactional sociolinguistics 6, 22, 70, 90
Interpretative repertoire 224–5, 228, 250
Intertextuality 49, 51, 53–5, 57–8, 61, 185, 274, 276, 284, 313
Involvement 23, 28–9, 34, 49, 54, 56, 99, 101, 102, 110, 159, 164–5, 175, 222–3, 253–4, 272, 276, 285, 298, 319–20

Masculinities 2, 126–7, 151, 161, 173, 186, 217, 219–20, 247, 249, 254–7, 261
Media representations 46, 147, 149, 171–4, 178, 313
Motorsport 9, 43, 46, 59–61
Multilingualism 17–8, 20–2, 27–9, 33–4, 38–9, 311
Multimodal discourse analysis 6, 9, 43–4, 48–50, 58, 61, 313

Nationalism 172, 174, 179, 181–3, 189

https://doi.org/10.1515/9783110789829-017

Objectification 127, 137–8, 140, 149, 181, 206, 312

Participatory team management 9, 24, 83–4, 90–1, 99
Psychological safety 108, 117–9

Queer linguistics 194–5, 198

Racial justice 43–4, 46–7, 49–50, 52–61
Racism 2, 23, 43–7, 53, 57–8, 273, 293, 303, 313
Recontextualisation 35
Religion 3–5, 45, 185, 274, 285, 293, 301, 314
Repetition 18, 29–31, 33–4, 39, 57, 165, 209, 311

Segregation 23, 25, 127, 196, 198–9
(Self-)exclusion 218–9, 224–5, 227–8, 248–9
Sexualisation 10, 26, 129–30, 132, 134–5, 138–40, 148–50, 153, 158–9, 165, 312–3, 317
Social media 1, 8, 9, 43–6, 48, 56–62, 183–7, 243–4, 276, 291, 293, 303, 315–7
Social semiotics 43–4, 47–9
Solidarity 65, 67–8, 77–9, 99, 107–8, 112–3, 115–6, 118, 121, 150, 157, 165, 203, 311

Sports media 7–8, 10, 44–5, 48, 148–50, 157, 162, 164–6, 197, 291, 313, 318
Storytelling 112–3
Subject positions 11–2, 79, 224–6, 250, 271, 273–5, 277, 279–82, 286
Superdiversity 20
Synthetic personalisation 49, 53, 57–9, 61, 313

Teasing 106–8, 114–5, 199, 261
Thematic analysis 6, 218, 224–6
Trans inclusion 194, 196–7, 203–6, 208–12, 313
Transgender 2, 5–6, 8, 10–1, 127, 159, 193–4, 201–5, 305, 313, 319
Translanguaging 8, 18, 21–3, 28–9, 33, 29, 311
Trivialisation 10, 127, 138, 140, 148–9, 151, 159, 165, 173, 180, 313, 317

Veil 272, 276, 279, 282–3, 312
Video 49–50, 52–3, 87, 98–9, 224, 276, 293

White privilege 21, 39

www.ingramcontent.com/pod-product-compliance
Lightning Source LLC
Chambersburg PA
CBHW050514170426
43201CB00013B/1951